HU SHIH AND INTELLECTUAL CHOICE
IN MODERN CHINA

Michigan Studies on China
Published for the Center for Chinese Studies of
The University of Michigan

MICHIGAN STUDIES ON CHINA

Alexander Eckstein
China's Economic Development: The Interplay of Scarcity and Ideology

Allen S. Whiting
The Chinese Calculus of Deterrence: India and Indochina

Ernest P. Young
The Presidency of Yuan Shik-k'ai: Liberalism and Dictatorship in Early Republican China

Rhoads Murphey
The Outsiders: The Western Experience in India and China

Donald J. Munro
The Concept of Man in Contemporary China

Daniel H. Bays
China Enters the Twentieth Century: Chang Chih-tung and the Issues of a New Age, 1895–1909

Evelyn Sakakida Rawski
Education and Popular Literacy in Ch'ing China

Thomas G. Rawski
China's Transition to Industrialism: Producer Goods and Economic Development in the Twentieth Century

Donald S. Sutton
Provincial Militarism and the Chinese Republic: The Yunnan Army, 1905–25

Paul S. Ropp
Dissent in Early Modern China: Ju-lin wai-shih *and Ch'ing Social Criticism*

Hsi-sheng Ch'i
Nationalist China at War: Military Defeats and Political Collapse, 1937–45

Chad Hansen
Language and Logic in Ancient China

Min-chih Chou
Hu Shih and Intellectual Choice in Modern China

The research on which these books are based was supported by the Center for Chinese Studies of The University of Michigan

Hu Shih and Intellectual Choice in Modern China

MIN-CHIH CHOU

Ann Arbor   The University of Michigan Press

Copyright © by The University of Michigan 1984
All rights reserved
Published in the United States of America by
The University of Michigan Press and simultaneously
in Rexdale, Canada, by John Wiley & Sons Canada, Limited

1987 1986 1985 1984   4 3 2 1

Grateful acknowledgment is made to the following publisher for permission to reprint copyrighted material:

Harvard University Press, for material from Jerome B. Grieder, *Hu Shih and the Chinese Renaissance: Liberalism in the Chinese Revolution, 1917–1937* (Cambridge, Mass.: Harvard University Press, 1970), and Lec Ou-fan Lee, *The Romantic Generation of Chinese Writers* (Cambridge, Mass.: Harvard University Press, 1973). Reprinted by permission of the publisher.

Library of Congress Cataloging in Publication Data

Chou, Min-chih, 1940–
Hu Shih and intellectual choice in modern China.

(Michigan studies on China)
Bibliography: p.
Includes index.
 1. Hu, Shih, 1891–1962. 2. Scholars—China—
Biography. I. Title. II. Series.
CT3990.H78C47 1984   951.04′092′4 [B]   83-21599
ISBN 0-472-10039-4

Paperback ISBN : 978-0-472-75074-0

Preface

Hu Shih (1891–1962) was my only hero during my high school and college years. When Hu returned to Taiwan to assume the presidency of the Academia Sinica, I entered high school. When he died, I was an undergraduate at Tunghai University. During those years, I read some of his popular essays, a few of his more serious writings, and nearly everything then written about him. Despite this, I did not have a clear understanding of what he represented or what his ideas were. But that mattered little. In my mind, he was a defiant hero with extraordinary powers of persuasion, urbanity, and a touch of charisma. Everything he said seemed logical and reasonable to me. When he died in early 1962, I took long walks through the darkened campus, feeling sad and lonely.

When I came to the United States for graduate studies, I plunged myself into my studies. After my initial period of adjustment, however, Hu came back to me. I read more of his popular essays and scholarly writings; and gradually my opinion of him began to change. Detached from my cultural milieu, I became less sensitive to the social, political, and intellectual atmosphere of the Chinese society under which Hu produced his writings. Judging him by universal standards of intellectual excellence, I concluded that Hu was a vain and superficial man whose ideas were either erroneous or irrelevant. This stage of my thinking lasted for quite a while and reflected my harsh criticism of him. Still later, as I was revising my dissertation, I re-read Hu's writings. More mature, I began to realize that I underestimated the pressures under which he worked and the problems he confronted. I examined him again, this time in the context of his time, and my perception of him changed once more.

Hu Shih was one of the leading scholars of the century and an outstanding promoter of the New Culture movement. Deeply schooled in classical scholarship, he made major discoveries in his research into Chinese history, culture, and thought. All have served as points of departure for others. Commenting on an extremely wide range of issues in contemporary China, his ideas reflected many of the concerns of his time. To be sure, Hu had his partisan, emotional, and even vicious moments in his treatment of past and contemporary scenes. But those moments should not be dismissed outright, for they provide valuable insight into the atmosphere of his age. Although he seemed too utilitarian and polemical to be classified as a great thinker, most of his ideas were interesting, many had enormous common sense, and some were full of wisdom and reflected genuine human concerns commonly shared by all thinking men.

My main interest, however, is not only Hu's ideas per se, but also what they have revealed in light of his life's journey. What I propose is a study of his opinions in the context of his time; of why he thought as he did and how he dealt with the myriad problems he and his country confronted. To analyze the temper of Hu and his time, I will penetrate as deeply as possible into his thinking. While this study is not a psycho-history, it does deal extensively with his aspirations, fears, and desires. My contribution to the scholarship of modern China rests in my probe of Hu's subconscious conflicts and of the dilemmas and struggles of the Chinese elite. The voluminous writings Hu left, including the substantial autobiographical materials, enable us to attempt an intimate understanding of his struggles. Mine is by no means a complete biography of Hu. Details about his life have been richly supplied by Grieder in his fine book.[1] My concern focuses only upon certain aspects of his life. To explore each of these in greater depth, I have decided on a thematic, instead of a chronological, approach.

This study is divided into several parts. The first section deals with Hu's reorientation in his formative years. Before his twentieth birthday, Hu had witnessed several major historical events. He was seven when the 1898 coup d'etat occurred; nine when the Boxer movement erupted; fourteen when the Russo-Japanese War broke out and the millennial civil service examination system died; and twenty when the Republican Revolution took place. These developments had noticeable effects on him. The entire country was in precipitous disintegration; and in an unpredictable surrounding, Hu had to find a new direction. Hu's experiences during this period suggest that a fundamental transformation of Chinese outlook was taking place at the turn of the century—a transformation earlier and much more profound than most historians have assumed. When he arrived in the United States, the choice of an academic major became a major struggle—something that his predecessors did not experience.

The second section discusses Hu's attempt to adjust to the new environment of American society that was different from the one he was accustomed to. His brief conversion to Christianity and his marriage crisis were emotional and painful. They reveal much about his predicament at a time when Chinese society had lost its consensus before it could establish a new system of values.

Hu's political attitude will constitute the third section of this study. Like his compatriots, Hu was debilitated by the twin evils of foreign imperialism and misrule by his own government. These crises elevated Chinese nationalism to an unprecedented level, something scholars of modern China have always emphasized. What has not yet been discussed in detail is the cosmopolitan outlook in certain figures of the May Fourth generation that reached its maturity in the mid-1910s when the May Fourth movement began.[2] Hu's patriotism became conditional. On the one hand, he refused to be identified with any exclusive nationalistic movement. On the other, he vigorously criticized imperialism. While unable to abandon his feeling toward his native land, he did adopt a wider empathy, relating both to China's interests and the principle of fairness. In general, so devastating was contemporary Chinese politics that politics ceased to be a career choice for some of the elite Chinese, contrasting sharply with the traditional Chinese attitude that government service was the most desirable and honored route to success and personal satisfaction. Unwilling to participate in and unable to improve politics, Hu Shih and others engaged themselves in cultural and intellectual endeavors exclusively, supporting the status quo and hoping that things would turn for the better.

This aspect—Hu's attitude toward intellectual reform—will form the fourth section of the book. A focus upon intellectual activities has more than one purpose, and this orientation toward intellectual reform was not as inherently conditioned by traditional outlook as some scholars have previously argued—Hu stressed intellectual reform, the only means available to him. With his country facing fundamental crises, Hu sought to change the general pattern of Chinese thinking. This, he believed, would improve China's chance to survive in the modern world. Living in a society that offered little emotional reward and almost no meaningful prospect, intellectual pursuit in remote subjects became an escape. It helped him block out grim reality. The question as to how antitradition Hu Shih was has been debated, dictated to no small degree by personal feelings of the debaters. Hu was, in general, antitradition; but at times he displayed genuine affection and concern for the continuity of the past. Specifically, Hu's perception of tradition, more variegated than most scholars would have us believe, defies any categorical explications. In his scholarly writings, Hu tried to present a fair and objective picture of the past, if not always successfully. Linking China's contemporary plight, which overwhelmed him, to traditional values, in his popular writings he was harsh and caustic toward the latter. And yet addressing Westerners he was sometimes tenderhearted toward his heritage. On this last point, no doubt he was somewhat defensive because of the threatening surroundings, as Levenson would have suggested. But there was more to it. When Hu addressed Westerners on Chinese tradition, he was usually far removed from Chinese reality, thus less affected by it. And some of his more favorable remarks on the subject appeared during his ambassadorship to Washington, apparently with the purpose of improving China's image in the West when his fatherland was engaged in a life-and-death struggle with Japan.

Certainly Hu Shih's opinions were his own, and his life experience had its uniqueness. But there must have been individuals who were bound up with him by a shared experience. That Hu had many admirers indicates that these admirers shared at least some of his views and aspirations. Of course, he also had a number of detractors: their numbers signify his wide influence and acknowledge his power. In this sense, then, Hu Shih was, at least to some extent, representative of certain important trends of his age. Thus, a comparison of Hu with his immediate predecessors, which will be addressed in the last portion of this book, should tell us to some degree how much Hu and the like-minded departed from the earlier generation. These departures were often subtle and nuanced. Significantly, Hu had a more profound sense of the crisis and dilemma of his age than his forerunners had had of theirs. For the first time in modern China, the effect of the disintegration of the old order and the intrusion of the modern West not only transformed the intellectual outlook but also irrevocably changed the mental makeup of

Hu's generation. Paralyzed by the overwhelming historical forces coming violently from different directions, Hu became an alienated protester. With no control over his own surroundings, his choices and judgment became characterized by ambiguity and ambivalence. While he never ceased expressing his deep concern about the social, political, and intellectual issues of the time, it was also a brutal fact that he derived little personal satisfaction from what was then Chinese society. He became an existential individualist, seeking the meaning of life all on his own. Thus, while the May Fourth period witnessed the continuation of many trends initiated by the reform generation of 1898, it also distinguished itself, among other things, by a heightened self-consciousness and self-criticism, a spirit of excruciating protestation, a sense of estrangement, and a highly ambiguous feeling toward its surroundings. It was in these aspects that the May Fourth period can be regarded as a new era. (More materials by and on Hu Shih have been published since the completion of this study. An important item is the three-volume *Collection of Correspondence to and from Hu Shih* [*Hu Shih lai-wang shu-hsin hsüan*], edited by Division of the History of the Republic of China, Institute of Modern History, the Chinese Academy of Social Sciences. This and other materials, however, do not warrant me to alter the substance of my arguments in the book.)

Turning to more personal matters, I find myself confronted with obligations of gratitude to a number of individuals and institutions. I am deeply indebted to Professor Albert Feuerwerker of the University of Michigan for instructions and guidance given over a period of years and for his assistance in the publication of this book. I am most grateful to Professor Frederick W. Mote of Princeton University who read and re-read the manuscript with meticulous care and who offered perspicacious criticisms.

Dr. Michael S. DeLucia, Mary-Margaret Kellogg, Professor Kang-i Sun Chang, Professor Earl Minor, and Jeannette Mirsky read the manuscript in whole or in part, and I am grateful for their comments and suggestions. I wish to thank professors Ch'en Ta-tuan, Kao Yu-kung, and James T.C. Liu, all of Princeton University, and professors Guy S. Alitto and Leo Ou-fan Lee, both of the University of Chicago, for their counsel and encouragement.

Mr. Hu Tsu-wang kindly gave permission to have the unpublished diary of his father reproduced for my research, and I am grateful for his kindness. I obtained most of the material for this book at the Asia Library of the University of Michigan. The Kuomintang Archives in Taiwan, the Department of Manuscripts and University Archives of the Cornell University Libraries, Cornell University, and the Library of Congress provided me materials that were not available elsewhere. To all of them I offer my sincere thanks.

I wish to thank my wife, Yu-ning, for her unfailing support and encouragement over the years and for her practical help with this book.

Finally, I must make an acknowledgment to Hu Shih himself. Hu repeatedly led me to new insights that I did not expect, and he forced me to reconsider more than once many of the issues discussed here. Studying him has been an extremely rewarding experience for me, and I have no doubt that I am the greatest beneficiary of this study. Hu's only protection from me has been the passage of a little over two decades since his death. If he cannot agree with all the conclusions presented here, he can at least rest assured that I have tried my best to achieve a sympathetic understanding of him and his time.

Contents

Part I	**The Education of a Modern Chinese**	
Chapter 1	Formative Years	3
Chapter 2	Travel Abroad	20
Chapter 3	From Agriculture to Philosophy	30
Part II	**Cultural Confrontation**	
Chapter 4	Christianity	39
Chapter 5	Marriage	58
Part III	**Political Views**	
Chapter 6	Cosmopolitanism	83
Chapter 7	Chinese Politics	107
Part IV	**Intellectual Views**	
Chapter 8	The Literary Revolution	149
Chapter 9	Attitudes toward Chinese Culture	166
Chapter 10	Classical Scholarship	189
Part V	**Epilogue**	
Chapter 11	The May Fourth Generation in Historical Perspective	203
	Abbreviations	221

Notes	223
Glossary	263
Bibliography	267
Index	293

Part I
The Education of a Modern Chinese

Chapter 1

Formative Years

Hu Shih was born on December 17, 1891, in Shanghai. Since his immediate forebears were from Anhwei province, he was, in accordance with Chinese custom, regarded as a native of Anhwei. His father, Hu Ch'uan, a minor official in the Manchu government and a moderate scholar, was married three times. Hu Shih's mother, his father's third wife, was seventeen when she was married in 1889 and twenty-three when widowed. Hu was four years old at the time of his father's death. His half sister was seven years older than her stepmother and his eldest half brother two years her senior. After the father's death, family life was beset with financial difficulties, frequent quarrels, and intrigue. Yet, Hu Shih was free from feelings of personal bitterness; most of his friends remembered him as affable and flexible in temperament.[1]

Hu Shih was precocious. His father began teaching him when he was not yet three. Before he was four, his formal schooling started in his native place, Chi-ch'i, Anhwei. By then he had acquired nearly a thousand characters. "I was then a sickly child and could hardly climb a doorstep of six inches without assistance," he recalled. "But I could read and memorize better than all the other boys in the school."[2] Considering his age, Hu's reading in those years was impressive. It included: the *Classic of Filial Piety* (*Hsiao-ching*), the *Four Books* (*Ssu-shu*), the *Classic of Songs* (*Shih-ching*), the *Classic of Changes* (*I-ching*), the *Record of Rituals* (*Li-chi*), and the *Classic of Documents* (*Shu-ching*). As his father had done earlier, his mother also insisted that the teacher explain the meaning of the texts he studied, instead of the customary learning by rote. For this additional instruction, she regularly paid the teacher more than the annual tuition fee of two silver dollars.³ Hu Shih's good foundation in classical scholarship was at least partly owing to this early training.

When he was nine years old, in 1900, Hu acquired another aspect of traditional culture—the illicit delights of vernacular fiction. Until about the turn of the century, fiction had been looked down upon as morally and intellectually worthless, although there were few Chinese who did not spend hours in their childhood relishing the tales of gallantry, intrigue, and romance found in the vernacular fiction. Hu's introduction to this world happened unexpectedly as was the case of many other youngsters. One day he chanced upon a torn portion of *Water Margin* (*Shui-hu chuan*) in an uncle's house. He read through it on the spot and afterward consumed whatever was available. There is pride in his confession that by the time he left for Shanghai, at age fourteen, he had read over thirty novels, including such classics as *Romance of the Three Kingdoms* (*San-kuo yen-i*), *Dream of the Red Chamber* (*Hung-lou meng*), and *The Scholars* (*Ju-lin wai-shih*). Familiarity with the details of these novels made him popular with the girls who asked him to tell them stories.⁴ And some years later, he put his knowledge of Chinese fiction to good use in the Literary Revolution of 1917 that he helped start.

Another significant development in Hu's early years was his formulation of a primitive atheism. The women in the Hu household were devout Buddhists, and Hu could remember their religious practices of which he strongly disapproved. "I was brought up in an idolatrous environment," he would recall years later.⁵ The first revolt came in 1902 when he was eleven.

> One day, while I was reviewing the *Hsiao-hsüeh chi-chu* by Chu Hsi, I came to a passage on the homilies of Ssu-ma Kuang. In it there is a discussion of Hell: "When the body has decayed, the spirit fades away. Even if there be such cruel tortures in Hell as Chiseling, Burning, Pounding and Grinding, whereon are these to be inflicted? . . .
> After rereading this line I became so elated that I leaped from my seat. The horrors of Hell described in Buddhist tales . . . rose before my eyes, but I was no longer afraid.⁶

This experience was soon further strengthened. In chapter 136 of *The Comprehensive Mirror for Aid in Government* (*Tzu-chih t'ung-chien*), the historical compilation made by Ssu-ma Kuang (1018–86) of the

Sung period (960–1279), Hu discovered an anti-Buddhist tract written in the sixth century by Fan Chen (fl. 483–505) who championed the theory of the destructibility of the soul whereas the imperial court patronized Mahayana Buddhism. Hu quoted Fan's argument:

> The body is the material basis of the spirit, and the spirit is only the functioning of the body. The spirit is to the body what sharpness is to a sharp knife. We have never known the existence of sharpness after the destruction of the knife. How can we admit the survival of the spirit when the body is gone?[7]

Hu expressed his conviction by attempting in 1904 to smash Buddha images in his village;[8] he never relented during his entire career his anti-Buddhist passion.

In the spring of 1904, a stepbrother of Hu Shih's left for Shanghai to seek a cure for tuberculosis. His mother decided that he should accompany his brother to obtain a modern education. The decision was an important one. By the turn of the century, the tides of change had penetrated from storm centers along the coast to Hu's native province. Hu's claim that "out of her great love for me she [my mother] sent me away . . . and allowed me to seek my own education and development in the great world all alone"[9] was an obvious simplification. By 1904, Sun Yat-sen (1866–1925) had become a well-known revolutionary, and K'ang Yu-wei (1858–1927), Yen Fu (1853–1921), and Liang Ch'i-ch'ao (1873–1929) familiar figures. The once revered civil service examination system, coming under increasing attack, was to disappear in a year. In a matter of eight years, the imperial system, which had survived for more than two millennia, would pass from the scene. Hu's departure from his mother of thirty-two was more than a parting—it speaks of the extraordinary impact of the new ideas. To accept his account that his semiliterate mother initiated the decision makes clear the deep changes in China.

When Hu Shih left home on a seven-day journey to Shanghai, "armed only with a mother's love, a habit of study, and a little tendency to doubt," he left a whole world behind. From his departure in the spring of 1904 when he was thirteen and a half until his mother's death in November, 1918—a span of more than fourteen years—he was able to visit her on only three occasions for no more than six or seven months.[10]

Shanghai was a city of approximately one million inhabitants. There Hu, no longer preparing for the traditional examination, received an education with a radically different emphasis. Although the classics were not entirely eliminated in his schools, they were nonetheless considerably diluted. It was the Shanghai experience which greatly expanded his horizon and which led him to still another world—the United States.

Hu Shih years later described Shanghai at that time as "only a commercial town of limited vision."[11] But though a port of commerce, by the early 1900s Shanghai had also become an intellectual center. In the city was found perhaps China's most famous publishing enterprise, the Commercial Press, along with several other sizable publishing houses and influential newspapers such as the *Shen-pao, Shih-pao*, and *Shih-shih hsin-pao*. The metropolis was the point of convergence for not only commodities of all sorts but also an increasing number of students leaving for or returning from universities abroad. Shanghai in these years rivaled Peking as China's foremost center of new ideas and political activities. In this milieu Hu Shih spent six formative years.

During his sojourn in the city, Hu attended four schools, performing brilliantly. The frequency of transferring from one school to another provided a good barometer for the atmosphere of the age. It attested to the transient and agitated mood. The Ch'ing empire was in its twilight years. Intellectual opinions were fluid, political realities capricious, and traditions crumbling irretrievably. To ambitious, ingenious young men, the situation offered great opportunities while creating deep confusion. At the same time the rapid demise of conventions and norms seemed to unleash boundless energy. Many people engaged in activity, though often without a sense of certainty. Hu Shih in general was remarkably self-assured, and he took advantage of the new avenues opened to him; yet he was not without moments of doubt and even despondency.

At the *Mei-ch'i* school, the first of the four, the curriculum was radically different from what he had experienced in Anhwei. In addition to Chinese, it consisted of English and arithmetic. Because of his excellence in Chinese, Hu advanced four grades by the end of the sixth week. He then enrolled in the *Ch'eng-chung* school where the courses included Chinese, English, arithmetic, physics, chemistry, and biology. He often placed first in his class and made impressive progress in English and arithmetic. Having stayed there for a year and a half, Hu transferred to the China National Institute (*Chung-kuo kung-hsüeh*) where Chinese, English, advanced algebra, analytic geometry, and biology were the standard courses for his grade. Hu ended his student days in Shanghai at the New China National Institute (*Chung-kuo hsin kung-hsüeh*) without fulfilling the requirement for a diploma.[12]

During these years Hu Shih devoted himself to mastering English and mathematics. He had studied neither prior to coming to Shanghai, but in two years he excelled in both subjects. By the time he transferred to the China National Institute, his superiority in English had been so firmly established that, though one of the youngest in the school, his revolutionary schoolmates asked him to serve as interpreter in negotiating with the customs service for the release of some contraband smuggled from Japan by a female student. In 1908, not yet seventeen, he was offered a job teaching English at the New China National Institute.[13] The persistent emphasis on mastering English was indicative of the values of that time.

Equally instructive was Hu's struggle with mathematics. Remembering, when he entered *Ch'eng-chung* school in 1905,

> I became most interested in arithmetic at this time, frequently studying the subject after the light in the dormitory had been put out. The bed room had no table. To do the homework, I put a candle on the bed frame outside the mosquito net and laid a piece of flat stone resting on the pillow.[14]

Hu told that he worked hard in order to skip a grade, which he did.[15] But there was a deeper motive. By focusing on mathematics he was trying to suppress his early passion for literature and history and channel his efforts to a career in the sciences. However, because of his profound interest in and precocious command of Chinese, the experience became almost traumatic.

Students at the China National Institute in 1906 began a trimonthly magazine named *The Struggle* (*Ching-yeh hsün-pao*) to spread new ideas and agitate for political action. Hu Shih was a regular contributor and, before the magazine folded, became its editor, often responsible for an entire issue. This journalistic venture introduced the fifteen-year-old student to Fu Chün-chien, the adult editor of the publication. Shortly after, Hu had to leave school to recuperate from beriberi. During his convalescence, he by chance picked up an anthology selected by Wu Ju-lun, one of China's last classical stylists. Hu was enthralled by the anthology's fourth volume devoted to the ancient style poetry (*ku-shih*). This led him to other poets, such as the idyllist T'ao Yüan-ming. On returning to school, Hu learned that Fu Chün-chien was relinquishing his editorial duties to return to Hunan. Hu wrote him a farewell poem; Fu responded with one of his own. Written on a piece of Japanese stationery, it contained the following lines:

> You and I, the heroes of the world,
> Friends and mentors, fellow connoisseurs of literature.

Hu Shih's literary talent must have been very impressive for an older man to pay him so splendid a compliment. It so embarrassed Hu that lest others see the poem and laugh at him, he hid it.

> But the poem encouraging a lad had already done the damage. Thenceforth, I read poetry in earnest and dreamed of becoming a poet. Sometimes when the teacher was solving a formula of the advanced algebra, I was devouring *Shih-yün ho-pi* covered under the text of Smith's advanced algebra. I was . . . completing an unfinished travelogue. Just a year or two ago, I had secretly lighted the candle deep into the night and lain on the pillow to study algebra. But my enthusiasm for mathematics surrendered to my new interest in writing poetry. The few months' bout with beriberi led me to discover a new world and determined my future life. From that time on I took the road of literature and history. Later, on many occasions I tried to correct this situation and return to the road of science. But I had become too interested and eventually failed to go back.[16]

This is a dramatic account. What Hu Shih did not mention was that his interest in literature was already deep-rooted before his bout with beriberi. His promotion through four grades in six weeks because of his ability in Chinese and his association with *The Struggle* were sufficient testimonies of his intellectual abilities. Hu's resolution to be a scientist may not have been a haphazard one. Rather, it indicated the rapidly dwindling attraction of Chinese culture and that the centrifugal forces in the nation were being felt by a growing number of people. More and more Chinese tried to stay away from the humanities and social sciences. Benjamin I. Schwartz's and D. W. Y. Kwok's studies show that at the turn of the century the youngsters had already begun to consider science a value system, not just a subject matter of study.[17] Hu Shih never revealed his teenage notion of science, but he did use science to refute a major Confucian tenet, as we shall see shortly. Hu's obsession with science was merely a reflection of the overwhelming trend of the age. How many of the May Fourth generation were there, who early displayed a palpable propensity in literature, history, and philosophy but who refused to concentrate on these disciplines at the beginning? The names of Kuo Mo-jo (1892–), Chiang Meng-lin (Chiang Monlin, 1886–1964), Wang Kuo-wei (1877–1927), Lu Hsün (Chou Shu-jen, 1881–1936), Ch'eng Fang-wu (1894–), and many others immediately occur to us.[18]

Hu Shih's was an age of radical opinions. Growing up and educated in such a climate, he could not but be deeply affected. Several individuals played important roles in his intellectual development. Lin Shu (1852–1924), considered a conservative in the May Fourth period, was a widely read pioneering translator of Western fiction prior to the inception of the New Culture movement. In view of the status of fiction in the mind of the literati, Lin's project was of deep significance. "Even by using classical style to render Dumas or Dickens into Chinese, he displayed a modernist aesthetic assumption that fiction is a fully developed art form, worthy of the best canons of style."[19] That Lin, who knew no foreign language, undertook such a gigantic task is evidence of how predominant the West had become in the Chinese consciousness. Furthermore, the capriciousness of his reputation amply attested to the changing criteria in modern China. It was Lin's translations that acquainted Hu Shih with a number of European novels, including those of Scott, Dickens, Dumas père and fils, Hugo, and Tolstoi.[20]

The two men who had a lasting imprint on Hu, however, were Yen Fu and Liang Ch'i-ch'ao. At the China National Institute, Hu read Yen's translations of C. L. Montesquieu's *De l'esprit des lois*, John Stuart Mill's *On Liberty*, and Thomas Huxley's *Evolution and Ethics*.[21] Of the last item Hu Shih wrote:

> Within a few years of its publication *Evolution and Ethics* gained such widespread popularity in the country that it became reading material for middle school students. . . . All they understood was the meaning of the formula "survival of the fittest" as it was applied to international politics. . . . Nomenclatures such as "evolution," "struggle," "elimination by evolution," and "natural selection" gradually became common in journalistic prose and slogans on the lips of patriots. . . . Furthermore, some people even adopted these terms as their own or

their children's names. Is not Ch'en Chiung-ming's style "Struggle and Survive" (Ching-ts'un)? One of my schoolmates was named "Struggle and Survival Sun" (Sun Ching-ts'un), and another "Natural Selection Yang" (Yang T'ien-tse).[22]

Hu Shih's own experience was equally fascinating. Up to that time his formal name was Hu Hung-hsing. "Then one morning I asked my elder brother to think up a style for me. As he was washing his face, my brother said, 'Why not use "fitness" (shih) in "survival of the fittest"?' I was delighted and began to adopt the name Shih-chih [to fit]." It became his permanent name when he went to Peking in 1910 to take the Boxer indemnity scholarship examination.[23]

Social Darwinism became the vogue in China then because it seemed to the Chinese both to explain China's plight and to offer a panacea for it. To many Chinese, this philosophy was a universal law which would solve even the most troublesome riddle. China was in such a serious crisis because it had failed to live up to the law of "survival of the fittest" and "struggle."[24] Some leaders in late-nineteenth- and early-twentieth-century America construed Social Darwinism to justify overseas expansion and conservative policies at home, whereas in China it was a radical ideology calling for a fundamental departure from the dominant ethos. In the United States, Social Darwinism indicated a tremendous amount of self-confidence; in China, it reflected a sense of self-deficiency and served as a weapon to invalidate the traditional outlook.[25]

Hu Shih began reading Liang Ch'i-ch'ao in his first year in Shanghai. From Liang, Hu acquired an elemental understanding of Hobbes, Descartes, Rousseau, Kant, Bentham, and Darwin. The *New Citizen* (*Hsin-min shuo*), serialized intermittently from 1902 to 1904, imparted to him such notions as civic virtue, the national consciousness, the infinite possibility of progress, the spirit of adventure, popular sovereignty, martial spirit, individualism, and the right to self-government.[26] Liang offered some of his most radical opinions during this period. "Time and again I have thought about this matter," he wrote, "and there is no characteristic of present-day Chinese society which should not be utterly destroyed from its foundation, the old eradicated and the new proclaimed."[27] These writings convinced Hu that "aside from our own, there are other well advanced peoples and highly refined civilizations."[28] Liang's writings also cultivated in him an awareness of

China's cultural tradition. Hu read Liang's "General Trends of the Development of Chinese Scholarship" which "opened a new vision of the world to me. It made me realize that China has learning beyond [that found] in the *Four Books* and the *Five Classics*." As a result of Liang's inspiration, Hu began reading Chinese philosophy at this time, and some years later attributed his own writings on Chinese thought to his sense of challenge aroused by the unfinished quality of Liang's work.[29]

His years in Shanghai provided Hu Shih not only an environment to learn, but also his first opportunity to express his opinions. The bulk of his writings appeared in the aforementioned student journal, *The Struggle*.[30] It was for the most part in the vernacular, as were many of Hu's writings published therein. It is now common knowledge that Hu was not the initiator of the vernacular (*pai-hua*) movement. Recent scholarship has conclusively demonstrated that Chinese leaders had advocated its use as early as the 1870s and that such reformers as Liang Ch'i-ch'ao, Ch'en Jung-kun, Ch'iu T'ing-liang, Huang Tsun-hsien (1848–1905), and Wang Kuo-wei were pioneers of the vernacular movement.[31] Hu Shih himself mentioned seven *pai-hua* newspapers, not including *The Struggle*, published at various places at the time.[32] The experience of Lin Shu captures the mood of the age. Lin, who eventually was to become a fierce opponent of the vernacular movement of the May Fourth era, was in 1900 a widely read *pai-hua* writer for a Hangchow vernacular newspaper.[33] It is apparent that the teenage Hu Shih was following a powerful trend in using the vernacular. It was indeed an age in which all types of new ideas were being experimented with.

Hu Shih's writings covered a variety of topics. A major concern was to discredit Buddhism. Quoting Fan Chen and Ssu-ma Kuang once again, Hu denied the existence of spirit after death and assaulted the concept of moral retribution. While acknowledging that "cause" and "effect" do exist, he insisted that no one could act to control them. "Eating makes one full, and drinking, drunk. . . . Heaven can neither prevent man from doing evil nor punish him for it." In essence, he equated Buddhism with superstition. It was antievolutionary, inculcated a slavish personality, perpetuated ignorance, and deepened China's poverty. Worse yet, belief in superstitious religions, according to Hu, demonstrated the inability of the Chinese to think. Speaking through one of the characters in his novel *The Island of Unchanging Reality* (*Chen-ju tao*), he wrote:

We poor Chinese have never been willing to think; we only know how to follow the trend and conform. That our countrymen are foolish to the extent as they are is, in my view, simply the result of this unwillingness to think. So the great Confucian scholar of the Sung, Ch'eng I-ch'uan, said, "Learning originates in thinking," and these four simple words certainly constitute an immortal saying.[34]

Hu's conclusion became inevitable:

God and Buddha are not only useless but are tremendously deleterious. *They must be destroyed* . . . to eliminate a great cancer. Gentlemen, you do not have to be frightened. *I am here!* If there were indeed god or Buddha, would I still be here editing this journal? . . . Ah, gentlemen, do not be afraid. *Let us destroy! Let us destroy!*[35]

This view, as Hu admitted, was "frankly iconoclastic and atheistic."[36] His empirical and rationalist attitude, he related, came essentially from the Ch'eng-Chu brand of the Sung Confucian thought. Not only did he read Chu Hsi's *Hsiao-hsüeh chi-chu* but also the *Four Books* annotated by the Sung master. Furthermore, Confucian thought never took religion seriously, and most Confucian thinkers maintained a skeptical attitude toward religion. Without doubt, Hu deeply though unconsciously was influenced by this secular bent in Confucianism.

But the problem is more complicated. Whether Hu Shih had read certain specific treatises of the Sung or whether he had been heavily influenced by Confucian thought in general is perhaps less significant than would appear. Whatever the surface similarity, the difference between Hu and Confucian thinkers was quite pronounced. A secularist or an agnostic is not necessarily antireligious, and many of the Confucian philosophers were not. Confucius, an agnostic, while refusing to discuss gods, was reverent toward and retained a distance from them. Moreover, he and many other Confucian thinkers were deeply religious in the philosophical sense, incessantly searching for the meaning of *t'ien*. Confucian scholars who attacked Buddhism were as against that religion as they were upholding Chinese culture. In brief, their criticism of Buddhism was, in part, an attempt to uphold the solipsistic status of the Confucian thought.

Hu Shih, on the other hand, assaulted Buddhism as an integral component of Chinese culture and mentality. He was, in the final analysis, a typical "modern" Chinese. Anti-Buddhist sentiment in the late nineteenth and twentieth centuries was strictly a "modern" issue. The popular Buddhism as practiced by the illiterate and semiliterate people then was a superstition-ridden religion devoid of intellectual content. Hu Shih's first contact was with this aspect of Buddhism, and this initial impression was long-lasting. He focused upon the Buddhism embodied in the womanfolk of Chi-ch'i. But Hu would not have been so aware of the superstitious practices had there not been a rising tide of iconoclasm in the nation. He was only thirteen and had not read the radical opinions of the reformers and revolutionaries. However, his two brothers were studying in Shanghai and a brother-in-law was doing business there. Traveling between the hometown and the metropolis, they periodically brought back to Hu Shih the prevailing views. This tide of iconoclasm dictated that a Chinese had to be anti-Buddhist to be "modern." How many "modern" Chinese in those years can one find who were not anti-Buddhist in their impressionable age? How many "modern" Chinese did not display the urge in their youth to destroy Buddhist "idols"? When he attempted to smash Buddha images in his village, Hu was merely following the footsteps of many famous "modern" leaders, including Sun Yat-sen.

Hu Shih's source of inspiration in dealing with other issues came increasingly from modern science. In his discussion of cause and effect, he took it as his task to argue for moral neutrality, refuting the Mencian notion of the innate goodness of human nature and Hsün-tzu's opposite stance. Instead, he accepted Wang Yang-ming's opinion that human nature "is neither good nor evil but capable of both goodness and evil." Hu recalled:

> I was then reading *The Science Readers*. Obtaining a highly superficial knowledge of science, I readily proceeded to use it to my own purposes. Mencius said, "The tendency of human nature to good is like the tendency of water to flow downwards. There is no man's nature which is not good, and there is no water which does not flow downwards." I said, "Mencius had no knowledge of science.... He knew neither the principle that water seeks its own level, nor the principle of gravity.... [W]ater is capable of going either up or down, resembling human nature which is neither innately good nor evil but which is capable of both goodness and evil.[37]

This argument, contrary to Hu's claim, was first advanced by Kao-tzu, with whom Mencius debated, but it nonetheless illustrated the direction of Hu's thinking. He was gradually moving away from the rationalist and skeptical attitude toward a more empirical, naturalist stance, and he based his reasoning on a new source of authority—modern science. Man's moral perfectibility, a perennial concern of Chinese philosophy, no longer occupied a place in his youthful mind.

Hu Shih also directed his attention to social issues. Again, he reflected his generation's preoccupations—the problem of marriage and of the continuation of the family name. Quoting Montesquieu's *De l'esprit des lois* via Yen Fu's translation, Hu defended parental guidance in marriage because, he held, parents were more experienced. But parental guidance had to be balanced by the feelings of the children involved. Thus, Hu proposed an eclectic solution, instead of advocating the practice of arranged marriage. Hu was thinking in social terms, and his opinions here must be understood in such a context. He urged that China's parents take their children's marriage as "the most serious matter of their families and clans" as well as

> a serious matter of the nation. . . . For several thousand years, our race has been deteriorating day by day, morals have been declining day by day, and physique has become weaker day by day. All these have been owing to the indifference of parents toward their children's marriage.[38]

A parallel commitment punctuated Hu's attitude toward the obsession with having descendants. In "On the Unreasonableness of the Custom of Insisting on Having Male Descendants," a vernacular essay written for a *pai-hua* newspaper in Anhwei, Hu declared,

> I now wish to recommend a most filial son to our four hundred million compatriots. Who is this son? He is "Society" . . . .
> Look at those heroes and noble-minded. They are immortalized and will never be forgotten. The whole society worships and commemorates them. Whether they have heirs or not will not affect our memory of them. . . . If a person has deeds that are beneficial . . . then society as a whole becomes his filial heir. You must remember that sons and grandsons, whether your own or adopted, are unreliable. Only the filial heir whom I have recommended to you is unfailingly sure.[39]

Hu's proposition reminds us of Liang Ch'i-ch'ao's "My View of Life and Death," an essay written in 1904. Drawing his inspiration from Buddhism, Confucianism, Christianity, and the concept of evolution, Liang maintained that the "small self" (the individual) is mortal while the "great self" (society), which is the aggregate of the total individual inheritance, is not. Since social progress and an individual's immortality depend upon that individual's contribution to the welfare of his posterity, he should make his utmost efforts to advance the interests of the "great self." Yet Liang, instead of repudiating the Confucian familial ethics, became even more convinced of their functional validity.[40]

In view of the similarity of Liang's and Hu's essays and of the proximity in time of their appearances, Hu Shih probably was influenced by Liang. In comparison, however, Hu's stance was a more radical one. Taken as a whole, his was an unambivalent rejection of one of the Confucian familial ethical tenets. Undoubtedly, his personal experiences played an important role. The death of his father when he was four, the difficult position of his young and widowed mother, the less than congenial atmosphere at home, the degenerate lifestyle of his opium-smoking brother, and the fate of a second brother, who was adopted out of the family, probably made him question the wisdom of the Chinese familial ethos. However, the more fundamental reason for his repudiation of the notion of having male descendants had to be attributed to the new value orientation of China's emerging intelligentsia. The social message in Hu's proposal was merely a reflection of the general concern of the age. Hu's "Society," Yen Fu's liberalism, and Liang Ch'i-ch'ao's various formulas were all designed to accomplish progress and independence for China.

Furthermore, Hu's notion of "Society" may also have been a personal, subliminal quest for immortality. In China, by the early years of the twentieth century, the nation and the family were actively competing with each other for an individual's loyalty. It had become more and more common for youth to seek a modern education in the major cities far away from home. Hu Shih did so at the age of thirteen. Instead of being with his parents, under their loving and protective care and fulfilling his filial duties, Hu was living with much older schoolmates from different regions of the empire, pondering national affairs and broad social and intellectual issues. Thus, family to him was no longer a clearly tangible locus of affection and loyalty. While this by no means indicated that feeling toward one's family had dissipated, it did suggest that family was no longer an exclusive concern for Hu

Shih. However, transferring one's loyalty from family to nation in those years was no easy matter. Where, after all, was the nation? The empire, to which Hu had no particular feeling of attachment, as we shall find out later, was crumbling and the republic, though to appear in just a few years, was perhaps a distant possibility to many contemporaries. Worse yet, whereas Hu seemed to have been committed to Yen Fu's and Liang Ch'i-ch'ao's ideas, China as a nation had reached no unequivocal consensus. In such a confusing milieu, a sensitive mind became a lone voyager and his own hero, pitting his ego against the world, seeking his own solutions and striving to satisfy his own yearnings. The family was too "narrow" and an obstacle to national progress. And yet there was no clear focus for national loyalty. Therefore, Hu Shih committed himself to "Society," an external and abstract entity which is independent of and can exist with or without a nation. Such a commitment enabled him, symbolically, to overcome chaos and the feeling of transience, to free himself from the bonds of the familial restrictions and traditional values. At the same time, "Society" represented a higher level of commitment than family.

In sharp contrast to his social and intellectual messages, Hu Shih's politics was moderate. The schools which he attended, particularly the China National Institute, were centers of revolution. Many of his teachers and schoolmates were devoted revolutionaries; some of them died for their causes.[41] Though he was involved to a certain degree, Hu was for the most part detached from the mainstream of radical politics.

In 1905 Hu Shih and three other students were selected to take a civil service examination sponsored by the Shanghai *yamen*. Three of them, Hu included, turned down the honor. Hu attributed his decision to the prevailing political atmosphere. The time was indeed one of great agitation. He was earnestly reading Liang Ch'i-ch'ao's radical writings and spelled with schoolmates in transcribing a copy of Tsou Jung's anti-Manchu tract, *The Revolutionary Army* (*Ke-ming chün*). When the Russo-Japanese War broke out, Hu and his friends became dejected with the Ch'ing neutrality and impotence. The assassination attempt on the former governor of Kwangsi, Wang Chih-ch'un, in the International Settlement, and the killing of a Chinese carpenter by a Russian sailor further heightened their political consciousness. Hu even sent a letter of protest to the Shanghai *taotai*. "How could we who were reading and transcribing *The Revolutionary Army* subject ourselves to the official examination?" Hu reasoned.[42]

Hu Shih's self-explanation should not go unchallenged, however. His decision not to take the examination was reached not so much from his political conviction as from his intellectual priorities, which will be discussed in some detail. In fact, neither Tsou Jung's *The Revolutionary Army* nor the drastic activities, including bombings and assassinations, undertaken by his teachers and schoolmates succeeded in converting him into a revolutionary.

In addition, Hu Shih was requested by his revolutionary friends at the China National Institute to negotiate with the customs service for the release of some contraband smuggled from Japan by a female student. However, he received the assignment because of his unusual English ability, not because of his politics. By the time the group arrived at the customs service around midnight, the office had been closed. Hu also took part in a major strike in 1908 against authorities at the China National Institute. The issue was student rights, and the incident resulted in a massive withdrawal of students, including Hu himself, and in the establishment of the New China National Institute. Years later, a former administrator of the Institute recalled that Hu was the one "most intransigently opposed to the school authority."[43]

Hu Shih's political moderation may be explained in part by his temperament and intellectual precociousness. Exceptionally bright, he was always younger and smaller than his schoolmates. From the beginning, he was thinking in dichotomous terms concerning intellectual exercise and physical expression. In his native Anhwei, Hu's brilliance and scholarly manner earned him the nickname Sir. And

> with the prefix Sir added to my name, I could not but behave like a Sir. Playing rough games with rough boys was out of the question. One day, as I was playing "throw copper coin" with a group of boys outside the door, an old gentleman of my father's generation passed by and saw me. Laughingly, he said, "Even Sir Men [Hu's early name] plays the coin game?" Instantaneously I felt so embarrassed and ashamed that I flushed up to the tip of my ears. I felt that I had greatly degraded my status as Sir.[44]

At the China National Institute, Hu Shih was very much left alone by his revolutionary schoolmates. He was not recruited to the ranks of the *T'ung-meng hui,* and for more than three years was not even forced, as were many others, to cut his queue. Hu did not learn the reason for this until twenty years later when a friend of his told him that the

T'ung-meng hui members in the school had decided that Hu had great scholarly potential and that as such they wanted to protect him from other distractions.[45]

From the start, then, Hu Shih demonstrated palpable traits of a "moral intellectual" in contrast to those of an "action intellectual." Traditional notions of propriety and emphasis on moral-intellectual accomplishment dictate that a gentleman not be engaged in manual labor or be associated with the populace. He is expected to be composed and not be overwhelmed by excessive emotions. His forte is moral suasion and intellectual discourse. If force is employed, one's conviction cannot be genuine. This explains, in part, why protest of the traditional style was essentially moral-intellectual in nature. Both Hu himself and others assigned him the role of a moral intellectual which he played all his life. This trait as manifested in Hu's attitude toward politics was of great importance. It is clear that even at this early stage Hu had already drifted away from the traditional values toward Western liberal ideas. But his thinking in terms of his political outlook disclosed the bent of a traditional moral intellectual—a detached observation and, in times of crisis, moral protest, but always peripheral to the practical workings of politics.

Traditional differentiation between the gentlemen and the people at large also imbues one with a deep-seated elitism. A Confucian scholar is the standard dispenser of new ideas and norms, the paternalistic spokesman of those below him, and the tireless champion of moral perfection. Personal purity is his foremost concern. When the atmosphere of social and psychological insecurity prevails, he often makes a meticulous, though unconscious, distinction between knowledge and action, devoting himself exclusively to moral-intellectual cultivation. Inevitably, the separation of knowledge from action generates a conservative political style and a craving for the status quo. Adverse political reality usually hardens his determination to preserve his independence. Whereas misrule arouses his indignation and offends his sense of decency, he is neither willing nor able to resort to radical means to change the reality. Invariably, he becomes a perpetuator of status quo and is profoundly suspicious of radical changes. A vicious circle is created: to continue his moral and intellectual pursuit, political stability becomes a prerequisite, thus intensifying his misgivings about any turmoil. More often than not, he is a moral conscience rather than an activist committed to revolution.

At this time, Hu Shih was simply indifferent toward politics. Later he would have to face the brutal reality of Chinese politics, and it was here that his detached elitism was reinforced by the Western values he adopted. Western education lengthened his distance from Chinese reality; and while his thinking remained essentially Chinese, his ideas would become mostly Western. Thus, Hu would come to look at Chinese politics from the outside as a Western-educated Chinese elite and judge its merits to a great extent by a foreign criterion.

The contrast between Hu Shih's intellectual radicalness and political moderation cannot be overemphasized. It was nothing short of extraordinary. While he was advocating the smashing of Buddhist idols and rejecting the central tenets of Confucian thought, he did not cut his queue until he had arrived in America in September, 1910.[46] Throughout his life, the disparity between his intellectual and political stance remained one of his most salient characteristics.

Hu Shih's stay in Shanghai in those six years was an exceptional intellectual venture and a period of uninhibited personal growth. But for all its reputation, its strategic position as a leading center of new ideas, the abundant opportunities it offered, and the modern conveniences it possessed, Shanghai was not able to completely satisfy Hu Shih and a good number of his contemporaries. In fact, the Chinese society simply could not give what he and many others were looking for. Inevitably, Shanghai was only to serve as a stopover for Hu on the way to a new adventure.

Chapter 2

Travel Abroad

Having stayed in Shanghai for six years, Hu Shih went to Peking to take the Boxer indemnity scholarship examination and, passing it, left for the United States in August, 1910. He was four months short of his nineteenth birthday. Recalling this major event twenty-one years later, he wrote:

> In 1908 my family was in great financial difficulty because of business failures. At the age of seventeen I found myself facing the necessity of supporting myself at school and my mother at home. I gave up my studies and taught elementary English for over a year. . . . In 1910 I taught Chinese for a few months.
> Those years (1909–10) were dark years in the history of China as well as in my personal history. Revolutions broke out in several provinces and failed each time. Quite a number of my former schoolmates at the China National Institute . . . were involved in these plots and not a few lost their lives. Several of these political fugitives came to Shanghai and stayed with me. We were all despondent and pessimistic. We drank, wrote pessimistic poetry, talked day and night, and often gambled for no stakes. We even engaged an old actor to teach us singing. . . .
> Despondency and drudgery drove us to all kinds of dissipation. One rainy night I got deadly drunk, fought with a policeman in the street, and landed myself in prison for the night. . . . I decided to quit teaching and my friends. After a month of hard work, I went to Peking to take the examination for the scholarship founded on the returned American portion of the Boxer Indemnity. I passed the examination and in July sailed for America.[1]

This self-analysis is too simplistic to be taken seriously.[2] Though financial difficulties, despondency, and drudgery may well have prompted Hu to seek a change of environment, they should not have had any logical relationship with a trip to America. What this decision of Hu's at a tender age divulged was his changed value commitment and China's mental and intellectual horizon.

By the time Hu Shih took the Boxer indemnity examination in 1910, China had been undergoing a fundamental revolution in values. Recent scholarship has convincingly demonstrated that major ideas of the New Culture movement of the future May Fourth era had already become ingrained at this time. Benjamin Schwartz observes that

> in many respects, the generation of K'ang Yu-wei, Yen Fu, Liang Ch'i-ch'ao, T'an Ssu-t'ung, Chang Ping-lin, Wang Kuo-wei and others was, in fact, the breakthrough generation; they were the real transformers of values and the bearers of new ideas from the West. . . . By the first decade of the twentieth century the mystique of revolution and that whole general disposition which we call radicalism (in its pre-Leninist forms) had also won a foothold.[3]

To leaders of the reform generation of 1898 and the May Fourth generation of the 1910s, China's Westernization was an inevitable fact. The only point in dispute was not whether, but to what extent, China should adopt the Western way.

From the outset the intellectual reorientation was directed toward Anglo-Saxon culture. Yen Fu was convinced that "Great Britain was the model par excellence of wealth and power" and that "it is Great Britain's commitment to liberal values which has made that nation the most powerful state in the world."[4] Liang Ch'i-ch'ao was equally uninhibited. As early as 1896 he intimated that the United States was the foremost power.[5] And in the *New Citizen*, he remarked that the Anglo-Saxon race occupied more than one fourth of the land on earth, ruled over a quarter of the world population, and daily expanded their sphere of influence. As a consequence, English had become the most widely used language.[6] Liang concluded,

> In view of these facts, we should know who is the best nation in the world. Compare the five races of different colors and there is no question that the white race is the best. Compare the different peoples within the white race and there is no question that the Teutons are the best. Compare the different nations that are composed of Teutonic peoples and there is no question that the Anglo-Saxon is the

best. This is no snobbish nonsense. It results from the inescapable working of the law of natural evolution.⁷

In view of the eminence of Great Britain and the United States in China, the large number of Chinese studying in Japan represented only a surface phenomenon. One may well question whether Japan was indeed the intended destination of these students. More likely, such external factors as geographical proximity, economic considerations, cultural congeniality, and linguistic similarity were the major reasons that Japan came to have the largest aggregation of overseas Chinese students. Certainly, Chinese were awed by Japan's astounding success, but its success merely confirmed the superiority of Western values and only enhanced China's admiration of the West. Chinese students went to Japan, then, not so much for the sake of learning the Japanese way as for the sake of acquiring Western knowledge via Japan. Perceiving Japan as no more than a transmitting station, many of them would leave it for an English-speaking country when the opportunity arose. Ting Wen-chiang (V. K. Ting, 1887–1936) went to Japan in 1902. But when Wu Chih-hui (1865–1953) wrote that opportunities for education in Great Britain were better, Ting persuaded his parents to allow him to go to England, departing in the spring of 1904.⁸ Many more examples can be offered. This brings forth a more basic issue: how indelible was Japan's influence on China in those years? Chang Hao writes of Liang Ch'i-ch'ao's case,

> While Japanese influence did help determine many of Liang Ch'i-ch'ao's practical concerns, it is, however, far from clear that it was as significant in determining his basic values and ideas. At the very least . . . the Japanese factor cannot compare with indigenous Chinese tradition and Western learning as an independent intellectual source.⁹

During the last decade of the nineteenth century, English rapidly became the most popular language among Chinese youth. Chiang Meng-lin began his study of English and Japanese prior to the reform movement. Before long he entered a Catholic school to concentrate on the former; still later his father sent him and his brother for English lessons from an American lady. In 1904, having acquired his *hsiu-ts'ai* degree, Chiang "longed for a better and more [W]esternized school for by this time I could see that the wind blew in the direction of [W]esternization, irrespective of whether China had constitutional reforms or revolution."[10] More instructive, many Chinese studied English, not Japanese, while they were in Japan. In 1898 Wang Kuo-wei enrolled at the Institute of Eastern Language (*Tung-wen hsüeh-she*) in Shanghai, founded by Lo Chen-yü (1866–1940). There Wang "attained proficiency in Japanese and a good foundation in English." After the Institute was dissolved in 1900, he continued his study of English on his own. In the autumn of 1901, financed by Lo Chen-yü, Wang went to Japan for further studies. In Tokyo he attended *Butsuri Gakko* (school of physics) where he studied English during the day and mathematics at night.[11] At the *Ch'iu-shih* Academy in Hangchow, Ch'en Tu-hsiu (1879–1942) studied French, English, and naval architecture. About the turn of the century he went to Japan where he attended an English language school.[12]

Enthusiasm for the English language was in part associated with the desire to go to either England or America for Western knowledge. Even as early as the 1900s, America was the more popular. The phenomenon was intriguing and invites a closer examination. Possibly, America was in the Chinese mind a symbol of equality and independence, and its growing strength as a Pacific power increased its prestige in China. Further, as a spacious and expanding country, it was thought to offer more choices. Craving for a trip to the United States began before the civil service examination system had been abolished. In 1902 Tuan-fang (1861–1911), the reform-minded governor of Hupeh, instructed Shih Chao-chi (Alfred Sao-ke Sze, 1877–1958) to take a group of government-supported students, Tuan-fang's son included, to study in the United States. Ku Wei-chün (Wellington Koo, 1887–), who would emerge as one of modern China's most eminent diplomats, went along with the group even though he did not have a scholarship.[13] Recollecting in 1904, the year he obtained the *hsiu-ts'ai* degree, Chiang Meng-lin wrote, "In spite of the persuasions of friends studying in Japan, I stuck stubbornly to my belief. I entered Nanyang College with a view to preparing myself for American universities. As for the textbooks on Western subjects were in English, it suited me splendidly." In August, 1908, Chiang "secured my ticket and boarded an American Mail liner for San Francisco. . . . There were about a dozen Chinese students on the same boat."[14] In 1903, while traveling through America, Liang Ch'i-ch'ao remembered seeing the names of 50 Chinese students, among whom were three girls. In 1905, there were 130 Chinese students in America; in 1906–7, 217; and in 1909, 183.[15]

The number of Chinese students in the United States during those years was negligible compared to the total number of Chinese studying abroad, but the meaning it signified was not. Equally suggestive were the cases of those who were not able to fulfill their wishes of pursuing further education in America. Kuo Mo-jo reported that, in 1907 while still a middle school student,

> I was extremely dissatisfied with the school curriculum, but aside from it I could not find anything [to satisfy my intellectual appetite]. I was agitated and anxious to an intolerable degree.
> By then the craze for going to America had been gradually spreading. Of course, I entertained great fantasies about Europe and America.[16]

Unfortunately, Kuo had to settle for a trip to Japan. This example makes one wonder how many others who had similar objectives made the same compromise.

With this historical perspective in mind, we can surmise that even before it was done away with in 1905, the examination system was no longer perceived as a symbol of status or a desirable avenue for personal satisfaction. In fact, leading intellectuals had long urged its abolition. As early as 1895, Yen Fu suggested that the writing of eight-legged essays be replaced with Western learning. "China will not survive without a radical transformation. What then is the foremost important step? I say that the very prerequisite is to abolish the eight-legged essay."[17] A year later, Liang Ch'i-ch'ao appealed to the Imperial Court to abrogate the examination system.[18] Thus, at least a decade before its demise, the prestige and relevance of this institution had been severely undermined. When it was finally abolished, "there was no serious protest."[19] In view of the craze for going abroad and a persistent concentration on the English and Japanese languages before the disappearance of the examination system, can we not argue that many of China's elite had long anticipated its fate?

Hu Shih came to America not because of financial difficulties or political goals. These factors certainly darkened his mood and confused his youthful mind, but never altered his goal. Financial difficulties, if indeed they had been serious enough, would have prevented him from making the trip. Politics was even a lesser consideration to him: he was for the most part observing others' political involvements and revolutionary activities. The primary factor which prompted him to journey to the United States was his intellectual priorities in the changed circumstances.

It was indicative that the only foreign language Hu studied in Shanghai was English. Since he pursued it diligently, we must assume that he was well motivated. The abolition of the civil service examination system had no meaningful impact on him, for neither in his autobiography nor in his available writings published in Shanghai did he even mention it. The disappearance of this institution was a major event in modern Chinese history only from our perspective, not in terms of the life experiences of the contemporaries. Hu did not seem to have difficulty in deciding to forgo the opportunity to take the examination in 1904. In that year, there were 130 Chinese studying in America, and he may well have been one of a growing number who were vaguely entertaining the idea of going to the United States. Hu began teaching English in 1908 when he was merely seventeen—a fact which amply demonstrated the heavy demand to learn that language. One cannot escape the conclusion that some of those who were taking English may have had in mind the ambition of going to one of the English-speaking countries.

From the available writings of Hu Shih, we know that he was highly conscious of the impact upon values which Anglo-Saxon culture had brought about. In "Patriotism," he exhorted the Chinese to

> preserve the glorious history of the fatherland. . . . If we discard our own history, we will be a despicable people and willingly obsequious slaves. Some people have indeed forgotten their own history. They are so willingly flattering that they constantly speak of foreigners as superior in every way and of China as worthless. . . .
> . . . We should make efforts to glorify the literature of the fatherland; we should not be so base as to take it as an unusual accomplishment when we know a few A.B.C.D.s [the rudiments of the English language]. If we do so, can we be considered human beings?[20]

In "The Chinese Government," Hu wrote:

> The United States, with a conspiratorial mind, was considering returning [part of the Boxer] indemnity to China. Now that this has

been done, the Chinese government is exceedingly grateful for the gesture of magnanimity, looking up to America as if it were the all merciful, the kindest Buddha. Now a United States fleet is coming to China for a visit. . . . The Chinese government is dispatching a special commissioner to Amoy to make sure that the Americans will be obsequiously served.[21]

These writings provide extraordinary insight into both Hu Shih's inner world and China's mental state. Hu perceived his country as being self-debasing, lacking in self-esteem and decency. His very admonition and emphasis suggest that the Chinese government may indeed have been servile to America and that some Chinese may indeed have taken the knowledge of rudimentary English as a feat. Hu Shih was deeply disturbed and anxious to arrest China's cultural and psychological crisis. For all his good intention and determination, however, was he himself immune from the burden which many of his compatriots experienced? Was he subliminally airing the worst fears in himself? Was he not trying to block off a negative identity in himself— "that is, of everything in himself which he tried to isolate and subdue and which yet was part of him"?[22]

Hu's dilemma was not to be solved easily. After leaving the New China National Institute, he engaged himself in carnal pleasures and intemperate habits. A sense of direction and certainty was lost. There were no longer established norms and values to which one could adhere, and his refusal to take part in the civil service examination bespoke the centrifugal tendencies then. The ringleader of Hu's debauching friends was a German language teacher by the name of Ottomeir, an offspring of a German-Chinese marriage. Ottomeir managed to learn to speak Cantonese and Shanghai and Peking dialects; he had an intimate knowledge of Chinese games of leisure. Hu and a few friends from Szechwan were Ottomeir's next-door neighbors. Not far away were still more young men with revolutionary backgrounds, including T'ang Ts'ai-ch'ang's son. Their usual schedules were incessant mahjongg games, drinking, and visits to female entertainers. "In less than two months, I learned them all," Hu reminisced.[23] The gambling could easily last a whole day, and so could their drunkenness. Then, one rainy night in the spring of 1910, trouble befell Hu. A group of them were drinking in a pleasure house. After getting deadly drunk, Hu left alone by a ricksha. When he regained sobriety, he found himself in a jailhouse. His cotton jacket was soaking wet and muddy, and one of his shoes was missing. He recalled:

> A sergeant was sitting beside a desk, and a muddy patrolman, standing, was answering his questions.
> "Is this the man?"
> "Yes, it is."
> "Go on."
> The muddy patrolman said: "Close to midnight last night, I was on duty at Hai-ning Road. It was raining heavily. Suddenly (he pointed at me), he walked toward me, knocking at the wall with his leather shoe. . . . No sooner had I turned on my flashlight than he began to berate me."
> "How did he berate you?"
> "He called me 'slave of foreigners!' (*wai-kuo nu-ts'ai*)"[24]

A policeman in foreign-dominated Shanghai was a symbol of foreign supremacy, and Hu, even in his drunken state, remembered to call him a "slave of foreigners." Hu must have been engaged in painful struggles within himself. Subliminally, however, the goal had never been in doubt. Immediately after the night in jail, he resigned his teaching position and went to Peking for the Boxer indemnity scholarship examination. His crisis epitomized a most excruciating and humiliating experience that numerous Chinese were to go through. On the one hand, Hu condemned America as "conspiratorial" and admonished his fellow countrymen not to take the rudimentary knowledge of English as an unusual accomplishment. On the other hand, he could not avoid identifying himself with the "conspiratorial" conqueror, and he would spend years mastering a foreign language the importance of which he tried to minimize. Scoring a full mark on Chinese and sixty on English, Hu placed tenth for the first group of subjects. Two hundred and seventy passed the hurdle and gained admission to take the second group of tests which included higher algebra, plane and solid geometry, trigonometry, chemistry, biology, Latin, modern languages, and European history. Hu did relatively poorly on these and placed fifty-fifth. Altogether, seventy were selected for the American journey.[25] Judging by the number of examinees, the examination should be considered competitive. And there should be no doubt that only the brightest participated in the competition. Take Hu's schoolmates at Cornell as examples. In 1913, three Chinese, Hu included, were elected to Phi Beta Kappa; a year later, four Chinese joined the Sigma Xi honor society of sixty-seven.[26]

Hu Shih left no record for us to detect his mood then, but two others in the same group did shortly after the examination. In part they wrote:

> [T]he United States of America generously remitted a portion of the Boxer indemnity to the Chinese government with the implicit proviso that inasmuch as the remission is an act of international conciliation and probity, the Celestial government should invest the money in some means whereby the existing *entente cordiale* between the countries in question may be forever maintained. The Pekin [sic] government, in due recognition of the American magnanimity, decided to spend the sum solely for the education of Chinese youths in the U.S. institutions of learning. . . .
>
> The seventy fortunate ones were now as gay as they were "ungay" before the announcement of their appointment. The doors of the Board of Education and the Board of Foreign Affairs were thrown wide open for them, and congratulations were tendered to them by every one of these high dignitaries. "Boys, go back to Shanghai immediately and get ready to sail for the Chinese Mecca of Education on August 16." . . .
>
> Shanghai now came into view. No sooner had the ship anchored another demonstration of joy was presented by the kinsmen and associates of the seventy passengers on the boat. Guards on the wharf had great difficulty to resume order within their jurisdiction. The tower of Babel must have fallen down in ancient times. What a medley of tongues used in greetings! After this rush, porters, drivers, tailors, and barbers had their share. So generous were they in offering us their services that we felt we were great sailors coming back from a victorious battle. Our doorkeepers soon became ill-tempered, because they had to accept so often for their young masters the numerous invitations to dinners, tea parties, and what not.[27]

What more poignant revelation was there that divulged so deeply China's self-image and its perception of America? The two authors described themselves as "the seventy fortunate ones," "young masters," "great sailors coming back from a victorious battle." The greetings and celebrations tendered to them could not have been more elaborate. The United States was no longer regarded as a barbaric country but as "the Chinese Mecca of Education." In a matter of five years, the American connection had supplanted the civil service examination as one of the most indispensable criteria for personal advancement and vainglory. Both "the seventy fortunate ones" and officials of education and foreign affairs unequivocally acknowledged this. More important, the two authors not only approved the return of the Boxer indemnity itself, but also gullibly perceived the intention of the American government as an act of "magnanimity" and "of international conciliation and probity."[28] Perhaps most startling was that the predominance of the West had penetrated even to the minds of porters, drivers, tailors, and barbers who, without clearly knowing the meaning of a trip to America, nevertheless sensed its enormous importance. Did not their "generous" services reflect more than an ordinary degree of reverence?

Was Hu Shih's mood much different from that of the two authors quoted above? His bound-footed, semiliterate, widowed mother apparently did not register any complaint about his partaking in the Boxer examination, and one of his brothers accompanied him on the trip to Peking. To realize his plan of going abroad, Hu had more than his share of problems to deal with. He had to borrow money to pay a debt, to cover his expenses to, in, and from Peking, and to help his mother settle more permanently.[29] He had to depart the country in such a hurry that he did not even have time to bid farewell to his mother.[30] All these illustrated his aspirations and determination. The anticipation of the journey to the United States must have been a fulfilling and exciting experience. It was in such a mood that Hu sailed for America on August 16, 1910.

Chapter 3

From Agriculture to Philosophy

In September, 1910, immediately upon his arrival in Ithaca, Hu Shih enrolled in the New York State College of Agriculture at Cornell University. For the next year and a half he studied biology and botany, plant physiology, and pomology. Not until the spring of 1912 did he transfer to philosophy. Hu spent five academic years at Cornell, departing for Columbia University in late September, 1915, to concentrate on Chinese philosophy.

Given his forte in the humanities, Hu's decision to major in agriculture was a strange and strenuous one. An examination of the motives behind Hu's academic choice should tell us something more than his academics.

Over the years Hu Shih was reluctant to reveal the true reason for his decision to major in agriculture and then to transfer to philosophy. First, he attributed the selection of agriculture to his craze toward science. He wrote in a free verse shortly before his departure from the United States in the summer of 1917, that when he first arrived in America, his ambition was to "plow" and "sow." Considering humanities trivial and irrelevant to national salvation, he often dreamed of planting vegetables and trees.[1] Agriculture, as a practical science, certainly had its appeal. Many perceived it as an effective tool toward revitalizing the Chinese nation. But even in an age of highly charged emotions and strong nationalistic feelings, the novel discipline of science had its limits. Did the Chinese youth have any personal ambitions? How could such an impersonal, high-sounding cause as "save the nation" have generated such a fanatically sustaining power? How often was Hu Shih thinking of the nation when he struggled with mathematics under candlelight deep into the night or when he was taking plant physiology and pomology?

Interestingly, after they transferred from science to other disciplines, these Chinese again tried to justify their respective *new* subjects. Looking back in 1917 at his academic choice, Hu Shih asked rhetorically and then immediately answered his own question: "Many things are necessary for the salvation of the nation, and which of them ought not be undertaken? But I am by nature suited for only one or two things."[2] Likewise, Lu Hsün in 1906 explained his decision to transfer from medicine to literature.

> Before the term was over I had left for Tokyo, because after seeing these slides [which showed a Chinese about to be executed by the Japanese as other Chinese stood around him watching the spectacle] I felt that medical science was not such an important thing after all. People from an ignorant and weak country, no matter how physically healthy and strong they may be, could only serve to be made examples of, or to become onlookers of utterly meaningless spectacles. Such a condition was more deplorable than dying of illness. Therefore our first important task was to change their spirit, and at that time I considered the best medium for achieving this end was literature. I was thus determined to promote a literary movement.[3]

Chiang Meng-lin came to the United States to enroll in agriculture at the University of California, Berkeley. After one semester, a friend of his suggested in 1909 that he take a major in the social sciences which, the friend said, were even more vital for China than was agriculture and which would give him a broader outlook. Chiang was apparently already struggling with himself about his academic choice. His friend's advice, therefore,

> set me thinking, for I was at the crossroads and must sooner or later make a final decision. . . .
> Early one morning, on my way to a barn to watch the milking, I met a number of fresh-looking youngsters—pretty girls and lively boys—on their way to school. Suddenly an idea struck me: I am here to study how to raise animals and plants; why not study how to raise men? Instead of going to the barn I went into the Berkeley hills and sat under an old oak tree overlooking beautiful sunlit San Francisco Bay and the Golden Gate. As I gazed into the bay, thoughts on the rise and decline of the successive dynasties in China presented themselves one after another. All of a sudden I saw as if in a vision

children emerging like water nymphs from the waters of the bay and asking me to give them schools. I decided to take education as my major, in the College of Social Science.[4]

These revelations, while interesting, do not explain much. What, after all, *is* the most important subject? To be sure, this group of Chinese was overwhelmed by a sense of responsibility, but we cannot seriously believe that none of them had any personal motives. Their justifications were hindsight wisdom and only revealed how popular science was, but not why it was popular to such an extent.

The craze toward science marked a deepening feeling of alienation among China's intelligentsia. Since traditional subjects could no longer satisfy their curiosity, the conventional route to fame was to be avoided. The new challenge no longer lay in probing the human mind or acquiring traditional wisdom, but in breaking riddles of the universe and taking on novel adventures. This, of course, should not be construed to mean that Chinese intelligentsia had no more feeling of attachment to their country and society. To solve the predicament of their urge to remain detached and yet committed, many of them chose a career in science, a subject presumably neutral in value. A scientist, while always beneficial to mankind, can more easily avoid entanglements in human affairs. What was Hu Shih telling us in his rejection of the civil service examination, his dogged struggle with mathematics under candlelight and his dream of "planting vegetables and trees"? Kuo Mo-jo's account was particularly suggestive. He went to Japan in 1914 to enroll in the First Higher School of Tokyo. Although demonstrating talent in literature, he was convinced that belles-lettres, history, and philosophy were useless. At the same time, he was repelled by the idea of studying law, political science, and economics. Determined to be a natural scientist and yet strongly averse to mathematics, Kuo elected medicine as a compromise.[5] Disinterest in law, political science, and economics, all of which entail an intimate association with social and political affairs, was an indication of Kuo's profound sense of estrangement. Medicine, on the other hand, would enable him to avoid a close contact with society and simultaneously give him a useful skill to serve it.

More than two decades after he first enrolled in agriculture, Hu Shih offered another explanation for his decision to major in that subject. This time it was an economic consideration. "The College of

Agriculture then charged no tuition fee and I thought I might be able to save a part of my monthly allowance to send to my mother."[6] This explanation was sheer nonsense. Financial problems were indeed one of Hu's concerns, and he did occasionally help his mother. In March, 1914, for example, he borrowed from an Ithaca businessman, Fred Robinson, two hundred dollars, half of which he immediately sent home.[7] In the final analysis, however, finances were never an important, much less the determining, factor in any of Hu's decisions. They did not deter him from going abroad, nor did it alter his academic plan in any manner. Further, he helped his mother financially only symbolically, possibly to soothe his own conscience. When he made the transfer to philosophy, he had to pay four semesters' tuition fee at once for the total sum of $200. "But I felt at home in my new studies and have never regretted the change."[8]

Hu decided to transfer to philosophy for a simple reason. It was, as he acknowledged much later, his "early interest in philosophy, in Chinese philosophy and historical subjects" and his "interest in literature."[9] Hu's year and a half in agriculture was understandably painful. He recalled: "I had had no experience on a farm and my heart was not in agriculture. The freshman courses in English Literature and German interested me far more than Farm Practice and Pomology."[10] One of the Cornell regulations at the time stipulated that students with a grade point average of eighty on the required eighteen hours would have the freedom of taking two additional hours of elective outside their majors. Given such an opportunity, Hu elected Professor James E. Creighton's history of philosophy in the College of Arts.[11] In fact, in the fall semester of 1911, half a year before the transfer, Hu took the following courses: history of philosophy, aesthetics, ethics, history of fine arts, logic, American politics, political parties in America, and psychology.[12]

It was interesting that, with such a clear propensity in the humanities and with no aptitude for farm practice or pomology, Hu was able to remain in the College of Agriculture for as long as he did. It should be noted that it was common for many May Fourth figures to live a double life: the life of what they wanted to be and the life of what they actually were. Examples abound. After graduation from the Sixth Higher School in Tokyo in 1918, Kuo Mo-jo entered the medical school of Kyushu Imperial University at Fukuoka. But instead of being a source of pride and joy, medical school proved to be a torture, so much so that he had the urge on more than one occasion to switch to literature. His close friend Ch'eng Fang-wu, however, dissuaded him by arguing that one does not have to specialize in literature to become a litterateur. Ch'eng himself majored in ordnance but was a devoted connoisseur of literature. Toward the end of his medical education, Kuo simply ceased to attend classes. His first poems were published in the early autumn of 1919 in the literary supplement of the *Shih-shih hsin-pao,* and his most famous ones were written the following year. In the spring of 1921, through Ch'eng's efforts, Kuo obtained a position on the editorial staff of the T'ai-tung Publishing Company where he worked in the summer during his years at medical school. Between 1922 and 1924, Kuo and his associates founded and edited the *Creation Quarterly* (*Ch'uang-tsao chi-k'an*), *Creation Weekly* (*Ch'uang-tsao chou-k'an*), and *Creation Daily* (*Ch'uang-tsao jih-pao*). In this period, besides producing literary works of his own and editing Creation Society publications, Kuo translated Goethe's *The Sorrows of Young Werther* and part of *Faust,* the *Rubaiyat of Omar Khayyam,* the first book of Nietzsche's *Thus Spake Zarathustra,* and a number of poems by English and German Romantic poets. Kuo also rendered classical Chinese poetry into the vernacular. It was amazing that he was able to acquire his medical degree in April, 1923, although he never practiced the trade.[13]

The case of Chao Yüan-jen (Chao Yuen-ren; Y. R. Chao, 1892–1982) was equally indicative. Having passed the Boxer indemnity scholarship examination in 1910, he enrolled at Cornell in the autumn of that year, entering the same class with Hu Shih. Chao majored in mathematics and physics, while devoting much of his time to studying phonology and music where his real interest lay. Moving to Harvard in 1915, he concentrated on physics and at the same time studied philosophy and musical composition. After receiving a Ph.D. in physics in 1918, Chao taught the subject at Cornell in the academic year 1919–20. During those years, he composed music and published a series of articles in the *Chinese Students' Monthly* on the phonetic transcription of the Chinese language. Returning to China in 1920, Chao began teaching mathematics at Tsinghua University. What prompted him to switch disciplines, according to one account, was quite accidental. In that year, he was asked to accompany Bertrand Russell on his tour of China. Interpreting Russell's lectures into various Chinese dialects with great fluency and accuracy, Chao's friends encouraged him to concentrate his future studies in the field of linguistics, to which he readily consented.[14] This account, however, reads like an anecdote. One may well wonder how much longer Chao would have been able to continue in mathematics had he not acted as Russell's interpreter.

Hu Shih followed an identical pattern. While he was going against his interest, his diary of the first year and a half was filled with notes on the books he read and summaries of the essays he wrote. The reading covered an extraordinarily wide range, from the pre-Ch'in classics to poetry, history, novels, Shakespeare, Francis Bacon, Wordsworth, Plato, Darwin, Goethe, Henry George, Dickens, and many others. In addition, Hu regularly practiced calligraphy, studied Latin with an American friend, and composed poetry in both Chinese and English.[15]

These Chinese, of course, were exceptionally bright individuals who could spend an unusual amount of time on different subjects without jeopardizing their academic standing. While devoting much of his time to phonology and music, Chao Yüan-jen was still outstanding enough to be elected to Phi Beta Kappa in 1913 and to Sigma Xi honor society a year later.[16] The importance of maintaining this "double life" cannot be overemphasized, for only when sustained by their true interests could these individuals manage to stay in their academic choices for as long as they did.

Once settled in the College of Arts and Sciences, Hu Shih began to excel. There was a marked improvement in his academic standing.[17] In the spring of 1913, a year after his transfer, he was elected to Phi Beta Kappa. By enrolling in the summer school for three consecutive years, he was able to complete the requirements for the B.A. degree in February, 1914. In May of that year, he was awarded a graduate fellowship to enter the Sage School to continue his study of philosophy.[18] In early May, 1914, his essay "A Defense of Browning's Optimism" won him the Hiram Corson Browning Prize, established in honor of Robert Browning by the late Cornell professor of English, Hiram Corson.[19] Two years later, Hu won another major award with his essay "Is There a Substitute for Force in International Relations?" in a contest sponsored by the American Association for International Conciliation.[20]

Hu's brilliance was readily acknowledged. On the occasion of his winning the Hiram Corson Browning Prize, a newspaper commented: "The strange anomaly of a Chinese student excelling all English-speaking students in English is attracting wide attention to Mr. Suh Hu, the only Chinese student who has ever won first prize in English at Cornell University."[21] Louis P. Lochner, a leader of the Cosmopolitan movement and a lifelong friend of Hu's, showed his enormous admiration for his friend when he wrote in January, 1914, to persuade Hu to stop smoking.

> I was dead in earnest when I told you last summer that I thought it was a mistake for you to smoke as incessantly as you did. . . . The fact is that I have seldom taken as intimately to a foreign friend as I have to you, and I honestly and without flattery believe that you are a rare genius. I think it is your duty to society to preserve your intellectual powers to their fullest extent, and for that reason I think you ought to take every precaution to keep in good health.[22]

Chang Loy of Harvard University, himself an exceptional student, complimented Hu as "the most scholarly of all the Chinese students in America."[23] The ultimate tribute to Hu was paid by his erstwhile professor of English, Martin Sampson, who, so overwhelmed by his brilliance, said: "It is entirely possible that a thousand years from now Cornell may still be known as the place where Hu Shih went to college."[24]

Hu must have felt at home in his new academic pursuit. But academics were only part of his total experience in his American journey. He was to encounter difficulties and crises, as well as moments of joy and triumph.

Part II
Cultural Confrontation

Chapter 4

Christianity

One of the first Western cultural elements which Hu Shih encountered was Christianity. The contact began early in his student days at Cornell University. In February, 1911, he started private Latin lessons with his friend Mr. Ace. The next month, Hu went to a religious gathering at the invitation of Ace.[1] In the months that followed, Hu's religion-related activities must have been frequent, for on June 13, he suddenly departed for a summer convocation of the Chinese Christian Students' Association at Pocono Pines, a scenic resort in eastern Pennsylvania. The meeting attracted about thirty-five Chinese and two hundred Americans and lasted from June 14 to 19. It was during his stay at Pocono Pines that Hu became a Christian convert.[2]

Hu gave this intimate account of his conversion in his diary:

> June 18. Sunday. The fifth day. The topic of the discussion session was "Ancestor Worship." Bible class. Father Hutchington lectured on Chapter 20, Sections 1 through 16 of *Matthew*. It was extremely lucid and moving. In the afternoon Shao-t'ang expounded to me the meaning of Christianity for about three hours. I was deeply moved. From now on, I am a Christian convert! In the evening, Mr. Mercer recounted his life experiences, which again were extremely moving. I cried, and so did others. When the lecture was over, seven persons stood up, declaring themselves Christian converts. I was one of them.[3]

Three days later, while still at Pocono Pines, Hu added more details about his conversion in a letter to a close friend in China, Hsü I-sun:

> When I entered the China National Institute, Ch'en Shao-t'ang (a Kwangsi man) was one of the classmates. A year later, he unexpect-

edly left for *Shou-chen* mission to concentrate on the English language and was subsequently baptized as a Christian. He came to the United States two years ago, and we met again. His behavior is like a Ch'eng-Chu scholar, evoking awe and love. His unshakable faith in God strikes me deeply, and yet his intellect and vision are by no means inferior to ours. It is obvious that religion can achieve a fundamental transformation in a person's character.

Last night, Mr. Mercer, an associate of Dr. John R. Mott [who headed the International Committee of the YMCA], confessed that while a student at college, he acquired a number of evil habits . . . leaving nothing untried. As a result, his father severed relations with him, and he became a drifter without means for subsistence. After an attempt to drown himself, Mercer was rescued by police and sent to a church where he was converted to Christianity. And he soon began his charity work. Some years later, Mercer by chance revealed his experience. When his father read the newspaper report about it . . . they were reunited. Mercer's father was a prominent lawyer, and a relative of the Mercers' was the immediate past president of the United States [Theodore Roosevelt?]. Growing up in the White House, Mercer's education was without doubt the very best. Yet he ended up as a vagabond. Eventually, it was the transforming power of religion which did everything that education, wealth, family, friends, and the test of poverty failed to accomplish. . . . When Mercer was describing his reunion with his father and his father's passionate cry, "My boy! my boy!" my eyes were filled with tears, and so were all the other listeners'. When the confession was over, seven persons (They were all Chinese. Among the Chinese participants of the convocation, only eight or nine were not Christians.) stood up and declared themselves Christian converts. I was one of them.[4]

As a growing number of Chinese students arrived in the United States in the early years of the twentieth century, various church groups began to conduct proselytizing campaigns directed at them. Many years later, Hu Shih still remembered their approach: it was

> to show the Chinese students . . . the best aspects, the more refined and fundamental aspects of American life, civilization and culture . . . to enable the Chinese students to see the real life of Christian home, to bring the Chinese students in contact with the best men and women in the American communities, to make them understand what an American home and American character are like—what Christian life is like in its family and civic activity.
>
> At Cornell . . . many Christian homes threw open their doors to Chinese students. The duty of such Christian leaders was to invite Chinese students . . . to visit their homes; . . . to organize Bible

classes for the Chinese students if there was felt a need for such classes; to introduce them to local churches if that was desired by the students.[5]

The summer convocation held at Pocono Pines was one of the activities sponsored by these organizations. The proselytizing campaign was particularly effective because Hu Shih himself was vulnerable. At the time of his conversion in June, 1911, he was merely nineteen and a half, away from home and studying agriculture with apparent disinterest. Understandably, his life was lonely and difficult, involving many adjustments. Various religious organizations, thus, filled a critical vacuum by providing friendship and practial help. Just at this time, Hu encountered a personal tragedy. On June 8, five days before leaving for Pocono Pines, he received word that Ch'eng Lo-t'ing, a close friend whose family had given him financial assistance to go to Peking for the Boxer scholarship examination, had died a premature death. According to Hu, the tragedy saddened him greatly and was instrumental in prompting him to attend the convocation. He wrote on June 17, 1911,

> I learned from I-sun the sad news about Lo-t'ing. I have since been feeling numb and empty. Further, after the semester ended, I could find nothing meaningful to do. Every time when I quieted down, I felt that life was such that it offered little consolation and happiness. I came to [the convocation] mainly because I wanted to immerse myself in the strength of religion to alleviate my sadness and pessimism.[6]

These, however, were contributing but by no means determining factors that explained Hu Shih's decision to attend the assembly and his positive response to Christianity. By his own account, he had developed an atheistic tendency since age eleven or twelve. It prompted him to attack Buddhism and religious beliefs in general, denounce the notion of the existence of spirit, and advocate the smashing of religious images. In view of this background, his conversion was too sudden. Hu did not mention any inner struggle, nor did he challenge, as in the case of Buddhism, the validity of Christian doctrines.

To be sure, Hu Shih perceived Christianity as an ethical-moral system. He admired Ch'en Shao-t'ang's awe-evoking behavior as a result of religious influence and was profoundly moved by Mercer's confession. Thus, without stating so, Hu regarded character cultivation and transformation as the greatest merit of this Western religion. It may be argued that he was unwittingly influenced by the prevalent Chinese attitude of equating the function of religion (*chiao*) with that of education (*chiao*) and that because of his overriding attention to the ethical-moral function of Christianity, no serious conflict ever developed between his atheistic inclination and his conversion to Christianity. This reasoning is persuasive to an extent, but the real question remains. Why did he fail to see the "superstitious" elements in Christianity while devastatingly attacking "superstitious" Buddhism? Moreover, by stripping Christianity of its religious nature and admiring it as an ethical- moral system, Hu put Christianity and Confucianism in the same category. Here again the discrepancy in his attitudes is obvious. Although he praised generously the character-transforming power of Christianity, he did not give similar accolades to this aspect of Confucian philosophy. Mentioning that Ch'en Shao-t'ang's behavior reminded him of a typical Ch'eng-Chu scholar was an offhand, unintentional compliment to Confucianism.

In view of these contradictions in Hu Shih's thoughts and his failure to employ a consistent standard, one must conclude that he saw Christianity as an integral part of the "superior" Western culture. Just as he did not come to the United States because of financial difficulties, he did not go to the Christian gathering at Pocono Pines solely to alleviate his depression. American church groups worked to impress Hu with "the best aspects, the more refined and fundamental aspects of American life, civilization, and culture," and he was receptive. In the final analysis, then, it was the admiration for Western culture which caused him to go to the convocation and to convert. He accepted Christianity because he had already accepted Western culture, and his perception of this religion as a superior ethical-moral system revealed how highly he regarded Western culture in general.

Oliver Brachfeld has this to say about some Jewish Christian converts:

> I have had occasion to make a close personal study of anti-semitic Jews who had become converted to Christianity. Some were uneducated persons, some university professors of the highest intellectual qualities. In all alike I saw the same mechanism at work—the desire to break away from "the side regarded as devoid of value" and to belong to the "side recognized as alone possessing value." The spirit-

ual aspect of their conversions seemed to be a psychological superstructure, a mere function of the desire for compensation.[7]

Did Hu Shih's behavior manifest such a desire? His double standard and conversion to Christianity spoke much about his mentality. This diary entry, written when he was at Pocono Pines, gives us a further clue to his psychological makeup.

> June 17 [1911]. Saturday. Bible class. The discussion topic was "The Influence of Confucianism " over which Dr. Gilbert Reid presided. It was a shame. Later, Dr. Beech remarked that the sad thing nowadays was that few [Chinese] were devoted to the classical scholarship. He then praised profusely the philosophy of Chu Hsi. Hearing this, I felt as if a knife were at my back.[8]

This is an ambiguous passage. We cannot tell what that shame was, nor do we know what precisely Hu was referring to when he felt a knife at his back. Nevertheless, the passage does reveal enough for us to conclude that he was extremely uneasy about his own heritage, so much so that a discussion of Confucianism and Chu Hsi thoroughly debilitated him. When all is considered, Hu did seem to have developed "a . . . propensity for doubt and shame" as a result of "a sense of loss of self-control and of foreign overcontrol."[9]

After returning to Ithaca from Pocono Pines, Hu Shih immersed himself in a number of activities related to Christianity. Between June, 1911, and December, 1912, he attended Bible classes, offered by William Wistar Comfort (1874–1955),[10] read the Bible thoroughly, went to religious sermons, and occasionally devoured other religious writings, such as John Bunyan's *Pilgrim's Progress,* H. Begbie's *Twice-born Men,* and Harry Emerson Fosdick's *The Second Mile.*[11]

But Hu Shih was too sensitive and self-critical to let his double standard continue unexamined. His religious fervor began to dwindle quickly. From December, 1912, to October, 1914, he attended church ceremonies only sporadically and no longer mentioned Bible classes or reading religious materials.[12] Simultaneously, he began to doubt and challenge Christian doctrines and practices. The first such occasion came in October, 1912. Accompanying a Chinese girl to a boarding house, Hu ran across a Methodist minister, "whose views were preposterous and confused, resembling a Chinese village woman discussing hell."[13] In December of that year, he told an American friend of his that he did not believe in baptism or the sacrament.[14] Then, on Christmas Eve,

> someone told me that there would be a Mass in a Catholic Church. I went there. . . . After being seated, I noticed that there were many statues in the middle of which was a crucifix. . . . These were idols! What is the difference between these and the Chinese idols? . . . The worshippers, before taking seats, would bend one knee (resembling our greetings). . . . Scores of youngsters walked in procession and sang hymns. On the altar, the preacher closed his hands to extend greetings. All these were just like the repulsive Buddhist ceremonies. The prayers and hymns of the Catholics were all incomprehensible. It was after awhile that I realized that they were in Latin. I dare say that few understood them. . . . When listening to the solemn religious music and prayers in such a solemn atmosphere at a deep, snowy night, one could hardly not be affected and awed. This is the spell-binding power of religion! This is the spell-binding power of religion![15]

Hu passed a similar judgment on Protestantism. Visiting Boston in September, 1914, he attended a religious ceremony at the First Church of Christ Scientist. This church, he said, was "the most superstitious of all the sects," and most of its beliefs and practices were just like the superstitions of the Taoist religion.[16]

Inevitably, Hu began to broaden his criticism of Christianity. At Amherst, Massachusetts, in November, 1914, he met Henry E. Jackson, pastor of the Christian Union Congregational Church at Upper Montclair, New Jersey, and a prolific religious writer. After reading one of Jackson's books, Hu wrote him:

> The death of Socrates as described by Plato often appeals to me more strongly than the death of Jesus. . . . It seems to me that one must first have the *Christian point of view* in mind in order to be able to say that what Jesus did during the crucifixion was greater and nobler than what Socrates did at his death. . . .
> . . . I have greater admiration and love for Jesus if he were a man than if he were the Son of God. It would not be remarkable at all for the Son of God to act as Jesus did act. But it *was* and will always be remarkable that a *man* should have acted as Jesus did.[17]

Responding to Jackson's rejoinder, Hu further argued:

I admit that *to the Christian* the death of Jesus does mean a great deal more than the death of Socrates. But why? Because . . . centuries of powerful *tradition* have made it so. . . . It is something purely *subjective,* and has no *objective validity.* [18]

Hu Shih here clearly renounced his Christian connection which had preoccupied him intensely only a short while before. The death of Jesus had a meaning only *"to the Christian,"* and he was not one, and he refused to see things from the *"Christian point of view."* Earlier, he considered the value of Christianity to be its power to transform men's character. Now when comparing the didactic value of philosophy and religion, he no longer doubted where his allegiance lay. In the same letter to Jackson, Hu asserted that Socrates' philosophy

> has had a *tremendous influence* upon the Greek and Roman world, and in the modern time upon our world. The ideal of the modern world is no longer the Christian ideal of self-abnegation, but the Greek ideal of self-development; no longer the Christian ideal of Faith, but the Socratic ideal of Truth.[19]

With Christianity demystified in his mind, Hu Shih also became aware of commercialism, ignorance, condescension, and other deplorable qualities in many missionaries, and a willingness to employ naked force by "Christian" nations in their dealings with weaker countries. Speaking at the First Baptist Church in Ithaca in early February, 1913, he challenged that missionaries be "good students,"

> eager to *learn* things when they are placed in the field. The Christian churches have sent out many teachers, but unfortunately too few students. *The missionary may have a faith to teach,* but you must admit, *he has many, many things to learn.* Unfortunately there are people who come to a foreign country with the inveterate view of uplifting, nay, of *civilizing* a barbarous people! They therefore come to us with that arrogant and patronizing air of a superior people.[20]

Later, in March, 1915, he issued another admonition at a Presbyterian church in Ithaca.

> The Christians are Christians in giving charities and in their private and civil dealings. But they are not Christians when they come to international relations. They "strain at a gnat, and swallow a camel!" [T]he professedly Christian nations recognize no authority but

that of the "mailed fist"; . . . they have no regard for the right and claims of the weaker nations; . . . they place national and commercial gain and territorial aggression over and above the dictates of justice and righteousness. . . .

There was a time when the missionaries were paid according to the number of converts they had made. But that is not what China wants, nor is it what the churches should emphasize in sending their missionaries.[21]

These criticisms, delivered in Hu's host country, required a great deal of courage. After warmly embracing Christianity for two years, what made Hu turn so sharply against it?

By October, 1912, when he first voiced reservations about Christianity, Hu Shih had been in the United States for a little more than two years. He was apparently more settled and at ease with himself. The bedazzling impact of American society, the sense of awe and admiration, began to dwindle. Daily contact with Western culture very likely helped restore a better sense of balance and a healthier psychological distance from which he began to reassess Western ideas and values. Moreover, now that the West had already formed a significant part of his consciousness, there was no need for further commitment and identification. Western culture was no longer mysterious and incomprehensible, but something intimate, ready to be accepted, modified, or rejected. Hu's improved mental and intellectual state no doubt led him to question some of his initial judgments and reassert his independence. He finally gave up his unhappy study of agriculture and transferred to philosophy in the spring of 1912. He began his activities in the Cosmopolitan Club in February, 1911, and in September moved into its headquarters where he lived for three years. In May, 1913, he became president of the organization on the Cornell campus. At the same time, he developed a great interest in American politics, organizing a study club to hold weekly discussions on Western political thought and institutions. These activities will receive attention in due course. Suffice it to say that they and the beginning of Hu's critical views toward Christianity paralleled and overlapped one another and may be construed as indications of his maturation, his increasing self-awareness, and his struggle to achieve a sense of mastery in a challenging environment.

Hu Shih's criticism of Christianity may also be interpreted in light of developments in China. During the Yüan Shih-k'ai years (1912–16) of the Republic, a movement to establish Confucianism as the state religion gathered momentum. In 1912, the Confucian Society (*K'ung-chiao hui*) was founded in Shanghai by a number of prominent figures, including Yen Fu. In July, 1913, members of the Progressive Party (*Chin-pu tang*) proposed an article in the draft constitution that Confucianism be established as the state religion.[22] And Yüan Shih-k'ai initiated a number of maneuvers, some of which had religious overtones, to promote his political ambitions. Although Hu Shih did not pass judgment on these developments until January, 1914, he could not have failed to notice them, being a person "best informed of the affairs back home."[23] On January 23, 1914, he wrote in his diary,

> Many people nowadays are discussing the issue of religion. Some of them have proposed that Confucianism be established as the national religion. I have been concerned with this issue recently. In my letter to Hsü I-sun, I raised a number of questions. Since I do not have answers for them, I now record these questions here for future reference.[24]

That suspension of judgment, however, lasted only a few days. On February 4, Hu commented on Yüan Shih-k'ai's order to pay sacrificial rites to Confucius as "an unnecessary fuss made by the simple-minded."[25] Regarding Yüan's edict paying homage to Confucius, Hu retorted in November, 1914, "While clearly propagating religion, Yüan makes all the disclaimers. This is still another fallacy [of this edict]."[26]

It is impossible, however, to establish a relationship between Hu's opposition to the Confucian movement and his criticism of Christian doctrines and missionary practices. The two synchronized, and Hu's writings yield no clue as to whether the one ever influenced the other. Nevertheless, it is interesting to note that the beginning of his anti-Christian stance paralleled the founding of the Confucian Society in 1912 and that his criticism of Christianity lasted approximately as long as the Confucian movement. Did his negative image of a *Chinese* religious movement play a role in forcing him to be more reflective on religion in general? Hu did complain, as we recall, that the Catholic statues were just like "the Chinese idols," that the Catholic rituals "were just like the repulsive Buddhist ceremonies," and that the practices of the First Church of Christ Scientist in Boston resembled the Taoist superstitions. It was possible that he rebelled against Christianity because in part he could no longer reconcile his own inconsistencies, brought out sharply by his misgivings about the Confucian movement. It must be emphasized, however, that the emergence of this more consistent attitude should be viewed as an integral part of his maturing process.

It is wrong to assume that Hu's rebellion against Christianity and his criticism of many of the missionary practices were without qualifications. For all his reservations, Hu did not reject the Christian culture per se. Robert Jay Lifton points out that to the West-educated Asian intellectuals, the West has a "strong initial attraction, followed . . . by profound . . . disillusionment." But "there are many 'Wests' to draw upon for ideological commitments. The connection with the West is never entirely broken."[27] While Hu's disillusionment with missionary misconduct was profound and his criticism of Christianity fundamental, he never lost faith in Western culture itself, of which Christianity, in Hu's mind, was an integral part. What he wanted was to strip Christianity of its religious elements and accept its secular values. He conceded the importance of spreading "the essentials of Christianity." By this, however, he did not mean "The theological dogmas as the doctrines of virgin birth, of original sin, of atonement, etc., but the truly Christian doctrines of love . . . of forgiveness, of self-sacrifice and of service."[28] Nor was Hu hesitant to point out to his Christian friends what he regarded as the petty matters in their religion. "Take the divergent differences of the various denominations. It is almost impossible for us to conceive that the followers of a common faith should display so many variations and diversities both in doctrine and in practice."[29] The true value of missionary work, then,

> is to render practical service, under which we may enumerate education, social reform, and medical and surgical missions. Along these lines the Christian missionaries have accomplished a great deal, especially the medical missions which . . . are the crowning glory and success of the missionary propaganda.[30]

It should not be overlooked that Hu singled out medicine, which rendered a most valuable service with the least value implications, as "the crowning glory and success of the missionary propaganda."

Hu Shih's approval of the missionary secular service was probably reinforced by a sense of personal identification. After all, he did share with the missionaries many of the nonreligious values. Moreover, was not Hu himself a "missionary" carrying these values? Was not he himself about to return to China to preach them? If the missionaries would discard their theological dogmas, their commercial approaches, their superciliousness, would not they and Hu be rendering similar practical services? "The foreign missionary," he wrote in March, 1915,

> *like a returned student from abroad,* always carries with him a new point of view, a critical spirit, which is often lacking when a people have grown accustomed and indifferent to the existing order of things and which is absolutely necessary for any reform movement.[31]

In defending missionary work, then, Hu was subliminally justifying his own worth and commitment. Anticipating his own "proselytizing" endeavor, he probably could not but harbor some empathy toward the missionary work in areas of medicine, education, and social reform. Both he and the missionary would play an enlightening role in China.

During the first few years after his return home in July, 1917, Hu Shih was reticent about the issue of Christianity. This was understandable. He had apparently exhausted his arguments for and against the missionary work. Furthermore, there were more urgent tasks awaiting him in his homeland. In a word, Hu was content to leave the issue of religion behind him.

But it was not to be. These were extraordinary times in China. Between 1922 and 1927 an anti-Christian movement broke out, led by segments of the student population and certain intellectual leaders. Though small in scale, the movement, invoking such popular concepts as science, Marxism, and nationalism, was nonetheless a boisterous one. It waned after Kuomintang's unification of the nation in 1927; yet anti-Christian sentiment itself never completely vanished.[32] As one of the luminaries, Hu Shih could not avoid the issue. For a decade beginning in the middle of the 1920's, he again addressed himself to the problems associated with Christianity.

One of the most serious problems, as Hu conceived it, was that many of the missionary activities compromised China's integrity as an independent nation. Though not an ardent nationalist, Hu was nevertheless sympathetic with the rising national consciousness. He warned the Christian establishments in China of this phenomenon and pointed out the difference between the fanatic antiforeignism of the

Boxers and twentieth-century nationalism. "Chinese used to fear 'intervention' and 'dismemberment'; they had no alternative but to swallow shame and sustain humiliation. But it has been different in recent decades." The 1911 revolution, the First World War, the Russian revolution of 1917, and other pivotal events helped heighten Chinese self-awareness. Hu believed that some of the Chinese views were "extreme," particularly the proclamation of a Marxist journal that the Boxer movement was "the sorrowful yet courageous prelude to the history of Chinese revolution." At the same time, he was quick to remind foreigners in China that "their [those who held seemingly 'extreme' views] proposals to deal with the foreign powers are by no means as virulent as their slogans," and he was hardly in disagreement with the goals of Chinese nationalism—educational autonomy from foreign interference, abolition of extraterritoriality, and other foreign privileges. "This nationalistic reaction is natural and understandable," considering the eighty-year oppression of the Chinese by foreign powers and the numerous privileges enjoyed by foreigners in China. "The Boxers could be extinguished because such a superstitious, barbaric movement could not stand on its own," Hu reflected. "But the present nationalistic movement . . . is rooted in the sense of justice of a whole people. . . . Such a movement cannot be terminated by naked force."[33]

Another cornerstone of Hu Shih's criticism of Christianity was his secular, rationalistic attitude. His reasoning against Buddhism and later against Christianity when he was in America was a typical manifestation of this thinking. In the 1920s, the tide of rationalism and "scientific" outlook swept much of the Chinese intellectual circle and, in Hu's view, constituted a second challenge facing the missionaries. According to him, Chinese rationalism, which had its indigenous root in Taoism and Sung-Ming Neo-Confucianism, was reinforced by modern science. Of course, Hu himself was responsible to a large extent for the popularity of the new "scientific" view of life in May Fourth China. Earlier, in 1923, he declared his "scientific philosophy of life" which, in part, stipulated that the universe is natural and purposeless, that human struggles are merciless and therefore no benevolent God or Buddha exists, and that all a man should hope for is a fulfilled life on earth.[34] Hu employed this argument against all the "untenable" beliefs, including religion. Regarding Christianity, he wrote,

> Now some of us want to question if the fundamental doctrines of Christianity can be validated; we want to ask if there indeed is God or spirit after life. . . . Twenty-five years ago, missionaries overcame the challenge of the Boxers and the Red Lanterns (*hung-teng chiao*). Now, faced with "the challenge of rationalism," are they going to sneak by, or are they going to face it squarely?[35]

Concerning missionary abuses, Hu complained in 1925 that some missionaries went to China to teach primarily because they were not able to make a living in their own countries; some went to recuperate health; others went to visit scenic places; and still others went to engage in the antique business. "There are certainly not a few commendable personalities among the missionaries in China today," Hu concluded sarcastically. "But we can be certain that the churches' selection of missionaries is less strict and discreet than the appointment of the China inland managers by the Standard Oil Company (*Mei-fu kung-ssu*) or by the British-American Tobacco Company."[36]

What Hu had in mind, thus, was an extravagant wish: that missionaries abandon their relentless pursuit of converts. In early April, 1922, when asked by Dwight Edwards of the Princeton-Yenching Foundation to preside over a lecture at the YMCA in Peking, he declined bluntly, saying that he had no positive feeling "towards Christianity in its institutionalized form" and that he was "opposed to all proselytizing in religion."[37] In Hu's view, missionaries should put their best efforts into nonreligious areas, such as education. But even here Hu's demand was not unqualified.

> Can Christian education concentrate their financial resources and human talent to run a few truly outstanding schools, rather than a number of mediocre and even poor ones? . . . Who cannot build a third or fourth rate school? Why do you missionaries have to come from tens of thousands of miles away to do this for us?[38]

Hu knew only too well that a mediocre institition would invariably place greater stress on preaching than on education. But even outstanding ones were suspect. He further argued, "Can't these mission schools abandon their proselytizing altogether and instead concentrate on education itself?"[39]

These proposals were so fundamental that even Hu Shih himself acknowledged the extreme difficulty of their realization. "I am fully aware," he conceded cynically, "that to persuade the mission institutions to abandon proselytizing is far more difficult than to persuade Chang Tso-lin and Wu P'ei-fu to disarm themselves." Hu still hoped, however, that missionaries would be more discreet and fair-minded. "Using an educational institution to propagate Christianity, exploiting the simple-mindedness of the young people to promote a religious goal is tantamount to fraud and is an immoral act." He warned that "those who were enticed to become converts in their early years usually become rebellious when they are more mature and knowledgeable. The exceptionally intelligent ones who were induced into the religion may even become revolutionists like Voltaire." Hu pleaded that mission schools abolish Sunday worship and religious courses in their curricula; that they not entice students' families or discriminate against non-Christians in their institutions; and that they devote themselves to true freedom of belief, speech, and thought.[40]

These opinions were expressed between 1922 and 1925 during the height of the anti-Christian movement. During the next decade, Hu continued to maintain his stance, but in a much milder manner.[41] Taken as a whole, Hu's battle with the Christian establishment in China was not devoid of a personal touch. It was probably not a coincidence that he said that "those who were enticed to become converts in their early years usually become rebellious when they are more mature and knowledgeable." Was he not speaking of his own struggle? Was he not accusing the missionaries of fraud for "luring" him when he was a freshman at Cornell? In principle, Hu probably would have been happier if missionaries had never set foot on Chinese soil. But that was not reality, and reality in China was complicated. Thus when he was delivering those scathing criticisms of the missionary community in China, he had to remind his compatriots of the significant contributions the missionaries made to China's modernization. Realizing how indispensable the missionaries were and what his own government was capable of, he began an active campaign in the late 1920s for the missionary cause. Take foot binding as an example. He said in 1928,

> In human history, no other nation [than China] has ever had such a barbaric institution!
> In all the classics of the sages and wise men, we cannot find any

solution for it. For a thousand years, the Neo-Confucian masters, while daily discoursing on *jen* and *i,* could not even see the inhuman sufferings of their mothers, wives, and sisters.[42]

It was, Hu told us, missionaries who emancipated Chinese women. In terms of children's status and treatment, again "our country is the most barbaric," and it was foreigners who played the enlightening role. Hu was devastatingly cynical. He was "profoundly grateful to the imperialists for awakening us from our dark, tranced nightmare." He wanted to "burn incense and perform rituals" to thank missionaries for bringing to China modern Western culture and humanitarianism. He offered his "sincere gratitude to the so-called 'cultural imperialists' for founding the 'natural foot society.' " While the schools and hospitals which missionaries established were not particularly good ones, missionaries still played the role of "vanguard" and "pioneers." Therefore, "we should forgive their past shortcomings."[43]

It was apparent that Hu Shih was concerned that the anti-Christian movement might undo the missionary work in China and therefore impede China's march toward modernity. This sentiment was widely shared in intellectual circles. One would be surprised to learn how many luminaries defended missionary activities in the name of religious freedom. The defense was such that "the sensationalism of the attack [on Christianity by the anti-Christian groups] belied actual strength."[44] To be sure, many of these defenders genuinely believed in religious freedom, but their practical consideration should not be overlooked.

Concern with the continuation of missionary service in China, however, could only explain Hu's defense in general, not his unusual pungency. To acquire a better understanding of Hu's position, we must put his remarks into a broad historical context. In Hu's view, his adversaries included not only cultural conservatism and anti-Western nationalism, but also those politicians who invoked pseudointellectual notions for expedient purposes. Shortly before he proposed in October, 1929, to offer incense and perform rituals to express gratitude to the "cultural imperialists," Yeh Ch'u-ts'ang, the Kuomintang's minister of propaganda, unabashedly boasted that "China originally was a golden world built on exquisite virtues." The party, having by this time unified the nation, initiated a number of conservative and oppressive policies to consolidate power. Party indoctrination and thought control were vigorously carried out; intellectual dissent was met with suspicion and intolerance; party-controlled newspapers and official documents were written in the classical; telegrams were composed in the parallel.[45] Hu Shih complained that the party took a conservative cultural stance based on a narrow national sentiment, refusing to accept Western culture because Western culture came to China along with gunboats. "[T]he rational New Culture movement can hardly compete with this emotional conservative attitude," Hu conceded.[46] His lavish praise of the missionary contributions to China and savage attack on Chinese tradition was clearly in part a reaction to the Kuomintang conservatism.

> We can deny the existence of God, but we cannot criticize Sun Yat-sen; we can refuse Sunday worship, yet it is compulsory to recite *tsung-li*'s [Sun Yat-sen's] will and attend Monday morning ceremony to pay homage to him. Recently, a scholar published a history textbook, showing a moderate skepticism of the credibility of *san-huang wu-ti* [China's legendary rulers]. This evoked an outcry of the government, and Tai Chi-t'ao tried to have the Commercial Press fined a million dollars.[47]

Hu's was an agonizing and helpless protest against a conservatism backed by party organizations and state power. This conservatism had little impact among the student population and the New Cultural leaders, yet it was also most formidable and virtually unchallengeable. Indeed, much of the sadistic cultural iconoclasm in the May Fourth period can be attributed to the feeling of impotence and frustration on the part of the New Culture leaders in the presence of the crushing weight of tradition as well as the overwhelming conservative political power of the warlords and the Kuomintang. Without any other effective means at their disposal, the iconoclasts assaulted Chinese culture to compensate for their impotent feeling and undermine the ideological foundation of an oppressive government, hence tantamount to a direct rejection of that government itself. In the process of their vengeful attacks, Hu Shih himself and the like-minded showed in abundance the qualities which they condemned and despised—utter absurdity and irresponsibility.

This was a time of intense emotions, of an enormous sense of urgency, and of tremendous centrifugal forces. Few were able to maintain a proper balance. Therefore, we should not take literally the attacks and counterattacks of various groups. In all fairness, Hu Shih probably did not consider China "the most barbaric," nor did he intend to offer incense or perform rituals to thank the missionaries among whom were antiquarians, misfits, and unscrupulous opportunists. Conversely, few twentieth-century Chinese truly believed that "China originally was a golden world built on exquisite virtues." In spite of his political expediency, Yeh made such a ridiculous assertion because, in part, he was genuinely alarmed by the excess of various kinds of cultural iconoclasm and by the apotheosis of the West in China. He believed that he was responding to an irrational force.[48] Notwithstanding this analysis, it should be noted that, although Yeh Ch'u-ts'ang and Hu Shih did not literally mean what they said, their remarks did reflect their basic convictions. Each must have believed that his was the only right solution.

To be sure, Yeh's prescription for China's problems was largely irrelevant, but his diagnosis carried more than an element of truth. Hu Shih himself did not always take a discriminating attitude toward the West; Ch'en Tu-hsiu's case provided an even better example of the unthinking acceptance of anything Western. Ch'en passionately defended Christianity and the missionary even before the inception of the anti-Christian movement. In "Christianity and the Chinese People," published in February, 1920, he put nearly every blame on the Chinese side for whatever went wrong. Of the ten factors which caused friction between the missionary and the Chinese, he believed that "the majority of the blames belong to the Chinese; foreigners have been responsible for but one or two of them." Indeed, he continued, the great contribution of Christianity lay in its dynamism and moral force. "The fundamental teachings of Christianity are trustworthiness and love. The rest is of no consequence . . . these fundamental teachings, scientists have not discredited and will never be able to discredit." The Chinese, therefore,

> should try to cultivate the lofty and majestic character of Jesus and fill our blood with his warm, moving spirit. Only then will we be saved from the pit of chilly indifference, darkness, and filth into which we have fallen.[49]

In his early 1922 essay, "Christianity and the Christian Church," Ch'en acknowledged that the evils of the church could be piled as "high as a mountain," among which was its complicity in the recent world war. Nevertheless, "when we criticize Christianity, we should differentiate it from the Christian church." Admittedly, there were shortcomings in the religion, but these were but "small shortcomings in the larger body of Christian doctrines."[50]

These words, coming from Ch'en Tu-hsiu, were particularly revealing. In late 1920, shortly after he wrote the first essay, he was already an avowed Marxist. Before the second essay appeared, Ch'en had become fully committed to the Marxian cause. Christianity as a religion never bothered him as a Marxist. When he rejected religious beliefs as "untenable" human illusions, he meant Buddhism, the Taoist religion, and Confucian-oriented superstitions. In assessing Christianity and missionary deeds, he was able to isolate the Christian ideals, to make a fine distinction between the abstract and the practical, between ideas themselves and their manifestations. Nowhere do we find such subtle judgments in his evaluation of Chinese values and ideas. In his Chinese world, ideas and the practical level of ideas—politics, economy, and society—were inseparable and always reflected each other's worst qualities.

Finally, Hu Shih's bitterness and cynicism may be explained from still another angle. Torn between his ambivalent desire to retain the services of the missionaries and his detestation of their arrogance and opportunism, between his inability to rationalize China's incompetence and the ubiquitous presence of foreigners in China, Hu felt debilitated. A psychological way out was to internalize some of the views of the foreigners in order to explain away his own impotence, to identify with the foreign conquerors, by whom he felt threatened, in order to share their power and prestige. Anna Freud explains this mechanism of defense.

> A child introjects some characteristic of an anxiety object and so assimilates an anxiety experience which he has just undergone. . . . By impersonating the aggressor, assuming his attributes or imitating his aggression, the child transforms himself from the person threatened into the person who makes the threat. . . . As the child passes over from the passivity of the experience to the activity of the game, he hands on the disagreeable experience to one of his playmates and in this way revenges himself on a substitute.[51]

As can be seen, Hu's criticism of China strikingly resembled the prevailing foreign opinions of China: that China was simply incapable of modernization itself and that it had to await enlightenment from a foreign source. For Hu, to condemn his native land in the worst possible terms meant that since the situation could not possibly be worse, he actually had it under control. To sing praise of missionaries in such a seemingly obsequious manner was to symbolically sever his emotional tie with China, to transcend the Chinese reality so that he would not be affected by it, and to minimize the devastating impact of foreign dominance. In this way, Hu was able to achieve a symbolic sense of mastery over overwhelmingly distressing circumstances. For all its ostensible benefits, however, this mechanism of defense was also an excruciating exercise of the subconscious. Anna Freud goes on.

> The moment the criticism is internalized, the offense is externalized. This means that the mechanism of identification with the aggressor is supplemented by another defensive measure, namely, the projection of guilt.
>
> An ego which with the aid of the defense mechanism of projection develops along this particular line introjects the authorities to whose criticism it is exposed and incorporates them in the superego. It is then able to project the prohibited impulses outward. Its intolerance of other people precedes its severity toward itself. It learns what is regarded as blameworthy but protects itself by means of this defense mechanism from unpleasant self-criticism. Vehement indignation at someone else's wrongdoing is the precursor of and substitute for guilty feelings on its own account. Its indignation increases automatically when the perception of its own guilt is imminent.[52]

This helps explain Hu's frequent violent rage.

Hu Shih's bittersweet feeling toward the missionary and his own country made him both a critic of and a spokesman for both sides. Take the example of Yenching University, the best mission school in China. When the university was in its planning stage in the 1910s, Hu was one of those who helped pick its name. When the anti-Christian movement broke out in the spring of 1922, he defended religious freedom in behalf of Yenching and other Christian colleges. Hu showed his support of Yenching's educational substance and ideas through his frequent appearances in its classes and assembly meetings, and he interceded in the 1930s in securing money for the university from the central government. Hu developed a lasting friendship with John Leighton Stuart (1876–1962), president of Yenching from 1919 until his appointment as the United States ambassador to China in 1945.[53] Much of this, of course, was done for the sake of China which Hu loved so dearly and about which he delivered so many cruel and pungent remarks.

Chapter 5

Marriage

Although his mother was enlightened enough to have sent him to receive a modern education in Shanghai when Hu Shih was only three months past his twelfth birthday, she nevertheless followed the time-honored tradition in selecting her son's future mate. A month before the journey to Shanghai in February, 1904, he was betrothed to Chiang Tung-hsiu,[1] a bound-footed, semiliterate girl who was a few months older than he.[2] Hu and Chiang never met each other until more than thirteen years later when he returned from America in 1917.[3] By then, he had won a Phi Beta Kappa membership and several literary prizes, acquired a good reading ability of German and French,[4] and established himself in the avant-garde of the New Culture movement. Upon arrival in China, he was appointed to the faculty of Peking National University. It was remarkable, therefore, that Hu did fulfill the nuptial promise in December, 1917.[5] But this was not done without a prolonged struggle and vigorous protest. Even after the marriage, he could not conceal his disappointment and bitterness.

Marriage had become a problem for many educated Chinese in the first years of the twentieth century. The issue did not escape Hu's attention. Indeed, his earliest writing on the subject appeared as early as 1906–8 from which we are able to have a few glimpses of his views on this matter. In "On Marriage," he lamented that the welfare of many Chinese was tampered with by their parents' impulse, by the intermediaries, and by the soothsayers. Reading Montesquieu's *De l'esprit des lois* through Yen Fu's translation, Hu noted that Montesquieu favored parental guidance in marriage because they were more experienced and could make better judgments. But while endorsing parental guidance, Hu also believed that it should be balanced by children's opinions. He warned parents that they should

> not foolishly believe in the go-betweens, the sightless fortune tellers, and the divinations of the mud and wooden idols. . . . Ha! ha! [otherwise] you cannot blame the youths for advocating *family revolution*.[6]

At the time, the nation was approaching the republican revolution and had been in the rapid process of a basic metamorphosis. Understandably, Hu's writing contained such unprecedented language as the "family revolution." The essay was significant in still another way. In the autumn of 1908, his mother and Chiang Tung-hsiu's family were making preparations for their marriage. It was postponed, for a total of nine years as it turned out, because of his "vigorous objection."[7] If Hu was alluding to his own betrothal in the essay, the matter certainly did not occupy a central place in his mind. When he was writing on marriage, Hu entertained no idea of challenging his mother; he even expressed disapproval of "the people of new learning" who advocated "free marriage."[8] Characteristically, his concern was the sociopolitical implications of marriage.

> If couples are not in love, if families are not in harmony, how can they have good children? For thousands of years, our race has been sinking day by day, our morality has been deteriorating day by day, our physique has been getting weaker day by day. All these are because our parents have been too indifferent to their children's marriages. They have been too *unautocratic*. . . . I anxiously *hope* that parents will take the marriages of their children as the most important events of their families and clans. Moreover, they should take their children's marriages as an important national affair.[9]

But Hu's views were to change soon. He was rapidly expanding his intellectual horizon, and his marriage could not be postponed indefinitely. How long was he able to take his personal affair in such an impersonal manner?

When Hu Shih went to Cornell University in the autumn of 1910, he was put into an alien surrounding. The contrast between the two cultures became sharp, and alternatives became available. It was in this milieu that his marital crisis began to surface.

The first entry on marriage in Hu's diary appeared in September,

1911, a year after his arrival in Ithaca. At that time, he partook in a debate contest the topic of which was: "Should China Today Practice Free Marriage?" He was the opposition and lost.[10] A year later,

> It suddenly occurred to me that I should write a book the title of which would be "In Defense of the Chinese Social Institutions," evaluating the strengths and weaknesses of the works on the subject by foreigners. This would be a worthy thing to do in defense of the fatherland.

Three of the nine main chapters listed in the outline were marriage, the family system, and the status of women.[11] In early January, 1914, his views began to harden. The position of Chinese women, Hu argued, was actually higher than that of their Western sisters, because

> our country protects women's integrity and chastity. We do not let them disgrace themselves in marriage. . . . Girls do not have to engage themselves in socialities, busying themselves in finding their own mates. This is because we respect women's modesty. Not so in the West. When girls come of age, their obsession is to find mates. Parents often order them to learn music and dancing and have them socialize with men. Those who know how to please men or who can lure men into their traps will get married. Those who are dull, simple, reticent, and upright, or who refuse to disgrace themselves by luring men will remain forever unmarried. Such a system debases a woman's integrity and forces her to flirt with and hunt for men. This is the evil of the Western free marriage.[12]

Love was certainly possible in an arranged marriage, Hu insisted.

> Love in Chinese marriage is duty-made. After the betrothal, a woman has a special tender feeling for her fiance. She feels embarrassed when occasionally hearing his name mentioned; she becomes eager and attentive when his activities are discussed. . . . A man feels the same toward his fiancee. Upon being married, the couple, realizing that it is their duty to love each other, often make special efforts to be considerate and loving. Thus, when imagination and obligations have become a reality, true love can indeed follow.[13]

Was Hu Shih resorting to his defense mechanism to rationalize his own betrothal and forthcoming marriage? Did he display a typical "emotional commitment" to an outworn Chinese institution? There was no question that the liberal dating and free marriage made him highly conscious of his unique situation, and the assault on the American way of life may well have been intended to conceal his psychological weakness. He used strong language in his writings, accusing American women of "flirting," "luring," and "trapping" in the marriage market. It was likely that he said these things in part for personal reassurances. Psychological tension, however, should not be taken as the inclusive cause for Hu's criticism of free marriage and defense of arranged marriage. There were other considerations which transcended the category of "emotional commitment."

Hu Shih was reserved in his personal behavior. Set apart from the rest because of his exceptional intellect and having no brothers or sisters of his age, he led a lonely childhood. Although close to his mother, grandmother, aunts, and half sister, he had few friends.

> Therefore, at the time when I was leaving home [for Shanghai] at the age of thirteen, I was as timid and bashful as a girl. I would extend my greetings without a murmur and respond to questions in a single word or two. . . . In ten years since I left home in 1904, I have had no opportunity to establish friendship with a girl. Even in this country [America] most of the women whom I befriend are in their middle ages.[14]

Little surprise, then, that liberal dating made him uncomfortable. The arranged marriage, he wrote in June, 1914, "relieves the young people from the terrible ordeal of proposing for marriage, which, I imagine, must be awfully embarrassing."[15]

Often, it is easier to accept new ideas in the abstract than to apply them to personal conduct. As ideas, they are remote and nonthreatening. Generally, Western ideas first came to China on the abstract level. Only later did they come to affect personal behavior. Most members of the new generation in early-twentieth-century China had accepted free love in principle, but it cannot be said that they could practice it without inhibition or embarrassment. This conflict between the theoretical acceptance of something new and the personal practice of it reveals the discrepancy between the conscious belief and the unconscious adherence to what is considered the "norm," between thought and the habit of thinking. Robert Jay Lifton observes that contemporary Japanese youth tend to remain very much in the bosom of their families. . . . This continuity in family life seems to be the balancing force that permits Japanese youth to weather their confusing psychological environment as well as they do. But the continuity is only partial. On matters of ideology and general social outlook, most Japanese students feel completely apart from their parents.[16]

Similarly, while accepting free love, many Chinese at the time still regarded the Western style of dating and physical contact as indications of lack of propriety. The differences between the two cultural styles were obvious in spite of the increasing convergence of the conscious beliefs of the two. Seen in this light, Hu Shih, while defending his personal affair with emotion, probably sincerely believed that American women were flirting, luring, and hunting in the marriage market. On the other hand, the arranged marriage "imposes upon the young people a duty to be constant, faithful, and pure."[17]

As noted earlier, Hu Shih reached an eclectic position concerning marriage when he was a teenager in Shanghai. He perceived marriage as more than an individual affair; it was something involving family and society. As such, it should be decided jointly by parents and children. He retained this notion when he was in America, arguing that "Marriage is [not] an individual affair, but has a social import. . . . [S]o the rationality of the Chinese marriage system is to be found in the fact that marriage concerns not only the young couple but the whole family as well."[18] Small wonder that he expressed disapproval of the failure of some Americans to support their parents.[19] The genuineness of these opinions was attested to by still another item in his diary *not* on marriage. In September, 1914, Hu was visiting Harvard University where he had a long conversation with a Chinese student, Sun Heng. He took issue with Sun's suggestion that freedom and equality were the two panaceas to rejuvenate China, and he intimated that "the problem is not that China has no such concepts as freedom and equality. It is that it does not understand them." Hu went on:

> I would say that the tendency of the current Western political philosophy is shifting from laissez-faire to intervention, from individualism to a socially oriented outlook. . . . Aren't there eugenic laws governing marriage? . . . Aren't there prohibitions against drinking? . . . Aren't there laws on inheritance? . . . How sad will it be if we simply pick up others' leftovers without a discreet and discriminating examination?[20]

Looking at it as a whole, Hu's defense of the arranged marriage was undoubtedly motivated to a degree by the problems of his own betrothal. His basic views on marriage, however, were formulated before his arrival in the United States; and they remained fairly consistent up to this time. His views had been shaped by the family- and society-oriented Chinese thinking and intensified by the urgent atmosphere in China. His thinking helped explain his favorable attitude toward those American policies regulating drinking, inheritance, and family health. Furthermore, Hu's reserved personality played no small part in his aversion to free dating.

The American influence, however, was too great for Hu to resist. After more than three and a half years, his defense and self-discipline began to weaken. On June 8, 1914, he recorded this in his diary:

> The frontiers I have crossed in the last ten years have been of the intellect, almost completely neglecting the development of emotions. . . . Living in this country and attending a co-educational institution, I should utilize the opportunity to make female friends in order to cultivate my character and mitigate my cold personality. . . .
> . . . For the past four years, I had never been to the Sage College (a women's dormitory) to date a girl. I often boasted of this. Reflecting on it now, I only have regrets. For the first time tonight I visited a girl. In the future I plan to do this more often.[21]

The girl to whom Hu alluded was Edith Clifford Williams, a fellow student of fine arts and daughter of H. S. Williams, a professor of geology at Cornell. Beginning in November of that year, Hu described their joyful conversations, long walks in the woods and under the moonlight. They visited each other between Ithaca and New York after she went to New York to study painting in his last year at Cornell in 1914–15. In the autumn of 1915, he transferred to Columbia, perhaps in part to be close to her.[22] Even when both were in New York, they corresponded frequently, totaling more than a hundred letters from him to her in 1915 and 1916. The Williams family apparently had no objections to their friendship, for Hu was their house guest on several occasions.[23] There was not the slightest doubt that Hu and Edith Williams were in love. The following *tz'u* poem, composed on August 20, 1915, showed his feelings.

Lin chiang hsien

The sound of the stream is gentle and trifling behind trees,
  And birds are busily singing for us.
Together we walk the secluded path along the slanting bank,
  I pick berries for you, and you put flowers on my hair.

Sitting side by side by the water,
  The shade stops the shining sun.
Engaged in deep conversations of our own,
  We completely ignore the evening crows returning to their nests.
There are only you and me,
  How can we tolerate a third party?[24]

Edith Williams was an exceptionally intelligent and sensitive woman, indifferent to convention and without vanity. Expressing his high regard of her, Hu said in January, 1915, "The lady's extraordinary vision is head and shoulders above that of an ordinary woman. I know of many, many women, but there is only one who has such intellect, vision, decisiveness, and compassion."[25] Her role in his development cannot be exaggerated. Well-read, reflective, and iconoclastic, she had an indelible influence on his cosmopolitan thinking, led him to a variety of sources which broadened his view, cultivated a moderate interest in arts in him, and constantly challenged and outwitted him. Predictably, Hu's notions about women, family, and marriage began to change. On June 7, 1914, one day before his date (we must assume that they had known each other for some time), he began to have second thoughts on the Chinese familial ethics. Earlier, he had faulted Americans for not supporting their aged parents, but

> now when I think the matter over, our family system also has its severe shortcomings. . . . Under our family system parents regard their children as a kind of old-age pension. . . . Children regard inheritance from their parents as a matter of course. . . . One man becomes a Buddha and the whole clan goes to heaven; one son makes a name for himself and all the relatives put the bite on him, like ants swarming over a bone . . . —what slavishness is this! Here, indeed, is the root of the nation's downfall! . . .
>
> . . . Western individualism inculcates an independent character and fosters the ability of self-reliance. Our "familial individualism" nurtures a selfish attitude toward outside groups and a habit of dependence among their own members. I do not see why ours is better than theirs.[26]

Three months later, Hu argued against concubinage, early marriage, obsession with having male descendants, and the transmission of inheritance within family.[27] He also took an increasingly liberal view toward the position of women. For instance, in July, 1915, when the *Cornell Daily Sun* criticized the demonstration of suffragettes at a boxing match in New York, he chided the student newspaper for its "conservative spirit" and "reactionary opposition."[28]

Hu expressed his view concerning male descendants as early as his days in Shanghai. In America, he had certainly noticed the feminist movement and pondered women's status before his courtship with Edith Williams. Be that as it may, for three and a half years in America, he mentioned none of these themes until he began dating her. Therefore, this concurrence should not be construed as haphazard. Edith Williams, in fact, was the major impetus, as he acknowledged in October, 1915.

> Since my acquaintance with Miss Williams, my lifelong views toward women and male-female relationship have gone through a significant transformation. Of course, I always have deep convictions about the importance of women's education, but I used to think that its purpose was to create for society sagacious wives and good mothers who would in turn provide a good education for their families. Now I realize that the highest goal of women's education is to create women able to live free and independent. When a nation possesses free and independent women, it can improve the morality and uplift the character of its citizens. This is because women have a special transforming power. When we take good advantage of it, we will be able to invigorate the weak and inspire the timid, to transform people to form better habits. It is important that patriotic people know how to . . . take advantage of [the resources of the free and independent women.][29]

Part of this notion of women's role reminds us of Yen Fu's well-known theme that the release of individuals' potential and energy would contribute to societal progress. Moreover, three months after the first date, Hu put forward two more proposals relating to the family system: "One is having no posterity, the other leaving no bequests to them."[30] The points here echoed his previous suggestion that the Chinese take "Society" as their heir. Both were in part meant to be a corrective to what he considered one of China's foremost cultural diseases. Hu listed the evils of the insistence on having male descendants and of leaving family estates to children and concluded: "I often wonder that isn't the belief 'there are three unfilial acts of which having no posterity is the foremost' the most important reason why we have had no great figures in literature, science, and politics in two thousand years?"[31]

But although Hu Shih shared with Yen Fu, Liang Ch'i-ch'ao, and other late Ch'ing reformers the burning desire for national well-being, the similarities ended here. For Hu, to be "sagacious wives and good mothers" was no longer good enough for women. To create "free and independent" individuals had become "the highest goal of women's education." Further, he expressed his opinions as an alienated protester. His proposals for not having posterity and for not leaving bequests to children had a personal touch, and his assertion that Chinese parents "regard the son and his wife as a kind of old-age pension" was perhaps not an innocent, impersonal remark. Nor was it a coincidence that he unleashed his bitterness toward Chinese marriage at no other time than when he was dating Edith Williams.

Hu was at this time contemplating the possibility of not fulfilling his nuptial commitment to Chiang Tung-hsiu. Having had the companionship of Edith Williams and having liberalized his notion of women and marriage, he became convinced that a union with Chiang would be a fatal sacrifice and suffocate his future. In early 1915, he complained to his mother about his fiancee's lack of education.[32] But escaping from Chiang Tung-hsiu would not be an easy matter. In order not to betray her and his own conscience, he had to give up Edith Williams as well. To stay single, then, would not only be the most potent protest but also provide a way out of his predicament. Reading Francis Bacon in September, 1914, Hu quoted passages from, respectively, Bacon's "Of Marriage and Single Life" and "Of Parents and Children."

> He that hath wife and children hath given hostages to fortune; for they are impediments to great enterprises, either of virtue or mischief. Certainly the best works, and of greatest merit for the public, have proceeded from the unmarried or childless men; which, both in affection and means, have married and endowed the public.
>
> ... [S]urely a man shall see the noblest works and foundations have proceeded from childless men, which have sought to express the images of their minds, where those of their bodies have failed; so the care of posterity is most in them that have no posterity.[33]

"What great courage!" "What a vision!" Hu commented. Similarly, in *Tradition of Tso* (*Tso-chuan*) he found that meritorious service, virtuous conduct, and immortal wisdom or writings would enable a man to live in time and space, "to die but not to be forgotten" (*ssu-erh pu-hsiu*). These three immortalities, Hu maintained,

> are the posterity of those who have no posterity. Sakyamuni, Confucius, Lao-tzu, and Jesus did not rely on descendants to perpetuate their names. Washington had no sons, yet Americans revere him as their national father. . . . It is their works that make Li Po, Tu Fu, Byron, and Tennyson live on. With or without posterity, what is the difference?[34]

Two months later, in November, 1914, Hu compiled an impressive list of the great men who remained unmarried: René Descartes, Blaise Pascal, Benedict Spinoza, Immanuel Kant, Thomas Hobbes, John Locke, Herbert Spencer, Isaac Newton, Adam Smith, Voltaire, William Pitt, Count Camillo Benso Cavour, and Edward Gibbon.[35]

Hu spoke his mind when he listed these names. In late August, 1915, he was invited by a lawyer by the name of James R. Robinson to spend a weekend in Robinson's cottage on the Cayuga Lake. There Hu met a Mrs. Frederick Fitschen and developed a deep feeling toward "family" and "children."

> Mrs. Fitschen is good at music. Her six children, ranging from fifteen to three, are learning either instruments or singing. Yesterday afternoon when Mrs. George R. Williams and I were paying them a visit, Mrs. Fitschen entertained us with a "family concert." The eldest daughter Eileen played harp, eldest son Paul, piano, second son John, cello, younger son George, violin, while Mrs. Fitschen herself conducted. . . . Such a family can truly be said as happy and harmonious. It almost made me forget my "no-posterity-ism" (*wu-hou chu-i*).[36]

Yet Hu Shih did not have the good fortune of having a wife as graceful, well-educated, and talented as Mrs. Fitschen. The only alternative then was to eliminate the root of his disappointment: to remain single. Feeling disenchanted, he rejected one of the most honored Confucian tenets—that of biosocial immortality. He no longer felt the need of living on through, and emotionally with, his children and their children by imagining an endless chain of biological attachment. Instead, he was profoundly apprehensive that the forthcoming marriage with Chiang Tung-hsiu and having children with her would result in the annihilation of his creativity and in rendering his life meaningless. Unwilling to commit himself to her and unable to marry Edith Williams, Hu began to develop a narcissistic tendency and desired to be a lone hero, living on in infinity. Hu did so by imagining being a participant in the general flow of human creativity on the highest level and by trying to form a spiritual union with the great men in history who remained single. Through this quest for meaning and mastery over an overwhelming situation, Hu was presumably able to acquire a sense of inner peace and immortality.[37]

Hu was destined to be disappointed. From the beginning, the pressure on him to fulfill the marriage vow had been relentless, and he was not to join the ranks of the unmarried great men in history.

As previously noted, Hu's mother was widowed in 1895 at twenty-three when Hu was less than four years old. Until his journey to Shanghai in 1904, for nine years his mother was solely responsible for his daily life and education. The following account illustrates her relationship with Hu.

> Every morning at dawn my mother would wake me up.... I was never able to find out how long she had been awake.... She would tell me what mistakes I committed and what improper things I said the previous day. She would urge me to be studious and tell me in detail my father's strengths.... When she recalled a sad memory, tears would stream from her eyes. Only when it was bright enough would she dress me up and hurry me to attend the early class [before breakfast]....
>
> An autumn evening after dinner, I went out to play with only a light vest on. My mother's younger sister ... was staying with us. Afraid that I might catch cold, she urged me to put on the jacket she was handing me.... I responded casually, "What *niang* [meaning mother; Hu used it as a homophone of *liang* (cold)] is it? I don't even have a father." ... Deep at night my mother made me kneel down on the floor.... She was angry and trembling, and she would not let me go to bed. As I was crying kneeling on the floor, I rubbed my eyes with my hands. My eyes were infected which lasted for a year. Various doctors were consulted, to no avail.... She heard that eye infection could be cured by licking. One night she woke me up and really licked my eyes! This was my strict mentor! This was my loving mother![38]

In 1904, she was courageous enough to let her only child go to Shanghai for a modern education. Before his nineteenth birthday, Hu departed for America. In between he spent no more than half a year with his mother. Although one of her main hopes was that he would return home early and marry the girl to whom he was betrothed, she was understanding enough, in a letter of October, 1912, to permit him to stay in America until 1915.[39] Yet by the summer of 1915, Hu was on his way to Columbia University to pursue further studies and perhaps to be close to Edith Clifford Williams. While his mother's embarrassing financial situation was never a deterrent to his ambition, it nevertheless worried him. In August, 1911, he contemplated writing a book on German grammar in Chinese in order to supplement his mother's income.[40] In March, 1914, he learned that she had to pawn some of her jewels for the occasion of the lunar new year.[41] At this time,

> Shou-huan's family, because of financial difficulties, was willing to sell their set of *Synthesis of Books and Illustrations of Ancient and Modern Times* (*T'u-shu chi-ch'eng*) for eighty *yüan*. Knowing that I would love to have it, my mother took a loan and purchased it. Even in such an embarrassing situation, she was considerate to her son to this extent.[42]

The pressure was such that two days later Hu borrowed from an Ithaca businessman, Fred Robinson, two hundred dollars, half of which he sent home.[43]

Hu's relations with his mother, hence, were filled with memories of sacrifices on her part, loving care, strict discipline, and a sense of awe and guilt. By marrying Chiang Tung-hsiu, he would repay his debt and show his gratitude to his mother.

Understandably, the repeated procrastination of the marriage promise considerably dampened Hu's mood. As early as the autumn of 1908, Hu's and Chiang's families made all the preparations for the wedding, including firecrackers. It was cancelled owing to his strenuous objection. When Hu came to the United States, he knew that the sojourn would be a long one. The repeated break of promise was not easy to live with. Elmer Eugene Barker (1886–1964), who earned his B.S. and Ph.D. in botany at Cornell, was at one time Hu's housemate, and became his good friend, wrote of Hu: "more than once he confided to me 'She [Chiang Tung-hsiu] is now twenty years old, by Chinese standards already a spinster. If I ask her to wait three or four years longer it will be almost a disgrace for her.' "[44] Yet her wait turned out to be even longer; and Hu knew that this would be the case. While he was in America, Chiang Tung-hsiu often went to his home to keep his mother company and help her with the household chores. All these evoked Hu's guilt feeling, and he expressed it through one of the Nineteen Ancient Poems.

> I traveled a thousand miles to join you,
> But now we are far apart, separated by mountain slopes.
> Thinking of you makes me old;
> Why is your high carriage late in coming?
> I grieve for the fragrant orchid,
> Whose flowers radiate brightly.
> But if no one plucks them in blossom time,
> They will wither with the autumn grass.[45]

Hu's anxiety was aggravated by still another development. Chiang Tung-hsiu's mother had been ill since April, 1915, and died the following January.[46] Even on the deathbed, she expressed regret that the marriage had not been consummated. "Because of me . . . Madam died with this unfulfilled wish. I truly cannot escape responsibilities."[47]

It was in such a mood that Hu began actively to seek a compromise. The exchanges between him and Edith Williams were revealing. On November 3, 1914, she posed this question to him: "If our views are in conflict with our parents', shall we make a compromise in order to have peace with them, or shall we go our way as to break the relationship without regard?" Williams was not on the best terms with her mother, and the question could have a double intent. "This is the foremost question in our lives, which cannot be answered in a word," Hu responded. According to Westerners, of all the responsibilities, the one toward oneself was most important. "How can I reluctantly believe what I do not believe simply on account of others, or do what I do not wish to do?" Such an attitude was not entirely selfish, Hu maintained, for it fosters independence of judgment, progress of ideas, and betterment of politics.[48] Easterners, on the other hand, took a more conciliatory stance. He noted that the Han scholar Mao I, despite his distaste for public office, accepted appointment to please his mother. "I call such an attitude 'altruistic tolerance.' " Hu continued,

If parents abruptly lose their beliefs in their old age, it will be like losing their support in life. The agony of that will be indescribable. It is not as easy for those who have reached the evening of life to change their ideas as it is for we young people to abandon old beliefs for the new.[49]

Between the two, he concluded, "I will follow Easterners in my family affairs, but in my ideas on society, the nation and politics I will follow Westerners."[50]

Three days later, Edith Williams showed him passages from Marquis de Condorcet (1743–94) and John Viscount Morley (1838–1923). Morley's passage reads:

> Now, however great the pain inflicted by the avowal of unbelief, it seems to the present writer that one relationship in life and one only justifies us in being silent where otherwise it would be right to speak. This relationship is that between child and parents. . . . This, of course, only where the son or daughter feels a tender and genuine attachment to the parent. . . . In an ordinary way . . . a parent has a claim on us which no other person in the world can have, and a man's self-respect ought scarcely to be injured if he finds himself shrinking from playing the apostle to his own father and mother.[51]

Hu's decision was apparently conveyed to Edith Williams, and she wrote him on February 3, 1915:

> The only "propriety" between those persons of the highest type—that is those who have had their eyes opened to the beauty of a still higher human development, and souls stimulated to the constant effort of realizing it—is propriety of thought. It is quite simple, isn't it? . . .
> . . . And in the association (or friendship) of man and woman, surely this all holds good, if the truth of sex attraction is clearly understood and valued for just so much as it is good for, and if, when it consciously appears not of use, it is consciously put away by wilful turning of the attention to the higher side of that friendship.[52]

These were poignant exchanges. In fact, all along Hu had been struggling with himself. May we not construe his opinions on the arranged marriage as an attempt in part to convince himself of its rationality? What did he mean when he wrote that arranged marriage "imposes upon the young people a duty to be constant, faithful, and pure"? What did he mean in writing "when imagination and obligations have become a reality, true love can indeed follow"? Was he not trying to be "constant, faithful, and pure"? Did he try to use his "imagination" and resort to his sense of "obligations" to create love? As he was having the exchanges with Edith Williams, Hu was simultaneously trying to convince himself of the impracticality of free marriage. Picking a mate in a free marriage was by no means easy, he intimated. Often, after much time, effort, and money, the "ideal woman" still could not be found. Further, "intellectual compatibility" between man and wife was simply impossible. Besides intellect, health, personality, and appearance should also be important considerations in a marriage. "Intellectual companionship, if not available in the family, can be had from friends. This is why I am [no longer] opposed to my [forthcoming] marriage."[53] He was happy to learn that Chiang Tung-hsiu had had her feet unbound, and he encouraged her to do more reading and to learn to write.[54] While still complaining about her education, he finally reconciled to the inevitable fact. A letter to his mother, dated May 19, 1915, read in part:

> Everything I said in my Number 3rd letter concerning Tung-hsiu's education was expressed in the emotions of the moment, with no intention of rebuking Tung-hsiu, much less of placing any blame on my mother. In the matter of my marriage I harbor no grievances whatever. I know full well that in this matter my mother has indeed expended every effort to arrange for me a happy family life. . . . I have seen many who can read and write, but who have not the capacity to be good wives and sagacious mothers (*liang-ch'i hsien-mu*); and how could I complain and ask for the perfect? . . . If a married couple can be at the same time teacher and friend (*k'ang-li erh chien shih-yu*), this is indeed one of life's great joys. But genuine equality in learning between husband and wife is not often found even in this country—how much less in our country where there is no education offered to women? If I were to hold up the standard of "intellectual compatibility" in seeking a mate, there is no doubt that I would live a solitary existence to the end of my days.[55]

This was truly a solemn encounter between the mother and the son, two persons living in different worlds and embracing irreconcilable values. Realizing her son's exceptional brilliance and the obvious disparity between him and Chiang Tung-hsiu, Hu's mother was not without regrets. "This [the betrothal] is something created by circumstances," she said. "I only hope that you would understand how difficult it is for me."[56] In the meantime, Hu continued to prepare himself for the inevitable. In July, 1915, a month after his correspondence with his mother, he related a story about the marriage of C. L. Crandall, an engineering professor at Cornell.

> Crandall's wife is blind. . . . I also know her. . . . Their betrothal preceded her blindness. . . . Madam did not want her handicap to burden someone she loved and insisted that the betrothal be nullified. Crandall refused and married her. His love and respect of her lasted throughout. Now they are old. . . . This is Westerners' faithfulness and integrity. I record it here because it is so commendable.[57]

Hu Shih's intention as to what he himself would do became clear. In the same month he recorded the Crandall episode, he composed this *tz'u* poem to express his sentiment to the fiancée whom he had never met.

Absence

Those years of absence I recall,
   When mountains parted thee and me.
And rivers, too. But that was all.
   The same fair moon which shone on thee,
Shone, too, on me, tho' far apart;
   And when 'twas full, as it is now,
We read in it each other's heart,
   As only thou and I knew how.

And now the moon is full once more!—
   But parting thee and me there lies
One half the earth; now as before
   Do these same stars adorn thy skies.
Nor can we now our thoughts impart
   Each to the other through the moon,
For o'er the valley where thou art,
   There reigns the summer sun at noon.[58]

In January, 1917, half a year before his homecoming, Hu wrote a *pai-hua* poem entitled "Receiving a Letter from Tung-hsiu While I Am Ill."

> Her letter comes while I am ill—
> Fewer than eight lines of quite unimportant chatter,
> Yet it makes me happy!
>
> I do not know her, Nor does she know me.
> Why, then, do I think so often of her?
>
> Is it not that we are destined to share
> A relationship from which affection grows,
> And so we are not strangers?
>
> An overseas voyager, not knowing his native land since birth,
> Still has a sentimental feeling toward it.
> This is also because there is a natural affection.
>
> Do you not love freedom?
> This is an idea that no one understands.
> To consent to being unfree
> Is also freedom![59]

This was what Hu had set out to do. If Crandall, an accomplished professor, could marry and love a blind woman, Hu could marry and love a bound-footed semiliterate. This was his way of consenting "to being unfree" in order to achieve the ultimate freedom. He had enough "imagination" and a sense of "duty" to learn to love his future wife. Speaking of Gandhi, Erik H. Erikson writes: "A soul that sensitive, proud, and self-centered can find a vocation only by *not* succeeding in ordinary ways."[60] Similarly, by obeying convention to that extent when a growing number of Chinese began to reject it, Hu had accomplished the ultimate unconventionality. By marrying Chiang Tung-hsiu, he would join the ranks of the C. L. Crandalls. By committing himself to such a marriage, Hu had presumably transcended the level of the Newtons, the Adam Smiths, and others in history who chose to remain single.

Hu Shih returned to China in July, 1917, and, in December married Chiang Tung-hsiu, ending a nine-year engagement.[61] Yet consenting "to being unfree" was not an easy matter. The marriage did not end his agonies, and the issues of women's status, family, and marriage continued to preoccupy him. During the two years following the nuptials, he produced nearly a dozen pieces of writing on these subjects, including the only play and short story he ever wrote. In these writings, we again see the enormous tension to which Hu was subjected.

Indicatively, one of Hu's first targets was none other than the arranged marriage. "In a country which has no freedom of marriage," he challenged in 1918, "how can we speak of love?"; "There is no chastity involved if there is no love or tender feeling between the couple."[62] Naturally, such a sweeping indictment would have to be modified in order to justify his own experience.

> The love created out of obligation as I have spoken of in that poem ["Receiving a Letter from Tung-hsiu While I Am Ill"] sometimes does exist. Otherwise, China's old-style marriage could not have survived [for so long].... But such love is entirely imaginary and idealistic, which can disappear completely if realities so dictate.[63]

The best Hu would do was to make his own marriage an exception to the rule. There was no need for him to defend the arranged marriage since he had been married; the burden was to unleash his bitterness toward the outmoded institution which tormented him. At the same time, he expressed his uninhibited admiration for the freedom and independence of the American women which, he maintained, set them apart from their sisters in other countries. What best symbolized their freedom and independence was their preference for bachelorhood and the high rate of divorce in America. Hu's perception of the first quality was interesting.

> When [American] women acquire more knowledge, they begin to look down upon pedestrian men. One only occasionally comes across an intellectual equal. This is why many women prefer staying unmarried to marrying pedestrian men.[64]

As a typical example, he gave none other than that of Edith Clifford Williams without, of course, mentioning her name. Well-read, unconventional, and defiant of her mother, Edith Williams was never married. "Her personality can truly be regarded as a concrete example of 'independence,'" Hu said.[65] If love or respect no longer exists, Hu further argued, a divorce would be justified. With this criterion in mind, "most [of the divorces in America] have legitimate reasons."[66]

Hu did not hesitate to apply these standards to the Chinese scene. Seizing the opportunity extended by the American colleges alumni association in China for a literary contribution, Hu produced a one-act farce on marriage in early 1919. In the matter of her "greatest event in life," the young protagonist, Tien Ah-may, had to combat her mother's superstition in soothsaying and her father's unquestioning belief in genealogy. After protesting, "Oh! oh! Father! You have destroyed the idols of superstition, but you bow to the idols of tradition!" she eloped with her boyfriend.[67] In December of that year, a female student named Li Ch'ao, after a heartbreaking confrontation with her family about her education and marriage, died in her twenties. Hu immediately made her a martyr by writing in *Hsin-ch'ao* a six-thousand-character biography of her, "which should be considered a long one in China's biographical literature." He did this for the young woman he did not even know, "because the suffering of her entire life can be regarded as a portrayal of numerous other Chinese women.... She can be counted as an outstanding victim in the history of women's movement in China."[68]

Significantly, all the women in Hu's writings ultimately achieved "freedom." It was Edith Williams who left her mother and insisted on her bachelorhood; it was Tien Ah-may who eloped and defied her parents; it was Li Ch'ao who "emancipated" herself by dying a martyr's death. Did Hu have some unmentionable desiderata? It was his misfortune to have been born into the Chinese society and to have been plighted to Chiang Tung-hsiu without his consent. Having failed to challenge convention himself, he encouraged *women* to elope, to defy, and to remain single. American women were so admirable partly because they looked down upon "pedestrian" men. Conspicuously, Hu did not mention those intelligent *men* who refused to marry pedestrian women. When the unfortunate Li Ch'ao died, he elevated her to the status of martyrdom in a national magazine. What was the prospect for men then? In "One Big Question," a short story Hu wrote in 1919, marriage was almost a death trap for men. A man had no freedom to remain single and could not resort to elopement, divorce, or desertion. In this story, the protagonist was a young man locked up in a marriage arranged by his former teacher. He had three children in quick succession and sank into destitution. In a matter of a few years, his health deteriorated, creativity dimmed, and his entire future was thrown away. "What is life for?" was the only question he was able to ask.[69]

Hu's attitude toward "parents" continued to be ambiguous.

Shortly after his mother died on November 23, 1918, he wrote a sentimental poem and a warm biography in her memory.[70] At the same time, he used the occasion to make a number of departures from the time-honored proprieties of the funeral ceremony and launched a frontal attack on the myth of parental infallibility and of children's unquestioning love and respect for parents. Since human feelings, parents' behavior, and a son's attitude of deference are different, "A flexible mourning period would be best. A long one may last several years, a short one three months or three days. Or there may be none at all."[71] Whereas Hu's suggestions were by no means unusual, the timing of the essay was perhaps more than fortuitous. Jerome Grieder observes: "Thus did the woman [Hu's mother] whose attachment to the old ways had proved too strong to sever in life serve her son as a symbol of the attack on traditional customs."[72]

What Hu Shih could not do to his mother during her lifetime, he did to his son in a naked manner. In June, 1919, three months after the arrival of his first son, Hu Tsu-wang, he celebrated the occasion with this poem.

> I really did not want a son,
> Yet the son came anyway.
> The signboard of "no-posterity-ism,"
> I can no longer hang.
>
> Like flowers blooming on trees,
> Seeds are fortuitously conceived when flowers fall.
> That seed is you,
> That tree is I.
> The tree has no intent to conceive the seed,
> Nor have I any favor to you.
>
> But since you have already come,
> I cannot but feed you and teach you.
> This is my duty toward humanity,
> Not a special favor to you.
>
> When you grow up,
> Don't forget how I teach my son.
> I want you to be an upright man,
> Not a filial son of mine.[73]

Responding to one of his critics, Hu continued,

This child did not himself freely propose to be born in my family. We, the parents, did not have his consent but casually endowed him with life. . . . How can we claim any merit? . . . We feel toward him only a certain contrition. . . . To put it in an extreme manner, giving birth to a son is like sowing the seed of potential calamity for him as well as for society. He may form bad habits and die young as a ruffian. He may even sink further and end up as a running dog of a warlord clique. Therefore, when we feed him and teach him, we are merely lessening our guilt and redeeming ourselves after we have sown the seed of calamity. How can we speak of favors and blessings? . . .

I would like to elevate the status of parents so that they will no longer perceive themselves as the creditors who "lend on usury" (*fang kao-li chai*).[74]

This was a pessimistic view and an excruciating protest. Hu showed little hope for the future of or confidence in the most fundamental human relationship—that between parents and children. Interested mainly in sex, as he saw it, parents endow lives "casually." Worse yet, giving birth to a child in China was like sowing the seed of potential calamity, for any child in such a society might well end up as an ephemeral ruffian or even a running dog of a warlord. These made the parents potential criminals. They would become real ones if they should expect anything from their children. The only thing they could and should do was to redeem themselves. The prospect for parents and children alike in the China of 1919 was indeed a dismal one, and a sensitive parent could not help being worried. It is also understandable that many of the values of Chinese parents were perceived by the cultural radicals as entirely intolerable. But Hu's unusual cynicism requires further explanation. Did he subliminally think that his own mother "lent on usury" in the matter of his marriage? He was determined not to lay any claims on his son, as his mother did on him. But he was not able to confront his mother directly. Now that he himself had become a parent, he indicted all parents, including himself, in order to divert the feeling that he was accusing his deceased mother. He was so disenchanted that he severed, symbolically, relationship with not only his own son but the future generations as well.

Of course, Hu's caustic opinions cannot be explained entirely in psychological terms. His deep sympathy for the suffering of women was largely derived from conviction and personal experience. He was aware that the betrothal was unfair to him as well as to Chiang Tung-hsiu. While he had to endure such a marriage, she had to wait nine years, by no means certain of her fate, and play a distant second fiddle for the rest of her life. He was fortunate enough to have received the best education at two leading universities, whereas she went through the ordeal of foot binding and suffered from the lack of schooling. Thus, Hu's sense of fair play overcame the bitter feeling he entertained. Although paying lavish tributes to the willingness of American women to divorce and their preference for bachelorhood, he set a demanding guideline for himself and those in similar circumstances. He spoke disparagingly of the

> returned students of recent days who, having breathed a bit of the air of enlightenment, get divorced first thing upon returning home—not stopping to think that their own civilized manner was bestowed upon them by good fortune, and paid for with a good deal of money; and that if their wives had enjoyed similar opportunities they too could have breathed the air of civilization, rather than suffering such derision![75]

In this spirit, Hu challenged the belief that women should remain unmarried or commit suicide for their deceased fiancés or husbands. Chastity, he insisted, should involve a consistent standard for both sexes and be dictated only by personal feeling and integrity. His writings on the topic were in part prompted by a few cases in which young women committed suicide for their deceased yet unmet fiancés. A Shanghai local official even had the audacity to recommend that one of the women be officially commemorated.[76] Similarly, Hu held that those who were raped need not feel morally ashamed of themselves, much less die because of it, for, as far as integrity was concerned, being raped was no different from a man being robbed. Since neither was the action of one's free will, one need not feel responsible for the result.[77] Rather than being submissive, Hu encouraged Chinese women to fight for their freedom and dignity. Though embittered by his own experience, he never forsook his commitment to societal well-being. The philosophy of life of the American women, he observed, "transcends the idea of being good wives and sagacious mothers"; their "spirit of independence, which at the first glance seems to be an extreme individualism, is in fact an absolutely indispensable prerequisite for a benign society."[78]

In February, 1919, inspired by the death of his mother, Hu wrote a widely read essay entitled "Immortality—My Religion." In it, he tried to modify and broaden the concept of "Three Immortalities" expounded in *Tradition of Tso*. The notion that one becomes immortal because of meritorious services, virtuous conduct, or monumental intellectual achievements is too vague, elitist, and without a deterrent to those who choose not to do good deeds, he argued. In its place, he proposed the concept of "social immortality." Everyone lives on in the continuous stream of society and is immortal. Man is the product of everything that has gone before, and his actions will inevitably affect the lives of all those who follow after. The "greater self" and the "lesser self," then, are inseparable, and the true worth of an individual is measured only by his contribution to the greater self. Therefore, "I must constantly consider how I can best develop the present 'lesser self' so as to discharge my responsibilities toward the greater self of the infinite past and leave no evil legacy to the greater self of the infinite future."[79]

Hu's theory of "social immortality," Grieder points out, "derived at least in part from a personal need for reassurance."[80] Indeed, the marriage was such a blow to his ego and sense of fulfillment that Hu wanted to be sure that even a mediocre event like it would have its imprint on history and make him part of the "immortal greater self." Here again Hu's personal experience and his concern for society converged. More than once he told his friend Lewis Stiles Gannett (1891–1966),

> If we are to lead we must obey the old conventions. Ours is an intermediate generation which must be sacrificed both to our parents and to our children. Unless we should lose all influence, we must marry as our parents wish, girls selected by them for us, whom we may not see before our wedding days—and we must make society happier and healthier for our own children to live in. Let that be our reward and consolation.[81]

From accounts from his friends, in his letters and diaries, we can assume that over the years Hu Shih did develop a tolerance and an understanding of Chiang Tung-hsiu who was somewhat coarse and domineering. How much affection Hu developed, however, is a matter of debate. The marriage lasted until his death, without much excitement.[82]

Part III
Political Views

Chapter 6

Cosmopolitanism

When he was a young student in Shanghai, Hu Shih wrote journal articles urging his compatriots to be patriotic.

> When everyone loves his country, it naturally becomes a strong country. . . . Look at the Britons and Germans! Who dare provoke them? Who dare touch them? Because they all love their countries. . . . Now look at the Chinese! They are humiliated and looked down upon everywhere. Ah! this is because our countrymen do not love their country. And that [the high international status of the Britons and Germans] is the *advantage of being patriotic*.[1]

Hu had nothing drastic in mind, asking only that the Chinese revive the study of China's literature and history and endeavor to improve China's education.[2] As he grew older, however, he came to realize that it was extremely painful for a Chinese to be patriotic. When he became involved in the Cosmopolitan movement shortly after he arrived in America, this cruel fact came to preoccupy him.

The Cosmopolitan movement grew out of student activities. In the last years of the nineteenth century, the tide of internationalist idealism began to run high. In 1898, Dr. Efisio Giglio-Tos founded the Fédération Internationale des Étudiants, "Corda Fratres" (Brothers in Heart), in Italy. Soon after, it attracted a following in the United States. An "International Club" was founded at the University of Wisconsin in 1903, followed by the Cornell Cosmopolitan Club and similar organizations elsewhere. By 1912, such clubs numbered close to thirty across the nation. In 1907, the Association of Cosmopolitan Clubs was formed and was recognized four years later as the American affiliate of the Fédération. In August, 1913, the eighth International Congress of the Fédération held its convention in Ithaca, to which the Cornell Cosmopolitan Club played host.³

The young cosmopolitans were strongly averse to a narrowly conceived nationalism and espoused universal human values which transcend national and cultural frontiers.⁴ The Fédération in its "fundamental articles" laid upon its members the responsibility to promote international understanding and to help dissipate among all walks of people the prejudice and hatred that make nations hostile toward each other.⁵ Reflecting the concerns of its members, the eighth International Congress of the Fédération passed resolutions, proposing, among other things, the adoption of Esperanto as an auxiliary international language and the establishment of a worldwide penny post to facilitate international communication. In other matters,

> the Congress . . . expresses its hope that the students of the world may be fired with zeal to carry on the work of the cultural, social, political, and economic uplift of the people of their respective countries.
>
> While the Congress greatly admires those students of the European states who during the recent wars have fought so noble [sic] and died for their fatherlands, it expresses its sincere hope that in the near future the movement of internationalism may reach these countries and bring to them good tidings of understanding, good will and peace among the nations; and that it may in the future prevent the necessity for the sacrifice of the best minds of a nation.⁶

Hu Shih became interested in the Cornell Cosmopolitan Club activities as early as February, 1911, half a year after his arrival in Ithaca.⁷ In September of that year, he moved into the club headquarters where he had his room for three years.⁸ At the end of 1912, he was one of the club's delegates to the annual meeting of the Association of Cosmopolitan Clubs held in Philadelphia⁹; and a year later he was on the delegation to the eighth International Congress of the Fédération in Ithaca, representing the Cornell Cosmopolitan Club as well as the Chinese Students' Alliance.¹⁰ In September, 1913, he was a member of the delegation of the International Congress that was received in Washington by President Woodrow Wilson and Secretary of State William Jennings Bryan.¹¹ In 1913–14, Hu was elected president of the Cornell club and at the same time served on the Central Committee of the Fédération.¹² In December, 1914, he again represented Cornell at the national convention of the Association of Cosmopolitan

Clubs in Columbus, Ohio, serving as chairman of the resolutions committee.[13]

Activities associated with the Cosmopolitan movement proved enormously beneficial to Hu. In July, 1916, he won a major award and a $100 prize for his essay "Is There a Substitute for Force in International Relations?" in a contest under the auspices of the American Association for International Conciliation.[14] Through these activities, he became a good friend of students from many countries and of several leaders of the Cosmopolitan movement. Among the latter were Louis Paul Lochner (1887–1975), who helped found the International Club at Wisconsin in 1903 and who later served as secretary of the Central Committee of the Fédération and editor of the *Cosmopolitan Student;* and George William Nasmyth (1882–1920), who became a Congregational minister and an ardent pacifist.[15] The various delegation and committee duties afforded Hu Shih opportunities to formulate his vision of an ideal world. In 1912, in a speech at the Cosmopolitan Club of Syracuse University he quoted Immanuel Kant's motto: "Always treat humanity as an end, never as a means."[16] To commemorate the tenth anniversary of the Cornell Cosmopolitan Club, he composed a sonnet in December, 1914.

> "Let here begin a Brotherhood of Man,
>   Wherein the West shall freely meet the East,
>   And man greet man as man—greatest as least.
> To know and love each other is our plan."
>
> So spoke our Founders; so our work began:
>   We made no place for pleasant dance and feast,
>   But each man of us vowed to serve as priest,
> In Mankind's holy war and lead the van.
>
> What have we done in ten years passed away?
>   Little, perhaps; no *one* grain salts the sea.
>   But we have faith that come it will—the Day—
>
> When these our dreams no longer dreams shall be
> And every nation on the earth shall say:
> "*Above all nations is humanity!*"[17]

Hu's cosmopolitanism can be seen from three different angles: his perception of his host country, his reaction to foreign, particularly

Japanese, threats to China, and finally, the ambivalence in his attitude toward China.

Examining American society as an outsider, Hu Shih was keenly aware of inconsistencies in American foreign policies and its racial prejudice. Hu spoke out on several occasions, challenging the double standard. In May, 1914, during the Mexican-American crisis, the *Ithaca Journal,* in abridged form at its masthead, printed Stephen Decatur's motto, "My country! In her intercourse with foreign nations may she always be in the right; but our country, right or wrong." Following a lively but inconclusive discussion of the motto among some Cosmopolitan Club members, Hu sent a letter to the paper offering his own opinions. The maxim, he charged, implied "a double standard of morality—one to our fellow countrymen and another to foreign or 'outlandish' people."[18] Hu later modified his position slightly, when it was suggested that the motto was not meant to advocate an unthinking embrace of anything that one's country stood for, but that it merely reflected a feeling of allegiance to the motherland even when its conduct turned out to be disappointing. Hu insisted, however, that the prevailing attitude in international affairs was one of hypocrisy.[19]

A more difficult task was to criticize the racial prejudice in the Ithaca community. In early October, 1914, a group of female students at the Sage College, a women's dormitory on the Cornell campus, petitioned the university president, Jacob Gould Schurman, to protest the presence of two blacks in the same dwelling. Schurman was about to make segregated arrangements for the two when Hu delivered a letter of protest to the *Cornell Daily Sun.* The editor declined to publish it for fear that it would damage the university's reputation; but he did, upon Hu's insistence, relay the message to Schurman. Largely as a result of Hu's action, Schurman rejected the petition of the white students.[20]

Hu's belief in cosmopolitan ideals also led him to become, beginning in the summer of 1914, an ardent supporter of Woodrow Wilson. In his early years in the United States, Hu greatly admired Theodore Roosevelt. During the presidential campaign of 1912, he sported a Bull Moose button.[21] On October 30, the Cornell Cosmopolitan Club conducted a straw ballot among its members. Interestingly, whereas Wilson was the overwhelming choice over Roosevelt (34 to 13), the Chinese gave six votes to Roosevelt and seven to Wilson. Though he did not reveal his choice, Hu must have voted for Roosevelt, for the very next day, the *Cornell Daily Sun* had a similar straw vote. "I too went to cast my ballot," Hu said, "and the person I voted for is Roosevelt."[22] Hu was likely attracted by Roosevelt's intelligence, moralistic views, and imposing personality. How much he approved of Roosevelt's Progressive programs—such as women's suffrage, industrial regulation, tax reform, and workmen's compensation—is difficult to determine. Hu expressed his opinions on these issues nearly two years after the straw ballots. He displayed his distaste for the laissez-faire policy in September, 1914, and expressly supported women's suffrage in late 1915, after he had begun dating Edith Clifford Williams and had transferred to Columbia University.[23] The best we can say is that Hu probably was in favor of Roosevelt's reforms in principle when he participated in the straw voting.

It is more fruitful to examine Hu's support of Roosevelt in terms of his adjustment to the American environment in general. At the time of the straw ballots, he was a few weeks short of his twenty-first birthday. He had transferred from agriculture to philosophy a year earlier, and his positive appraisal of Christianity then formed a sharp contrast to his negative views of Buddhism and Taoism. Although he moved into the Cornell Cosmopolitan Club headquarters in September, 1911, this move resulted in part from a quarrel with his landlady.[24] Nor had he systematically expressed his cosmopolitan ideals. In other words, Hu was still in the process of regaining his poise after the initial cultural shock of living in a foreign country. When he assessed Roosevelt and Wilson, he did not think it important to consider their stance on international affairs or their racial attitudes. Without commitment, Hu mentioned Roosevelt's position on the Panama and Colombia questions and Wilson's favorable response to the Philippines' quest for independence.[25] Nowhere did Hu discuss Roosevelt's racial views, his East Asian policies, or his willingness to resort to war to resolve international disputes.

But this was to change. Long before the end of Wilson's first term, Hu shifted his allegiance. It was perhaps significant that this happened in mid-July, 1914, less than two months after the debate on "My country! right or wrong." What was previously unimportant now became his central concern—consistency in international conduct and a sense of righteousness in relation to other nations. If Hu's ballot for Roosevelt attested to his identification with American interests, his allegiance to Wilson signaled the emergence of his independence and the embrace of a wider identity. But the inner struggle, which went on for nearly four years, was apparently not an easy one.

Shortly after the outbreak of the First World War, Hu commended Wilson as

> the supreme product of Western civilization, who strives to make moral ideals the basis of politics. This is what I call "consistency.". . .
> If all the politicians in the world were like Wilson, then this unprecedented war certainly would not have occurred.[26]

After the sinking of the *Lusitania* in early May, 1915, Hu duplicated the full text of a speech Wilson delivered at a naturalization ceremony. Without mentioning the incident, Wilson exhorted the naturalized citizens "not only always to think first of America, but always, also, to think first of humanity, You do not love humanity if you seek to divide humanity into jealous camps." In Wilson's view,

> the example of America must be the example not merely of peace because it will not fight, but of peace because peace is the healing and elevating influence of the world and strife is not.
> There is such a thing as a man being too proud to fight. There is such a thing as a nation being so right that it does not need to convince others by force that it is right.[27]

Greatly excited by this Wilsonian idealism, Hu stated that "the declaration of such an uncompromising humanitarianism displays a truly inimitable vision."[28] In a similar vein, he praised Wilson's proposal of "A Peace without Victory" as a "noble ideal" and the League to Enforce Peace, which Wilson did not favor, as an organization which would "open a new era in international relations."[29]

But the problem for Hu was not as simple as adopting a new identity. For China *was* his fatherland which he loved dearly. While he found the Wilsonian ideal immensely appealing, he was by no means able to sever his natural tie. Gandhi, Erikson tells us, was also attracted to "one of those more inclusive identities" through his contact with British culture. He was "willing neither to abandon vital ties to his native tradition nor to sacrifice lightly a Western education."[30] As we shall see, the brutal opinions of the West and Japanese aggression in those years tested Hu Shih's cosmopolitan ideal to the very limit.

Loyalty toward one's country, of course, does not necessarily invalidate one's cosmopolitan ideals. Hu believed, indeed, that a sense of national identity was compatible with a cosmopolitan vision and would actually enhance one's self-awareness. In October, 1912, reading George Grote's *A History of Greece* and comparing it with Edward Gibbon's *The Decline and Fall of the Roman Empire,* "it suddenly occurred to me," Hu wrote, "that the reason why the Roman empire fell was that, having been a unified country for too long, they only had the concept of the world but no longer a sense of their nation."[31] But there is a crucial difference between a patriotic feeling and a narrow nationalism. Cosmopolitanism, Hu held, "is patriotism balanced by a humane outlook." He was delighted to have encountered a similar notion in the line of Alfred Tennyson's poem, "Hands All Round."

> That man's the best cosmopolite,
> Who loves his native country best.[32]

Still later, in August, 1914, Hu read a passage by Thomas Carlyle which, he said, precisely reflected his own views.

> We hope [that] there is a patriotism founded on something better than prejudice; that our country may be dear to us, without injury to our philosophy; that in loving and justly prizing all other lands, we may prize justly, and yet love before all others, our own stern Mother-land, and the venerable structure of social and moral life, which Mind has through long ages been building up for us there.[33]

A well-guided national sentiment, then, helps refine and strengthen but should never displace a cosmopolitan goal. "Patriotism is a fine thing," Hu wrote in October, 1914, "but it must be understood that above the nation there exists a higher goal, a greater community. As Goldwin Smith says, 'Above all nations is humanity.' "[34]

Thus, Hu's embrace of cosmopolitanism was an attempt both to find his indigenous roots in a threatening surrounding and to search for a broader identity. When, in 1913, the eighth International Congress of the Fédération Internationale des Étudiants met in Ithaca, Hu pleaded with his fellow Chinese to be involved in the international student movement, for

> our mission . . . is . . . to understand and be understood. . . . But we must not confine our observations and associations to the Americans

alone when hosts of young men from all parts of the world are within our reach. . . . [The movement] broadens our sympathy and ennobles our vision. . . .

. . . This movement is not exactly a pacifist movement, yet it is the most fruitful and hopeful work for the propaganda of peace. . . . [A] better and more humane international relationship . . . in the ultimate end will no doubt also benefit our own fatherland. It is our duty to join any movement which proposes to combat the evils of narrow nationalism, race prejudice, greed, injustice and aggression. Are they not also *our* deadly foes?[35]

Clearly, the greatest and most immediate threat to China came from Japan. Hu perceived this unequivocally and remarked on January 27, 1915, nine days after Japan delivered the notorious Twenty-one Demands to Yüan Shih-k'ai: "My cosmopolitanism should first of all be aimed at Japan. This is called catching the ring-leader."[36] Hu's reactions to Japanese aggression ranged from advocating nonresistance to proposals for a more just and efficient execution of international law.

Shortly after war broke out in Europe, Hu had a conversation with George W. Nasmyth who had just returned from England and a tour of Belgium in the wake of the German invasion. Nasmyth said to him,

What I saw on the continent has further convinced me of the futility of force. I never believed in the doctrine of nonresistance preached by Tolstoi and the Quakers . . . but now I can see their unusual wisdom. Can't you see that Luxemburg was intact because it did not resist and that Belgium was in ruins because it did?[37]

Bertrand Russell, Hu noted, also urged the adoption of nonresistance as "a distant religious ideal" and as "the course of practical wisdom." "Only pride and fear stand in the way," Russell continued. "But the pride of military glory might be overcome by a nobler pride and the fear might be overcome by a clearer realization of the solidity and indestructibility of a modern civilized nation."[38] These arguments elicited from Hu an immediate sympathetic response. Right after the conversation with Nasmyth, he noted that water, as expounded in Lao-tzu's writing, has no discontentment because it competes with nothing else. And yet precisely because of its noncompetitiveness, water has the greatest ability to yield and conquer. Jesus and Sakyamuni, Hu further observed, also teach the virtue of forgiveness and nonviolence.[39]

Hu's nonresistance had its "practical wisdom," at least in his own mind. He pessimistically but correctly predicted that China's neutrality in the world war would be easily violated.[40] In view of China's military weaknesses, Hu approved of its nonresistance in the course of Japan's invasion of Tsingtao, for to fight would have incurred greater loss, as was the case of Belgium.[41] At the height of the Twenty-one Demands crisis, he objected vehemently to any military engagement, which many Chinese students in America demanded.

> I say, talking of fighting Japan at this present moment is insanity. For how can we fight? . . . What shall we fight with?
> . . . *It is pure nonsense and foolishness to talk of fighting when there is not the slightest chance of gaining anything but devastation, and devastation, and devastation!*
> . . . [T]o resist the tide of an ocean with a single hand is no heroism. . . . [T]o strike an egg against a rock is no heroism![42]

Hu's reasoning here, while pragmatic, should not be construed as expedient. Fundamental to his belief was that building up the military would only increase the possibility of war.[43] More important, when Hu was debating with other Chinese in the *Chinese Students' Monthly* against a military action to counter Japan's Twenty-one Demands, he originally included a section on the doctrine of nonresistance in his article "A Plea for Patriotic Sanity." But he deleted the section at the last moment after the article had been typeset, apparently fearing that such an opinion would further provoke his compatriots.[44]

Threats to China, however, did not come from Japan alone. Hu Shih soon found himself combating brutal opinions in the United States which favored Japan's actions. In February, 1915, a person signing the byline "A Friend of China" wrote in the *New Republic:*

> From a purely domestic point of view, an increasing Japanese preoccupation in China is bound to relieve in no small degree the embarrassment we have found in dealing with an active Japanese question in California. . . .
> The independence of China since the joint intervention of the Powers in 1900 has been due not to the inherent strength of the Chinese government nor to the substantial and admirable qualities of

the Chinese people, but to the balance of conflicting international interests. . . .

The Republic . . . has proved . . . a dismal failure. . . . She is incapable of developing herself. Her history is a record of foreign conquest. . . .

It is far better for China and for the world at large that there should be a responsible and effective direction of her affairs. That direction Japan will be able to give.[45]

Three weeks later, Hu's rebuttal appeared in the same publication. He reminded "A Friend of China" that

we are now living in an age of national consciousness. . . . In this twentieth century no nation can ever hope peacefully to rule over or to interfere with the internal affairs of another nation, however beneficial that rule or that interference may be. . . .

. . . [T]he transformation of a vast nation like China cannot be accomplished in a day. . . . Three years have hardly passed since the formation of the republic. Can we yet say, O ye of little faith! that "China as a progressive state has been tried and found wanting," and that "She is incapable of developing herself"?

[E]very people has the right to determine its own form of government. Every nation has the right to be left alone to work out its own solution.[46]

As time went on, Hu began to modify his doctrine of nonresistance, and by June, 1916, he came to endorse a just and internationally sanctioned use of force against aggression. In October, 1914, through George W. Nasmyth, he was introduced to Norman Angell's argument in *The Great Illusion* that war was unprofitable as well as morally indefensible. The emphasis on the economic aspect led Hu to observe that Angell was an idealistic "materialist" who engaged in one-sided reasoning.[47] In June, 1915, however, Hu came to know Angell better when the Conference on International Relations, jointly sponsored by the Carnegie Endowment for International Peace and the World Peace Foundation, met on the Cornell campus. Hu now concurred that any war is "as wasteful in economics as it is disastrous in morals."[48] Later, he read two essays of John Dewey published in early 1916 which further influenced his thinking. Dewey suggested that to call war a resort to "force" was to misunderstand it. War is inefficient and wasteful, and "must be adjudged a violence, not a use of force." On the other hand, "force is the only thing in the world which effects anything." He concluded that the "belief that war springs from the emotions of hate, pugnacity and greed rather than from the objective causes which call these emotions into play reduces the peace movement to the futile plane of hortatory preaching."[49] At the same time, Hu became interested in the pacifist views of Mo-tzu who argued on moral and economic grounds against war.[50] These pragmatic reasonings persuaded Hu to favor a more coherent international law and its efficient enforcement. "It is futile," he wrote in mid-1916,

> to look for an international policy which shall not involve a use of force; . . . even the so-called doctrine of nonresistance is *not* really a condemnation of force as such; and . . . the search for a "substitute for force" can only mean seeking a substitute for the most crude form and most wasteful use of force.[51]

The solution was to

> convert the now isolated and conflicting energies of the nations into some organized form—into some form of international association under a prescribed course of reciprocal duties and rights.[52]

Partly because of this conviction, by early May, 1917, Hu was no longer opposed to China and America joining the war.[53] This, however, did not mean that he had abandoned his cosmopolitan ideal. For the "international association" to succeed and be meaningful, Hu insisted, there had to be

> a radical change of the attitude of nations toward one another. . . . [W]e shall teach that the sovereignty of a state is a *right* the existence and validity of which entirely depend upon a tacit or explicit recognition and respect on the part of the other nations. . . .
> . . . Instead of "Right or wrong, my country!" we must regard the state as merely one of the many groups to which the individual belongs. . . . [T]he state is only a means to the well-being and free development of the individuals that compose it.[54]

These arguments of Hu's, it should be emphasized, were not high-sounding principles the purpose of which was to benefit China alone. In December, 1918, having by this time returned to China and thus facing only his home audience, he again insisted that the "international association" (the League of Nations?) envisioned by politicians in the

West was the ideal means to solve the problem of force itself, whereas a military approach would only compound problems.[55]

In the defense of China, Hu would only go thus far. Given the actions and opinions against China, his reactions were remarkably consistent. If he had any burdens, excessive nationalism was not one of them. In fact, against the overwhelming adversity and the ever-worsening condition at home, he did not always think that China was defensible on practical and even on moral grounds. Thus, on another level, his cosmopolitan outlook painfully divulged his psychological tension and ambivalent feeling toward his native land.

By his own pronouncement, Hu was an optimist. He frequently exhorted himself and others to look forward and be confident. His award-winning essay of 1914 was characteristically entitled "A Defense of Browning's Optimism." Recollecting his student days in America, Hu wrote that he was most impressed with "the naive optimism and cheerfulness" of the American people and that as a result he came to believe that "in this land there seemed to be nothing which could not be achieved by human intelligence and effort."[56] But how could a sensitive Chinese be such an optimist at a time when nearly everything in his country was going wrong? We should not take Hu's own words for granted without further analysis.[57] His statements were personal testimonies of his faith in himself and in the American system, a faith that exceptional talents like *himself* indeed could achieve anything by intelligence and effort in the land of opportunity. In a personal sense, he was enormously optimistic and confident, but he was almost fatalistic in terms of the general surroundings. The very fact that he exhorted himself and his friends to be optimistic bespoke his painstaking but futile effort to overcome his pessimism and feeling of despair, which invariably colored his views of the Chinese situation in international politics.

In his own mind, Hu frequently conceded the impossibility of defending China against brutal reality. In April, 1911, when certain Filipino students demanded independence for the Philippines, they were ridiculed by their American counterparts who pointed out that Japan would appropriate the archipelago if the United States should let it become a nation. Hu was too saddened by the American argument to speak. "I could only nod as a reply. Ah! Alas! do a vanquished people have the right to speak in their own behalf?"[58] Four years later, a

Japanese applied a similar logic to the Chinese situation, literally debilitating him. A certain Dr. T. Iyenaga wrote in the *New York Times:*

> Japan did violate the neutrality of China in exactly the same sense as England and France would violate the neutrality of Belgium by making it the scene of military operations of their efforts to drive out the Germans from the much-harassed country. . . . [T]he Germans in Kiao-Chau [Kiao-chow] had been taking military measures in the Shantung Province far beyond the zone within which China asked Germany and Japan to limit their operations. It would, then, have been suicidal for Japan to confine her military action within the so-called war zone. . . . If the Allies finally win, Japan will have proper claims to make for the blood and treasure expended for the capture of Kiao-Chau and in running the great risk of having for her foe a power so formidable as Germany. Even should Japan decide to retain Kiao-Chau, it would not be a violation of China's integrity, for Kiao-Chau was not a part of China; its complete sovereignty, at least for ninety-nine years, rested in Germany.[59]

Despite the persuasion of a friend, Hu chose not to rebut. "What Iyenaga says, though absurd, is the reality. In today's world of might, this kind of absurd argument has become the definitive opinion."[60] Hu was also well aware that any opinion in agreement with his own was usually the least popular opinion. In November, 1915, the *New York Evening Post* editorialized that "a world-settlement" meant

> a minimum of cutting and trimming here and there in Africa and Asia to make the Western adjustment as smooth as may be. . . .
> It is still true that when we speak of the world-war and of the world as it will look after the war, we think almost exclusively of the nations of the West.[61]

This time Hu responded, endorsing the stance of the *Post*.[62] Nevertheless, he added that his effort was no more than "an attempt to clap with one palm. Knowing that it will be useless, I just could not help trying."[63]

Cosmopolitanism was symptomatic of Hu's struggle to achieve a distant nonviolent vision, to transcend the transient, and to conquer the unconquerable. In March, 1915, when the Twenty-one Demands crisis was critical, Hu was pondering the utopian visions of Plato, Kant, Francis Bacon, Thomas More, and St. Augustine, and cited Tennyson's poem envisioning the formulation of "the Federation of the world."⁶⁴ Hu also took issue with Napoleon who likened China to a sleeping lion. "I don't think that using the parable of a sleeping lion to describe my country is as pertinent as the parable of a sleeping beauty," he insisted. "In the future if China has anything to contribute to the world, it must be in the areas of culture and morals, not the military."⁶⁵ Hu's most agonizing moment occurred on May 6, 1915, one day before Japan was to deliver the ultimatum to Yüan Shih-k'ai on the Twenty-one Demands.

> Last night I could not sleep at all. Rising at about one o'clock, I telephoned the *Cornell Daily Sun* for news from the Far East. They did not have any. Still unable to sleep, I got up at five, walked down the hill to buy a copy of a Syracuse newspaper. . . . Standing on the iron bridge and looking down at the water below . . . I suddenly came to think that Lao-tzu's likening water to nonresistance has its extraordinary vision. He says: "Nothing is better than water. It benefits the myriad of things and yet it competes with nothing else. Nothing in the world is weaker and softer than water, yet nothing hard or strong enough can destroy it.". . . If water has to compete with stone, give it time, water will prevail.⁶⁶

This represented Hu Shih's extraordinary self-control and his excruciating efforts to master an impossible situation. As Erikson has suggested in the case of Gandhi, embracing the cosmopolitan vision and the doctrine of nonresistance, Hu Shih could, symbolically, make the formidable foes—Japan and the Western powers—acknowledge "the power of the weak."⁶⁷ And Lifton writes that

> the "psychological non-resistance" involved is in the service of a greater harmony and can . . . represent a good deal more than mere passivity. . . . The implicit formulation accompanying psychological non-resistance, in other words, includes a vision of ultimately indestructible human continuity, a vision which enables one to look beyond immediate upheaval while psychologically "rolling with a punch," and to reassert inner imagery of connection, integrity, and movement.⁶⁸

This vision was what Hu subliminally tried to attain. He found many examples. Confucius did not fight when confined to adverse and impoverished conditions. Jesus registered no complaints when being crucified. Lao-tzu did not reciprocate with bitterness. "This is great bravery, bravery of the bones and of spirit."⁶⁹

Underlying Hu's pessimism was a profound feeling of ambivalence toward China. Although he often defended China's interests with passion, Hu was not always sure that his fatherland was worth his convictions and aspirations. If "we must regard the state as merely one of the many groups to which the individual belongs," and as "a means to the well-being and free development of the individuals that compose it," then China in the early twentieth century offered neither. Hu was too honest to deceive himself. In October, 1913, reflecting on the impeachment of the governor of New York, William Sulzer, Hu wrote: "Ah! how dare I privately criticize the political merits and demerits of a foreign country! I am too busy lamenting the filthy politics and corrupt officials of my own land."[70] Later, in July, 1914, following the discussion of "My country! right or wrong," Hu again turned to China.

> Confucius says: "Father conceals for the son, and son conceals for the father. Therein we find uprightness." This is sage's saying. . . . I too am not without selfish wishes. . . . Am I not frequently concealing for my country? Everyone has the mind to differentiate right from wrong, but it is a different matter whether the mind is strong enough to overcome a blind patriotic feeling. . . . Reading history, when I come to the Opium War and the Anglo-French invasions, I always think that China was upright. But when I come to the Boxers, I never believe that the Boxer bandits were upright.[71]

As time went on, Hu's choice became increasingly difficult. The following item from his diary in March, 1917, best illustrates his torment.

> Wang Jen-ch'iu [Wang K'ai-yün] is dead. Ten years ago I read his correspondence (*Hsiang-ch'i-lou chien-ch'i*) in which he had the following passage to his daughter-in-law: "They [foreigners] invaded our capital without being able to destroy, much less to dismember, us. Even if they had been able to dismember us, what is wrong if we had abandoned our chaos and embraced their moral order? . . ."
> I was angered. I thought that this old man made such an outrageous remark because he did not love his country. But in ten years my own ideas have changed. . . .
> I often say that statism (ethnic statism) has only one defensible foundation . . . that is: . . ."the self rule of a race is in the end more preferable to an alien rule.". . .
> If the choice is between Yüan Shih-k'ai and Wilson, then people will pick Wilson. If one picks Yüan simply because Wilson is of a

different race, then he must be poisoned by nationalism. This is what is meant by "abandoning chaos and embracing moral order."

I misjudged Wang Jen-ch'iu. He is dead now. I record my thoughts here as a self-repentance.

If the premise "the self rule of a race is in the end more preferable to an alien rule" cannot be established, then nationalism and statism cannot either.

But can such a premise be established?

The issue cannot be stated in a blanket manner. The central focus of this premise is "in the end." "In the end" suggests that if it [a benevolent self rule] cannot be expected now, it may be expected in the future. When argued in this way, it will never be refuted. But it is really an *ad infinitum* evasion.

Today, people realize the difficulty in proving the validity of this premise. Therefore, they have established a different one. Wilson has said in his second inaugural address: "That governments derive all their just powers from the consent of the governed, and that no other powers should be supported by the common thought, purpose or power of the family of nations." This is the theory of republican politics and can also be regarded as the premise of nationalism. If the Indians refuse to acknowledge the British rule, then a revolution will be justified. . . . If the two million Germans in America consent to the American rule, then there will be no revolution.

But what are the prerequisites for the governed to give their consent? If we render or withhold our consent on ethnic grounds, then we are resorting to nationalism and nationalism's *ad infinitum* evasion as the premise. This would be a "circuitous" logic. If we base our premise on the merit of the government, then we actually return to the [Wilsonian] premise.

Narrow nationalists today, while blatantly talking about loving one's country, really do not understand why one's own country should be loved or what nationalism actually means. . . . I record the above observations here to remind people that nationalism alone cannot be a valid premise.[72]

If, looking at China from such a distance, Hu had serious reservations about its ability to rule itself or to provide its citizens "the well-being and free development," it is understandable that, when he returned home, the reality became even more unbearable. The following poem, composed in June, 1918, a year after the homecoming, amply attested his mood.

My son, for twenty years I have taught you to love your country,

> But such a country how can you love! . . .
> You should not forget that it was the crass soldiers
> of our own country who
>   raped the Third Aunt, caused the death of A Hsing,
>   forced your wife to die, shot Kao Sheng to death.
> You should not forget: who cut off your fingers,
>   who beat your father to death,
>   who burned down the whole village . . .
>
> Ah! . . .
> Fire is spreading here,
> Run, don't perish with us!
> Come back for awhile.
> Don't forget,
>   When your old man was dying, all he hoped for
> was that the nation would soon be annihilated—
>   annihilated by the Cossacks, annihilated
>   by Prussia—anyway, it could not have been
>   as bad as it is now.[73]

Hu Shih here thoroughly rejected the Chinese government and its legitimacy—the entire Chinese state. And, at least in the abstract, he no longer considered the nation

> a "terminal community," with the implication that it is for present purposes the effective end of the road for man as a social animal, the end point of working solidarity between men.[74]

In all fairness, however, Hu was not ready to "abandon our chaos and embrace their moral order," nor did he hope that China be "annihilated." He still had a strong feeling for the Chinese nation as "a community of people" who "share deeply significant elements of a common heritage" and who "have a common destiny for the future."[75] Thus, he was tormented by his quest for a more inclusive identity and his devotion to China. In September, 1916—when Yüan Shih-k'ai had been dead for three months and the country was in utter chaos and confusion—Hu wrote these lines to console himself after a sleepless night:

> You love her deep in your heart, don't say you don't love her.
> You love her deeply, yet you are looking on when someone is trying to
>   harm her.

> If someone is trying to harm her, how are you going to treat her? If people love her, how are you then going to treat her?[76]

He continued,

> You may wonder why I need any self-justification for worrying about my country. I would say that it is because I am a self-proclaimed "citizen of the world" who does not subscribe to a narrow nationalism and who considers it particularly unworthy of being an emotional "patriot."[77]

The truth of the matter, of course, was more complicated than Hu would have us believe. A more poignant revelation is found in his comments on his translation of Maupassant's "Deux Amis," completed in January, 1917.

> Reading it casually, one would think that this short story is no different from the patriotic novels of the idealistic school. Upon close analysis, its salient features become self-evident.
> 1. In his depiction of the siege of Paris, Maupassant does not deal with one or two imposing patriots but rather concentrates on two unconcerned and indifferent drunkards who at the time of national crisis are obsessed with the joy of fishing. . . .
> 2. . . . At the time of roaring bombardment, these two fishermen are enjoying fishing and talking politics in grand terms and chastising their government. Here we can see that Maupassant has no intention to depict a narrow patriot. . . .
> 4. These two fishermen, while not particularly patriotic, eventually die for their country. Whereas unconcerned with and indifferent to national affairs, they die precisely because they refuse to be traitorous. This is Maupassant's extraordinary vision. . . . This is a "natural" patriotism which in time and history anyone with conscience possesses and which does not need a narrow nationalism as a prerequisite.[78]

These comments best attested Hu's agony and self-conquest.

"I have lately abandoned the pacifism of nonresistance," Hu Shih wrote in July, 1936.[79] Little wonder that he did. By the middle of the 1930s, no one doubted that Japan would eventually subjugate China, and Hu finally decided that an all-out war of resistance was inevitable. The process of reaching this conclusion, however, was an arduous one.

At one level, Hu had a remarkable faith in international goodwill and sense of justice. Shortly after the First World War, he claimed that the Allies' victory was "not the result of 'resolving problems by force,' but rather the result of 'resolving the problem of force.'" He steadfastly believed that the League of Nations, not yet proclaimed until 1920, would be the ultimate answer for world peace.[80]

Obstinately, Hu refused to accept imperialism even as a partial explanation for China's plight. In October, 1922, he defended Japanese and Western imperialism-capitalism in these words:

> The hopes of foreign investors for peace and unity in China are in no way less than the hopes of the Chinese themselves for peace and unity in China. . . . That foreigners supported Yüan [Shih-k'ai] indicated that most of the capitalists hoped for peace and order. We can say that they were myopic, but we cannot accuse them of being motivated by evil intentions. . . .
>
> . . . International investment becomes a problem only when the country in which the capital is invested is not at peace, not stable, and not capable of protecting the interests and security of the investors. Therefore, people say that Mexico, China, Persia, and countries in the Near East are "the last stakes of diplomacy and sources of international chaos.". . . Frankly speaking, China is no longer in any great danger from foreign aggression. . . . Nowadays foreign powers, be it Japan, America, or England, cannot help letting the Chinese people resolve their own political problems and reconstruct a unified nation.[81]

This was as friendly an interpretation of the motives of foreign interests in China as one could expect from a native Chinese. Certainly, Hu directed these words mainly at the Chinese Communists with whose premises and approaches he strongly disagreed. In their arguments, there was always an excess of emotion. While he no longer spoke of inner strength, moral cultivation, and self-reflection as the primary goals of life, Hu, like his moralistic predecessors, put an enormous emphasis on these qualities. Habitually, he blamed China for most of its problems. Moreover, Hu's thinking reflected his psychological weakness and practical concern. Since imperialism was too powerful to challenge, chastising China was an easier way out and helped overcome his feeling of impotence. In practical terms, blaming imperialism would, in Hu's view, distract China's attention and waste what little precious time and energy it had. After all is said, however, none of these considerations could completely explain Hu's belief in international goodwill and the rationality of man. As late as August, 1930, only a year before the Manchurian Incident, Hu said to a friend of his that Japan "has many virtues that other nations do not possess. This is why it has reached its present status in one leap." Hu further observed that "the key to the peace in Europe lies in the German-French cooperation, so the key to the peace in East Asia lies in Sino-Japanese cooperation. This will certainly be the guiding principle of China's future diplomacy that cannot be ignored."[82] In time, however, Hu's faith was rudely shattered.

Hu Shih put forward his proposals for a Japan policy less than a year after the Manchurian Incident of September 18, 1931. The most important thing, as he saw it, was for the League of Nations to sponsor a direct negotiation between China and Japan. He was willing to let Japan retain its privileges in Manchuria under previous treaty agreements and, to avoid further hostility, to demilitarize the region. However, he insisted that Manchukuo, proclaimed on March 1, 1932, be revoked and that China's territorial and administrative integrity be respected.[83] Although only two months later, Japanese foreign minister Uchida Yasuya (Kosai, 1865–1936) declared that "Japan is determined not to return to China the territorial and administrative integrity in Manchuria,"[84] Hu retained his faith in the League of Nations and hoped that world opinion would force Japan to come to a peaceful settlement with China. With such a hope in mind, he hailed Stimson's nonrecognition doctrine as an "ideal political philosphy" and as constituting a "moral sanction" against aggression.[85]

As Japan penetrated more deeply into China, Hu was ready to make more concessions. In October, 1932, he was prepared to accept an autonomous Manchuria as part of the Chinese nation.[86] However, while he still favored the League as mediator, he was against any further retreat on China's part and rejected the idea of direct negotiations with Japan when the latter refused to revoke Manchukuo. "No matter what, we cannot be the first to bend on our knees to recognize what Japan created by violence and what the rest of the world has refused to recognize."[87] What Hu had in mind was not a militant response, but rather a gradual, determined effort to rebuild the country so that someday China would be able to rid itself of the yoke of foreign invaders. He pointed out that it took Belgium four years to rebuild the country from the German devastation in the First World

War and France forty-eight years to recover its territory lost in the Franco-Prussian War of 1871. "What does four or five years or forty or fifty years mean in the life of a nation of thousands of and tens of thousands of years?" Hu argued rhetorically.[88] And as late as November, 1933, he was still thinking of a collective, international approach to insure world peace. China's future, he said, depended upon a rational international organization

> which would prevent the strong from being aggressive toward and preying upon the weak and which would allow the weak to present their cases with dignity and to live in peace. . . . This ideal situation is not entirely impossible.[89]

A little earlier, Hu strongly rebutted a suggestion that China go to war. He was still clinging to his pacifist stand. It would be against his conscience, he said, to urge the young people to risk their lives in the face of the merciless modern weapon. " 'To war' is only two words, but few of us have sufficiently pondered their meaning."[90]

It should be noted that Hu's pacifism and cosmopolitan approach had its "rational" and pragmatic elements. He favored Japan's privileged position in Manchuria because Japan had been enjoying those privileges all along,[91] and to demilitarize Manchuria would be the only sensible course of action to him. "The reason is quite simple," he wrote. "Were not there two hundred thousand soldiers there on the night of September 18 last year [1931]? . . . For the safety of the place, for the welfare of the people in Manchuria, I propose to demilitarize Manchuria."[92] Hu was heartbroken when, in March, 1933, a Japanese advance team of "a hundred twenty-eight men and four tanks" overran Jehol, a province of six hundred thousand square kilometers defended by over a hundred thousand soldiers.[93] And he heard more than once from Ting Wen-chiang, who was a respectable lay military strategist, that "[some] Chinese military officers cannot even read military maps."[94]

These conclusions of Hu's underscored his utter pessimism. While he doggedly believed in man's reasonableness and sense of fair play, he also saw the darker side of human nature. As a rule, the strong would never let pass an opportunity to prey upon the weak, and world affairs were ultimately determined by self-interest and might. This ostensible contradiction in his propensity is not difficult to explain. His elitism and intellect often led Hu to believe that everyone else was as rational, reasonable, and guided by a sense of moral justice as he. The practical Chinese affairs and the cruel reality, however, frequently drove him into despair. Although he vigorously defended China's right to survive as a nation, nevertheless his judgment typically revealed his pessimistic outlook. Reading his political essays, one cannot escape the conclusion that, as Jerome Grieder aptly writes, "In his admiration for Japanese energy Hu seemed at times almost to concede that the Japanese had earned the right to behave as they did toward their lethargic Chinese neighbors."[95] In his angry moments, Hu could hardly conceal his contempt for his own country. One day after the Manchurian Incident, he sighed: "It has been nearly forty years since the Sino-Japanese War. Yet ours is still such a country. . . . How can we not suffer in the hands of others?"[96] On another occasion, he wrote that China was in such a plight because "our ancestors have committed too many curses and accumulated too deep a retribution."[97] On March 2, 1933, he repeated by far his angriest remark which he often shared with his friends: "If China is not exterminated, then there are no heavenly principles in the world."[98]

What was a Chinese to do in such a terrifying bind? The invincible Japanese troops kept marching on without respite, while the Chinese were not even able to put up a token resistance; and the rational international order which Hu Shih envisoned remained wishful thinking. Whereas Hu would not let his beloved country bend on its knees, he himself offered an extraordinary plea for mercy. In October, 1935, when asked by his Japanese friend Murobushi Koshin to write an article for the *Japan Critic,* He spoke to the Japanese people directly.

> It is a matter of course that, when two nations are at war, one defeats the other. However, the two nations do not have to harbor deep hatred. In less than five years of the Russo-Japanese War, Japan and Russia became allies. In less than ten years of the Sino-Japanese War, most of the Chinese were on Japan's side in the Russo-Japanese War. . . . Therefore I say that a victory does not have to evoke hatred [from the other side]. But it is a different matter when one takes advantage of another's weakness, attacks when the other side is already in danger, making the other side incapable of fighting a war or defending itself. This is beneath the dignity of bushido, and it provokes the deepest hatred. . . . Is a scorched China Japan's fortune? . . .
>
> I am most deeply awed by Japan's achievements, and I have often envisioned Japan's future. Industrious and patriotic, with a ten-thousand-generation, unbroken imperial line, the influence of the bu-

shido spirit, the prevalence of aesthetic feelings, and a tireless devotion to learning, the Japanese can be said to have combined the strengths of both the English and the German peoples. Japan should be able to peacefully develop into a best liked and admired country in East Asia.[99]

This was Hu's last plea, but all was too late. A month later, he reached the conclusion that "if we retreat one inch, the other side will advance ten feet. There will be no end to our humiliation, and it will be impossible to protect us intact."[100] When he wrote Murobushi Koshin again in the same month, Hu was in a sad but determined mood, and for the first time he revealed that he was abandoning his pacifist stand. To be a friend or an enemy in international politics, Hu observed, implied an equal relationship between two parties, and China clearly was not qualified for either. Yet in order to survive, China should try to be on the best possible terms with those nations which were not harming or hindering it. If no nation was willing to do this, then China should be prepared to deal with whatever enemy there was. Hu related to Murobushi Koshin his final realization:

> You do not approve of Judaism. But Judaism has a curious doctrine that urges men to "love your enemy." For twenty-five years, I have deeply believed in this doctrine of Judaism. Yet I am ashamed that my belief in the *tao* is not sincere enough and that my faith in the *tao* is not firm enough. In recent months, I have had doubts whether this doctrine is really what an ordinary flesh and blood like me can adhere to for life.[101]

At the same time, in November, 1935, Nelson T. Johnson, American ambassador to China, summed up a conversation he had with Hu Shih, Lin Yutang, and Chang Loy of the Chinese customs service.

> Dr. Hu Shih led the conversation, saying that it was "almost a probability" that the Chinese would resort in the near future to military action against the Japanese. . . . The reason for the belief of these three gentlemen that the Chinese may fight is summed up in the phrase, quoted by Mr. Lin Yutang, "when a dog is driven to the end of a blind alley he will turn and fight."
> Dr. Hu Shih . . . said that he has always been a pacifist, is still one, was one of the few who urged a direct settlement between Chinese and Japanese shortly after the Mukden incident, and was the only Chinese who expressed approval in print of the conclusion by the Chinese authorities of the Tangku Truce of May 31, 1933. He feels

now, however, that there is no hope of compromise with the Japanese and that the ambitions of the Japanese military leave for China no alternative but to fight for self-preservation. He added that heretofore he had felt that persons such as he, who would not be called upon to bear arms in case of a conflict with Japan, should not urge a course which would bring suffering to many Chinese but that now the situation was so serious that he no longer held this view.[102]

Speaking of the spirit of the Age of Enlightenment, Peter Gay has written:

> The philosophe was a cosmopolitan by conviction as well as by training. Like the ancient Stoic, he would exalt the interest of mankind above the interest of country or clan; as Diderot told Hume in an outburst of spontaneous good feeling. "My dear David, you belong to all nations, and you'll never ask an unhappy man for his birthcertificate. I flatter myself that I am, like you, citizen of the great city of the world.[103]

How much Hu Shih wished that he had been able to be part of such good spirit and companionship! He himself was a cosmopolitan by conviction as well as by training. But China in the twentieth century was different from eighteenth-century Europe, "whose various inhabitants have attained almost the same level of politeness and cultivation."[104] China was not an equal of the powerful nations, nor was it perceived as polite and cultivated. Sadly, Hu could only protest injustice, plead for mercy, and try not to betray his conscience by being a "natural" patriot. In spirit, then, he was more akin to the Japanese Hiroshima atomic bomb survivors who spoke with such empathy and helplessness.

> I feel strongly that there should be no separate nations—no demarcation of borders between countries. . . .
>   Nowadays people begin to talk again of patriotism. Let patriotism be tied up with love for a particular place. Those who come from Texas can love Texas. Those in Hiroshima can love the Inland Sea. If one loves Texas, one can also love California—there is no war between Texas and California.[105]

But like a dog "driven to the end of a blind alley," Hu finally gave up his cosmopolitan ideals when his country's very survival was in imminent danger.

Chapter 7

Chinese Politics

"Wherever I live," Hu Shih wrote in late 1916,

> I consider its political and social life just as I would the political and social life of my native place. Whenever there is some political activity or an undertaking of social reform, I delight in learning of it. Not only that, I also get personally involved in it, studying its positives and negatives, strengths and weaknesses, identifying myself with the party I support, and sharing its joys and sorrows.[1]

Throughout his years in the United States, Hu made several efforts to understand its political system. While at Cornell, he went to political rallies and attended meetings of the Ithaca Common Council to familiarize himself with the workings of American local government. He was deeply impressed by the democratic spirit of American politics and the sense of participation of Ithaca citizens.[2] During the presidential campaign of 1912, he identified himself with Roosevelt while paying close attention to the election in general, subscribing to three New York papers that supported three of the major candidates—the *Times* (Wilson), the *Tribune* (Taft), and the *Evening Journal* (Roosevelt). Taking Samuel P. Orth's course on American party politics, Hu read corrupt practices legislation of all the states.[3] In November, 1912, he organized a group of Chinese students to study American and European politics.[4]

Hu's interest revealed his political ideas and style. There were telling incidents. He became interested in the women's movement during the latter part of his Cornell days and his Columbia years. In late October, 1915, shortly before the general election in the state of New York, he went to Fifth Avenue to watch a suffragette parade. "In

107

general," Hu opined, "a parade has two purposes. One is to promote its cause, and the other, to draw attention. In a word, it is a public showcase, the so-called advertising." Having watched it for more than three hours, he began to note that "the most moving aspects of this parade" were the orderly conduct of over forty thousand participants, their solemness, the sizable number of female teachers, and the perseverance of the paraders in the bitter cold.[5] On the same day, upon learning of the fate of the suffragette movement in New Jersey, Hu reflected:

> New Jersey is the state of American president Wilson. Two months ago, Wilson announced his endorsement of the suffragette issue and, on the election day, returned to the state to cast his ballot. His cabinet members from the state were also in favor of this issue. Yet it failed to pass. Even the endorsement of the highest national leader could not sway his fellow citizens in the state. This really attested the independence of Westerners who are not easily influenced by those in high positions or with coveted titles.[6]

On another occasion, one evening as he was reading in his room in Furnall Hall, overlooking Broadway, Hu was distracted by a commotion in the street below.

> Going to the window I looked down and saw an automobile filled with women, all of them suffragettes. . . . Slowly a crowd gathered. The flute stopped and the girl arose to invite the crowd to a rally that was to be held in front of the library. I went along too. . . . Suddenly in the crowd I caught sight of Professor John Dewey. . . . I thought at first that he was perhaps only passing by, but when the speeches were over he . . . got into the car and drove off with all the suffragettes, and then I realized that the professor was helping them in their campaigning. Alas! a scholar of the twentieth century should not act thus.[7]

When the results of the suffragette issue in New York were announced on November 3, 1915, Hu commented "The anti-suffragettes won . . . but those who voted for the issue numbered more than five hundred thousand. This is a glorious defeat."[8]

These observations of Hu's were suggestive. To be sure, it was not unusual for him to be particularly impressed with the independence of Westerners, the orderly conduct of the paraders, and the sizable number of female teachers among the suffragettes—qualities that constituted sharp contrasts to political behavior in his own country. Yet this hardly explains Hu's political style. By his own acknowledgment, he had been in favor of the suffragette movement.[9] But he chided in no uncertain terms Dewey's active support of it and seemed indifferent to the result of the vote on the issue. How are we to reconcile Hu's liberal beliefs in general and his conservative approach in particular instances?

As Hu implied, an intellectual's role in politics was to render judgment. Thus, Dewey's support of the suffragette movement should have stopped short of an active involvement. To Hu, political means—style, spirit, and dignity—were more important than issues. He paid more attention to the behavior of the suffragettes than to the results themselves. Once the means were properly adhered to, the defeat, while disappointing, was a "glorious one."

Hu Shih's political style can be further elucidated in terms of the tendencies of a liberal. A liberal, Bernard Crick writes, usually

> expects too much. He wishes to enjoy all the fruits of politics without paying the price or noticing the pain. He likes to honour the fruit but not the tree; he wishes to pluck each fruit—liberty, representative government, honesty in government, economic prosperity, and free or general education, etc.—and then preserve them from further contact with politics. . . . He overestimates the power of reason and the coherence of public opinion; he underestimates the force of political passions and the perversity of men in often not seeming to want what is so obviously good for them. . . . He tends to think in terms of an enlightened public opinion working on clear and simple representative institutions. . . . This liberal will join in political crusaders to clean up this or that, but he abhors the political regular. If he has a party at all . . . then it is a party of anti-party.[10]

Indeed, Hu underestimated the emotions and selfish motives in politics and naively believed in the power of reason and in the good will of those involved. He assumed that disagreements, however fundamental, would be temporary and that consensus was always within reach. Therefore, he was not so much disturbed by the antisuffragettes' votes as he was impressed by their "independence." Moreover, since any political issue was a clear-cut one, one did not have to do anything to advance its cause. The suffragettes, then, were doing something superfluous; they were "advertising." These liberal tendencies probably reinforced Hu's elitism. As Grieder aptly puts it, the society which Hu envisioned was the one "in which all are leaders and none are led."[11]

Little surprise, Hu Shih had profound misgivings about any "radical" ideologies or activist politics. In November, 1916, he recalled a visit to the home of his friend, Paul B. Schumm. "His father, George Schumm, subscribes to anarchism and enjoys the philosophies of Proudhon, Herbert Spencer and the like. Yet he is honest and benign and does not look like a person who believes in anarchism."[12] On his way back to China in the early summer of 1917, Hu was clearly annoyed by what he saw as the crude, ignorant, radical Russian exile youths on the ship who "blatantly talked socialism and anarchism."[13] Hu obviously believed that an honest man like George Schumm should not have been an anarchist. In the second case, Hu's emphasis on intellectual finesse and dignified approach led him to dismiss outright any political commitment based on passion.

While Hu's thinking was an important factor in determining his political style, objective circumstances played a pivotal role. Hu had strong feelings toward America and its people, and he repeatedly said that he considered Ithaca his second home. America, however, was still only his *second* home, and he had no illusion that he was anything more than a peripheral observer with no power to shape the outcome of American politics. As much as he was interested in the women's movement, the most he could do was to praise the courage of the suffragettes. Indeed, his interest in American politics was partly an intellectual exercise, with a detached excitement and objectivity, hoping that lessons thus acquired might someday benefit his own country. He explained in November, 1916, "the place in which we live is really our society, and its public affairs are all worth our attention." Further, the habit of attending to public affairs was in itself important.

> If, when residing in a certain place, we are unconcerned with the interests and aspirations of that place, when we return home, will we be able to suddenly become enthusiastic about the interests and aspirations of a given place in our own country?[14]

Hu Shih's seven-year sojourn in the United States coincided with the Republican Revolution, Yüan Shih-k'ai's monarchism, the beginning of warlordism, and the continued foreign encroachments on China. Though thousands of miles away, Hu still expressed extensive opinions on political events back home.

The Republican Revolution of 1911 broke out a year after Hu's arrival at Cornell. Considering the pivotal nature of the event, his diary had few comments at the outset, and for several days, they remained strictly factual. Not until October 17 of that year did he pass the first judgment when, commenting on Yüan Shih-k'ai's acceptance of the imperial appointment, he called Yüan "a despicable fool."[15] Surprisingly, however, Hu was reticent on the *revolution* itself. Indeed, slowness to accept political change was one of the outstanding characteristics of Hu's thinking.

It was nearly three months later that Hu endorsed the Republican Revolution. Writing in the *Cornell Era* in January, 1912, he argued in favor of democracy in China in historical terms. There was, said he, "a quiet, peaceful, oriental form of democracy" in classical China. Did not Mencius regard the people as the most important and the sovereign the least? The Republican Revolution, therefore, was not entirely alien or without a theoretical foundation. Significantly, Hu ruled out the possibility of offering a crown to any individual, be he Yüan Shih-k'ai, Sun Yat-sen, or Huang Hsing (1874–1916).[16] Responding to an inquiry from the *Outlook* in August, 1915, Hu further wrote:

> Young China believes in democracy; it believes that *the only way to have democracy is to have democracy.* Government is an art, and as such it needs practice. . . . The Anglo-Saxon people would never have had democracy had they never practiced democracy.[17]

Shortly after Yüan's death in June, 1916, Hu concluded that "the whole episode [the monarchical movement] may furnish the world with a fresh proof of China's sincerity in her democratic aspirations and in her strife for an upright and enlightened government."[18] All along, Hu took issue with Yüan's foreign advisers Ariga Nagao (1860–1921) and Frank Johnson Goodnow (1859–1939), charging the latter as "a reactionary" "who has helped to kill the first constitution of the Chinese Republic."[19] Hu pleaded:

> Professor Goodnow and many other well-meaning constitutional authorities think that the Oriental people are not fit for democratic form of government *because they have never had it before*. On the contrary, Young China believes that it is precisely because China has not had democracy that she must now have democracy.[20]

In his battle with his foreign audiences, Hu resorted to the only recourse at his disposal: to invoke remote theoretical democratic precedents in Chinese history and to insist on the future prospect of democracy in China. He entertained no illusion as to what the condition in China really was, readily admitting that

> the Chinese democracy . . . now exists only in name. For almost two years the country has had no parliament, no provincial legislatures, no district councils. There are no political parties, no freedom of press, no freedom of speech.[21]

And in December, 1914, Hu, quoting at length a letter from a friend who had just returned to China from America, concurred that there was little chance for democracy to succeed in China. China, the letter went, was far from acquiring the qualities of a republic. Not one in a hundred could read, and perhaps not one in a million could discuss domestic politics or international diplomacy. "China at best was a republic of a handful of elite, not a republic of true democracy."[22]

Confronted with this grim reality, Hu decided to put aside politics and concentrate on nonpolitical areas. In a letter to Hsü I-sun in China, dated January 25, 1916, Hu argued that the proper way at the time was to cultivate men of talent by emphasizing education. His own plan after returning home was to devote himself to the task of social education, so that enough talent would be trained "over a period of one hundred years." Hu conceded that at a moment of great crisis his proposal seemed a slow and doltish process. However, he had decided that there were no shortcuts in national or world affairs. A slow and doltish plan, then, would be the only possible solution.[23]

Hu's assumption was that education would create upright and intelligent citizens who in turn would engender a congenial political atmosphere. In such a society, consensus and harmony would be a matter of course, and politics would become more or less superfluous. In May, 1915, reading Liang Ch'i-ch'ao's latest article, "The Foundation of Politics and the Guide for a Political Commentator," Hu quickly came to the conclusion that "Liang's ideas are in accord with mine." Liang rejected the relevancy of the issue of the form of government. China had experimented with monarchism, republicanism, dictatorship, and other formulas, but none worked. "Therefore," Liang held, "there must be something above polity for a more fundamental solution." He insisted that only those with property and superior moral standards should engage in political activities so that politics would not become a means for other ends. Specifically, the top leadership should consist of men of knowledge, reputation, and tolerance; the middle-ranking officials should have and stay within their specialties; and the majority should simply obey the leaders and be genuinely interested in national affairs. "Other than social education," Liang concluded, "what else would enable us to achieve this? . . . If we do not adhere to this means, if we daily engage people in senseless and groundless political activities, how are we going to prevent chaos and perishing?"[24]

These views divulged Liang's feeling of disillusionment with Chinese politics. Liang was horrified by corruption and consumed by the possibility of perishing, so much so that he sought means outside politics in order to rescue politics. But though disenchanted, he was still deeply concerned about the leadership quality and wanted the masses to be interested, if not involved, in politics. And "change" could mean a better future to him. After all, Liang did organize one of the major military campaigns that helped end Yüan Shih-k'ai's monarchical ambition. Hu Shih, on the other hand, was far less sanguine. The possibility of any political change appalled him. In January, 1916, he expressed his views on revolution to Edith Clifford Williams and her father, referring in particular to the military actions against Yüan Shih-k'ai.

> I do not condemn revolutions, because I believe that they are necessary stages in the process of evolution. But I do not favor premature revolutions, because they are usually wasteful and therefore unfruitful. . . . It is for this reason that I do not entertain much hope for the revolution now going on in China, although I have deep sympathy for the Revolutionists.
>
> Personally I prefer to build from the bottom up. I have come to believe that there is no short-cut to political decency and efficiency. The monarchists have no desire for political decency and efficiency. The Revolutionists desire them, but they want to attain them by a short-cut—by a revolution. My personal attitude is: "Come what may, let us educate the people. Let us lay a foundation for our future generations to build upon.[25]

Hu, of course, had no love for Yüan Shih-k'ai. What he desperately craved was a sense of order in a chaos that defied normal comprehension. Subconsciously, he assumed that *any change* would be for the worse—causing further domestic decay, inviting more foreign incursions, and disturbing what little equilibrium there was. Therefore, any moment of stability, however fleeting or illusive, was to be treasured. This inevitably meant that he supported the status quo. Although he had "deep sympathy for the Revolutionists," they, in his perception, were disturbing peace and order. He despised the monarchists who, ironically, represented stability. Thus, while they "have no desire for political decency and efficiency," Hu was ready to give them another opportunity. Unable to decide upon any immediate course of action or even to pass a clear judgment, he took a millennial approach—the cultivation of men "over a period of one hundred years"—to try to rescue China's crisis. A nonaction and a status quo were preferable so that he would be able to "build from the bottom up," to "lay a foundation for our future generations to build upon." What this amounted to was an indefinite postponement of action under any circumstances and an unconditional refusal to sanction any action against any government. Herein lay the psychological foundation of Hu Shih's cultural and intellectual reform.

Hu's response to contemporary events underscored his dilemma. He was reticent at the time of the 1911 Revolution when its outcome was not yet certain. Whereas there was no question as to where his allegiance lay, he endorsed republicanism publicly in January, 1912, only after the revolution had become a fact. While virulently attacking Yüan's maneuvers, Hu nevertheless tolerated Yüan in the hope that things would get better or, at least, be at a standstill so that he could devote himself to the task of the cultivation of men. Hu was delighted to learn in November, 1914, that Sun Yat-sen, Ts'ai Yüan-p'ei (1876–1940), and Wang Ching-wei (1883–1944) had agreed by signing a peace accord not to organize another military campaign against Yüan.[26] When the antimonarchy forces began their attacks in the last days of 1915, Hu chided them as "premature," "wasteful," and "unfruitful." For all his sympathy toward the revolutionists and his commitment to republicanism, what the anti-Yüan forces created was merely another disruption and disturbance. Yüan died on June 6, 1916, and Hu's verdict was typical of his thinking: "The only and most hateful thing about Yüan's whole life is that he sat and let opportunities go by."[27] Characteristically, Hu was not so much interested in Yüan's evils as in lamenting the opportunities he missed.

While passing these judgments, Hu left the basic question unanswered: how was he going to cultivate men of talent and build from the bottom up under such political conditions? He was one of a growing number of Chinese intellectuals in the early twentieth century who tried in vain to convince themselves that cultural and intellectual reform was more fundamental than political reform. Inevitably, Hu came to the painful realization that there was no easy solution for the anarchy in China.

In June, 1917, on his way home from the United States, Hu reflected pessimistically on the condition in China. He had been, he said, preparing himself for some constructive undertakings in the homeland. "The work of destruction has been accomplished in general," and therefore there was no need for him to take part in it. "Frightening news," however, kept pouring out as he was sailing home, and "the present situation," after all, probably "will not allow me to undertake the labors of construction after my return."[28] This turned out to be the beginning of a bad omen. Before his ship had reached Shanghai, Hu received the news of Chang Hsün's (1854–1923) restoration attempt and the ever confusing warlord fighting. Before long, he was involved in debates with the warlords, the Kuomintang, the student activists, and the Communists. The journals with which he was associated, *Nu-li chou-pao, Tu-li p'ing-lun,* and *Hsin-yüeh,* unavoidably became political. He even held some political posts, including ambassadorship to Washington (1938–42), delegation to the United Nations (1945), and membership in the National Assembly (1947–62). Yet Hu became entangled in politics with great reluctance.

Shortly after he returned to China, Hu reached the resolution of "refraining from political involvement for twenty years, from talking politics for twenty years."[29] Instead, he decided to devote himself to the task of

> laying a foundation based on thought and literature to reform Chinese politics. . . . [S]eeing the poverty and paucity of the publishing world, the inertia of the education circles, I realized that Chang Hsün's restoration coup was quite a natural phenomenon.[30]

Although this was to a degree an honest assessment of the situation, the case was more complicated than Hu's analysis allowed.

Lin Yü-sheng, in *The Crisis of Chinese Consciousness,* has argued that one of the most important characteristics of Confucian thinking was "the stress placed on the function of the inward moral and/or intellectual experience of the mind." This "cultural-intellectualistic approach," to use Lin's own words, could be traced to Mencius and Hsün-tzu and was palpably manifested in Ch'en Tu-hsiu, Hu Shih, and Lu Hsün.[31] These and other thinkers believed that

> a change of basic ideas *qua* ideas was the most fundamental change, the source of other changes. In other words, two levels of change characterized their approach: first, change of world view, which would then bring about a second basic level, change of the system of symbols, values, and beliefs—this cultural change, in turn, would precipitate other political, social, and economic changes.
>
> Their belief in the power of ideas implied another assumption: the close relationship . . . between understanding and action. These intellectuals tacitly—perhaps unconsciously—assumed that their prime need was to express fully to the people . . . what they believed and to advocate the best programs for implementing those beliefs; then the people, being also endowed with the faculty of understanding, would grasp the meaning and perceive the benefits of those truths and those programs, and act accordingly.[32]

There is more than an element of truth in Lin's observation. But in the process of his analysis, Lin overstates his case. Knowledge (ideas) and action (political involvement) have a much closer relationship than he would have us believe. While assuming the preponderance of ideas, Chinese thinkers also believed that ideas will have no meaning unless complemented by actions. The former give direction and substance to actions, while the latter complete the meaning of ideas. The idea of ordering and harmonizing the world (*chih-kuo p'ing t'ien-hsia*) remained the highest goal of a Confucian gentleman and prompted countless literati to seek an occupation in politics. Both Confucius and Mencius lamented their lack of opportunity to implement their ideals; such scholar-statesmen as Ou-yang Hsiu (1007–72), Wang An-shih (1021–86), and Tseng Kuo-fan were emulated heroes. In the Ming and Ch'ing, the importance of action was actively exalted. Wang Yang-ming's theory of "unity of knowledge and action" (*chih-hsing ho-i*) and the school of statecraft (*ching-shih hsüeh-p'ai*) elevated the status of action to a new height.

No school of Chinese thought precluded the necessity of political involvement. Politics was shunned only when conditions made a commitment to it impossible; Chinese intellectuals adopted a cultural and intellectual approach to the exclusion of everything else as a retreat and usually because it was the only means to fulfill their sense of obligation to society and at the same time to protect their independence. External factors, then, were overwhelmingly important in determining whether or how deeply one becomes involved in politics. Lin Yü-sheng does acknowledge that outside conditions "can account for the changing intensity of the cultural-intellectualistic approach," though he insists that they "cannot explain its origin."[33] "Intensity," indeed, is the key word here. Lin's concession hardly explicates why Hu Shih would not even *talk* politics for twenty years.

Certainly, Hu's disinterest in politics was to some extent dictated by his commitment elsewhere. He reflected on his intellectual activities in the past few years. He had always believed, he said, that China needed men of talent of all kinds and that he had to be comprehensive, covering as many things as possible. That, he soon decided, was too ambitious and unrealistic. Since no one could possibly be omniscient and omnipotent, one's contribution to society was to try one's best in one's chosen field.[34] By 1916, before his departure from America, Hu had "already found my lifetime vocation in Chinese philosophy."[35]

However, Hu's interest in scholarship cannot fully explain his decision to completely sever himself from politics. By resolving not to talk politics, he recognized that politics was after all an essential human activity and implied that he might become involved in it after the twenty-year moratorium.

Yet, Hu was destined not to be able to fulfill his wish. In December, 1918, Ch'en Tu-hsiu, Li Ta-chao (1889–1927), Kao I-han, and Chang Wei-tz'u established a small magazine, the *Weekly Critic (Mei-chou p'ing-lun)*, as a forum for political debate. Hu was not close to the publication; his contribution to it consisted mostly of literary pieces. But in June of the following year, when Ch'en Tu-hsiu was arrested by Tuan Ch'i-jui's (1865–1936) men, Hu agreed to take over editorial responsibility for the journal. At this juncture, Hu felt that he "could no longer avoid political discussions." The nation was in turmoil; "the Anfu Clique was at the height of its power, and the spoils-sharing Shanghai peace conference had not yet dispersed. The so-called new elements in the nation, however, while being silent on concrete political issues, talked expansively about anarchism and Marxism." It was the indignation aroused by these phenomena, Hu said, that "drove me to speak out on politics."[36]

What Hu referred to here was his running battle with Li Ta-chao and a few Marxists in the country. Earlier, in July and August, 1919, his essay "Study More Problems, Talk Less of 'Isms,' " a pointed criticism of Li, appeared in the *Weekly Critic,* together with lengthy rebuttals from Li and Lan Chih-hsien and Hu's rebuttals of the rebuttals.[37] In these writings, Hu was discussing politics in a rather particular sense. While he himself did not engage in an analysis of specific issues, he challenged his fellow countrymen to deal with concrete political problems. "All valuable ideas seek solutions for concrete problems." On the other hand,

> The great danger of "ism" is to make men satisfied and complacent. Thinking that they have found the panacea for a "fundamental solution," they would no longer make efforts to seek solutions for this or that concrete problem.[38]

Chinese Marxists, in Hu's mind, were engaged only in dangerous abstractions and vague generalizations, and their proposals had little to do with China's reality. Hu's experimentalism, of course, was also an ism. But Hu insisted that, more than anything else,

> it is a method which provides means to study problems. . . . All the isms and theories are . . . merely hypotheses awaiting proof, not infallible doctrines. Experimentalism emphasizes concrete facts and issues; it does not acknowledge any fundamental solutions. It only acknowledges progress bit by bit and drop by drop. Only when every step has intelligent guidance, when every step involves positive experimentation will we have true evolution.[39]

Although Hu resorted to the authority of John Dewey and his experimentalism, such a way of argument was essentially polemical in intent. "Temperance with their cravings and refusals do determine men in their philosophies, and always will," as William James said.[40] Dewey's ideas only served to confirm, reinforce, and embellish Hu's own. Hu's ideas on China's practical problems were formulated early, and it was he who often influenced Dewey, not the other way around. During his visit to China in 1919–21, Dewey often echoed, "almost verbatim," what Hu Shih and Chiang Meng-lin had told him.[41] With or without the knowledge of Dewey's philosophy, Hu would have been divided by differences in both sentiment and opinion from what he regarded as a sweeping and oversimplified solution put forward by Chinese Marxists.

We have too often associated Hu's gradualism with his philosophical conviction. What needs to be emphasized here is the psychological dimension underlying his cautious approach to politics. Hu did not want to talk of an overall political solution because, deep in his mind, he knew too well that there was *no* solution at all. Refusing to talk politics in broad terms was in part to shield himself from any crushing disappointment. Hu offered this terrifying vision in June, 1922.

> We do not acknowledge that in politics there are fundamental solutions. . . . We do not entertain fanciful hopes so we will not have big disappointments. As we look at our age, we find so many evil causes . . . that there certainly will be no satisfactory major reforms. We should put aside our luxurious hopes for politics. . . . Instead, we should hope "to gain a foot when there is only a foot to gain, to gain an inch when there is only an inch to gain."[42]

Hu Shih could debate Chinese Marxists without getting into any specific details because the latter in 1919 could do little more than talk and were harmless. Real politics, however, was different. As Hu acknowledged in August, 1920, "At the outset, we had no intention to talk practical politics, but practical politics has never ceased bothering us."[43] At this time, Hu's good friend Ting Wen-chiang criticized his vow of not talking or getting involved in politics for twenty years: "Don't be tricked by Hu Shih-chih who tells us that political reform must be preceded by [a reform in] thought and literature." Ting chided Hu,

> Your proposal is a kind of fantasy. Your literary revolution, intellectual reform, and cultural reconstruction will not be able to withstand the assault of corrupt politics. Good politics is the prerequisite for all peaceful social reforms.[44]

Thus confronted, Hu was forced to concede that "when politics is not benign, nothing else can be done: education cannot be managed; industry cannot be managed; even a small business cannot be managed."⁴⁵ He had to abandon the logic, if not the sentiment, of his cultural-intellectual approach.

> "Without a good society, how can we have a good government?"
> "Without a good government, how can we have a good society?"
> Such a set of chain, how *can* we untie?
>
> "If education is not good, how can we have good politics?"
> "If politics is not good, how can we have education at all?"
> Such a set of chain, how *can* we untie?
>
> "If we do not destroy, how can we begin construction?"
> "Without construction, how can we destroy?"
> Such a set of chain, how *can* we untie?⁴⁶

The result of the discussion among Hu, Ting, and a handful of other friends was the establishment of the *Endeavor* (*Nu-li chou-pao*). In the first issue, published on May 7, 1922, Hu set the theme of the new enterprise with a poem entitled "The Song of Endeavor."

> "This situation won't last long."
> My friends, you are wrong.
> Unless you and I do something about it
> This situation can last a long time.
>
> "Somebody will have to do this kind of thing."
> My friends, you are wrong again.
> You should have said,
> "If I do not do it, who else will?"
>
> Nothing in the world is impossible
> Until, one day, you and I, who call themselves good men,
> Should also say, "It is impossible to do anything."
> Then, indeed, it would become impossible.⁴⁷

But was Hu able to translate his proclamation into concrete actions? Ting Wen-chiang poignantly reflected upon the terrible predicament of a Chinese intellectual in an age of violence and absurdity in an imagined conversation between himself and a "foreign friend." The dialogue began as the friend expressed surprise that Ting had given up politics and gone into business.

I replied with a sigh: "it is impossible to be an official any more. For the past ten years . . . I have always advocated that good men make efforts to take official posts. But . . . to be an official was something too difficult for a good man to learn; and . . . after holding official posts, many good men became corrupt. . . . Moreover, since I set my mind to be a good official, I was unwilling to accept bribes or take a second job. So after ten years as an official, I still have no money to spare. . . . I have finally come to the realization that as long as politics is not enlightened, as long as there are no posts suitable for good men, my desire to be an official is rather dilute. Also, witnessing that the work accomplished with many years of hardship by those of us who wished to be good officials could be completely undone by an order of an ignorant bureaucrat or a professional politician, I realized that my work was built upon sand with no solid foundation at all. Therefore, I changed my paths and went into business.". . .

I was silent for some time, and replied with an effort: "I, too, know that politics cannot be abandoned. This is why besides business I have been discussing politics in my spare time."

A: Ah! politics is to be practiced, not to enliven our conversation. It requires all of one's energy; it is not a pastime of one's spare time.

I: What you said is of course correct. But it is not easy to devote one's entire time and energy to politics. I think that Chinese politics in the past ten years is corrupted by those professional politicians who have no other professions. They take politics as their ricebowl and make things ever worse. What we want is to earn our own ricebowl first before we plunge into politics so that we can stand above personal interests, unaffected by the idea of obtaining a ricebowl. . . .

A: But your plan can only be tried at a time of peace and stability. . . .

I: . . . But the apathy of recent years is really a reaction. . . . You should know that prior to the 1911 Revolution, people had a common goal . . . believing that after the Manchus were driven out and the Republic was established, heaven would be in peace. . . . The experience of the past eleven years has completely destroyed this belief. . . . People no longer have faith . . . not knowing how China can make good, or for what they should sacrifice and fight. . . . First, there was disappointment, then negativism, and finally numbness.[48]

Understandably, Hu Shih's struggle was an excruciating one. When a friend of his urged in May, 1922, that he form a party of his own, he argued that "forming a party is not our business, much less a business of mine. . . . Some people say that we 'love our feathers' too much. . . . If we did not, would there be a place for us to talk today?"[49] In August, 1926, he became more favorable toward the idea of forming a political party, giving out even the general principles of his "Liberal Party."[50] By April, 1928, however, he had decided that such a task was after all not his cup of tea. "Having a few individuals independent of political parties is to nurture a little vital constitution (*yüan-ch'i*) for the nation."[51]

What Hu settled for was the role of a political commentator unaffiliated with any parties. The precarious road which he pursued reminds us of the form of dissent of an ethical idealist in traditional times, "who restlessly occupied the interface of private and public: not so attracted by quietism as to abnegate political responsibility, and not so involved in office as to forego moral indignation."[52] But although the style looked familiar, the substance of Hu's thinking was different. What he was speaking of were political parties and the role of a political commentator, both in the modern sense. His mentality could no longer be described as that of a Confucian moral protestor, and the goal of politics in his mind was not so much to establish a cosmic moral order as to provide dignity and well-being for the governed in practical terms.

Hu was well aware that his style would be a liability to partisan politics. "By temperament and ability," an independent-minded political commentator was perhaps not suited to organize a political party, Hu pointed out. Such a person usually had the ability to write, to analyze things, and to pass judgment on politicians, but he could rarely execute plans or handle people.[53] Compounding Hu's personal limitations was his deep-seated aversion to Chinese politics. "In China, which is not accustomed to party politics and which in recent years has held it in detestation, what is needed today is certainly not partisan, but independent, political commentators," he claimed. These commentators would be so impartial and detached, Hu said, that no vested interests could ignore their exhortations.[54] Hu, in other words, wanted to influence politics while he himself remained above politics.

Hu's political commentaries in the *Endeavor* and elsewhere covered a wide range of topics. Representative of Hu's view and that of the leading liberals was "Our Political Proposals," signed by Hu and fifteen others in May, 1922. The sixteen signatories contended that the objective of a "good government" was a minimal requirement. A "good government" meant, in its negative aspect, the existence of proper organs to oversee and prevent corruption and self-seeking activities in politics. On the positive side, it should utilize political organs for the welfare of society and the protection of individual freedom. To realize these demands, they asked for a "constitutional government," an "open government," and "politics with a plan." While they took for granted the obviousness of the ultimate goal, the signatories realized that mere demands and talks would not do much good. Therefore, "the first step toward political reform at the present time is that good men must have a fighting spirit. All the elite members of the society, for their self-preservation, for society and the nation, must come out to do battle with the forces of evil."[55]

The signatories of the manifesto were determined to rally "public opinions" and "fight a deciding battle."[56] They immediately faced an impossible situation, however. T'ang Erh-ho (1877–1943), a medical doctor, became deputy minister of education in July, 1922, occupying the post for only five days before resigning over a budget dispute. The "Good Men Government," a dubious term given to the cabinet headed by Wang Ch'ung-hui (1882–1956), collapsed in mid-September, 1922, having lasted for only a month. Its minister of finance, Lo Wen-kan (1888–1941), was even imprisoned for allegedly accepting a bribe in connection with the signing of a treaty with Austria, a charge of which he was later acquitted. In January, 1923, Ts'ai Yüan-p'ei resigned his presidency of Peking University to protest Lo's arrest and the wicked politics.[57] All of them were cosignatories of "Our Political Proposals."

Hu took a highly ambiguous attitude toward these events. Though advocating a "fighting spirit," he knew full well that self-preservation was often the only option available. "Though some people blame him for acting too hastily," Hu wrote, "we do not believe that T'ang Erh-ho's decision was wrong. He came with a principle, and he left when it failed to be implemented. His decision to resign was quite appropriate, and we offer our sympathetic respect."[58] Hu saw Ts'ai Yüan-p'ei's resignation in the same light. "We support Mr. Ts'ai's decision," he declared. "And by doing so, we are showing our approval of a loud protest for the sake of justice and decency and in the spirit that 'one should not get into the same stream and defile oneself.' "[59]

Hu Shih then did not really believe that protest and refusal to work with the crooked politicians would have much effect. On January 23, 1923, Ts'ai Yüan-p'ei issued a public statement, condemning the unscrupulousness of the political behavior and urging others to refuse to have anything to do with politics.[60] The *Peking Morning Post* (*Ch'en-pao*) dubbed it "Ts'ai Yüan-p'ei's Principle of Non-Cooperation" and wondered if it would be as popular as Gandhi's nonresistance in India.[61] Hu responded to the question in his typical pessimistic way.

> [H]e [Ts'ai] is a person who "is never lax with his own behavior but who is extremely generous with and tolerant toward others." Unlike Gandhi, he will not be able to launch an active movement; rather, he can only prepare himself to join such a possible movement. . . . Individual conscience is his court of justice.
>
> India is a religious country where Gandhi is a recognized pontiff. This is why his "Non-Cooperation" can "sweep India." But in a filthy, dark, shameless country and among a people who are cowardly, who have no love for freedom, Mr. Ts'ai's non-cooperation simply will not succeed.[62]

Little wonder that Hu himself was extremely reluctant to accept any posts that were directly or indirectly related to politics. Throughout the 1920s, he had many offers to be a university administrator. With the exception of one, he resolutely turned down all of them.[63] His only favorable response created much bitterness in himself. On April 26, 1928, immediately after he consented to head his alma mater, the China National Institute in Shanghai, which by this time had attained the status of a private university, "I put a pair of handcuffs on myself today," Hu said. "This was certainly not a wise decision, and I have much regret as I come to think of it."[64] Several opportunities for political appointment came up in the late 1940s. In 1946 and 1948, the press regularly reported his imminent appointment to one post or another, including ambassador to the United States for a second term, minister of education, and even premier. Invariably, Hu responded to such reports by insisting that he had neither interest in nor talent for political office.[65] In March, 1948, there was speculation that Hu would be a candidate for the first vice-presidency under the newly promulgated constitution. He immediately denied such intention.[66]

Events took a more interesting turn a few days later when Chiang Kai-shek announced that "as long as the nation remains disunited, I am determined not to run for the presidency."[67] He then listed the qualifications for the first president under the constitution.

> [H]e must be a person who comprehends the essentials of the Constitution. . . . [H]e must be a person inspired by the ideals of democracy and imbued with a democratic spirit. . . . [H]e must be one who has a

profound understanding of our history, culture, and national traditions. . . . Finally, he must be one who follows world trends and has a rich knowledge of contemporary civilization. . . . Let a person outside of our Party with such qualifications be nominated as candidate to the presidency. Let all of us support him and help him to be elected.[68]

It is clear that this list was drawn to fit Hu Shih's qualifications. John Leighton Stuart, then American ambassador to China, reported that in answer to the criticisms of the Kuomintang and of himself, "the Generalissimo made it clear that he would not accept the office of President." On April 5, 1948, Chiang "openly advised party members to vote for Hu Shih and Sun Fo for president and vice-president respectively, maintaining [that] both are civilians."[69] Chiang told the Central Executive Committee of his party that on account of the contributions the party had made, it "does not need to keep the post and honor of the presidency." He himself would be ready to accept the presidency of the Executive Yüan.[70]

But Chiang was not successful in persuading Hu to accept the presidential nomination. In declining public office, Hu's standard answer was that, with a trace of sarcasm, a person who could not keep his study desk clean had no business in running national affairs. Regardless of the logic of such an argument, he was keenly aware of his lack of political acumen and of the fact that while the offer was a genuine one, Chiang's motives were complicated. Hu pointed out, as Stuart related, that

> the office of President, under the Constitution, may become, as in France, largely ceremonial while the President of Executive Yuan will exercise great authority. Also once appointed, the President of Executive Yuan should be secure in office as two-thirds vote of the Legislative Yuan is required to unseat him.[71]

Hu assumed the reasonableness of human nature and the ease of reaching a consensus. But he did so from his own point of view with an unshakable faith in his own ability to accept anything reasonable. He was deeply distrustful toward the motives of others. Under the circumstances, he simply would not become entangled in a hopeless situation, being outmaneuvered and compromised. As it turned out, the National Assembly, of which Hu was an active member, invested the presidential office with broad "emergency measures," "practically unlimited power," the day before the body elected Chiang Kai-shek on April 19, 1948, the first constitutional president by a vote of 2,430 to 269.[72]

Nonetheless, Hu Shih did hold several public offices. In 1946, he stood successfully for election to the Constitutional National Assembly that convened in Nanking in November–December to draft a constitution. Publication of the document on January 1, 1947, officially brought to an end the period of political tutelage. In November of that year, running as a nonparty candidate representing "educational circles," Hu was elected to the National Assembly created by the new constitution. Because no further elections to the assembly were held after the Nationalist government moved to Taiwan in 1949, Hu retained his seat in the assembly until his death fifteen years later. Both posts were among the least political, representing more his intellectual interest than his political ambition, and rendered more prestige than influence. These posts, in other words, were a compromise between a complete withdrawal from politics and a more active involvement.

Hu was meticulous in guarding his independence. Upon being appointed ambassador to Washington in 1938, he told Elmer Eugene Barker, with a sardonic pleasure, that he had "degenerated into being an ambassador."[73] While Hu "traveled far and wide in the United States and Canada, some 37,000 miles, making addresses and spreading good will and understanding for his country," he resolutely refused to be identified with Chiang Kai-shek's government. "When his government once sent him $30,000 to use for propaganda, he returned it with the comment, 'My speeches are sufficient propaganda and they do not cost you anything.' "[74] Significantly, most of Hu's speeches during his ambassadorial tenure dealt with China's ideals in the remote past, its present aspirations and future potentials. By doing so, Hu made an implicit distinction between representing China and a contemporary Chinese government. What, indeed, could have been a better way to discharge his duties as a patriotic Chinese while at the same time disavowing Chinese politics? In August, 1942, Chiang Kai-shek unexpectedly recalled Hu mainly because he believed that Hu had been trying harder to justify American policy toward Chungking than to argue China's case in Washington.[75] Defending what he regarded as an incorrigibly corrupt and incompetent government was something that Hu would not do.

Hu Shih's relationship with the authority in power was always ambiguous. Committed to nonviolent change and unwilling to become embroiled in compromising situations, he was constantly in an angry mood and felt powerless. Hu scathingly criticized the government in power for its inability to provide basic human decency and to resist foreign aggression; he tirelessly demanded that it slowly but systematically improve itself and give people constitutional rights. However, unable to influence politics himself, Hu supported the status quo, clinging to the hope that misguided politicians would somehow come to their senses and that the little stability provided by the status quo would give him a few precious moments for his intellectual endeavors. At the same time, he kept his expectations to the very minimum, taking delight in any progress made by the existing power.

Although he expected little from warlord governments, Hu was unwilling to demand their overthrow by revolutionary means. Any improvement or sign of hope was eagerly welcomed. "Nowadays many people like to criticize Yen Hsi-shan (1883–1960), but Yen Hsi-shan has certain merits that other [warlords] lack," Hu pointed out in June, 1922. "He governs Shansi with plans," referring to Yen's efforts to achieve a compulsory education. This was why "people call Shansi a model province and Yen Hsi-shan a model *tu-chün*.[76]

Hu Shih felt neither trust nor affection for the Kuomintang. He had been a perpetual critic of the party ever since it nominally reunified the nation in 1927. In April, 1929, he bitterly complained of the gross violations of human rights by the government and urged the enactment of a constitution to provide a legal foundation for the government.[77] Responding to the Kuomintang's reasoning that the Chinese were not yet prepared for self-governing, Hu demanded that the party let the people participate in politics regardless of their level of sophistication. The democratic system, he held, had an educative function. While mistakes would be inevitable in the initial stage of political participation, the very experience of participation would help people attain better political judgment.[78]

Hu even challenged the cult of Sun Yat-sen—a sacrilegious offense which few Chinese would be daring enough to commit. He correctly pointed out that Sun Yat-sen's theory that "knowledge is difficult, while action is easy" (*chih-nan hsing-i*) had serious authoritarian implications. "The true meaning of this theory . . . is to make people believe in the foreknowers, obey the leader [Sun], carry out actions without departing [from the Party doctrines].⁷⁹ As to its cultural policies, the Kuomintang was simply "reactionary" and its ideas "ossified," Hu charged.

> When it completely loses the sympathy of the progressive intellectual world, the Kuomintang will be totally expended and drained.
> . . . Even if my bones are burned into ashes, someday somebody will still prefix the posthumous title "reactionary" to the Kuomintang.⁸⁰

Hu Shih's persistent criticism of the Kuomintang was in part brought about by the party's own doings. The duel between them gives insight into the nature of the Kuomintang rule, the state of Chinese politics then, and the terrible dilemma of Hu Shih and like-minded individuals. In March, 1929, Ch'en Te-cheng, director of the Shanghai Kuomintang branch and of its propaganda department, a diehard conservative and unyielding ideologue, proposed at the party's national congress to "severely punish counterrevolutionaries." The term *counterrevolutionary* was frighteningly broad, including "the Communists, other third party members, and all those who oppose the Three Peoples' Principles." Ch'en continued,

> once any provincial or special city party branch proves in writing that certain individuals are counterrevolutionaries, the court or another legally designated organ shall hand down sentences to them as counterrevolutionaries. These individuals may appeal. But the higher court or another legally designated higher organ, once receiving proof in writing from the party's central office [that these individuals are indeed counterrevolutionaries], shall reject the appeal.⁸¹

Enraged, Hu wrote a letter of protest to his friend Wang Ch'ung-hui, then serving as president of the Judicial Yüan, complaining that "in the judicial history of the world," no "civilized nation" ever resorted to such a method of proving guilt or innocence.⁸² At the same time, Hu sent a copy of the letter to the *Kuo-wen chou-pao* for publication, which was promptly stopped by the censor.⁸³ Upon learning of these developments, Ch'en Te-cheng immediately rebuked Hu's challenge. "Frankly," Ch'en wrote,

> the nation's highest fundamental laws are all derived from the bequeathed teachings of the *tsung-li*. To violate these teachings is to violate the law, which brings judgment by the law of the land. This is

an immutable principle and does not permit Dr. Nonsense (*hu-shuo po-shih*) to talk nonsense about it.[84]

It was at this juncture that Hu Shih, undeterred, began writing the highly critical essays in the *Crescent* (*Hsin-yüeh yüeh-k'an*), referred to above, attacking the Kuomintang as reactionary and in violation of human rights. These writings brought about a flurry of counterattacks by Ch'en Te-cheng, Ch'en's colleagues, and a number of party branches in Nanking, Peking, T'ientsin, and elsewhere. These party professionals demanded the closing of the Crescent Bookstore, Hu's arrest, his removal as president of the China National Institute, and the deprivation of his civil rights.[85] Typical was the resolution of Ch'en's propaganda department, dated August, 1929.

> As proposed by the propaganda department [of the Shanghai special city party headquarters]: Hu Shih, President of the China National Institute, has defiantly insulted our late *tsung-li,* calumniated our party principles, betrayed our government, and deceived the people. It is hereby resolved that the Party order the national government to severely punish [Hu].[86]

At the same time, measures with broader implications were undertaken. Citing Hu's "misinterpretation of the Party's principles," the training department of the Kuomintang wrote the central government, requesting that the Ministry of Education issue a warning to Hu. Further, the ministry was asked to instruct all college presidents in the nation to supervise faculties and students in carefully studying the party principles so that "similar erroneous opinions [such as Hu Shih's] would not occur again."[87] In late September, 1929, the national government ordered that the Kuomintang members be the first hired and last fired in the government bureaucracy.[88]

When the final verdict was handed down on Hu, however, it was a relatively light one. Hu carried considerable prestige and influence, both in China and abroad, and he had some influential friends who perhaps interceded in his behalf. On October 4, 1929, Hu was reprimanded by the Ministry of Education headed, ironically, by his Columbia schoolmate and onetime Peking University colleague Chiang Meng-lin. To show his defiance, Hu wrote to Chiang, rejecting the reprimand. Attached in Hu's letter were mistakes Hu found in the reprimanding letter made by Chiang's copying clerk.[89]

For all his courage, however, these violent reactions and the reprimand had their effect on Hu. The Kuomintang's tendency to resort to harassment, intimidation, torture, and imprisonment could not have escaped his attention, and even with his prestige and influence, Hu must have been concerned about his physical well-being. Immediately after the confrontation with the Kuomintang, Hu's attitude softened considerably; he never again criticized the party as severely as he had.

Nevertheless, fear for his safety did not change Hu's attitude toward the Kuomintang. It only held his hostility in check. What turned Hu into a conditional supporter of the party was his belief that there was no better alternative. Thus, he readily accepted the Nationalist government as the de facto ruling power and steadfastly clung to the view that revolution, such as the one advocated by the Communists, would exacerbate the situation and heighten China's crisis. In December, 1929, immediately after the reprimand by the Ministry of Education, Hu reflected, with the Communists in mind, that "when the atmosphere for armed struggle becomes common and when the multitude are not able to stop disorder, there will simply be more chaos and disruption which, once begun, will never end." China's real enemies, Hu further noted, were "poverty, disease, ignorance, corruption, and disorder," none of which could be overthrown by violent revolutions and all of which could be solved only by a patient cultivation of talent and a conscious adoption of scientific knowledge and methods.[90] Of all the alternatives then, the Kuomintang was in Hu's mind apparently a lesser evil.

As China's crises worsened in the 1930s, people's patience began to wear thin. Some simply became resigned to a feeling of helplessness, while the more active started to demand extraordinary measures to deal with the extraordinary situation. It is not surprising, then, that the debate on democracy and dictatorship broke out at this time. Hu Shih's role in this episode spoke much about his mood and his time.

Ever since the first years of the twentieth century, the idea of an enlightened despotism had had a strong appeal to more than a few Chinese. Before his suicide in 1905, Ch'en T'ien-hua declared that "to save China, there is no other way than to resort to an enlightened despotism."[91] In that year, Liang Ch'i-ch'ao wrote a long essay elaborating on Ch'en's idea. An enlightened despotism, Liang reasoned, would prevent self-defeating domestic competition and chaos and more effectively direct the national energy toward international competition.[92] The appeal of despotism continued among some of Hu Shih's contemporaries. In September, 1926, Fu Ssu-nien expressed his hope that China would have a capable "dictator who will impose some order and civilization on us."[93] In the 1930s, this thinking gathered further momentum and soon became an issue of lively debate.

One of the most vocal proponents of despotism was Chiang T'ing-fu (T. F. Tsiang, 1895–1965), a Columbia-educated historian who headed Tsinghua University's history department and later served as ambassador to the Soviet Union, the United States, and the United Nations. In May, 1933, he asked his fellow intellectuals

> actively to support the central government. If the central government is bad, we should try to reform it. But even if we cannot reform it, we still should support it for the simple reason that it is the central government. . . . [A] strong central government, even if it is not satisfactory, is better than three or four independent governments. . . . [I]f we want to have a good government, we must have a government to begin with. Many people say that we cannot achieve unity because our government is not good; I say that when political power is not centralized, we cannot have a good government.[94]

Chiang elaborated his views half a year later in "Revolution and Despotism." He started with a pessimistic note: "China seems to have reached the stage where revolution is the only way out, while revolution itself is not a way out." In the past twenty years, all the militarists, from Yüan Shih-k'ai to Chiang Kai-shek, had to direct their energy at their domestic enemies at the expense of constructive work. The question was not one of men's ability or motive, but one of circumstances. Revolution, Chiang T'ing-fu argued, would provide no solution for the problem, for even a genuine revolutionary party, under the circumstances, would have to look after its own interests, to expand its own territory, and, worst of all, to ally itself with different foreign powers at the expense of vital national interests. In the last regard, he maintained, Sun Yat-sen went even further than Yüan Shih-k'ai in yielding to the Japanese demand. Therefore, "when we speak of revolution today, we speak of civil war." And the more revolutions China had, the worse off the nation became. "Our present question is whether the nation can survive; it is not a question as to what kind of a nation we should have."[95] Chiang's conclusion became clear now. "Personal dictatorship," he wrote, was the only way to deal with China's crises. In fact, he held, China was already a dictatorship of not one individual but scores of individuals. Each province and even each city was a small dictatorship in which people had no freedom. The only sensible thing to do, then, was to establish a grand dictatorship in place of the dictatorship of individuals.[96] Chiang's idea was immediately endorsed by Ting Wen-chiang, Ch'ien Tuan-sheng, Wu Ching-ch'ao, and others.

In defense of democracy, Hu Shih put forward two major propositions. The first was the idea that democracy was the least sophisticated form of political life—"kindergarten politics" as he called it—and consequently the best suited to a politically inexperienced people like the Chinese. The second he called *wu-wei* politics, aimed primarily at discrediting the view that strong government was synonymous with good government.

Hu's attitude toward democracy in China was not without ambiguities. When assessing China's conditions in realistic terms, he expected little. As he quoted a friend of his when he was a student in America: "China at best was a republic of a handful of elite, not a republic of true democracy."[97] On the other hand, however, Hu was committed to the ideal of democracy and believed that China should have democracy. He developed a standard argument against his detractors. In 1915, he pleaded to his American audience, "Young China believes in democracy; it believes that *the only way to have democracy is to have democracy.* . . . The Anglo-Saxon people would never have had democracy had they never practiced democracy."[98] In late 1923, upon being asked to preface Chang Wei-tz'u's *Introduction to Politics,* Hu took issue with Chang's opinion that democracy alone was not enough to train good citizens.

> The most advanced democracies did not have their good citizens out of nowhere. . . . If they had waited until "the people are sophisticated enough" to adopt democracy, they would never have had any hope for democracy. . . . Political life . . . is no more than a kind of organized life which can be acquired by learning. But when speaking of "learning," there must be opportunities to "learn". . . . The democratic system is the most universal educative system because it is nation-wide and because all the citizens can participate.[99]

When the debate on democracy and dictatorship intensified in the 1930s, Hu carried his argument a step further. In response to his antagonists, he ventured that democracy "is but a kindergarten system best suited to train a people inexperienced in politics." The advantage of democracy was that it did not have to depend upon exceptional men of talent. Rather, it draws upon the collective wisdom of the people; and it was flexible and adaptive. Parliaments and local assemblies in the West were kindergarten institutions, and most of the Western politicians were men of pedestrian quality. Moreover, democracy afforded citizens opportunities to participate in public life and protect their rights. Dictatorship, on the other hand, "is the most complicated, most difficult of all human affairs in the world," for it required the exceptional genius and knowledge of one man to manage the business of an entire nation.[100] With this premise, Hu asserted in July, 1937, that "constitutional politics can begin at any time and place, but it must start from the kindergarten level and gradually move up. Constitutional politics is a habit of life, and the only way to learn it is to take part in this kind of life."[101]

In great part, Hu's opinions on this issue were shaped by his continuing faith in democracy. There were more than a few Chinese then who greatly admired dictatorships in the Italian, German, and Russian styles. Ch'ien Tuan-sheng openly predicted that democracy was no longer able to cope with the demand of fierce international competition and of complex economic issues of modern times and that totalitarianism would be with us for some time to come.[102] It is remarkable that in such an atmosphere Hu insisted that a dictatorship was impossible for China. National unity, said he, could not be imposed by force. The only way to unify China, "to put it simply, is to gradually foster a national centripetal force by means of political institutions, and to gradually create a 'public loyalty' in place of the 'private loyalty' that is prevalent today."[103] There was a genuineness in his declaration that democracy was but "common sense" politics. The American politics and presidential elections which he observed firsthand seemed to him so easy, orderly, and effortless.[104] He also noted that the majority of the voters in England and America, who rarely paid attention to serious matters but spent their leisure "reading sporting news and detective novels," were nevertheless not easily manipulated by shrewd politicians.[105] When Hu occasionally condemned Western politics as mediocre, he did so against the background of his elitist thinking and an abstract standard of what democratic politics should be.

Thus, Hu Shih achieved a major breakthrough here, at least in his theoretical thinking. Traditional politics was in essence politics of and by the elite who at best looked after the well-being of the multitude with condescension. Hu, however, came to the conclusion that it does not take exceptional talent to participate in politics, which is nothing but a commonsense human activity. As such, even the uninitiated could make reasonable political decisions.

Hu's theory of "kindergarten politics" had its practical side. Among other things, Hu sought to dramatize his opposition to any possible increase of the already dangerous dictatorial power that the Kuomintang held. Proponents of dictatorship had little admiration for the Kuomintang dictatorship, although a few of them, realizing the choices they had, expressed the hope that the party could be transformed into a more efficient dictatorial power.[106] But the implication of the dictatorial argument was frightening enough. In reality, who else but Chiang Kai-shek and what other party than the Kuomintang would be handed the absolute power? It was against this background that Hu expressed in no uncertain terms his disapproval of any possible dictatorship. He voiced his doubt in December, 1933, that

> at the present time China has any vital issue of great glamour to rally the emotions and reason of the people and enable the country as a whole to follow the leadership of a certain leader, or party, or class toward the creation of a new-style dictatorship.[107]

Hu was quick to remind his antagonists of the statement, jointly issued in December, 1934, by Chiang Kai-shek and Wang Ching-wei, proclaiming that it was neither feasible nor necessary for China to establish a dictatorship.[108]

Indeed, so distrustful of the Kuomintang was Hu that he demanded that the party be nothing but titular. Here came his theory of *wu-wei* politics. Let there be no doubt that Hu was not a believer of *wu-wei* philosophy per se: "Those who have paid attention to my writings or attended my history of philosophy classes know that I am most uncompromisingly opposed to *wu-wei* philosophy."[109] By advocating *wu-wei*, then, Hu was trying to underscore as forcefully as possible his conviction that the Kuomintang had neither the skill nor the wisdom to undertake the task of China's modern transformation. Construction works of national scope required modern and specialized knowledge that the Kuomintang politicians did not possess. Genuine and permanent work of national construction required true dedication, but the party men would only do enough superficial work to keep their jobs. Conditions in the country had become so outrageous that Hu Shih wanted the politicians to realize their own incompetence, so that they would perform a little "benevolent" politics of *wu-wei*.[110]

In his theory of "kindergarten" politics, Hu argued that everyone should be and was capable of participating as a political being; when he discussed *wu-wei* politics, he was referring not only to the general vision of politicians but also to the more technical aspects of undertakings of national scope that could be managed only by trained technocrats. Therefore, there was no contradiction between his "kindergarten" politics and *wu-wei* politics.

In Hu's eyes, every piece of the so-called construction work undertaken by the Kuomintang did more harm than good. Examples abounded. The construction of motor roads, not only in the urban areas but in the remote interior, was considered an index of economic progress. To build roads, city walls were demolished, precious arable land was taken out of cultivation, additional taxes were levied, and peasants were conscripted to work on the construction. Once built, however, the roads remained in constant disrepair. Worse yet, many of the city walls, torn down to make way for motor roads, had to be rebuilt hurriedly in order to ward off bandits.[111] Thus, peasants paid unbearable taxes to support a large bureaucracy which could do nothing to benefit them and to maintain troops that were only capable of plundering people. "Beset by such hardships, if the people do not flee, resist, or become Communists or bandits, then indeed they are damned bastards," Hu bitterly complained. To ease the plight of the people, the Kuomintang should not only reduce the number of bureaucrats but "stop all the so-called 'construction works.' "[112] In light of the Kuomintang incompetency and corruption, Hu became fond of Herbert Spencer's dictum that the only legitimate function of a government was to exercise police power.

> This is the modern version of *wu-wei* politics. The duty of the police is to maintain peace and order for the people and do nothing else. When the people have peace and order, they will automatically develop various construction works on their own.[113]

Interestingly, it was here that Hu's and his adversaries' opinions converged. Although Hu disagreed with his opponents on fundamental issues, they shared common assumptions. They were elitists thinking in elitist terms. What they all desired was a consensus; and what separated them was the question of process. Convinced that a dictatorial rule would, among other things, further divide the nation, Hu wanted the Kuomintang to limit its role to that of a policeman. He argued that his opponents' plan—to unify the nation by force—could only worsen things, as attested by the attempts of numerous militarists in the Republican era.[114] The proponents of dictatorship believed, on the other hand, that only an extraordinary force from above could eliminate dissension. Both Chiang T'ing-fu and Ch'ien Tuan-sheng believed dictatorship to be a "transitional" stage for China.[115] What the advocates of dictatorship envisioned was an enlightened superman whose authority no one could challenge and who, after national unity had been achieved, would reign more than rule. Chiang T'ing-fu's opinion here was strikingly similar to Hu's: "Once we have a strong and powerful central government to maintain domestic order, all the rest—industry, commerce, transportation, and education—will automatically improve"[116]; "All I want is for the central government to maintain the nation's order. . . . Once we have [such] a government, I believe that our condition will naturally become modernized."[117] Without explicitly saying so, the proponents of dictatorship, like Hu Shih, believed in the people's ability and tendency to march toward a commonly agreed upon goal. To both groups, party politics was unnecessary.

Indeed, the aversion to partisan politics and the elitist attitude toward politics of the debaters of both camps became mutually reinforcing. Hu Shih wrote in August, 1935, that he did not "approve of party politics"; nor did he believe that "democracy has to go through the stage of party politics." "Even if we could freely form parties at this moment, I would not join any." But "for the sake of fairness," Hu argued, the Kuomintang should grant people the freedom of organizing parties.[118] He then went on to dispense his advice in broad terms.

> In the past twenty years the tendency of politics throughout the world has considerably diminished men's superstitious faith in party politics, especially in this country which is basically hostile to [the idea of] party politics. We can expect that in the future, China under constitutional rule will not experience enthusiastic competition among political parties. If we examine the national crisis of the past four years, we

see that as national consciousness increases, partisanism declines. This is not merely a Chinese phenomenon. . . . Far-sighted statesmen should seize upon this tendency to create a consciousness of "nation above all" and a national, supraparty politics.[119]

The ideal of supraparty politics could be easily implemented, Hu Shih contended, if the Kuomintang would follow Sun Yat-sen's "Five-Power Constitution." "As I see it, the spirit of the Five-Power Constitution is the spirit of 'non-partisan politics,' " Hu opined. The judicial branch, of course, should abide by the principle of justice and therefore be nonpartisan, as should the examination branch which selects talent on merit and the impeachment branch which enforces justice. Theoretically, the legislative branch was the equivalent of the parliament in the West. However, as Sun designed it, this branch in China would do no more than enact laws, a specialized, technical skill that should have nothing to do with partisan views. Finally, much of the executive branch did not have to subject itself to partisan bickering, if public servants were selected by examination. China then could really move from one-party politics to politics without parties.[120]

Considering his background and the condition in China, it is understandable why Hu Shih harbored such distrust of party politics and why he so vigorously argued that Chinese politics be based on a national common interest transcending any partisan or personal interests. Nevertheless, as Grieder perceptively observes,

> the acceptance of divided interests is one of the hallmarks of the liberal approach to politics. The conciliation of conflicting definitions of the "common" interest provides the dynamic of political life, in the liberal view of it. Seen in this light, Hu's demand for the creation of a "supraparty politics" and his insistence on the need for unanimity of purpose expressed an illiberal, and even an incipiently authoritarian bias.[121]

In China, a political consensus was well-nigh impossible. The only group capable of expressing relevant opinions was the elite minority which nevertheless was too divided on fundamental issues. Therefore, any so-called common interest would merely be a reflection of the attitudes and aspirations of this small group, which, almost out of necessity, would try to impose these attitudes and aspirations on the populace as well as on the dissident members of the elite class. Hu's antagonists saw this reality more clearly than Hu, and they were prepared to pay a high price for the consensus and unity. Yet even here the difference between Hu and the advocates of dictatorship was not as fundamental as it appeared. Again, as Grieder writes,

> even his [Hu's] own eloquent and sincere defense of the right to dissent seems . . . less an affirmation of the usefulness of divided opinion for its own sake than a rejection of the authority of the Kuomintang to determine the limits of consensus according to priorities and prejudices with which Hu was in basic disagreement.[122]

But Hu's opposition to the Kuomintang dictatorship was limited to matters of principle; his realistic assessment of the political situation in China was different. Believing that no other political group of his liking could do better, Hu readily conceded to the Kuomintang all the power it wanted. Here we find still one more tacit agreement between Hu and his opponents. At a meeting of the Independent Critic Association on February 13, 1932, which Hu attended, all the members acknowledged that "the Kuomintang dictatorship at this time is in fact inevitable." Hu further reported that "Mr. Chou Ping-lin is quite pessimistic about the future of the Kuomintang. All the others are non-Kuomintang members [of which Hu was one] who nevertheless believe that the political groups outside the party are even more hopeless."[123]

Hu's only alternative, then, was to help the party reform itself. To Hu, the promulgation of a constitution would suffice to legitimize any government. He wrote in August, 1935: "The future power of the Kuomintang should be built on a newer, firmer foundation. That foundation is a constitution."[124] This conviction paved the way for him to accept unqualifiedly the Kuomintang constitution enacted a decade later. Speaking at a political rally in August, 1947, Hu proclaimed that the Kuomintang "has returned the political power to the people and enforced constitutional administration. While attending the National Assembly last year, I already realized the sincerity of the Government in this regard."[125] Thus, while virulently condemning the party, Hu simultaneously acquiesced in the Kuomintang dictatorship.

In a similar vein, Hu Shih's relationship with student activism was an ambiguous one. He viewed some of the student activities as worthy intellectual exercises and others as youthful follies. He considered student protest, although irresponsible, an expression of their concern with national affairs. When students became increasingly radical in the late 1940s, Hu criticized them and sided with the existing authority. Typically, he constantly urged students to overcome whatever difficulties there were by means of personal efforts and perseverance.

In early 1920, Hu was one of the proponents of a work-study plan in Peking which, he envisioned, would help modify the Chinese contempt for manual labor and ease the financial burden of students. The results, however, soon disappointed him. The work was so mechanical and physical that it was really a "drudgery," he complained, and students worked so long each day that they had no time to study. What was more, some students took the opportunity of work-study to "experiment with a new lifestyle." The Shanghai work-study group wanted to "enable young men and women of new thought to emancipate themselves from the economic and ideological yokes imposed by the old society and old family system." Hu reminded the students that "work-study is an extremely common thing—millions of Americans are doing it." If the students wanted to advance fancy causes, they should do so without using the name of "work-study."[126] It may seem strange that, as one of the foremost leaders of new thought, Hu would oppose the students' attempt to free themselves from conventions. But the disagreement here was really not so much a matter of ideas as a matter of style. To Hu, work-study should be strictly an intellectual exercise, and its benefits to students should be entirely educational. The students' experiment with a new lifestyle looked to him almost communistic, and their attack of the old system seemed to him like a demagogic movement defiling the good name of work-study.

The issue of work-study, however, was a minor one in comparison with the student movement. Between the May Fourth movement of 1919 and the Communist victory in 1949, students were never dormant for any significant period of time. Hu acknowledged that student strikes and demonstrations had their legitimate reasons: party men, rather than educators, were often appointed to college posts; nepotism and corruption were widespread; universities could not get enough funding and their presidents would refuse to assume duties because of it; and faculties often would not be paid for months. Under the circumstances, Hu observed, student activism was a manifestation of their "pure emotion" which was "very natural," "an expression of vitality," and a "good phenomenon." Further, student involvement in politics heightened students' consciousness, enhanced their abilities, and broadened their vision. As such, Hu vehemently denounced the use of force and means of terror by the government in dealing with student activists. He lamented in 1934, "the young people consider politics bad, but you prove their point by handcuffs and footchains; they think that the legal system is bad, yet you prove their view by court martial and fraudulent evidence." He urged that the government grant constitutional rights to the people to freely discuss issues and express opinions. What China needed was not more obedient citizens, but independent individuals who had the courage to criticize the government. In particular, young people should have the opportunity to work out their own problems, to find answers through trial and error.[127]

But Hu Shih never endorsed the student movements without strong reservations and deep suspicion. Student entanglement in politics, he opined, was basically an "abnormal phenomenon." If a society was functioning normally, politics should be left to grown-ups and students should be able to concentrate on academics alone. He hoped that the student movement would be a temporary thing induced by extraordinary happenings, and he counseled students to go back to the classroom and take up serious intellectual matters. On the one hand, Hu believed that the students' anger and actions were well justified, commenting that the student strikes were "sincere" and "respectable." On the other hand, he likened student movements to "mass movements." As mass movements based on "emotional impulses," they would "never last long." The tactic of strike, Hu warned, would cost students the sympathy of society, and the ones hurt by student strikes were the students themselves. "No major events of a society or a nation can be solved by anyone who has no learning."[128]

Hu Shih was aware that a fundamental political solution was necessary to bring things to normalcy but that such a solution was entirely beyond reach. Reflecting on the May 30th Incident and other tempestuous events of 1925, he maintained that public opinion would be a valuable asset to a nation's diplomacy only if that nation was already in a relatively strong position. In China's case, student protest and demonstrations simply would not do much good. National salvation would be a long struggle. The Chinese, Hu pointed out, would not be able to defeat imperialism with "empty hands and naked fists," nor would they be able to "curse" to death the "British and Japanese bandits."[129]

There was then little left to do except to discipline oneself. In June, 1932, Hu offered "three prescriptions for self-defense" to the graduating college seniors. Acknowledging the dismal prospect of college graduates, he advised them to find enough research topics to keep themselves up; and "to make our lives not too painful, and in order not to become decadent, we should broadly develop our avocational interests so that we will have something to rely on for our spiritual life and a place to spend our surplus energy." Finally, students should retain their confidence. As national affairs sank to despicable levels, he conceded, many people were lucky not to have committed suicide. To be optimistic in such an age which only "makes us feel pessimistic and desperate," one had to look to the distant future for consolation. Hu now came to his favorable story to support his position. France ceded Alsace and Lorraine and was forced to pay an indemnity of five hundred million francs to Prussia following the Franco-Prussian War of 1870–71. But Louis Pasteur (1822–95), unperturbed, continued his research in chemistry, which "at the surface had nothing to do with national salvation." His research benefited France so much that Huxley claimed that Pasteur's scientific contribution more than made up for the French indemnity.[130]

It is not surprising that Hu's advice was challenged. A college graduate asked how it was possible for one to develop avocational interests and maintain optimism when one could not even find work. "I have a fourth prescription to offer," Hu responded. "You should reflect on yourself first; you should not put the entire blame on others, much less on society." He complained that some students went to diploma mills for the sake of getting diplomas and that others took such easy courses that their diplomas were virtually worthless. Therefore, "blaming yourself is the only road to life, because only your own efforts are most reliable."[131] This fourth prescription, in turn, was challenged. Hsü Mei suggested that improving social conditions was necessary before college graduates, good or bad, would have a reasonable chance to find employment. This theory, Hu countered, made him "feel strange" although "I do not completely gainsay that Madam Hsü Mei's view has an element of truth." Then Hu, who tirelessly encouraged others to be optimistic, unwittingly divulged his deep pessimism.

> Madam Hsü Mei complained that I did not provide an answer for the "overall issue." My "prescription" essay indeed was not to provide an answer for the "overall issue". . . . In that essay, I recognized that my audience was the individual, not society. I have such self-understanding that I never speak to the "overall issue."[132]

Thus, Hu's elitism was profoundly reinforced by his pessimism. Unable to influence the general surrounding, Hu asked everyone else, like himself, to overcome adversity and achieve personal independence. Up to late 1935, he was able to offer general "prescriptions." Very soon, however, he was to lose this luxury and had to take a stand on specific incidents. After a seven-year sojourn overseas, Hu was appointed in September, 1945, president of Peking National University, a post he assumed a year later. By this time, a good portion of the student body in the nation was in open revolt, and the Kuomintang was increasingly resorting to brute force to suppress the unrest. It was in such an atmosphere that Hu had to make excruciating choices.

Hu voiced the hope that the university would be a place of free inquiry and independent thinking for students whose only concern, he said, should be their academic work. But this turned out to be an unattainable dream. Soon after Hu took over the presidency, the Marshall mission failed, the Kuomintang–Chinese Communist Party (KMT-CCP) negotiation collapsed, and the relationship between the Kuomintang and its critics deteriorated beyond repair. Typically, Hu took a middle position on the issue of student unrest under the circumstances. He insisted that intellectuals had a supervisory function in politics, and as such the government should resort to none other than the established legal means and procedures in dealing with those who criticized government policies. He openly denounced Chiang Kai-shek for Chiang's habit of blaming all student unrest on Communist subversion. In their protest and demonstrations, Hu maintained, most students were merely expressing a natural concern for national affairs. On the other hand, Hu urged students to restrain themselves and return to the classroom. Earlier, he had assured his students at Peking University that he would personally stand bail for any of them arrested because of their activities. Now, he reminded them that those whose convictions drove them to demonstrations and strikes had to be prepared to accept any possible consequences. By the late summer of 1948, Peking University, for all its prestige, had come under a virtual state of siege by the Kuomintang security forces. At last, Hu told those students who were ordered to appear before the special criminal courts established to try subversives that they must either surrender or face expulsion.[133]

Hu further revealed his legalistic bias and deep-seated elitism in his short-lived relation with the Chinese League for the Protection of

Civil Rights (*Chung-kuo min-ch'üan pao-chang t'ung-meng*). Established in 1932 and modeled after the American Civil Liberties Union, the purpose of the league was primarily to seek justice for the ever increasing number of political prisoners held by the Kuomintang. Hu Shih was chairman of the league's Peking branch from its inception at the end of 1932 to February, 1933. From the very beginning, serious disagreements developed between him and the radical faction of the league, represented by Soong Ch'ing-ling (1892–1981), widow of Sun Yat-sen and sister-in-law of Chiang Kai-shek, and Yang Ch'üan (1893–1933), who served as Ts'ai Yüan-p'ei's assistant in the University Council in 1927–28 and became secretary-general of the Academia Sinica in 1928 when Ts'ai assumed its first presidency.

Hu saw the function of the league as essentially educative and complained in February, 1933, that the radical members of the league

> perceive the issue of civil rights entirely as a political issue and refuse to see it as a legal question. . . . Only when we seek the protection of civil rights from the standpoint of law will we be able to guide politics onto the confines of law. The law is the only permanent and universal guarantee of civil rights.[134]

The league's demand for the immediate and unconditional release of all political prisoners was not a promotion of "the protection of civil rights but rather a demand from the government for the freedom of revolution. In order to survive, a government must, of course, sanction all activities aimed at overthrowing or resisting it," Hu argued. On the other hand, he urged that the government have "sufficient evidence" and "legal warrant" to arrest "political offenders." Once arrested, political offenders should be arraigned within twenty-four hours; the court should indict them only with "sufficient evidence" and hold open trials. And those convicted should receive "the most humane treatment" under allowable circumstances. "These are the legal questions concerning political offenders. Departing from this position, we can only resort to revolution, but a revolution cannot be considered a movement for the protection of civil rights."[135]

Indeed, the question of "political offenders" was one of the most crucial issues that separated Hu and his radical counterparts. Seeing the darker side of human nature, Hu believed that every government in power would naturally treat its challengers as political offenders.

Thinking on behalf of the Kuomintang, he apparently thought that the Chinese Communists belonged to the category of political offenders. Of course, practical considerations were always on his mind. As time passed, Hu became increasingly worried that the Communist insurrection would further cripple the feeble foundation of the Chinese government and provide opportunities for more foreign interference.[136]

For some years, Hu avoided commenting publicly on the KMT-CCP struggle. While he disliked the Communists, he permitted that they had the right to challenge the Kuomintang. With this ambiguous feeling, he urged both sides to be reasonable and patient. In December, 1934, he asked the Kuomintang to guarantee peaceful assemblies and speeches, and to release ideological and political offenders whose cases could not be backed up with solid evidence.[137] At the same time, he insisted that the Communists stick to peaceful means to resolve their differences with the Kuomintang. In the late summer of 1945, Hu dispatched a telegram from New York City to Mao Tse-tung, the text of which read:

> Mr. Mao: From the newspapers I have learned that you so kindly told Mr. Fu Shih-nien [Fu Ssu-nien] to convey your greetings to me, and I am grateful to you for this kindness. On the night of August 22 I had a long talk with Mr. Tung Pi-wu [Chinese Communist representative to the San Francisco Conference], to whom I expressed the hope that the Chinese Communist leaders, in consideration of the international situation and China's future, should strive to forget what is past and look forward to what is coming, and be determined to build up a second major party in China not dependent on armed strength by laying down their arms. If you are so determined, then the eighteen years of internal conflicts will be settled, and your efforts through the past twenty-odd years will not be nullified by civil war. Jefferson fought peacefully for more than ten years in the early days of the United States, finally succeeding in bringing the Democratic Party, of which he was the founder, to power in the fourth presidential election. The British Labor Party polled only 44,000 votes fifty years ago, but as a result of peaceful struggle, got 12,000,000 votes this year and becomes the major party. Those two instances should furnish much food for thought. The Chinese Communist Party, today the second major party in China, has a great future if peacefully developed. It should not destroy itself through intolerance. This was the gist of my talk with Mr. Tung Pi-wu, to which I particularly call your attention. Hu Shih. August 24th, 1945.[138]

This must be regarded as a most extraordinary historical document. Hu was not the only one who clung to the hope in such a late stage of the KMT-CCP struggle that a civil war could be averted. But was Hu really so naive as to liken Chiang Kai-shek's China to Jefferson's America and twentieth-century Britain? Did he really believe that the Communists would have a fair chance to become a "second major party" and that either they or the Kuomintang would "forget" the past and "lay down their arms"? Hu simply applied too much psychological analogy. So disinterested in politics was he that he assumed that everyone else was just as disinterested; trying to avoid and despising politics to such an extent, he took it for granted that others, like himself, would have no vested interests or ambition in politics. He himself was so ready to agree to any status quo, so craving for stability, that he assumed that the ends and means in Chinese politics were, or at least should be, clear-cut ones. The life-and-death struggle between Mao and Chiang, and indeed any political strife, appeared to Hu a foolish and childish game. Here we find the psychological foundation of Hu's assumption of political consensus. Hu was a pessimist hoping for the best while anxiously anticipating the very worst.

Hu Shih's supposedly neutral, intellectual position, however, collapsed once again. In less than two years, he was forced to make a choice. In July, 1947, he openly sided with the Kuomintang and denounced the Communists.

> Political parties competing for political power should follow the legal way of winning the support of a vast majority of the people. To overthrow the Government by force of arms is not a legal way but a revolution. For the sake of self-defense, the Government is duty-bound to suppress the Communist rebellion. . . . Difficulties which did not exist during the war of resistance have now come into being, and what was spared during the war of resistance has now been destroyed. Therefore the Communist rebellion must be suppressed. After eight years of war . . . poor and weak China has risen to the rank of one of the Big Four in the world. Certainly President Chiang hopes to maintain this international prestige.[139]

In view of the fact that the Communist Party had been outlawed since March of that year and that the State Council had proclaimed the Communists to be in open rebellion, Hu's counsel that the Communists adhere to the "legal" means to win political power must have seemed to many people quite inconceivable. A peaceful and reasonable man living in a violent age, Hu tried hard to have nothing to do with politics. When he had to make his stance clear, he made the least painful choice by supporting the existing political authority, which, in his own mind, was the only logical course of action.

Part IV
Intellectual Views

Chapter 8

The Literary Revolution

Of all his undertakings, Hu Shih had a lasting pride in the role he played as a promoter of the Literary Revolution of 1917. In the years that followed, he devoted a great number of his writings to explaining and justifying this revolution.[1] Partly because of his own effort, he is well remembered for his contribution to it. What follows, however, will not be a study of the origins of or Hu's role in the movement. Instead, my discussion will focus on what is revealed in his writings on the broad subject of the reform of literature.

Hu's literary program, written on August 21, 1916, and published in the October issue of *Hsin ch'ing-nien,* consists of the following eight points.

1. Don't use literary allusions.
2. Don't use cliches.
3. Don't be a stickler for parallelism.
4. Don't eschew colloquial words and phrases.
5. Pay attention to grammar.
6. Don't groan without being sick.
7. Don't imitate the ancients.
8. What you say must be about something.[2]

To put it in another way, what he proposed was to produce vernacular literature with themes consonant with contemporary concerns.

An important objective of the vernacular movement was to democratize education. As early as July, 1916, Hu asserted that "literature should not be the private possession of a few educated elite, but should be accessible to the great majority in a country."[3] He made this point clearer ten years later.

> We have realised at last that certain things must be given up if China is to live. If we really want education, general and universal education, we must first have a new language, a language which can be used and understood by tongue and ear and pen, and which will be a living language for the people.[4]

The rise of English, French, Italian, and German, Hu told us, was instrumental in the emergence of new literatures and of, indeed, new values in those countries. In his mind the adoption of *pai-hua* would have the same effect.[5] He maintained in 1926, "as language is the most important vehicle of thought and of expression, any radical and fundamental change in a national language could not but involve a great change in other phases of social and intellectual life."[6]

Be that as it may, however, Hu understood that no matter how potent language itself might be, it alone would not be able to achieve what he had in mind. He was thinking of a particular type of literature, as he hinted in July, 1916.

> I believe that literature should not be totally unrelated to human affairs. The immortal literature in the world always has had great influence on "manners and morals" (*shih-tao jen-hsin*). (This belief of mine should be viewed in a broad manner. Such works as *Water Margin* and *The Scholars,* such writers as Li Po, Tu Fu, Po Chü-i, today's Henrik Ibsen, George Bernard Shaw, and Count Maurice Maeterlinck are what I mean by "having great merit in influencing manners and morals." If perceived narrowly, literature must always talk about Confucius and Mencius, and the paragons in literature must always be loyal ministers and filial sons.)[7]

What precisely, then, did Hu have in mind? He maintained in 1915 that there are two kinds of literature—one with a specific purpose and one without. The first is aimed at ridiculing, exhorting, and perhaps improving the world, while the second reflects the author's aesthetic feelings. "Poetry and other types of writing that have both these qualities are the superior kind," Hu concluded after a long deliberation.[8]

A very catholic reader, Hu was particularly attracted to the realist and naturalist literature when he was in America. In April, 1911, reading *The Inspector General* by Nikolai V. Gogol, he wrote, "it depicts the Russian officialdom and exposes [its corruption and stupidity] more revealingly than Li Po-yüan's *Panorama of Officialdom* (*Kuan-ch'ang hsien-hsing chi*)."[9] In February, 1914, after seeing *Damaged Goods* by the French playwright Eugene Brieux, Hu commented,

> This is one of the famous plays of recent times. Focusing on syphilis, it depicts the harm of this disease and its bearings on society and family. . . .
> Ibsen's *Ghosts* also deals with syphilis, though it is not as forceful as *Damaged Goods*.[10]

In July of that year, Hu organized a reading club which was to meet every weekend and for which each of the five members was to read at least one Western literary work a week for discussion. "My readings for the first week are Hawthorne's *The House of Seven Gables* and Hauptmann's *Before Dawn*," Hu recorded in his diary.[11] Ignoring Hawthorne completely, he went on,

> The aforementioned second book is the earliest problem play by the German literary master Gerhart Hauptmann. . . . The theme of *Before Dawn* is the problem of drinking. . . . The work is as good as Ibsen's problem plays and better than Brieux's.[12]

On the same day, Hu read another of Hauptmann's works, *The Weaver*, "the very best of Hauptmann's products. Its depiction of the gap between the poor and the rich, of the misery of the weavers brings readers to tears."[13] After reading August Strindberg's *The Link* less than two weeks later, Hu observed that both it and Ibsen's *A Doll's House* render broad criticisms of the legal system in general.[14] In July, 1915, Hu noted that Leo N. Tolstoi's *Anna Karenina* and *Dream of the Red Chamber* are similar in structure and themes. The former, according to Hu, describes "the debauchery, extravagance, and ignominy of the Russian aristocracy."[15] Before he completed his education in the United States in 1917, Hu had "read all of Ibsen's plays and was particularly pleased with 'An Enemy of the People.' "[16]

It was no accident that Hu Shih paid special attention to realist and naturalist writings. He observed as early as July, 1914 that

> since the times of Ibsen, European playwrights of stature often concentrate on social plays, which are also called "problem plays," for

these plays all discuss important contemporary social issues. The best in this field used to be Ibsen of Norway who is now deceased. Today's masters are Hauptmann in Germany, George Bernard Shaw in England, and Brieux in France.[17]

In late 1916, Hu expressly concurred with Ch'en Tu-hsiu that "China's literature from now on should move toward realism."[18]

While never having spelled it out, Hu could not have overlooked the implications of realist and naturalist literature. René Wellek defines realism as "the objective representation of contemporary social reality." And in such a representation,

> didacticism is implied or concealed. . . . [I]t is a simple fact of literary history that the mere change to a depiction of contemporary social reality implied a lesson of human pity, of social reformism and criticism, and often of rejection and revulsion against society.[19]

Naturalism, which is often identified with realism, strives for "a mimetic, objective representation of outer reality (in contrast to the imaginative, subjective transfiguration practised by the Romantics)." Confronted with the evils of the Industrial Revolution, naturalists often depict depressing conditions of the deprived and impoverished and the scramble for money and power of the privileged. Although they believe man to be an object to be observed, described, and analyzed in total neutrality just as a scientist studies a machine, the very subject matter of the naturalists implies a moral judgment on human suffering, brutality, and injustice.[20]

If Hu studied Western realist and naturalist plays with an academic detachment, he approached fiction of realist and naturalist tendencies of the Ming and Ch'ing periods with a sense of involvement. One of the earliest and certainly among the most impassioned advocates of Ming-Ch'ing fiction, Hu had good reasons to like it. Of all the literary genres, fiction affords an author the greatest freedom to present his thoughts in detail. When used as a vehicle to express reform ideas, it is therefore a potent instrument. Further, most of the Ming-Ch'ing novels are written in the colloquial and demonstrate a distinct spirit of defiance and rebelliousness. Hu said in 1917 that

> the only literary genre in our country today that can be compared with the first rate literature in the world without causing us embar-

rassment is the colloquial fiction. The reason is simple. These novels do not imitate the ancients. . . . Instead, they all depict contemporary social reality of the day. As such, they are true literature.[21]

The moral was clear: Hu intended, by means of these novels, to promote the vernacular language and a new outlook.

One of the first novels under his scrutiny was *Water Margin*. He explained why it took several centuries for the story to develop to its completion.

The politics, villainous officials, and despotic policies of the Southern Sung angered and alienated the populace. Life was even more miserable in the north under the alien rule. Therefore, in both the south and the north, there emerged among the populace a psychology of intense hatred toward the wicked politics and officials. Such a psychology in turn fostered a feeling of worship of grass roots heroes. . . .

. . . The story of *Water Margin* thus is the consummation of four hundred years of complaint and bitterness of the commoners and the literati. . . . Shih Nai-an . . . made it into a purely anti-government book.

These and other observations led Hu to conclude: "I think that *Water Margin* is a book of wonders. In the history of Chinese literature, it occupies a far more important place than *Tradition of Tso* and *Historical Records (Shih-chi)*."[22]

Since *Tradition of Tso* and *Historical Records* are two of the earliest classics, by making this comparison Hu delivered an ultimate punch. His elevation to such an incomparable status of a novel that glorifies grass roots heroes and rebels also bespoke Hu's defiance. Rebels of different types and ideological persuasions in Chinese history, including Mao Tse-tung, were all fond of *Water Margin*.

Hu's study of *Dream of the Red Chamber* conclusively proves that the novel is essentially autobiographical. As such, he hailed it "a masterpiece of naturalism," for its principal author Ts'ao Hsüeh-ch'in recounted the decline and fall of his once prosperous family. "The true value of *Dream of the Red Chamber* lies precisely in this commonplace naturalism."[23] That in the end Lin Tai-yü died and Chia Pao-yü became a monk had its significance in Hu's eyes. "This kind of tragic ending will make readers . . . realize the evils of familial despotism, and make them reflect upon various issues about life, family, and society."[24] *The Scholars* is praiseworthy because it exposes the depravity of officialdom and the eight-legged-formalism mentality and because it nurtures the consciousness of defying authorities and conventions.

> Refusing to give you an official title is the only panacea by means of which a despotic ruler tries to destroy talent. There is only one way to resist this vicious trap: cultivate a new social psychology to make people aware of the ugliness of the examination system and officialdom; to make people realize that to be a "human being" is more precious than to be an "official," that knowledge is more valuable than the eight-legged essay, and that to have integrity is more important than to have wealth and position. . . .
> The entire intent of *The Scholars* is to cultivate such an understanding. . . .
> How can Fang Pao, Yao Nai and the like attain such an inimitable technique and such a transcendent moral vision?[25]

Hu's reference to Fang and Yao deserves attention. Fang Pao (1668–1749) and Yao Nai (1732–1815), chief exponents of the T'ung-ch'eng school, named after their home town in Anhwei, advocated the philosophy of Neo-Confucianism and the *ku-wen* prose style. This school dominated the classical literary mode during part of the eighteenth century. Largely because of Tseng Kuo-fan (1811–72), who ardently admired it, the influence of the T'ung-ch'eng school continued into the latter half of the nineteenth century. Among Tseng's proteges was Wu Ju-lun (1840–1903) who in turn taught Yen Fu and Lin Shu. In Hu Shih's view, "Yen Fu and Lin Shu are genuine T'ung-ch'eng men, while T'an Ssu-t'ung, K'ang Yu-wei, and Liang Ch'i-ch'ao belong to the transformed version of T'ung-ch'eng school."[26] Thus, by belittling Fang Pao and Yao Nai, Hu Shih not only rejected values represented by the T'ung-ch'eng school, but also criticized some of his major adversaries.

Hu insisted that *Journey to the West* (*Hsi-yi chi*) has no "profound messages or significant meanings" (*wei-yen ta-i*) except that it mocks people and despises the world. "In its humor there is a biting cynicism wherein lies precisely the literary value of *Journey to the West*." The novel depicts darkness, corruption, and lack of talent in the palace of heaven. In one place, it even contains "a declaration of revolution."[27]

One of the salient features of *Flowers in the Mirror* (*Ching-hua yüan*), according to Hu, is its social message. Written when Li Ju-chen was frustrated with his career in his evening hours, "this novel is of interest to us today as a monumental work of social criticism and propaganda. . . . The whole book may indeed be called a Chinese declaration of the Rights of Women." Overall, Hu believed that the novel was analogous to Jonathan Swift's *Gulliver's Travels,* since both ridicule baneful social customs.[28] *Panorama of Officialdom* is "a document of social history. What it depicts is the most important institution and vested power in China's old society—the officialdom; what it covers is the most corrupt, the most decadent period of this institution."[29] "The motif of *Panorama of Officialdom* is simply to tell everyone that officialdom is the filthiest, the most despicable thing in the world."[30] Similarly, *Tales of Heroic Young Lovers* (*Erh-nü ying-hsiung chuan*) can be construed as an unconscious mimicry of *The Scholars*. The description of social habits in *Tales of Heroic Young Lovers,*

> though not intentionally satirical, looks to us as if the author had been consciously depicting [the condition then], and therefore leaves us many valuable sources of social history. . . .
>
> Wen-k'ang's profuse praise of the civil service examination system makes us even more aware of its baneful effects; his sincere depiction of the praiseworthiness of the examination system amounts to an excellent confession of the psychology which worships wealth and power under such a system.[31]

To be sure, Hu Shih's studies of the Ming-Ch'ing novels have other important observations that are strictly academic, and many of them still serve as points of departure. In terms of his research on the authorship and origin of several of these novels, his studies "are a landmark of Sinology."[32] Be that as it may, however, in the process of his research, Hu painstakingly searched for and even read didactic lessons into these works. He lamented in 1918 that a grave illness in human life "was our unwillingness to look with open eyes at the real world." While our society was one of "male robbers and female prostitutes," we insisted that it was one of sage-kings. Our government was filled with corrupt officials and vile bureaucrats, yet we profusely praised it for its virtue and accomplishments. If we were determined to improve ourselves, Hu maintained, "we must first admit that our society is in fact a society of male robbers and female prostitutes."[33] These Ming-Ch'ing novels, then, served an excellent realist-naturalist purpose. Even the excessive condemning tone and explicit messages in *Panorama of Officialdom,* while diminishing the literary value of the work, were not without merit.

> When China was repeatedly being defeated, the cumulated illnesses of political institutions and society were exposed. . . . A condemning novel, though having shortcomings . . . can truly indicate a reflective attitude of the society and an attitude of self-blame. Such attitudes are prerequisites for social reform.[34]

If Hu Shih's literary view was narrow, it was because his conception of literature was overwhelmingly conditioned by his utilitarianism. Persistently, he considered literature to be no more than unearthing misery and injustice, registering protest, and offering reform ideas. In April, 1918, he exhorted his compatriots to write about

> factory workers, ricksha pullers, inland farmers, peddlers and shopkeepers of all sorts . . . the distressing metamorphoses of the family system, the agonies of marriage, the status of women, and the unsuitability of [current] educational practices.[35]

He extended this functional notion of literature to the area of poetry. In January, 1923, Hu took issue with the notion that poetry should not be used as a tool for propaganda, arguing,

> If poetry fails to express the cries of human suffering and misery, and contents itself as the mouthpiece of pretty lovers and saints, then it has neglected one of the sacred duties it was primarily intended to fulfil.[36]

It should not be surprising, then, that the only two pieces of creative writing Hu ever produced dealt with the agonies of marriage in twentieth-century China.[37]

Put in historical perspective, Hu Shih's evaluation of Ming-Ch'ing fiction was a radical departure from the past. Certainly, Liang Ch'i-ch'ao and Yen Fu advocated the importance of fiction as an instrument for social reform, and Wang Kuo-wei provided us with the first study of *Dream of the Red Chamber* from a literary standpoint. When everything is considered, however, Hu was most directly responsible for raising to respectability the status of fiction—a genre previously regarded by traditional scholars as no more than an occasional diversion from serious moral-intellectual pursuits. Hu was also one of the first to study systematically the major Ming-Ch'ing novels as a legitimate subject and to utilize them consciously for an ideological purpose. In terms of its attitude toward fiction alone, the May Fourth period can be considered a new era.

More than anything else, the literary revolution points to the profound alienation of Hu Shih and his generation. In fact, alienation was an integral part of the creative literature and the literary revolution in twentieth-century China. "In general," Leo Lee tells us, "it may be said that two major trends in nineteenth century Western literature held sway in China: realism and romanticism."[38] Lee has shown how disenchanted China's romantics were. We shall concentrate on Hu's feeling of estrangement.

The very conclusions and inferences that Hu drew from the Ming-Ch'ing novels were the best testimony of his alienation. His realist vision was a devastating indictment of Chinese society. His heroes were the grass roots antiheroes in *Water Margin,* the rejectees of the examination system in *The Scholars,* the iconoclastic Li Ju-chen of *Flowers in the Mirror,* the persecuted protagonists in *Dream of the Red Chamber,* the ill-treated women, and those in *Panorama of Officialdom* who curse officials as the filthiest creatures on earth. Needless to say, norms and institutions considered negative were singled out: concubinage, the sterile and empty eight-legged essay, the wicked and avaricious bureaucrats, the sanctimonious morals, and the systematic oppression of creativity and human dignity.

On at least three occasions beginning the early 1920s, Hu Shih quoted and consented in a statement of Huang Yüan-yung, a noted journalist-reformer, on the origin of the literary revolution. Huang wrote Chang Shih-chao in 1915:

> In my humble opinion, politics is in such confusion that I am at a loss to know what to talk about. Ideal schemes will have to be buried for future generations to unearth. . . . As to fundamental salvation, I believe its beginning must be sought in the promotion of a new literature. In short, we must endeavor to bring Chinese thought into direct contact with the contemporary thought of the world, thereby to accelerate its radical awakening. . . . The method seems to consist in using simple and simplified language and literature for wide dissemination of ideas among the people. Have we not seen that historians regard the Renaissance as the foundation of the overthrow of mediaevalism in Europe?[39]

This was a poignant revelation of one of the central spirits of the literary revolution. Huang Yüan-yung, who was a seasoned publicist heavily involved in social reform and politics before his assassination in San Francisco in 1915, came to the realization in his last year that it was hopeless to pursue a political route. Hu Shih, too, came to this disheartening conclusion, only much earlier in his life. The situation was indeed debilitating. Hu went on to reflect upon the exchange between Huang Yüan-yung and Chang Shih-chao.

> The recipient of this letter . . . published it with a reply in which he pointed out that "all social reforms must presuppose a certain level of political stability and orderliness, and the promotion of a new literature cannot be an exception." In the same year [1915] Huang Yuan-yung was assassinated in San Francisco; and in the following year Mr. Chang Shih-chao, who would not desert politics for the promotion of a new literature, took a prominent part in the campaign which finally thwarted the monarchical movement and caused the death of Yuan Shih-kai. But the downfall of Yuan Shih-kai did not bring the country nearer to the "level of political stability and order" as had been expected; nor did it remove all the evil forces which Yuan Shih-kai had planted throughout the country, and which soon ran wild and plunged the nation into disunion and civil strife lasting to the present day.[40]

Thus, the price Huang paid for being involved in politics was his own life; Chang Shih-chao was engaged in a game of futility. At the same time, "evil forces" continued to run rampant. Under the circumstances. literature in particular and intellectual activities in general became the only avenue open to Hu. Looking back, he said in 1924, "the success of the Revolution [of 1911] gave the Chinese people a sense of self-confidence, while its failures in the political aspects forced a number of leaders to turn attention to social and intellectual problems."[41]

But literature turned out to be as much a reform scheme as it was an outlet for Hu's disenchantment. This disenchantment was expressed in different forms, one of which was a spirit of meanness in his attitude toward China's literary heritage. Hu ventured his definition of a literary revolution this way.

> The history of Chinese literature is simply the history of a metabolism of language (instrument). . . . The vitality of literature depends en-

tirely upon its ability to express the sentiments and thoughts of a given period with a living medium. When the medium has become ossified, a new and vital one must be substituted for it: this is "literary revolution.". . . Therefore we can say that all the literary revolutions in history have been revolutions in literary instruments.[42]

When "instrument" became the only criterion by which to judge the worth of a literature, China's literary heritage was indeed pitifully poor. According to Hu, the only "living" literature China ever had were the philosophical dialogues of the Sung, the *tsa-chü* of the Yüan, the serialized fiction and the plays thereafter.[43] Most of the classical literature Hu dismissed as either academic or spurious, saying that "in the past two thousand years China has had no truly valuable and living classical-style literature. . . . What writers in this period have written is dead stuff, written in a dead language."[44] Classical Chinese language, he reminded us, had been dead by the time of Han Wu-ti (141–87 B.C.). Therefore, Hu's own history of the vernacular literature "is really a history of Chinese literature."[45]

When Hu was not judging the past by the present, he was criticizing Chinese tradition by a foreign standard.

> The methods of Chinese literature are too imperfect to serve as our models. Speaking of prose, there are only short essays but no well organized, argued, and structured long ones. In the area of verse, there are lyrics, but few narrative poems, let alone epics. Our play is still in its infantile stage. . . . There are but three or four good novels which nevertheless contain many shortcomings. Excellent short stories and one-act plays are completely absent. As for materials found in Chinese literature, they are even more unworthy to serve as models.[46]

Earlier, in June, 1917, Hu held that *Water Margin, Journey to the West, The Scholars,* and *Dream of the Red Chamber* are first-rate novels. But he immediately pointed out that he was speaking of their contents, not their structures. *The Scholars,* for instance, and its imitators—*Panorama of Officialdom, A Brief History of Enlightenment (Wen-ming hsiao-shih), Travels of Lao-ts'an (Lao-ts'an yu-chi), Flowers in the Sea of Sin (Nieh-hai hua),* and *Eyewitnessed Strange Phenomena of the Past Twenty Years (Erh-shih nien mu-tu chih kuai-hsien-chuang)*—are nothing but endless, unrelated plots strung together, which can be broken into numerous short stories or serialized ad infinitum.⁴⁷ Finally, the Chinese had no notion of tragedy, Hu lamented. Novels and plays as a rule end with a grand reunion. "This 'superstitious faith in grand reunion' is the ironclad proof of the weak thinking ability of the Chinese. . . . This is a literature that tells lies . . . that can never create a deep passion, a thorough awakening, or a fundamental reflection in the reader." Western literature, therefore, "will offer an absolutely sacred medicine to cure our lying, hypocritical, and shallow literature."⁴⁸

Certainly, one must take into account the circumstances under which Hu wrote these words. While the literary revolution encountered only feeble opposition, the unconscious weight of the classical literature and indeed of the entire tradition remained overwhelming. Traditional literature, from the standpoint of the early twentieth century, had become dull and tyrannical. Sentiments and themes expressed in it were stale, and diction outworn. Unlike modern academics, who have the luxury to step back, study, and enjoy the abstruse classical literature as a distant subject, those Chinese under its daily grind certainly felt differently. Classical literature, in other words, had become a high-handed implement that helped suppress freedom and imagination. In this sense, the literary revolution, as Hu said in 1933,

> was a movement of conscious protest against many of the ideas and institutions in the traditional culture, and of conscious emancipation of the individual man and woman from the bondage of the forces of tradition. It was a movement of reason versus tradition, freedom versus authority, and glorification of life and human values versus their suppression.⁴⁹

Hu took pains to point out that each generation has its distinct literature with a mission of connecting past achievements with future possibilities. As such, literature of earlier ages should not be imitated blindly or considered superior to literature of the present generation.⁵⁰ For this reason, he insisted that classical literature be no more than a subject for specialists, as were Greek literature and Latin literature in the West.⁵¹ This, of course, did not mean that classical Chinese literature had become entirely irrelevant. In 1920, Hu put forward a proposal for language teaching at the secondary school level. Students at this level, he said, should be able to write not only decent vernacular but understandable classical as well. Further, they should be able to read "easy" classical works, such as the *Twenty-Four Dynastic Histo-*

ries, The Comprehensive Mirror for Aid in Government, Mo-tzu, Tradition of Tso, and *Classic of Songs.*[52]

This having been said, however, it still took a bitter ideologue to make the pungent remarks that Hu did. So eager to protest, so anxious to be didactic, he found little value in the vast corpus of China's literary heritage that was not "vernacular" or utilitarian. When criticizing the Chinese literary tradition, his criteria were almost entirely Western. Differences in approaches, styles, and genres of Chinese literature became deadly defects in his eyes, and the lack of tragedy in Chinese literature turned out to be proof of China's mental and intellectual weakness. Hu saw a meaningful connection between the past and the present only at his most rational moments, which were few and far between. Persistently, he was convinced that the old had to be discarded in order for the new to develop. Many of Hu's observations concerning Ming-Ch'ing novels have been accepted by academic researchers today. What separates an academic and Hu is that Hu seemed to obtain a sadistic pleasure in accentuating the negative in the past.

Of all the Western literary figures, few equaled the popularity of Henrik Ibsen in May Fourth China. To promote his ideas, *Hsin ch'ing-nien* in June, 1918 published a special issue entitled "Ibsenism," for which Hu Shih, expectedly, wrote the lead article. This was an instructive event. John Northam writes of Ibsen,

> He is one of the first and greatest of those who sensed in the nineteenth century what was to become perhaps the dominant shaping force of the twentieth, namely man's feeling of alienation from his own society. He grasped through his imagination the fearsome fact that by the inevitable closeness and intricacy of its organization modern society had become . . . a force insidiously hostile to self-fulfilment. . . .
>
> This society, for all its power, is, in Ibsen's view, dead. . . . [I]t is his basic estimate that society by its very nature is not a source of creative energy. It is a structure made up of decayed truths, Mrs. Alving's "ghosts." Society requires continuity, and thus clings to values long past their period of true vitality; by doing so it necessarily becomes hostile to the creative aspirations of some individuals.[53]

Hu Shih did not pay a close attention to, nor was he interested in, Ibsen's own background or his misgivings about the European bourgeois conventionality. What attracted him was Ibsen's indictment of society. Hu charged: "Society is always inclined to be autocratic . . .

frequently resorting to its conforming power to destroy individuality and suppress free and independent spirit of the individual."[54] He attacked the very assumptions and practices of family, law, morality, and religion, ridiculing them as founded on a double standard, cowardice, slavish habits, and outworn convictions. Society, in a word, was an ugly place with few redeeming virtues. Hu spoke in the person of Professor Rubek, a protagonist in Ibsen's "When We Dead Awaken."

> I was young then—with no knowledge of life. The Resurrection, I thought, would be most beautifully and exquisitely figured as a young unsullied woman—with none of our earth-life's experience—awakening to light and glory without having to put away from her anything ugly and impure.
> . . . I learned worldly wisdom in the years that followed. . . . "The Resurrection Day" became in my mind's eye something more and something—something more complex. . . .
> I imaged that which I saw with my eyes around me in the world. I had to include it—I could not help it. . . . I expanded the plinth—made it wide and spacious. And on it I placed a segment of the curving, bursting earth. And up from the fissures of the soil there now swarm men and women with dimly-suggested animal-faces. Women and men—as I know them in real life.[55]

"This is the fundamental method of Ibsenism," Hu exclaimed.

> That "most beautifully and exquisitely figured as a young unsullied woman" symbolizes the idealist literature; and that "men and women with dimly-suggested animal-faces" is the realist literature. Ibsen's literature and Ibsen's philosophy is simply realism.[56]

What then was the recourse for an independent individual in such a world of animal faces? Hu wrote, quoting a passage from one of Ibsen's letters to the Danish critic Georg Brandes.

> What I chiefly desire for you is a genuine, full-blooded egoism which shall force you for a time to regard what concerns yourself as the only thing of any consequence, and everything else as non-existent. . . . There is no way in which you can benefit society more than by coining the metal you have in yourself. . . . There are actually moments when the whole history of the world appears to me like one great shipwreck, and the only important thing is to save one's self.[57]

Thus, to defy society and retain his independence, Hu cultivated a heroic and yet tragic sense of loneliness. "The strongest man in the world is the man who stands alone," Hu quoted Ibsen.[58]

It was this alienated feeling that characterized the dominant spirit of the literary revolution in the May Fourth period. Since "politics is in such confusion," to honor the age-old tradition of political service would require extraordinary courage and sacrifice. On the other hand, however,

> "Living in this world, one has to do something." The literary scene, therefore, provided such a milieu [for commitment] and offered an attractive alternative to political service for a sizable portion of modern Chinese intellectuals. It was also a change of focus from state to society.[59]

Hu underscored the importance of a new literature to such an extent because in one breath the new literature offered a reform scheme and a psychological compensation. It afforded him a sense of involvement and helped him overcome the feeling of impotence. As an alienated intellectual, the new literature satisfied his urge to disentangle himself from the social and political reality. As one of the forms of "participation" which require the least degree of involvement, however, literature enabled him to pursue reform while being an outsider. The vernacular language and the protest-exposé fiction, in particular, served this dual purpose well. Hu understood clearly that *pai-hua* was a departure from the dominant medium of expression and that its adoption signified a break with the ethos of the past. In his eyes, the Ming-Ch'ing vernacular novels of protest and sarcasm defied convention and rejected the preponderant values in society. And yet both *pai-hua* and the fiction were so useful. One offered a new instrument for mass education while the other offered didactic lessons. They were, in other words, both relevant and remote. By espousing them, Hu at once severed his tie with the establishment and became an engaged reformer. It was in this spirit that he justified his stance.

> Society is constituted of individuals. One more person saved is one more element prepared for the reconstruction of a new society. Therefore, Mencius said, "the frustrated attend to their own virtue in solitude." This is similar to Ibsen's "save one's self." Such egoism is in fact the most valuable kind of altruism.[60]

Here Hu Shih's mood was akin to that of a naturalist who is always torn "between pessimism and optimism."[61] From the start, Hu was confident that the literary revolution would score a sweeping victory. Indeed, the opposition proved to be disappointingly feeble and scattered. To stir up interest by controversy, Ch'ien Hsüan-t'ung (1887–1939) had to publish a letter in May, 1918, under the *non de plume* Wang Ching-hsüan. The letter, written in the old literary style and ostensibly from an ultraconservative reactionary, made a number of absurd charges against the new literature. It was answered, with prior knowledge, by still another member of the radical camp, Liu Pan-nung (1891–1934).[62] The arrogance and playfulness reflected in the ruse poignantly attested the mood of the May Fourth era. Psychologically, the New Culture leaders were on an all-out offensive. Hu Shih, too, was never concerned about the opposition. He wrote Ch'en Tu-hsiu in April, 1918, about an essay by Lin Shu in objection to the new literature: "I was delighted [that Lin wrote such an essay] and read it, thinking that it would be a worthy piece for those of us who attack the classical literature. But I was greatly disappointed."[63] By December, 1919, Hu was able to pronounce: "So rapid indeed has been the spread of the intellectual transformation that it even astounded those who have entertained the wildest expectations for its final triumph."[64] Even the conservative arguments of Mei Kuang-ti (1890–1945) and the *Hsüeh-heng* group, which were more articulate and sophisticated than Lin Shu, did not pose a serious challenge. "Truth" and the climate of opinion were on Hu Shih's side. He declared his final verdict in May, 1922.

> The voice of *Hsüeh-heng* probably utters the epilogue of the opposition to the literary revolution. I dare say that the revolution has passed the stage of discussion and that the opposition party has collapsed. From now on, we live in an age of creation of the new literature.[65]

But Hu's confidence was overshadowed by his pessimism. The emphasis on new literature to the exclusion of other endeavors was in itself a retreat from reality, and the cutting attacks of the Chinese literary heritage by Hu and other radicals reflected their feelings of impotence and estrangement.

We recall that Hu was especially pleased with Ibsen's "An Enemy of the People." This was to be expected. Tomas Stockmann, medical adviser to the town, is up against the whole world for his principle. The mineral baths, which bring prosperity to the town, are, to Stockmann's horror, filled with poisons and harming the people. When Stockmann tries to speak up, the entire town, feeling that its livelihood is threatened, turns against him, including the *People's Monitor*, a self-proclaimed liberal newspaper, and his own brother who happens to be both mayor of the town and chairman of its bath committee. Dr. Stockmann refuses to submit to the common wisdom that "the individual must subordinate himself to Society as a whole; or, more precisely, to those authorities responsible for the well-being of that Society." On the contrary, he believes that "the majority is never right—never, I tell you! That's one of those social lies against which every free, intelligent man ought to rebel." Now, "it's no longer merely a question of sewers and waterworks, you see; it's a question of cleaning up the whole community." As far as Dr. Stockmann is concerned, "there's only one fundamental truth, in my opinion—and that is that Society cannot live a healthy life based on truths that have become old and spineless." In the ensuing struggle, Stockmann loses his job and his daughter her teaching position. His home is smashed, his father-in-law withdraws the inheritance for his wife and children, and he is declared "an enemy of the people." For all these setbacks, however, Dr. Stockmann has the last word.

> Dr. Stockmann: Drive *me* away! Are you stark raving mad, Katrine? I'm the strongest man in the town! Don't you know that!
> Mrs. Stockmann: The strongest—? You mean *now?*
> Dr. Stockmann: Yes! I'll even go so far as to say that I'm one of the strongest men in the whole world!
> Morten: Are you really, Father?
> Dr. Stockmann: (dropping his voice) Hush! You mustn't say a word about it yet; I've made a great discovery, you see.
> Mrs. Stockmann: Not another, Tomas, dear!
> Dr. Stockmann: Another, yes—another! (gathers them round him and speaks in a confidential tone) And I'll tell you what it is: the strongest man in the world is the man who stands alone.[66]

Hu Shih was, in his own world, that strongest man, standing alone.

Chapter 9

Attitudes toward Chinese Culture

Between his teenage days in Shanghai and his sophomore year at Cornell, Hu Shih resisted his pronounced interests in the humanities and tried instead to be a mathematician and an agricultural specialist. When he finally transferred to philosophy, his talent began to flourish. It was in Chinese thought and literary studies that he found his lifelong vocation and built his reputation. In retrospect, he would have been a mediocre mathematician or agriculturist at best, and his decision to transfer proved to have been one of the high points in his life.

Over the years, Hu published an extraordinary body of writings. Covering a wide range of subjects, they demonstrated his diverse concerns and the complexity of his consciousness. A good number of his writings dealt with China's modernization, some of which Hu wrote in a detached, analytical frame of mind and others in a highly emotional, polemical spirit. Other writings were done by Hu in his capacity as China's official or unofficial spokesman for a Western audience; still other writings and research he did to relieve tension and seek pleasure in the face of harsh reality. To be sure, Hu himself was not always conscious of the purpose of his writings, and many served more than one purpose. It is fair to say, for example, that most of his writings and research on the subject of the distant past gave him a badly needed respite from contemporary affairs while at the same time providing him with a weapon to address his deep concerns. I classify his writings into these categories as outlined here mainly for the convenience of discussion. Hu's pleasure scholarship will receive our attention in the next chapter, while the other aspects of his writings will be our immediate concern here.

By Hu's own account, his practical scholarship was indelibly influenced by John Dewey. "Dewey taught me how to think," Hu said in 1930.

> He taught me constantly to pay attention to concrete issues at hand, to regard all the theories as hypotheses awaiting proof, and always to consider the consequences of ideas. They [Huxley and Dewey] made me understand the nature and function of the scientific method.[1]

Hu related on another occasion that Experimentalism had become "the guidance of my life and thought and the foundation of my philosophy." His dissertation, *The Development of the Logical Method in Ancient China,* and its expanded Chinese version, *A History of* [Ancient] *Chinese Philosophy,* were "all guided by this philosophy," as were his proposals for literary reform.[2] Over the years, Hu enhanced the impression of his close ties with Dewey by producing a number of essays on Dewey and pragmatism.[3]

While it is undeniable that Dewey played an important role in Hu's intellectual development, the matter was by no means as simple as Hu and others had led us to believe.[4] In fact, despite his frequent reference to Dewey, Hu understood that their relationship was an ambiguous one. He related in his autobiography that "when later my thinking followed the thinking of Huxley and Dewey, it was because since my teenage years I had placed great emphasis on intellectual method."[5] At another time, Hu intimated that he "found it very hard to pin down from what place, from what book or from what teacher" he acquired his approach.[6]

The truth was somewhere in between. While he did not receive any startling revelations from Dewey, he nonetheless obtained something quite significant: a confirmation by Dewey of the views he had held for a long time. Grieder perceptively summarizes the relationship between Hu and Dewey.

> [A]n examination of his ideas during those years [in the United States] . . . reveals no radical departure from the general tendency of the opinions Hu had reached during his Shanghai days. There is, indeed, some modification . . . and considerable embellishment. . . . But nowhere . . . is there evidence of a sudden and startling conversion to new beliefs, or of a fundamental revision of Hu's conception of the world. It is difficult to escape the conclusion that as a student in the United States Hu Shih responded readily and with enthusiasm to ideas for which his earlier education had prepared him, and that he

assimilated those aspects of contemporary Western thought which proved most compatible with attitudes already foreshadowed, if not yet firmly held, before his arrival in this new world.[7]

In his early years, Hu was influenced by the secular, iconoclastic spirit of Chinese thought, notably that of Fan Chen and Ssu-ma Kuang. His antireligious themes were both a testimony of this influence and a reflection of the mood of his time. After he went to Shanghai in 1904, Hu became an avid reader of Yen Fu's translations and Liang Ch'i-ch'ao's writings. Like many of his predecessors, he too advocated science, critical thinking, nationalism, the concept of progress, and a host of other ideas. It was also in his Shanghai days that, under the influence of the vernacular movement, Hu began his journalistic venture in *pai-hua* writing. Thus, long before he came into contact with Dewey, he had already accepted the ideal of practical statecraft and, through the writings of Chinese pioneers, Western pragmatic ideas.

In 1912, Hu entered the Russell Sage School of Philosophy at Cornell which, under the leadership of James Edward Creighton, was a "stronghold of Idealism." There Hu "read the more important works of the classical philosophers of ancient and modern times," but "their problems never interested me," he said of the reading he had been required to do in such idealists as Francis Bradley and Bernard Bosanquet.[8] Hu's thinking was developing in different directions. He wrote in January, 1914,

> What our country urgently needs today is not novel theories or abstruse philosophical doctrines, but the methods by means of which knowledge may be sought, affairs discussed, things examined, and the country governed. Speaking from my own experience, there are three methods which are miraculous prescriptions to restore life:
> 1. the principle of inductive reasoning;
> 2. a sense of historical perspective;
> 3. the concept of progress.[9]

At the time, Hu was paying close attention to Western textual criticism, pragmatism, and the evolution of the theory of natural rights.[10] Half a year later, with his schoolmates at Cornell, Chao Yüan-jen, Yang Ch'üan, and Jen Hung-chün (1886–1961), Hu founded the Science Society (*K'o-hsüeh she*) to "advocate science, promote industry, define nomenclature, and disseminate knowledge."[11] The journal of the Society, *Science* (*K'o-hsüeh*), enjoyed a rare longevity in the vicissitudinous publishing world of modern China.

An example of the variety of influences to which Hu was subject was the literary revolution. He had a rare moment of modesty when he attributed the origin of the movement to Dewey's inspiration. The story, however, was more complicated. Before Hu wrote a word on the subject, a number of Chinese had put forward their proposals for a reform in language and literature. The vernacular had been in use ever since the 1870s, and many reformers thereafter began advocating a wider adoption of this medium of expression. Prior to the May Fourth period, proposals for a "revolution in poetry" appeared, as did works on Chinese grammar. The importance of fiction as a tool for reform was also argued for.[12] Even the views of those who did not set their minds on reform anticipated Hu's position. A comparison of Wang Kuo-wei's opinion on literature and that of Hu would compel many to conclude that Hu perhaps conveniently neglected to mention his extraordinary debt to Wang. The atmosphere was such and the groundwork was so well laid that Wu Wen-ch'i maintained that

> the fetus of the new literature was conceived as early as after the Reform Movement of 1898. Gradually it developed and grew, and it was born in the May Fourth period. Hu Shih, Ch'en Tu-hsiu, and Ch'ien Hsüan-t'ung were but delivering doctors.[13]

It was in such a milieu that Hu undertook his journalistic activity in *pai-hua* writing. After he came to America, Hu read and referred to Ma Chien-chung's (1844–1900) monumental work on Chinese grammar and paid close attention to problems concerning Chinese language and literature.[14] At that time the issue of literary reform had become so pressing that he was constantly engaged in lively debates on the subject. In fact, Hu's first substantial piece of writing on the issue was a response to a challenge of another Chinese student in America. "Earlier," Hu wrote in August, 1915,

> a certain person by the surname of Chung widely distributed leaflets, attacking the Chinese language and proposing the adoption of phonetic scripts. . . . I think that this is a serious issue and that we should not be dictated by emotions when we examine it. I therefore suggested that "Chinese language" be the topic for discussion at the annual meeting [of the Chinese Students' Association].[15]

Hu's essay for the conference, "The Problem of the Chinese Language," set the tone for his proposal for a literary reform and contained the cornerstone of his argument that he would later reiterate.[16]

This was not all. Certain Western literary theories played no small role in providing Hu with ideas and sharpening his arguments. In July, 1916, Mei Kuang-ti accused him of parroting faddish trends in American literary circles, such as Imagism.[17] While vehemently denying the charge, Hu less than half a year later dutifully copied the six credos of the Imagists, noting that "there are many similarities between the Imagists' principles and my own."[18] It was readings Hu did on the Renaissance that led him to draw simplistic parallels between the *paihua* movement in China and the emergence of the vulgate national literatures in early modern Europe.[19]

Since the betterment of society was one of Hu's foremost objects, the congeniality of Dewey and pragmatism naturally attracted him. In the summer of 1915, Hu read, "with great eagerness, all the works of Mr. Dewey."[20] This was a highly significant development: Hu had his ideas confirmed by a leading authority who expressed them with subtlety and sophistication. Forever entangled in polemical debates of one kind or another, Hu never had the luxury of a quiet, uninterrupted environment to work out his own ideas in a cogent manner. To pay tribute to Dewey was then in part to promote what he himself had in mind. Dewey was his alter ego and a more articulate spokesman for his cause.

The key word to understanding Dewey's philosophy is *experience*. Dewey had serious misgivings about a priori or transcendental knowledge. Believing that nothing is fixed or static, he developed a new empiricism which combines the naturalistic bias of the Greek philosophers with a sensitive appreciation for experimental method as practiced by the sciences. According to Dewey, morals, values, and outlooks change as time and place change. He believed that his theory bridges the most noxious of dualisms in modern thought—the separation of science and values, knowledge and morals. Dewey's central concern was to acquire a sense of certainty toward the future. "Intelligent understanding of past history is to some extent a lever for moving the present into a certain kind of future." The solution of present problems necessitates constant reinterpretations of the past in accordance with present needs. History is written and rewritten as "new standpoints for viewing, appraising and ordering [of] data arise."[21] For Dewey, this reinterpretation would be a vigorous and aggressive endeavor.

We do not merely have to repeat the past, or wait for accidents to force change upon us. *We use* our past experiences to construct new and better ones in the future. The very fact of experience thus includes the process by which it directs itself in its own betterment.[22]

Aside from the content of his new history, Dewey's approach was familiar. "The 'new history' is an old story," Carl Becker tells us.

Since history is not an objective reality, but only an imaginative reconstruction of vanished events, the pattern that appears useful and agreeable to one generation is never entirely so to the next. There is thus a profound truth in Voltaire's witticism: "History is only a pack of tricks we play on the dead.". . . The kind of tricks we play is . . . likely to depend on our attitude toward the present. If well enough satisfied with the present we are likely to pay our ancestors the doubtful compliment of approaching them with a studied and pedantic indifference; but when the times are out of joint we are disposed to blame them for it, or else we dress them up, as models suitable for us to imitate, in shining virtues which in fact they never possessed, which they would perhaps not have recognized as virtues at all.[23]

The urge to write new history, in China or elsewhere, has never been absent. Chinese in traditional times periodically offered their "new" history, though generally in a similar attempt of striving to restore the golden age of the past. New history was particularly flourishing when times were out of joint, as they were in China in the latter half of the nineteenth century. Thus, beginning in the last years of that century, history written by the reformers became startlingly new. K'ang Yu-wei did critical studies of the authenticity of the classics and offered many revolutionary concepts in his *Study of the Forged Classics of the Hsin Period* (*Hsin-hsüeh wei-ching k'ao*) of 1891. In his *Confucius as Reformer* (*K'ung-tzu kai-chih k'ao*), published in 1897, he pictured Confucius as a political reformer, the author of the authentic classics, and the founder of the Confucian religion. T'an Ssu-t'ung (1865–98) was equally radical in his criticism of the past and hope for the future. In his revolutionary "A Study of Benevolence" (*Jen-hsüeh*), written during the last two years of his life, he evolved an ingenious combination of Confucian, Buddhist, and Christian ideas together with what he had learned about Western science. He hoped by this eclecticism to arrive at a new way of life more congenial to human beings.[24]

By the time of the May Fourth era, the intensity of writing new history reached a new height, and the content of the new history became still newer. Rarely did any of the cultural radicals in this period invoke Confucianism or Buddhism. The authority was the modern West. And at least in the case of Hu Shih, there was, true to the Deweyan philosophy, a far more conscious manipulation of past experiences to "construct new and better ones in the future." Hu asked in 1917,

> How can we Chinese feel at ease in this new world which at first sight appears to be so much at variance with what we have long regarded as our own civilization? ... How can we best assimilate modern civilization in such a manner as to make it congenial and congruous and continuous with the civilization of our own making? ... Where can we find a congenial stock with which we may organically link the thought-systems of modern Europe and America, so that we may further build up our own science and philosophy on the new foundation of an internal assimilation of the old and the new?[25]

The question necessarily led to a reassessment of Confucianism. Though he found a system of logic in Confucius's theory of "rectification of names" (*cheng-ming*), Hu believed that Confucianism put too much emphasis on human affairs at the expense of logic and science. As such, "the future of Chinese philosophy depends upon its emancipation from the moralistic and rationalistic fetters of Confucianism. . . . Confucianism was once only one of the many rival systems flourishing in Ancient China."[26] On the other hand,

> the emphasis on experience as against dogmatism and rationalism, the highly developed scientific method in all its phases of operation, and the historical or evolutionary view of truth and morality ... these which I consider as the most important contributions of modern philosophy in the Western world, can all find their remote but highly developed predecessors in those great non-Confucian schools.[27]

What Hu was referring to here were the philosophies of Chuang-tzu (369–286 B.C.?), Han-fei-tzu (d. 233 B.C.), Hsün-tzu, and, above all, Mo-tzu (470–391 B.C.). Mohism had "much in common with Utilitarianism and Pragmatism," and the logic of Mohists and Neo-Mohists was "the most systematically developed theory of logical method in the entire history of Chinese thought." Mo-tzu opposed Confucian formalism and ritualism, insisting that "the practical consequences of beliefs, theories, and institutions" be of the foremost consideration. Confucianism was obsessed with the ultimate ideal goal and the motive of behavior, while Mohism emphasized the "how" and "why" and the practical side of human conduct.[28]

But although he criticized certain aspects of Confucianism, Hu did not repudiate the entire philosophy. In fact, Hu spoke of Confucius the man and his social and political philosophy in generally favorable terms. Confucius was a man of vision and, like Socrates and Plato who tirelessly battled the Sophists, a proponent of conservative morals and ideals. At a time when there were cynics and escapists aplenty, Confucius was concerned and involved, a "practicing politician." His concept of *jen* denotes the noblest human ideal, and his notion of "gentleman" (*chün-tzu*) represents a model personality that generations of individuals strove to imitate. Many of the corruptions in the Confucian system were creations of his followers. The excessive moral judgment in Chinese historical writing had nothing to do with Confucius's original ideas. Confucius displayed a rich sense of history and a sensitive appreciation of the importance of music and literature. But he was not without faults. While he emphasized consistent, logical thinking, the how and the consequence of human conduct, these were not central to his philosophy. In fact, his notion of learning concerned almost entirely book knowledge at the expense of direct observation and experimentation. Partly because of his meticulous attention to motives in human conduct and partly because of his insufficient stress on logic, later Confucians worked out an extreme moralism based on intent alone. By adding rigid and minute details to a general code of conduct that Confucius developed, they created a repressive set of "propriety" and what amounted to a "religion of filial piety." Not until Mencius (ca. 370–ca. 290 B.C.) and Hsün-tzu (ca. 300–ca. 230 B.C.) did there emerge a philosophy in the school of Confucianism that had something significantly new.[29]

Throughout the 1920s and early 1930s, Hu vigorously attacked the speculative, metaphysical outlook of the Sung-Ming Neo-Confucianism and sang praise of what he regarded as the pragmatic, empirical learning of the early Ch'ing scholars. The latter, Hu maintained, displayed an inchoate scientific spirit and method by adhering to evidence and by skillfully employing both induction and deduction in their research. While Neo-Confucianism was heavily influenced by the negative, other-worldly Buddhist thought, the school of Han Learning in the eighteenth century was a successful revolt against metaphysical thinking in general and the Indian religion in particular.[30] In areas of culture, society, and politics, Hu continued to hold a positive view of Confucius. In an important article, "On *Ju*," published in 1934, Hu reconstructed the emergence and characteristics of this most powerful class in traditional Chinese society. The *ju*, he said, was originally a group of educated Yin people whose occupation was to preside over funeral ceremonies. Because of their profession, they were relatively poor; as a conquered people, they harbored a nationalistic and provincial sentiment and developed a nonresistant, obedient personality. It was in the hands of Confucius, the greatest leader of this group, that the class underwent a metamorphosis, By transfusing the effeminate, bigoted class with an assertive, independent spirit and by imbuing it with a sense of historical mission, Confucius transformed the provincial ideology of the *ju* into a cultural and spiritual movement with universal concerns and vision. In particular, Confucius proposed the concept of *jen* and an egalitarian philosophy of education that included everyone capable of learning. These were revolutionary ideas. A *ju* was no longer a weak person of limited concerns but a gentleman of broad vision, of courage and perseverance who was ever ready to take the entire world as his responsibility. So extraordinary were Confucius's contributions that the term *ju* later became synonymous with Confucians.[31]

Although science and pragmatism always occupied a central place in Hu's thought, other problems concerned him as well. His hope for a Chinese culture built on modern science and empirical values never diminished; but in the forties and fifties, part of his attention was increasingly drawn to China's tradition of individualism, liberalism, and political culture. Typical of this concern was a lecture he delivered in Taiwan in 1954. By examining the positions of three major figures in Chinese history—Lao-tzu, Confucius, and Mo-tzu—Hu voiced his political aspirations and philosophy in clear terms. Lao-tzu's concept of political *wu-wei*, he said, represented the first major philosophical development in China. This *wu-wei* philosophy, which decried overgovernment and repressive policies, and which preceded the concept of laissez-faire by two thousand three hundred years, was the cornerstone of Chinese politics, and proved to be an indispensable element for any dynasty to last. Confucius's concept of *jen*, a truly inimitable vision, was neither anticipated nor surpassed. The democratic philosophy of education, formulated by Confucius and elaborated by others, "created a healthy individualism." Apropos of Mo-tzu, Hu thoroughly gainsaid his earlier position by announcing his repentance, admitting that he overstated Mo-tzu's contribution. Instead of mentioning Mo-tzu's logic, Hu told his audience that Mo-tzu was a "reactionary," that his system was a "totalitarianism," and that he actually worked out a "spy system." This startling change of position on Hu's part came as no surprise. Chinese politics as practiced by either of the Chinese governments had little to please him, and his disappointment inevitably led him to reconsider his enthusiastic embrace of Mo-tzu. Hu confessed that he "bent the other way too far" in his early years. "Thirty-five years is a long time. My hair has grayed a little; naturally my ideas have matured somewhat."[32]

The above analysis is but a brief glimpse of Hu Shih's attitudes toward the major schools of Chinese thought as reflected at different stages of his scholarly activities. What is important is not so much his ideas per se as their sharp contradistinction with his views on Chinese culture expressed in his polemical writings. In the latter, he remorselessly assaulted and passed sweeping judgments against Chinese culture.

Hu began his mordant attack upon Chinese tradition immediately after he returned to China in 1917. In the late 1910s and early 1920s, he was eager to destroy any notion that traditional values were of any relevance in the modern world. In his joint reply with Ch'en Tu-hsiu to a reader's letter in the October 15, 1918, issue of *Hsin ch'ing-nien*, he wrote: "the old literature, old politics, and old ethics have always belonged to one family; we cannot abandon one and preserve the others."[33] In his preface to the *Collected Essays of Wu Yü* (*Wu Yü wen-lu*), written in 1921, Hu hailed Wu as "the old hero from Szechwan who beat Confucius and Sons single-handedly" and likened Wu to a scavenger who indefatigably cleaned the Confucian refuse in society so that the young would not be poisoned again.[34] Wu Yü (1871–1949) was one of the earliest anti-Confucian scholars in modern times. Because of its anti-Confucian stance, his *Intellectual Trends in the Sung and Yüan Dynasties* (*Sung Yüan hsüeh-an ts'ui-yü*) was banned by the Ch'ing government. By the May Fourth period, he had become one of the most potent and systematic critics of Confucianism. By paying Wu such a tribute, Hu Shih revealed his own anti-Confucian character.

Following the First World War, there were profound misgivings in both China and the West about the direction of the materialistic and scientific culture. In China, the challenge to the notion of the omnipotence of science culminated in a debate on science and the philosophy of life in 1923, an event that needs no elaboration here. Hu wrote two essays in this context. The first was a long prolegomenon to the debate literature, in which he stridently declared his "materialistic," "scientific" philosophy of life.[35] The second, entitled "Our Attitude toward Modern Western Civilization" and produced in 1926, was a virulent attack upon the Oriental mentality and culture. It was "poisonous" and "pathological," he said, to label Western civilization as materialistic and Eastern civilization as spiritual. Such an attitude, among other things, would merely aggravate the self-boasting psychology of the Chinese. "A spiritual civilization must be built on a material foundation," Hu pointed out, and only the deranged Orientals, unable to satisfy their basic material needs, elected to seek "illusory, spiritual" compensation by inflicting wounds on themselves. As such, they were fit only to be "subservient people." "In China, eight hundred years of Neo-Confucianism could not even see the cruelty of foot-binding suffered by two hundred million women." On the other hand, Western culture, characterized by rationalism, a spirit of self-reliance and democracy, had conquered nature, demolished superstition, and showed a genuine interest in human welfare. Hu even insisted that the basic character of Westerners was superior: they "do not struggle for power and aggrandizement; they struggle for freedom, equality, and justice."[36]

As Hu was writing the second essay, reality in China was changing rapidly. The Kuomintang reunification of the nation was followed by a national program founded on a crude personality cult, ill-conceived nationalism, and embarrassingly childish cultural themes. In the meantime, problems of dire poverty, chaos, and foreign aggression did not abate. On the first anniversary of the Manchurian Incident, Hu angrily proclaimed that China's miseries were the result of the evils and the retributions of its ancestors. The problem was far more than physical; it was deeply spiritual. Things such as foot binding and the eight-legged essay that constituted a spiritual madness and cruelty were the fundamental illnesses of the Chinese race.[37]

Hu's attitude, understandably, provoked vigorous protests. In 1934, a Shou-sheng urged that while the Chinese should not try to conceal their feeling of humiliation by invoking past glories, they nonetheless should have self-confidence under adverse circumstances. "That our reform has not been as expeditious as Japan's is that our traditional culture is too splendid. Creative people usually have strong personalities and are not easily receptive [to outside influences]."[38] Hu immediately matched this ill-conceived reasoning with his own diatribe.

> Our traditional culture is really too impoverished, and we cannot engage in such a dream talk as that it is "too splendid." We can put aside modern scientific culture and industrial culture, for we are shamefully poor in these areas. Let us speak only of the remote past. . . . The Greek and Roman literature, sculpture, science, and politics are enough to make us realize that our culture is too poor. . . . Even more than two thousand years ago our science had fallen far behind. (Why don't our patriotic youth compare the few principles of geometry in chapter "Ching-shang" of *Mo-tzu* with Euclid's geometry?) From then on, Europe has had whatever we have had, and it has had much more than we have ever had. . . . As to the unique treasures that we do have . . . parallel prose, regulated poetry, eight-legged essays, bound feet, eunuchs, concubinage, five-generation households, chastity arches, hellish prisons, court whipping, and law courts filled with torture implements . . . —though they are "splendid," though "they are all unique in their own right in the world," they are after all institutions and systems for which we cannot hold our heads up.[39]

Hu further pointed out that such virtues as loyalty (*chung*), filial piety (*hsiao*), benevolence (*jen*), and compassion (*ai*) were "universal ideals shared by all civilizations in the world." Being universal, they could not explain the particular nature of Chinese tradition, and thus the only thing that mattered was how these ideals were realized. In China, they had remained "empty words." "Our ancestors were only able to incorporate these appealing terms into their eight-legged essays, *t'ai-chi* diagrams, and *li-hsüeh* dialogues." As empty terms, these ideals were not able to prevent the evils throughout Chinese history. China, in Hu's argument, was beyond salvation. "We must repent behind closed doors and clearly recognize that the shallow contact with Western culture will not make our ancestors' and our own numerous evils and retributions disappear." Despite the elimination of foot binding and the abolition of many elaborate tortures, the barbarity and cruelty behind these institutions was still embedded in the psyche of the Chinese people.[40]

Hard pressed by his critics, Hu decided to make a few concessions.

"As a student of history, as a red-blooded Chinese, naturally I often would like to find some worthy qualities in the tradition," he allowed in 1934. After viewing China's past, Hu pointed out three characteristics he thought could be considered outstanding in the world. The grammar of Chinese language was the easiest and most reasonable. Having severed with feudalism early, Chinese social structure was rather egalitarian and democratic. Finally, the religiosity of the Chinese people was weak.[41] But these were no more than backhanded compliments. Lin Yü-sheng points out that grammar "had to do with a formal aspect of the language that could hardly be considered to have any bearing on the moral quality of the tradition. The second Hu explained in terms of historical circumstances, thus detaching its merits from the traditional Chinese mind."[42] Furthermore, Hu was not even able to offer this limited generosity without reservations. While Chinese grammar was simple, he contended, Chinese characters were difficult and most unreasonable. Because of its egalitarian and democratic nature in its early stage of development, Chinese society had few centripetal forces and was at best loosely organized. As such, most of the social movements were generated from the lower echelon: foot binding from dancers, opium smoking from vagabonds, novels and popular forms of literature from street singers. Precisely because of its weak religiosity, China readily succumbed to Buddhism and endured a lengthy dark period. But "these three things, after all, are still the most commendable attributes that China can ever boast of," Hu concluded. "Other than these, after twenty years of reflection, I really cannot think of anything else that is worth mentioning."[43]

Hu adhered to his caustic view of Chinese culture throughout his life. On November 6, 1961, a few months before his death, he spoke of the Oriental heritage with usual pungency at the four-nation Science Education Conference held in Taipei. A true idealism and spirituality, he asserted, was "sadly underdeveloped in our Oriental civilization." "What spirituality is there in a civilization which tolerated so cruel and inhuman an institution as footbinding for women for over a thousand years?" Therefore,

> a full realization of the total absence of spirituality and even vitality in such old civilizations seems to be a necessary intellectual preparation for a full understanding of the modern civilization of science and technology which glorifies life and utilizes human intelligence for betterment of the conditions of life.[44]

Attitudes toward Chinese Culture 179

How do we reconcile such extraordinary discrepancies between Hu's scholarly writings and his polemical writings? When he was engaged in scholarly writing, he had a sense of detachment, and he had to obey evidence, thus greatly limiting his freedom of expression. Though deeply concerned about China's contemporary difficulties, his approach was "primarily a pedagogical one."[45] In a detached mood with much of contemporary reality blocked out, Hu was able to propose to preserve the best in his heritage and adopt the best from Western culture. Writing for popular consumption, contemporary reality immediately assumed a much larger role, overwhelming him and ultimately becoming an integral part of his consciousness. Viewing everything from a contemporary and pragmatic standpoint, Hu inevitably traced all of China's diseases to its traditional values. Ideals and their practical manifestations became synonymous to him. Embittered by China's myriad crises and yet unable to do anything himself to arrest these crises, Hu vented his anger and frustration by lashing out at China's past.

Cultural conservatism further incensed Hu, whose most savage attacks on the Chinese culture were in part aimed at it. It was characteristic of the May Fourth period that cultural and intellectual debates seemed to reach an ever-heightening vicious cycle. When consensus disappeared, when the basic psychological locus was destroyed, opponents' opinions were always downgraded and their intentions and motives questioned. Under a psychology of siege, one always felt the need to make one's position vigorously known, invariably provoking violent responses. Under such circumstances, it would be futile to try to determine whether the conservatives or the iconoclasts were the culprits. Suffice it to say that both sides felt that they were engaged in battles with an extraordinary adversary. Even the unscrupulous political conservatives, backed by state power, by no means felt omnipotent, for they understood clearly that the climate of opinion of the educated class was on the other side. While Hu and his cohorts felt debilitated when faced with government-sponsored conservatism, they were at the same time supercilious and vituperative, always certain that they alone possessed the truth. By being so cruel toward his own cultural past, Hu not only emphatically rejected the crude conservative elements in the country, but also acquired a masochistic-sadistic pleasure and presumably overcame his feeling of impotence.

In the final analysis, however, Hu's iconoclasm, so violently, cynically, and persistently expressed, cannot be dismissed simply as extemporaneous reactions to outside factors. Nor can it be explained entirely in political or psychological terms. He must have believed deeply that traditional Chinese values were obsolete in the modern world. Hu could not even tolerate the articulate conservatism of such men as Liang Ch'i-ch'ao, Mei Kuang-ti, Liang Shu-ming (1893–), and Chang Chün-mai (Carsun Chang, 1886–1969), whose genuine concern about China's cultural and psychological crisis Hu often ridiculed and whose arguments he grossly simplified and even distorted. When Hu evaluated China's past in a scholarly manner, he was a historian of modernization; when he attacked it, he was a Chinese intricately entwined in China's contemporary plight. From two different perspectives, he naturally saw things differently. If these two positions were not consistent with each other, they certainly could and did exist simultaneously.

Hu Shih's tension as revealed in his scholarship and general views was not limited to the aforementioned aspects. Writings intended for the consumption of Western readers revealed still another dimension of his consciousness. Lin Yü-sheng observes that "sometimes—usually before a foreign audience" Hu spoke favorably of certain values in Chinese tradition.[46] There is an element of truth in this observation which nevertheless needs to be examined further. The number of writings Hu produced in English was enormous. Some of them disclosed an affection toward China's past; others he wrote to explain his country to the West with practical purposes in mind; still others were scathing assaults of the Chinese culture.

Even in his student days in America, Hu spoke up on several occasions on behalf of China. In January, 1912, immediately after the Republican Revolution, he wrote repudiating "the misconception that democracy is entirely a new thing to the Chinese" and arguing that "though China has been under monarchical government for thousands of years, still behind the monarchs and the aristocrats there has been dominating in China a quiet, peaceful, oriental form of democracy." Hu further asserted that Mencius, "the Montesquieu of the Orient," had said that the people should be regarded the highest and the sovereign, the least. "That the people are to be regarded most had been the essence of the laws of China. Most founders of the dynasties were men who won, not conquered, the people."[47] While we cannot rule out the possibility that he was apologizing for something which ancient thinkers in China pondered only in abstract terms, Hu's overriding concern was pragmatic. He was eager to convey the message to his Western readers that "there is no recognized royal family to set up in place of the departing house." No one like Yüan Shih-k'ai, Sun Yat-sen, Huang Hsing (1874–1916), or Wu T'ing-fang (1842–1922) would be fit to become a new emperor, and with the exception of Yüan, "They do not want to be Caesars . . . ; they want and the people expect them to be only Washingtons or Franklins." "Shall we," Hu then came to his real point, "after so much struggle and so much bloodshed, be so ridiculous as to offer a crown to some individual, and set him up as a national ornament, merely for the sake of fulfilling a theory of political history?"[48]

In May, 1914, Hu spoke at length about the movement to establish Confucianism as the state religion in China. The movement, he observed, could be traced back to the 1890s when K'ang Yu-wei began to reinterpret Confucianism "in a new light, in the light of 'change,' or progress." In Hu's own time, "the movement . . . is led by men of the truly progressive type," such as Yen Fu. Hu wrote these words in part as a rebuttal to the prevalent notion in America that "this movement is a backward step in the history of China's progress." He had by then developed serious misgivings about Christianity, and the criticism of the Confucian movement was lodged mainly by the religious establishments. By way of comparison, Hu was able to voice his reservations about Christianity. "The Confucian movement is no more a backward step than Mr. Yuan Shih-kai's proclamation asking the Christian churches to pray for China was a progressive step." Hu further dismissed the notion that the movement was a threat to Christianity. On the contrary,

> a reformed Confucianism . . . will mean in the near future a useful source of emulation to Christianity, and will inspire her to modify some of her creeds and formalities in order to be better adapted to the oriental conditions.[49]

Here Hu's emotional attitude was more apparent than real. While the missionary position offended him, it did not make him alter his basic views. Hu was not yet a cultural iconoclast in 1914, and his stance at the time was one of reformism. The Confucian movement, he acknowledged, was "a very imperfect one. Its greatest defect is that it is not so much a *reformation* as a mere revival of Confucianism." He posed the following questions, which made his position unequivocal, for the Confucians to consider.

> I. What does the term "Confucianism" actually imply? Does it simply comprise the doctrines contained in the Confucian Classics? Or shall it also include the State religion of ancient China? . . . Or shall it also include the metaphysical and ethical philosophies which sprang up in the Sung and Ming dynasties?
> II. Shall we accept all the Sacred Books as they are? Or shall we apply to them the scientific methods of modern historical research and criticism in order to ascertain their authenticity?
> III. Shall the new Confucianism be a religion in the Chinese sense (that is *Kiao* [*chiao*], or education in its fullest meaning), or a religion in the occidental sense?
> IV. How can we adapt the Confucian teachings to the modern needs and to the modern changes?[50]

Hu made it clear that the Confucian movement he had in mind should be a strictly intellectual movement.

> Confucianism can never hope to be revived by any official formulation of its rituals of worship, nor by a mere constitutional or statutory provision, nor by the re-introduction of the study of Confucian classics into the schools.[51]

Thus, Hu's defense of China before his homecoming in 1917, though often invoking remote ideals and institutions, was apparently motivated by his practical concerns. It was indeed China's ever dangerous and deteriorating position in international politics that prompted him to write on behalf of his native land. The Japanese aggression in the 1930s and 1940s constituted one of his constant concerns, and he took pains to put forth China's best face and to underscore Japan's shortcomings before his Western audience. He claimed in the early 1930s that behind the astounding successes of Japan's modernization program lay serious problems. Even the most farsighted Japanese leaders "could only see and understand certain superficial phases of the Western civilization." In their eagerness to preserve their national heritage and strengthen the state, the Japanese retained a great many worthy as well as less commendable elements of their indigenous culture. The latter included the lowly position of women, the Shinto religion, and, not the least of all, the "peculiar extra-constitutional powers of the military caste in the government." On the other hand, in China's modernization,

> If anything is retained of the old, or any of the old things are thrown overboard, both the conservation and the change have been voluntary and probably practical and reasonable. . . . In this way China has also succeeded in bringing about a cultural transformation, which, though painfully slow and piecemeal, and often lacking coordination and coherence, may yet culminate in solving some of our pressing and basic problems of life and culture, and achieve a new civilization not incompatible with the spirit of the new world.[52]

When he was appointed ambassador to Washington in 1938, Hu faced a painful choice. Unable and unwilling to defend contemporary China and yet representing his country during one of its most difficult times, he chose to follow what he considered to be the least compromising course of action: talking before the American public about distant Chinese ideals and achievements and China's potentials. Among other things, Hu spoke of the foundation of democracy and intellectual freedom tracing back to the times of Confucius and Mencius.[53] As discussed earlier, he intimated to Elmer Eugene Barker that his propaganda did not cost the Chinese government anything. We might add that, in his own mind, neither did it compromise him.

Hu was ever mindful of the implication a favorable presentation of Chinese tradition before a foreign audience could have. Immediately after he proposed to reinterpret Chinese philosophy in light of modern logic and science in his dissertation, he reflected that his effort in that regard was not "prompted by a desire to claim for China the honor of *priority* in the discovery of those [Chinese logical] methods and theories which have hitherto been regarded as exclusively occidental in origin. I am the last man to take pride in priority as such." Rather, his interest in Chinese logic was "primarily a pedagogical one," and one of the purposes of his research was to demonstrate to his fellow Chinese that "these [logical] methods of the West are not totally alien to the Chinese mind, and that on the contrary, they are the instruments by means of which and in the light of which much of the lost treasures of Chinese philosophy can be recovered."[54] Indeed, it was often in the "pedagogical" sense that Hu was able to retain a more detached, less emotional attitude toward the past. In his scholarly writings, he created a mental distance between himself and China's daily events. When writing in English, he was more often than not physically removed from his homeland, hence less conditioned by its bleak reality.

Even when he was writing for the Western reader, however, Hu was devastatingly negative in direct comparisons between Chinese and Western values. He wanted to make it forcefuly known where his own values lay. When "the despondent mood of a number of European writers has led to the revival of such old myths as the bankruptcy of the material civilization of the West and the superiority of the spiritual civilization of the Oriental nations,"[55] Hu unleashed his anger by virulently attacking the Oriental mentality and generously praising Western science, democracy, and social progress. In "The Civilizations of the East and the West" which, significantly, was the English version of three earlier essays, one in Japanese and two in Chinese,[56] he asked "all apologists for the spiritual civilization of the East [to] reflect on this. What spirituality is there in a civilization which tolerates such a terrible form of human slavery as the 'ricksha coolie'?" To those who pointed to the religious life of the East, Hu reminded them of "those Oriental religions whose highest deities appear on roadside in the shape of human sex organs." In contrast, he was "truly and religiously moved to bless the Hargreaveses, the Cartwrights, the Watts, the Fultons, the Stephensons, and the Fords who have devised machines to do the work for man and relieve him from much of the brutal suffering to which his Oriental neighbor is still subject." While Western science symbolized the desire to know, Oriental sages and saints simply "tried to suppress this intellectual longing of man." Whereas "the backward civilizations of the East" were doing all they could "to glorify contentment and hypnotize the people into a willingness to praise their gods and abide by their fate," the Western "religion of Democracy" and ideal of socialism were making Western civilization "fast becoming the world civilization."[57]

In 1929, a year after the publication of "The Civilizations of the East and the West," Hu suggested that China take "the attitude of whole-hearted acceptance" of modern Western civilization. There is, of course, nothing unusual about such a suggestion. What is noteworthy was Hu's brutal comparison between China and the West. Once again, he turned to his favorite subject: there had to be something "fundamentally wrong" for a civilization to have tolerated foot binding for such a long period of time. To justify his position, he insisted that

"Foot binding is not an isolated fact" and that his condemnations of Chinese values were by no means "sweeping" or "dogmatic" but rather were "the studied expressions of many years of actual observation and historical study."[58]

After all this is said, however, Hu Shih did from time to time display tender feelings toward his heritage and was often defensive before his Western audience. In the Chinese surrounding, Hu had a secure enough feeling as not to need a closer tie with the past. A savage assault on the past not only constituted no threat to his sense of identity but served as an outlet for his frustration. In his scholarly writings, the distance between himself and contemporary China was immediately lengthened, and he was able to maintain his balance. Addressing his Western audience on issues of China's modernization, Hu had still another frame of mind. The distance from China was far enough to evoke his nostalgia, and the pressure from the Western public, real and imagined, often created a need to justify his beloved country. Whereas many of his favorable writings in English were calculated defenses of China's cause in international politics, not all of these writings can be construed as such, and even those calculated defenses probably also fulfilled a purpose of psychological gratification. In his favorable essays, Hu consistently depicted a China that had in its possession what he regarded as the universal values—democracy, scientific spirit and method, egalitarian principles as demonstrated in the social structure and the civil service examination, a tradition of intellectual freedom, and a healthy this-worldly outlook. Knowing what he could and could not do, he emphasized these as remote ideals and practices which nevertheless would provide a solid foundation on which a modern China would be built.

In this regard, we find a distinct contrast between Hu's writings in English and his polemical writings in Chinese. In the latter, not only was he silent on many of the virtues discussed in the former, but the emphases in these writings were radically different. In his polemical writings, Hu never acknowledged China's tradition of democracy, intellectual freedom, and the struggle for political enlightenment. When he mentioned China's egalitarian social structure, he immediately counterbalanced it by pointing out its deadly effects on the development of China's leadership class. Though he briefly touched on such virtues as loyalty, filial piety, benevolence, and compassion in Chinese thought, he deprived them of their central place in Chinese culture by making them universal values treasured by all civilizations and by insisting that, never having been implemented, these concepts remained empty terms. In his polemical Chinese writings, Buddhism conquered China because China was able to produce no more than primitive religious systems. In his English writings, though China for a while succumbed to Buddhism, "the humanistic and rationalistic mentality of the [Chinese] race did not give up the fight in despair" and gradually built up "a secular philosophy and a humanistic civilization."[59]

Hu Shih's defensiveness was always conspicuous when he felt a direct threat. One of the first such incidents was his brief but spirited defense of the arranged marriage when he was in America, feeling keenly uncomfortable about his own betrothal. His views on scientific method and spirit provided a further illustration. In his polemical Chinese writings, scientific method and spirit hardly mattered; what was really important was the subject matter of study. "An identical method, when applied to different materials, will produce divergent results." Therefore, when Western science had been producing astounding inventions and discoveries, "our scholarship was still doing somersaults in worn-out papers," referring to the Han Learning of the Ch'ing period which he said was scientific in method and spirit in all of his scholarly writings. "Our highest achievement of the past three hundred years was merely the study of a few ancient texts. What good does such a thing do to life? What is its benefit to a nation?"[60] But while Hu himself could repeatedly say cruel things about China, negative observations from his Western counterparts often provoked him. In "The Scientific Spirit and Method in Chinese Philosophy," written in the late 1950s, he reversed the position spelled out in his polemical Chinese writings

> I have deliberately left out the scientific *content* of Chinese philosophy, not merely for the obvious reason that that content seems so insignificant compared with the achievement of Western science in the last four centuries, but also because I am of the opinion that, in the historical development of science, the scientific spirit or attitude of mind and the scientific method are of far more importance than any practical or empirical results of the astronomer, the calendar-reformer, the alchemist, the physician, or the horticulturist.[61]

These remarks were aimed at none other than two of the prominent critics of the Chinese mind—Wilmon Henry Sheldon who held that "the West generated the natural sciences, as the East did not," and Filmer S. C. Northrop who insisted that "a culture which admits only concepts by intuition is automatically prevented from developing science of the Western type beyond the most elementary, inductive, natural history stage."[62] Since both Sheldon and Northrop ruled out any possibility for the Chinese to develop science, Hu had to come to his final point. Though the actual content of Chinese science was negligible, the scientific method and spirit in Chinese tradition would make the Chinese, and "sons and daughters of present-day China, feel not entirely at sea, but rather at home, in the new age of modern science."[63]

Since Hu judged the worth of a modern culture to a large extent by its achievement in science, the questions of scientific method and spirit were naturally paramount in his mind. He occasionally went out of his way to justify his fatherland in this regard. While he never argued in his Chinese writings, scholarly or polemical, that Confucianism had anything to do with science, Hu did just that in at least one of his English writings. Confucianism, he told his American colleagues,

> if correctly interpreted, will be in no sense adverse to modern scientific thinking. Not only is it my opinion that Confucianism will furnish very fertile soil on which to cultivate modern scientific thinking but Confucianism has many traditions which are quite favorable to the spirit and attitude of modern science.[64]

Hu argued in broad terms to support his contention: the Confucian agnosticism and respect for truth, its attitude of skepticism, and the so-called development of scientific learning in China from the seventeenth to the nineteenth centuries.[65]

This argument was quite arbitrary in the context of Hu's writings in general. Elsewhere Hu praised the Confucian agnosticism and skepticism only as part of the Chinese humanistic outlook, in contrast to the religious mind of Indian Buddhism, not as part of China's scientific culture. And nowhere else did Hu link the Han Learning of the Ch'ing to the Confucian ethos. In fact, this scholarship, consisting mainly of detailed philological, textual, and historical studies, was very much free of value judgment, and Hu apparently did not fail to notice this aspect.

Not surprisingly, Hu Shih himself did not initiate the argument that Confucianism fostered scientific spirit and thinking; it was forced on him. His remarks were in response to the question "concerning the relationship between modern scientific thinking and Confucianism" raised at a symposium on world religion. That Confucianism was considered a religious system by the organizers of the symposium and that he was regarded as a Confucian by at least one participant offended him. Such circumstances rendered his position quite difficult. Hu had to disclaim himself as a Confucian, which he did, and he had to argue that Confucianism was not a religion but a philosophic system conducive to scientific thinking.[66] Having done these things, Hu felt secure no matter how his relationship with Confucianism was perceived by his Western colleagues.

The modern world was a threatening place for Hu Shih. To respond to the challenge, he sometimes had to be "in search of something in Chinese tradition from which he could derive a sense of self-respect as a Chinese to counteract his genuine sense of the inferiority of Chinese tradition in the face of his adopted Western values."[67]

Hu Shih's consciousness was very complex and manifested itself on several different levels, providing evidence for both his apologists and detractors to eulogize or discredit him. But to categorize him in any one manner is to draw a simplistic picture of a complicated man living in a difficult age. What we can say is that Hu's position, perceived as a whole, was ambiguous and out of focus. Hu's contribution was negative but nonetheless enormously important: to underscore in forcible language the obsolescence of many elements in Chinese tradition. But so preoccupied with either attacking or defending the past before different groups, so deeply affected by China's contemporary plight, so bitterly aroused by the injustice, suffering, and wrongs in China's past, and so sapped by petty quarrels with his compatriots was he that he left largely unfinished the equally urgent task of "an internal assimilation of the old and the new."

Chapter 10

Classical Scholarship

Whether Hu wrote to offer solutions for problems of China's modernization, to engage in polemical debates, or for the consumption of Western readers, it was a burdensome experience. For pleasure, for respite, and for a truce with himself, he turned to something remote and unengaging. It was in classical scholarship that Hu found what he badly needed: a few moments of joy and an escape from China's harsh reality. There were many reasons why classical scholarship was an attractive field to many modern Chinese. The primary reason was their intrinsic interest in it. Moreover, the paucity and poverty of scholarship on contemporary China, along with the absurd and yet voluminous political writings, made modern scholarship a scorned field. Conversely, the exquisite classical language, the sense of awe and mystery which classical scholarship evokes, the inveterate Chinese attitude of respect for the past and for the written records of the bygone era made the study of the distant past highly appealing.

But there was more. One of the most painful experiences for a Chinese intellectual was to learn to identify himself with the modern history of his own country. Fairbank puts the problem in this way:

> As in Western countries . . . intense nationalism . . . had its influence on the writing of history and our understanding of what happened. The Meiji period has been well documented by Japanese historians with a natural pride in Japan's accomplishments. In China of the same period the collapse of the old order left only a few loyal chroniclers and only a prolonged tragedy for them to record.[1]

The problem was indeed petrifying. How could a modern Chinese face the history of his own time and feel comfortable? Fairbank's passage partially explains why Chinese scholarship on modern China was so underdeveloped. How many humiliated peoples have ever written their own contemporary histories? But the problem here went beyond one of national pride and had deep psychological roots. A modern Chinese often felt that the world was beyond his comprehension and that he had lost control of his own destiny. As Susanne Langer has written, "[Man] can adapt himself somehow to anything his imagination can cope with; but he cannot deal with Chaos. Because his characteristic function and highest asset is conception, his greatest fright is to meet what he cannot construe—the 'uncanny,' as it is popularly called."[2] To avoid the history of modern China was to try to mitigate the feeling of impotence; to immerse oneself in remote scholarship was an attempt to seek something unchanging and permanent.

Classical scholarship rendered an indispensable function. As a subject, it was distant but delightful; it was abstruse and yet could be readily grasped, analyzed, and made sense of. It at once provided immense joy and offered one of a few available means by which a Chinese could try to create an inner world of his own. Classical scholarship, then, had a "psychic closing-off" effect. Robert Jay Lifton explains that "resembling the psychological defense of denial, and the behavioral state of apathy, psychic closing-off is . . . a distinctive pattern of response to overwhelmingly threatening stimuli." It "conveys a threefold process: numbing of affect, symbolic walling-off of the organism, and abrupt disconnection in communication between inner and outer worlds."[3]

Hu Shih understood early and clearly this particular function of classical scholarship. In December, 1914, he intimated,

> the German literary master Goethe said to himself: "Whenever there are major mind-disturbing happenings in politics, I always exhort myself to engage in some kinds of scholarship absolutely unrelated to these events in order to stabilize my mind." Therefore, in the most critical moment of the Napoleonic war, Goethe was daily involved in the study of Chinese culture. . . .
>
> This is really worth pondering. [Hsü] I-sun wrote me, saying: "Chu-ko Liang [181–234], who vowed to die on the line of duty, had the unusual wisdom to decide to be an eremite at Nan-yang. Because he was well aware that, despite his deep desire, he simply could not help the situation. As such, the best course of action on his part was to cultivate his strength in order that he might be able to emerge

again if opportunities should arise." This coincides [with Goethe's thinking].[4]

Hu offered Goethe as an example of self-discipline to Edith Clifford Williams who was feeling despondent after her application to be a nurse at the war front was turned down by the Red Cross. But let there be no doubt that Hu was also speaking of his own mind. In March, 1915, three months after he wrote the passage on Goethe and when the crisis of the Twenty-one Demands was building up, he advised his fellow students not to get excited. For no matter how much they loved China, they would not be able to help it anyway. "No telegrams or letters will ever stop the nation's calamity." Instead, calamities like the Twenty-one Demands should be faced "calmly."[5]

That many of his fellow students disagreed with him did not deter his determination. When Yüan Shih-k'ai's monarchism began, he resolved even more firmly not to be affected. Writing Hsü I-sun on January 25, 1916, Hu argued that neither the monarchical movement nor foreign encroachment or even "national destruction" was "worth our concern." He had an invincible logic: if China had the quality that would prevent it from perishing, then China would not perish; if China did not possess that quality, then our confused uproar would not prevent China from perishing. It would be better, Hu said, that "we make good resolutions and, starting from the very foundation, create new causes for our fatherland that will enable it to endure. Then, if China should perish, it would still be revived someday."[6] The "new causes" to which Hu alluded were the transformed qualities which he thought China should possess. He was forced to take an intellectual approach exclusively, "starting from the very foundation." This intellectual approach ostensibly had a quality of imperturbability toward any crisis, however grave or imminent it might be. Beneath the surface, however, it was a different story. Studies of philosophy, philology, and literature of the distant past that Hu was undertaking were aimed as much at saving his beloved country as saving his own sanity.

Having thus established his position, Hu clung to it throughout much of his remaining life. He never seriously contemplated becoming an eremite Chu-ko Liang. In 1925, he again gave the example of Goethe as a way of self-discipline and of gaining inner peace at a time of great turmoil.[7] In June, 1932, when China was moving steadily closer to an all-out war with Japan and the nation's mood was definitely turning darker, Hu offered some "prescriptions" to the graduating college students for their self-defense. To make the best of the circumstances, he advised, students should develop interests outside their occupations.

> With a hobby that you love, you will not feel dispirited after sitting behind a desk for six hours. Because you know that, after going home, you can do your chemical research, or paint landscape paintings, or write novels and plays, or continue your textual studies of history, or engage yourself in works of social reform.[8]

Although he mentioned "works of social reform," what Hu really had in mind was something less engaging, the potential practical application of which would nevertheless be significant. Nothing would be wasted in the end, he insisted, and anything intellectual could be justified, including the distant and seemingly unrelated classical scholarship.[9] His own choice was the highly obscure textual studies.

Hu Shih was exhorting the college graduates not to feel discouraged under extreme adversity. But it turned out to be a difficult task to keep his own spirits up. In May, 1948, when the entire country had plunged into the civil war, he wrote from Peking University to Chao Yüan-jen at Berkeley, California.

> Even at this time I still hope that Yüan-jen can come to teach at *Peita* (Peking University). Life here is not that comfortable, but it also offers many pleasures. (I am still playing with my *Commentary on the Book of Waterways* [*Shui-ching chu*] and can sometimes work on it for seven or eight hours a day!)[10]

In August, 1949, having by this time arrived in the United States, Hu wrote Chao again.

> I am thinking of returning to do a few things which I am capable of doing. But, first, I definitely will not accept any political offices. Second, I will not play with textual studies either. (You will probably notice the difference in the tone of the two sentences!)[11]

Hu Shih was, after all, quite conscious of what he had been doing. "Playing" with *Commentary on the Book of Waterways* and other textual works had little to do with what he regarded as national affairs, and the guilt feeling was noticeable.

In the United States, Hu's life as an expatriate was by no means pleasant: he was doubtful of his destination and future plans, embarrassed by his unemployability, and worried with his status as an alien. After strenuous efforts by his friends, he was appointed at Princeton University in May, 1950, as "Fellow of the University Library and Curator of the Gest Oriental Library with the rank of full professor." This was an honorary post with stipend to last for two years. In his agonizing moments, Hu submerged himself in rare books and remote classics. "Princeton's Gest Library is an 'antique book storage' which should be useful for me,"[12] he said with a sarcastic anticipation. After moving to New York City following the curatorship at Princeton, he concentrated once more on *Commentary on the Book of Waterways*. To his friends and visitors, he was fond of saying, with more than a slight trace of self-ridicule, that it was his "ivory tower."[13]

But the "ivory tower," the inner world thus created, was to be exposed from time to time. This ivory tower offered no more than a temporary peace; and the price paid for such a respite was heavy. We shall now look at the problems associated with the obsession with remote scholarship from a broader perspective.

Pai Hsien-yung, one of the most astute observers of the modern Chinese dilemma, gives us a poignant fictional account of a man who tries to create a world far removed from the contemporary age. Wu Chu-kuo, a professor of Chinese history at the University of California, goes back to Taiwan to visit Yü Chin-lei, a friend dating back to the days of Peking National University and a professor of English literature at the Taiwan National University. Their rendezvous turns out to be a sad occasion for painful confessions.

> Wu Chu-kuo . . . leaned forward toward Professor Yü and said, "Let me tell you something, Chin-lei. Most of the courses I give at universities abroad cover Chinese history only up to the T'ang or Sung Dynasty. I've never offered a course on the Republican era. Last semester, at the University of California, I gave a course on the 'Political Institutions of the T'ang Dynasty.' This was when student riots were at their peak in America. Our students were the worst. . . . They were sitting in the classroom, but they could not keep their eyes off the disturbances outside. So I put down my book and asked: "Is this what you call a 'student riot'? More than forty years ago, the students in Peking started a revolt which was many times more ferocious than yours." . . .
> Seeing that I had their attention, I slowly announced: 'The per-

son who led the group that beat up the envoy to Japan and that was later jailed is standing here in front of you.' The whole room roared with laughter, some of the students stamping their feet, others clapping. . . .

"They all asked at once how we attacked Chao's Pavilion. So I told them that we formed a human pyramid and climbed into Ts'ao Ju-lin's house on each other's shoulders. The first man who jumped over the wall lost his shoes and then, barefooted, ran like mad all over the court yard setting fire to everything in sight. 'Where's that student now?' they asked in unison, and I said, 'He is teaching in a university in Taiwan, teaching Byron.' They laughed hysterically."

Professor Yü blushed instantly and his wrinkled face broke into a boyish smile. . . .

"Well, last year, I was at a convention of the Oriental History Association in San Francisco. In one session there was an American student freshly graduated from Harvard, who read a paper entitled 'A Re-evaluation of the May Fourth Movement.' From the start this young fellow tore the movement to pieces. He reached his conclusions with a self-righteous eloquence. These fanatic young Chinese intellectuals, he said, in an iconoclastic outburst against tradition thoroughly rejected the Confucian system that had prevailed in China for over two thousand years. They were ignorant of the current condition of their country, they blindly worshiped Western culture, and had superstitious faith in Western democracy and science. This created an unprecedented confusion in the Chinese intellectual climate. Moreover, these young people, who had been brought up in a patriarchal society, had neither independent ideas of their own nor enough will power. As the Confucian tradition collapsed, they immediately found themselves without their only source of spiritual sustenance. Gripped by a sense of panic, they began to wander about like patricidal sons haunted by the spectre of a murdered father. They had overthrown Confucius, their spiritual father, and so they had to carry the burden of their crime. Thus began the long journey of their spiritual self-exile. . . . Then he concluded: 'Some Chinese scholars like to compare the May Fourth Movement to a Chinese Renaissance. But I consider it, at best, a miscarried renaissance!' By the time he finished reading the paper, there was a great deal of excitement in the room, especially among the Chinese professors and students, who turned to look at me, obviously expecting some sort of rebuttal. But I didn't say a thing, and after a while, quietly left the room."

"But, Chu-Kuo. . . .'

"To tell you the truth, Chin-lei, some of the youngster's conclusions wouldn't be difficult to refute. The only thing is . . . " Wu Chu-kuo spoke with a lump in his throat. He then gave a nervous laugh. "Just think, Chin-lei. For several decades, I have been a plain deserter living abroad. On an occasion like that, how could I have mustered enough self-respect to stand and speak up for the May Fourth Movement? That's why, too, in all my expatriate days, I've never talked about the history of the Republican period. That time at the University of California I saw how excited the students were in the middle of their movement, so I mentioned May Fourth on the spur of the moment only to humor them—it was no more than a joke. The glories of the past are after all easier to talk about. I can tell my students without feeling ashamed at all, 'The T'ang Dynasty created the most powerful, and culturally the most brilliant, empire in the world at that time.' And I have been talking like this all these years abroad. Sometimes I couldn't help laughing to myself and feeling like one of Emperor Hsüan Tsung's white-haired court ladies, who just kept telling foreigners the anecdotes of the T'ien-pao reign." . . .

Outside, the rain came down more heavily, and the cold kept creeping into the room through every available crack along the door and windows. Suddenly the front door opened and banged shut, and a young man entered from the vestibule. . . .

"Chü-yen, come meet Uncle Wu," Professor Yü called to the young man. Wu Chu-kuo glanced briefly at his fine, handsome face. . . .

"Uncle Wu teaches at the University of California. Didn't you say you would like to study there? Well, why don't you ask Uncle Wu about it?"

"Uncle Wu, is it easy to get a fellowship in Physics at the University of California?" Chün-yen asked with interest.[14]

Pai Hsien-yung, himself an expatriate, has his own motif, but some general observations can still be extracted from his story. We find some interesting parallels between Professor Wu Chu-kuo and Hu Shih. Wu teaches traditional Chinese history, as Hu taught ancient Chinese philosophy. Wu derives his few pleasures from dwelling on the glories and accomplishments of the T'ang and Sung, as Hu took delight in the remote textual studies. Wu was a red-blooded activist in the May Fourth period, as Hu was a conscientious spokesman for China's causes. They both had their burdens to carry. Hu's defense of China was accompanied by an uneasy feeling. Considering himself a "plain deserter," Wu cannot even muster "enough self-respect" to defend either his own position or the history of his fatherland. Hu wrote on contemporary China with violent rage and biting cynicism, while Wu simply wants to cease to be a contemporary being and lives in a world of nostalgic reminiscences and profound sorrow. On rare occasions when he does comment on contemporary issues, he does so with an ambiguous, self-condemning tone. The May Fourth will only be mentioned, not discussed or debated. And mentioning it is "no more than a joke."

Hu Shih and Wu Chu-Kuo might well have derived some psychological satisfaction from defending China's interests and dwelling on the past glories, as Levenson would have suggested. Be that as it may, this aspect should not be overemphasized. Certainly, they felt powerless and insecure in the general surroundings, and an emphasis on China's past achievements could have offered them a compensation. As individuals, however, they were conceited, highly sensitive, and self-conscious. All along, Wu Chu-kuo is well aware that "most of the courses I give at universities abroad cover Chinese history only up to the T'ang or Sung Dynasty," that "sometimes I couldn't help laughing to myself and feeling like one of Emperor Hsüan-tsung's white-haired court ladies, who just kept telling foreigners the anecdotes of the T'ien-pao reign." So Hu Shih was only too conscious of his defense of China, of his "selfish wish." The T'ang and Sung glories on which they dwelt and the defenses they developed were as much emotional needs to obtain psychological compensation as a conscious self-deception for a few moments of indulgence.

It is the good fortune of Wu Chu-kuo, who is talented enough to teach at Berkeley, and Hu Shih, who had more freedom than most of his compatriots, that they were able to be expatriates at certain points of their life's journeys. What does one do if one is not fortunate enough to be or does not choose to be an expatriate? One teaches Byron, as does Professor Yü Chin-lei, to maintain a distance between oneself and reality. But Professor Yü is much crippled by arthritis, as was his hero Byron a cripple.

But none of these defenses—immersing oneself in unrelated textual studies, teaching history of remote periods, and studying a subject which had nothing to do with China—were viable solutions. Although by manipulatiing and interpreting something remote and unrelated, these individuals gained a sense of command and control, yet precisely because these subjects were so unengaging, unrelated, and remote, they more sharply enhanced the feeling of impotence of these men. Here was a problem that they could not solve. Deprived of the most fundamental, indispensable prerequisite for reform—political power and stability—and forced to resort to intellectual approach alone, they were reduced to being either debilitated protesters or self-condemning complainants, characterized by an inveterate feeling of anger and alienation. Small wonder that some of them often thought of giving up their endeavors altogether. Hu Shih conveyed in 1928 this terrifying vision to China's youth:

> We hope that the youth who have the ambition to become scholars will turn their heads as early as possible and think twice. . . . Nowadays the saddest thing is that some youth follow our footsteps by crawling in the worthless worn-out papers. We hope that they will turn their heads as quickly as possible and learn as much as possible the knowledge and applications of the natural sciences. This is the road of life, whereas the one in the worn-out papers is the road of death.[15]

In the same year Fu Ssu-nien (1896–1950), being the director of the Institute of History and Philology of Academia Sinica, spoke in his very first address in that capacity.

> History and philology of course do have some bearings on education, but they are not necessarily the things which are of the national scope or have enduring values. A dozen or so scholastics of the old academy type who would waste away their lives on this unproductive activity would be enough to symbolize our nation's respect for scholarship of this kind. This thing is of no worth after all, and we naturally need not lure others into it.[16]

And Ting Ling, the celebrated writer, offered the following self-assessment in the spring of 1930.

> I sometimes feel that it would not be a serious loss if we gave it up entirely. We write, and a handful of people read. Time passes and there is no influence whatsoever. What is the meaning of all this except that we get paid for it? . . . Now I realize that we have done something harmful; we are dragging these young people onto our old path. Some sentimentalism, individualism, grumblings or sorrows with no way out! . . . Where is the way out? They will only sink deeper, day by day, into their raging moroseness, not seeing the relation between society and their sufferings. Even if they could improve their language and produce some good essays and poems that win praise from some old writers, what good, tell me, is that to them? And what good to society? Therefore, with regard to writing, personally I am willing to give it up.[17]

These were frightening revelations. The best minds of modern China openly denounced their chosen occupations, regarding their endeavors as worthless, and spoke of others in the field as being "lured." History, creative writing, and philosophy were dead ends for Hu Shih, ornaments for Fu Ssu-nien, and harmful and meaningless in the eyes of Ting Ling. Did they really take such dim views of their lifelong devotions? We would be seriously amiss if we should take their words at their face value and consider them to be their genuine self-appraisals.

Hu Shih, Fu Ssu-nien, and Ting Ling all had their own reasons for saying what they did. Ting's valedictory indicated "a swing from passive sentimentality to revolutionary frenzy."[18] Hu Shih and Fu Ssu-nien were in the main emphasizing the importance of science as a subject matter. But these explanations are not explanations after all. To be sure, sorrowful and sentimental literature had no meaning to Ting as a revolutionary. But why didn't she produce literature that was free from the problems she mentioned? Was not literature an important tool to serve "the people"? Why were Hu and Fu being so superfluous as to advocate the importance of science in twentieth-century China? Listen to Hu Shih's own words written five years earlier.

> During the past thirty years there is one term which has acquired a supreme position of respect in the country. Whether people understand it or not, whether they are conservative or progressive, they all dare not publicly reveal an attitude of contempt toward it. That term is "Science." Whether this almost universal worship is of value or not is another question. The least we can say is that ever since the Reform Movement of the 1890s, there is no one who calls himself a forward-looking person who dares openly belittle science.[19]

Did Hu Shih, Fu Ssu-nien, and Ting Ling really want to give up their devotions and turn away from the "road of death"? Far from it. They continued producing literature and writing on the pre-Ch'in history, ancient philosophy, history of Buddhism, and historiography. In fact, as they were writing these mordant things about their own occupations, they were also mourning the fact that not enough people took those disciplines seriously. Hu Shih in 1919 gave this advice to Mao Tzu-shui, a student at Peking National University and later a professor of Chinese literature at Taiwan National University.

> I believe that, as researchers, we should not take a narrow, utilitarian position. A scholar should consider his propensity in choosing a field and take the attitude of "truth for the sake of truth.". . . All the branches of knowledge are equal: discovering the original meaning of a character is as worthy as discovering a star.[20]

Hu further lamented, in 1921, that people of ability simply did not want to enter the field of Chinese studies.

> It is really quite important now for us to study the classical scholarship. But the young people in general are not interested in China's classical culture and scholarship. When we speak of those who study the classical scholarship, we are speaking of a small number.[21]

Still two years later, he compiled a "minimal" bibliography for those Tsinghua University graduates who were going overseas for further studies. The purpose of this bibliography, which was extraordinary by today's standard, was for them to gain a working foundation on Chinese culture.[22]

Apparently Hu Shih, Ting Ling, and Fu Ssu-nien were telling us something else then. What is revealed in their attitude is a most excruciating, most unspeakable desideratum. Being a writer, a historian, or a philosopher in a country like China was no more than being a scapegoat whose fate was doomed. To avoid this trap, Ting Ling chose to be a revolutionary who presumably would have better control over her life. Hu Shih, by personality and conviction, could never hope to become a revolutionary. But how much he wished that he had been a scientist so that he would not have felt so impotent and helpless, so that he would not have had to be entangled in the depressing, suffocating social and political web! In a country like China, chaotic, poverty-stricken, and arbitrarily ruled by one militarist after another, who else but scientists could make greater contributions while standing outside? A scientist deals with universal values transcendent of social and political boundaries; he can be a committed person regardless of political and social conditions. While a historian, a creative writer, a philosopher was virtually on "the road of death," committing serious offenses by "luring" bright and ambitious young people, doing harmful things in the worn-out papers, a scientist was universally respected and useful, even in China. Do we not find here one of the deepest reasons why science was worshiped to such an extent in China? Was it not one of the most deep-seated reasons why nonscience subjects were despised in such a blunt and crude manner?

It was too late for Ting Ling, Fu Ssu-nien and Hu Shih to shift fields, but it was never too late to take revenge or to vent their anger and frustration. Ting did so by embracing a larger cause and by repenting for her past. Fu did so by openly demeaning his profession in an official capacity. And Hu did so by admonishing future masters of China not to follow his road of death. Ting, Fu, and Hu, however, were national figures. The mundane majority must find a different way to deal with the problem. For the semicrippled Professor Yü Chin-lei, it is to teach such an unengaging subject as Byron and to rest his only hope on his son who, "Handsome and Talented" by name, is ready to apply to Berkeley for graduate studies in physics, one of the most abstract and therefore the least socially and politically oriented subjects.

It would be a terrible injustice to say that Ting Ling, Fu Ssu-nien, and Hu Shih were solely motivated by personal feelings. Undoubtedly, Ting's decison was in a significant part prompted by a sense of justice, and Hu and Fu apparently were convinced of their own beliefs. Still, such a position as Ting's and such writings as Hu's and Fu's cannot be explained entirely in terms of commitments and beliefs. Their feeling of impotence, therefore, must have been an important factor in determining their stances. And precisely because it was partly prompted by intense personal feelings, their attitudes toward their respective fields could never be clear-cut. Rather, the attitudes were bittersweet. While they kept complaining, they continued to be fascinated with their writings and studies. Though Hu Shih struggled hard to stay aloof and remain unaffected, he also needed a sense of belonging. Classical scholarship, which was more neutral and less engaging than modern history and yet the potential implications of which were broad enough, was one of a few things that helped him maintain a proper distance and provided him with a sense of Chineseness which was so alien and yet so dear.

Part V
Epilogue

Chapter 11

The May Fourth Generation in Historical Perspective

After spending nine years in semi-exile in the United States, Hu Shih returned to Taiwan in April, 1958, to assume the presidency of Academia Sinica. By then he was an old man in failing health. Less than four years later, on the afternoon of February 24, 1962, he died of a heart attack. "So ended a life that had begun, seventy years earlier, in a time so remote in mind and custom that the stages of Hu's journey must be measured not in decades but in centuries."[1] Certainly, Hu's peregrinations covered a wide range of territories and stretched far in time. But measuring his journey in decades would be more meaningful than measuring it in centuries. Indeed, a comparison of Hu's generation with that of 1898 reform movement will reveal a subtle but significant shift of outlooks, feelings, and sense of commitment in both intellectual and personal ways.

To be sure, many of the ideas that Hu espoused had been antedated by the reform generation. As Benjamin Schwartz sums up,

> in many respects, the generation of K'ang Yu-wei, Yen Fu, Liang Ch'i-ch'ao, T'an Ssu-t'ung, Chang Ping-lin, Wang Kuo-wei and others was, in fact, the breakthrough generation; they were the real transformers of values and the bearers of new ideas from the West. Nationalism (even including that variety of nationalism which stressed the responsibility of imperialism for China's ills), the idea of progress, liberalism, Social Darwinism, and indeed the whole Faustian-Promethean thrust of modern Western culture had all found their spokesmen within this remarkable group.[2]

What is stated here could not be more true, but Schwartz further observes, "However bold and open the generation of Yen Fu and Liang Ch'i-ch'ao may have been in confronting new ideas on the intellectual plane, in terms of its personal culture it lived comfortably and even deeply within the old culture."[3] It is only when we consider intellectual views together with personal positions of the May Fourth figures that we discern a generation shift.

When K'ang Yu-wei, Yen Fu, and Liang Ch'i-ch'ao were young, studying various modern subjects was not part of their experiences. Certainly they all advocated new learning; some even studied it. But they did so as part of their adult intellectual reorientation. By Hu's time, however, a modern education had become increasingly common as many of the age-honored traditions were rapidly losing their grips. Further, the idea of going abroad to study occurred to few of the reform leaders, and they did so only as a last resort. Yen Fu's study of modern subjects and his subsequent trip to England in 1877 were fortuitous rather than by design. With the death of his father in 1866, Yen's prospects of further education leading to an official career were abruptly cut off. "It was only in the latter half of the nineteenth century . . . that the pursuit of 'Western studies' emerged as one more bleak alternative for those whose path to an official career had been blocked."[4] And it was in such a mood that Yen went abroad. Hu Shih, on the other hand, rejected the civil service examination even before its abolition in 1905. He acquired little sense of satisfaction or direction from Chinese society, and going abroad was no longer unthinkable but was becoming accepted by more and more ambitious youth. Though not without sadness and confusion, he greeted with excitement the opportunity of studying in America.[5]

Understandably, American influence on Hu Shih was prominent, both personally and intellectually. He could never again be confined to the Chinese style and values, and his attachment to his adopted land and culture was a permanent one. The American policy makers of the Boxer indemnity remission saw clearly the inevitable acculturation of Chinese students. Edmund J. James (1855–1925), president of the University of Illinois from 1904 to 1920, envisioned that a massive American educational project involving the Chinese youth would "achieve in China nothing less than 'the intellectual and spiritual domination of its leaders.' "[6] Another American predicted that Chinese students will be studying American institutions, making American friends, and coming back here to favor America for China in its foreign relations. Talk about a Chinese alliance! The return of that indemnity was the most profitable work Uncle Sam ever did. . . . They [the Chinese students] will form a force in our favor so strong that no other government or trade element of Europe can compete with it.[7]

Hu Shih was first exposed to American wealth and power at the cozy and almost idyllic Cornell campus. There were many memorable moments and unforgettable people: the academic triumphs and honors, the frequent speaking engagements, the exquisite outings to the Finger Lakes area, Edith Clifford Williams who occupied so special a place in his life, Elmer Eugene Barker, whose admiration of Hu outlasted Hu's life, William Wistar Comfort, "a friend and admirer" of Hu,[8] who exerted a strong influence on Hu in his early days at Cornell, Fred Robinson who was generous enough to have offered Hu an emergency loan of two hundred dollars. All these and more have been detailed earlier. And there were the L. E. Pattersons who became Hu's surrogate parents and who were so close to Hu that his mother even asked for their intercession in Hu's courtship with Miss Williams.[9]

Because of these warm relations and a sojourn of five precious years there, Hu's feeling toward Ithaca was tender and loving. On September 21, 1915, on his way to Columbia University, he looked back at his days at Cornell with profound melancholy.

> I finally left Ithaca on September 20. I used to say that Ithaca was my "second home." Having now parted it, I come to realize that calling it my "first home" would not be an overstatement. I have been absent from home for some eleven-odd years. Home in my memory only consists of obscure streams and mountains, of vague faces. There are my mother, sisters, a teacher, and a friend; nothing else evokes my passion or memory. . . . But Ithaca's streams, gorges, mentors and friends are vivid in my mind. These five years are the most important period in my life. The friends I have made, the treatment I have received, the people I have met, the experiences I have had, and the knowledge I have acquired are the results of my own efforts and fortune, which cannot be compared with the externally imposed concept of native identity and which certainly will have a greater influence on my future than my childhood experiences. What is more moving is that the folks of Ithaca never took me as an outsider. Though not one of its citizens, I had the opportunity to observe its social and political events, customs, religious practices, the strengths

and deficiencies of its educational system. Because of all these, I regard myself as a member of the Ithaca community. Now I am parting it, how can I not be amorous?[10]

While he genuinely appreciated the opportunity to study abroad, Hu was fully aware of the devastating effect of not having a higher educational system of one's own. In early 1915, he put forward a plan for establishing first-rate universities in China.[11] A conversation on February 20, 1915, with his English professor at Cornell, John Quincy Adams, Jr., painfully revealed what Hu was going through.

> The professor asked: "Does China have universities?" I could not answer. . . . He said: "If China wishes to preserve its cultural heritage and create a new culture, it must have its own universities. . . . No national affair is as urgent as establishing universities. . . ." I told him my proposals concerning guidelines of establishing national universities. . . . The professor heartily expressed his approval. . . . Further, he said that if China should have a first rate university, he would donate the several thousand volumes of classical and modern English drama in his collection, which took the professor fifteen years to build . . . spending no less than five hundred dollars each year. I promised that I would render all my effort to promote [my plan], and in behalf of the universities in my dream, I thanked him for his noble friendship. . . .
> If someday I should be able to see a national university in China to rival this country's Harvard, England's Cambridge and Oxford, Germany's Berlin, France's Paris, I truly would not have any regrets when I die. Alas! Where would the place be in the world for a big country of four million square miles and of four hundred million people that has no universities! Where would the place be for a country that has no universities![12]

To his dismay, Hu learned that Columbia University's annual budget for the 1915–16 academic year was $3,897,350, "surpassing the annual budget of Shensi, Shansi, Honan, Sinkiang, Hunan, Kiangsi, Anhwei, Chekiang, Fukien, Kwangsi, or Kueichow."[13]

Hu never gave up the idea of achieving China's educational independence. In 1948, he once again put forward plans for establishing national universities of quality. Such a goal did not appear unreasonable to him. The University of Chicago was founded in 1891 by a grant of twenty million dollars from the Rockefeller Foundation, he pointed out; and the Johns Hopkins University, under the presidency of Daniel

Coit Gilman (1831-1908), became a leader in graduate studies. "What a private foundation could do," Hu maintained, "a legitimate country as a matter of course will be able to do more easily."[14] This seemingly simple objective, however, would remain his lifelong unfulfilled wish.

But problems involving China's higher education were more complicated than Hu envisioned. The lack of self-confidence of the Chinese people and the absence of an indigenous belief system contributed in no small degree to China's inability to achieve its independence. Anything with a foreign touch was automatically considered superior. Ting Wen-chiang wrote George Ernest Morrison, an adviser to Yüan Shih-k'ai, in May, 1912, concerning an incident during the 1911 Revolution.

> On arriving home [in T'ai-hsing, Kiangsu] I found that the people were also in a great panic, for the town had declared for the Revolutionaries after the fall of Soochow, and the disorderly element began to take full advantage of the change. The gentry asked me to organize a local guard, thinking that since I had been abroad I was capable of doing anything and everything in the world. . . . I was greatly astonished at the easiness with which order could be kept, for though the crops were especially bad last year and there were many unemployed people about town, we kept perfect order for more than a month with nothing better than rusty old swords.[15]

The feeling of omnipotence of the foreign-educated Chinese by their compatriots was cultivated partly by none other than the foreign-educated elite themselves. Spending several of their impressionable years in a foreign land could not but have an indelible effect on their psyche and outlook. The impact was far-reaching because the Chinese went as individuals of a subjugated nation to conquering nations for enlightenment. Going to the West usually in their teens, many of these individuals went through the transformation from late adolescence to early adulthood in Western surroundings and owed their entire academic credentials and much of their intellectual growth to Western universities. Many of them matured and discovered themselves as a result of their foreign experiences. Naturally, many of the foreign-educated Chinese formed an unbreakable bond with their host countries. To promote their host countries was in many ways to promote their own worth.

It was fashionable in the May Fourth generation to mention Dewey, Russell, Byron, Wordsworth, science, democracy, and a host of other catchwords. Not a few of the Chinese openly flaunted their foreign degrees and boasted their Western connections. After returning to China from England in 1922, Hsü Chih-mo (1896–1931) delivered one of his first lectures at Tsinghua University.

> Unfortunately, the important messages contained in the lecture, "Art and Life," escaped the attention of the young audience, because Hsü had chosen to flaunt his acquired British style by reading his paper in English with pedantic air of an Oxford don.[16]

Hu Shih had his share of this mentality. While his feeling toward Cornell was spontaneous, his attachment to Columbia was a more calculated one. For years, he misled his fellow countrymen into believing that he earned his Ph.D. at Columbia in 1917 while at best he received the degree in 1927, or he might never have had one. Compiling the *Columbia University Master's Essays and Doctoral Dissertations on Asia, 1875–1956* as part of the Columbia bicentennial celebration project, Howard P. Linton was surprised that he could not find any record on Hu. A few years later, Yüan T'ung-li, compiling *A Guide to Doctoral Dissertations by Chinese Students in America, 1905–1960*, was equally puzzled that many so-called Chinese Ph.D.'s, Hu included, simply had no records to be verified. But even then, Hu's degree was not a matter of public knowledge; not until the late 1970s did T. K. T'ang reveal some of its details.[17]

Hu Shih's tampering with his degree, defended by T. K. T'ang as a trivial matter, had its unfortunate implications. The degree he flaunted happened to be an American degree, and the intended recipients of this false information happened to be his compatriots. The language Hsü Chih-mo flaunted happened to be English, and the audience he intimidated happened to be his own students. Thus, we have a great historical irony here. Sending students abroad, intended to help China regain its independence, became a double-edged sword. It helped enlighten the nation on the one hand while on the other put it in a deeper cultural and psychological bind. The returned students became the first group of Chinese who acquired an intimate grasp of Western culture, society, and politics, whereas their attachment to the West also became irrevocable.

Close contact with and better knowledge of the West affected other aspects of Hu's life as well. Apropos of Christianity, he shared some common ground with his predecessors. Both Hu and the earlier reformers came under its influence, and they all judged it for its value in influencing morals. But the similarities ended here. According to Hsiao Kung-chuan, K'ang Yu-wei first came into contact with Christian ideas in Hong Kong in 1879. While the impact of Christianity on his thinking was strong, K'ang's knowledge of the religion was fragmentary and superficial. Perceiving Christianity from a secular point of view, he considered it inferior not only to Confucianism but to Buddhism as well. More important, "Christianity, together with Buddhism, strengthened K'ang's Confucian convictions and induced him to promote Confucianism as a religion."[18] This sense of confidence was indeed one of the sharp contrasts that separated the two generations. Even Wang T'ao (1828–97), one of the earliest Chinese exposed to Western culture at close range, was not deprived of this feeling. Wang was baptized in 1854 and spent a good part of his life working for or with foreigners.

> Yet, in the later decades of his life Wang T'ao voiced criticism of both the missionary movement and Christianity, and he consistently pointed to Confucius as the historical figure whose elucidation of *tao* came closest to perfection.[19]

In comparison, Hu Shih showed no such confidence. There is reason to believe that, encountering Christianity for the first time in a foreign culture, he responded to it more intensely than even Wang T'ao did, and his revolt against it was also more impassioned. But Hu never tried to solicit the authority of Confucianism to discredit Christianity, nor did he ever make a direct comparison of the two. While his criticism of Christianity and the missionary movement was severe, he did not favor a complete break with the missionary enterprise in China. This ambivalence was largely absent among members of the generation of the 1898 reform.

Hu Shih displayed ambivalent feelings in still another area, that of his attitude toward his own country. This ambivalence was not shared by the reform generation whose obsession was the nation-state. Yen Fu devoted almost his entire attention to the question of national wealth and power. As Schwartz puts it, to Yen, "values, institutions, ideas—the whole content of culture—must be judged in terms of one criterion: will it preserve and strengthen the nation-state?"[20] Like Yen,

Liang Ch'i-ch'ao "stood in the mainstream of Chinese nationalism." It would be a reflection of barbarism, he said, for human loyalty to stop short of or go beyond the focus of nation-state. "In this way, the nation-state became for Liang the 'terminal community.' "[21] The reform generation, of course, was more complicated than the above description can do justice to. K'ang Yu-wei, for instance, was a utopian who envisioned a universal community based on values that transcended national boundaries and vested interests. So meticulous and radical was his plan that Hsiao Kung-chuan calls him "justifiably China's first utopian writer who, by virtue of the boldness of his conceptions, was a worthy colleague of the great utopians of other lands."[22]

But K'ang was able to be bold and radical because his commitment was abstract. While all utopian ideas grow out of dissatisfaction with the present and all utopians are critics of their age, K'ang's utopianism was not a direct criticism of the cruelty of Chinese and foreign institutions, or of high-handed imperialism. He spoke of the evils, injustices, and wounds inflicted on each other by mankind in either historical or universal terms, and the utopia he envisaged would be realized only in the millennial future. Hsiao Kung-chuan points out that K'ang's thinking constantly moved on two levels. At one level, "he disengaged himself from concerns with immediate situations and sallied forth into theorizations and speculations which had little direct contact with reality."[23] K'ang's utopian thinking, in other words, did not lead him to question the nation-state as the ultimate focus of loyalty, and it lacked a personal immediacy and an existential experience.

Hu Shih and others of the May Fourth period were no less patriotic than K'ang Yu-wei and his generation, but Hu's patriotism was definitely more reflective than instinctive. In terms of the attitude toward the nation, the May Fourth period moved in two directions. On the one hand, nationalistic feeling reached a new height, affecting virtually everyone who could read and write. This phenomenon was so obvious that most historians have chosen to emphasize it. What is less visible was the growing cosmopolitan sentiment which, though confined to a small group of the better educated, was quite articulate and highly significant. We have noted Hu's outcry against his own country and the brutal reasonings of foreign critics of China. Kao I-han (1885–), too, seriously questioned whether one should be unconditionally loyal to one's own country. A nation, he held, is no more than a means for the fulfillment of individual potentials and for the realization of a world civilization.[24] Ch'en Tu-hsiu echoed the same sentiment, only more strongly: "A nation exists to protect the rights of its citizens and promote their well-being. If it cannot fulfill these duties, then even if one has a nation, one has nothing to be proud of, and even if one's country is destroyed, one has nothing to regret about." Were not Indians and Koreans, who were under the British and Japanese rule, respectively, better off than the Chinese? The Jews, who had no country of their own, were known for their ability to advance their economic interests and personal well-being. On the other hand, "in our vast country, only those Chinese living in the foreign settlements enjoy peace and freedom." While he did not reject it, Ch'en did insist that patriotism should be accompanied by a rational understanding as to what a nation means and what it should stand for.[25]

Many of the May Fourth elite passionately longed for a more tolerant and understanding world. In advocating their cause, they showed an appreciation of the plight of not only their own country but also all oppressed and humiliated peoples. At the same time, their feeling toward their own country became conditional, and they were never again able to defend it without reservation and often criticized it severely. For them the primary purpose of a nation-state was not to bring national glory but to offer them dignity and peace. Thus, cosmopolitanism, unlike K'ang Yu-wei's utopianism, was intimately related to the existential experience of the May Fourth elite and symbolized their urgent quest for meaning.

Speaking of their existential commitment, nothing set these May Fourth elite figures apart more unequivocally from the reform generation than their attitude toward their marriages. The latter, for all its radicalness in ideas, took much of the traditional culture for granted in personal life. Yen Fu attacked various facets of the family system in China, particularly the subjugation of women. But

> the stamp of tradition on what might be called his personal culture remained indelible. Whatever his opinion of this or that aspect of the traditional culture, he does not view it from the outside. In his own individual existence, as a matter of fact, he remains a traditional gentleman no matter how far his ideas on general political and social ideas may stray.[26]

In him, we find "no evidence whatsoever of revolt against any of the traditional ways in matters of emotional life," and "the demand for sexual freedom or romantic love" was irrelevant to the transformation of values that he advocated.[27]

K'ang Yu-wei was by far the most radical member of the reform generation; his views on marriage and women would probably disturb many liberated people today. A union between man and woman, he proposed, should never be made permanent but rather be limited to a short period of time. "It is only human nature that people succumb to temptations, that their passion extinguishes after a while, and that they always prefer new and more attractive partners."[28] K'ang charged that men treated women as "toys" and "slaves" who wore heavy makeup, tightened their waists and bound their feet to please men, and who had no human dignity, much less freedom of marriage or right to participate in politics. He argued for complete freedom for women, including the freedom of education, of selecting their mates, of holding offices, and of retaining their family names after marriage. Foot binding and other customs that enslaved women should be abolished.[29] But here again K'ang spoke of these ideas as distant future possibilities without a personal commitment.

> What has been said above is intended only to serve as a plan of future progress. If at present, when the education of women is incomplete and their personal character is not fully developed, we recklessly apply the rule of independence to women who would turn their backs on their husbands and give free rein to lustful passions, we would then open the road to chaos. "Linens for summer; furs for winter": to everything its appointed time. Until we have arrived at that time, we must not prematurely apply this rule.[30]

K'ang's personal conduct attested to what he meant. In 1897 he took a concubine because at forty he still had not had a son. Then in 1907, five years after he finished the final version of *Ta-t'ung shu* in which he spoke of the principle of equality between sexes and the rights of women, he took another concubine.[31]

K'ang's views on marriage and women, Hsiao Kung-chuan insists, were more radical and unconventional than those of the May Fourth generation who echoed many of K'ang's concerns. What Hsiao has overlooked is that K'ang could afford to be radical and unconventional because those matters seemed remote and unrelated to him personally.

To Hu Shih and others of his generation, freedom of marriage and women's liberation were no longer matters just for intellectual contemplation. The family system had become absolutely unendurable, and they responded with extraordinary immediacy to their own marriages and to the suffering of women. Hu regarded his arranged marriage as a violent affront to his freedom. A brief look at the attitudes of Hu, Liang Ch'i-ch'ao, and Liang's beloved disciple Hsü Chih-mo toward marriage, divorce, and free love will show how far the May Fourth generation had traveled along the road away from traditional values.

Hsü Chih-mo was married in 1915 to Chang Yu-i, younger sister of Chang Chia-ao (Chang Kia-gnau) and Chang Chün-mai (Carsun Chang). Within a few years, Hsü fell in love with Lin Hui-yin, daughter of Lin Ch'ang-min (1876–1925) who happened to be a close associate of Liang Ch'i-ch'ao and who, together with Liang, served briefly in the warlord cabinet under Tuan Ch'i-jui in 1917. In 1921, while living with his wife in Sawston, attending Cambridge University, Hsü daily exchanged letters with Miss Lin who was with her father in London. As a precaution, Hsü used a local grocery store as his mailing address. In March, 1922, Hsü obtained a divorce from his wife Chang Yu-i, despite objections from his parents and the birth of their second son only a month before. The understanding Chang Yu-i had already left Cambridge in the fall of 1921. Via Paris she went to Berlin where she delivered the child. On October 15, 1922, Hsü returned to China with the intention of marrying Lin Hui-yin and bringing her back to Cambridge. By this time, however, Lin Ch'ang-min had already agreed to marry his daughter to none other than Liang Ssu-ch'eng, eldest son of Liang Ch'i-ch'ao. The match had been informally made by the two families. When Hsü persisted with Miss Lin, Liang Ch'i-ch'ao became increasingly concerned and wrote a long letter to his beloved disciple on January 2, 1923. It was nominally to reprimand Hsü for his divorce, but the undertones of warning apparently referred to a matter of personal and immediate urgency. He entered a personal plea that Hsü

> not inflict pains on others in search of your own happiness. . . .
> . . . The sacrosanctity of love is something of which today's young people are fond of speaking. I have no objection to it, but I also think that there are many other things in the world that are sacrosanct. . . . Ah! Chih-mo, is there really such a thing as a perfect universe? . . . You should know that we will better appreciate the wonders of our lives when we take life as imperfect. . . .

> You are a man of emotions . . . Chih-mo, you should know that it is difficult to establish but easy to dissipate oneself. . . . If you indulge in unattainable dreams, you will, after a few setbacks, lose your interest in life and die in dejection and anonymity. But death is all right compared to the most frightening prospect of neither life nor death, of helpless decadence.[32]

Although he never mentioned any third party, there was no question as to what Liang's real concern was. Five days thereafter, he wrote a letter to his eldest daughter expressing the pressing need to formalize the engagement of Liang Ssu-ch'eng and Lin Hui-yin. In sending the ostensibly reprimanding letter, Liang Ch'i-ch'ao was really trying to dissuade Hsü Chih-mo from pursuing his own future daughter-in-law.[33] Thus,

> despite his reformist stance in politics and his titanic contributions in introducing Western culture, Liang Ch'i-ch'ao in private life was still very much a scholar of the traditional type. He would take comfort in the established ways of life with which he was familiar and in which he wanted to define the future happiness of his children. It was something of a great irony that this political reformer should have felt the urge to defend the sanctity of that most prevalent of old social conventions, the arranged marriage system, especially when the happiness of his own family was at stake.[34]

Before long, the indomitable Hsü Chih-mo became entangled in still another love affair. The heroine this time was Lu Hsiao-man, wife of Princeton- and West Point–educated Wang Keng. After an exasperating courtship, Hsü and Lu were married on October 3, 1926, in the Pei-hai Garden of Peking. Here the roles played by Liang Ch'i-ch'ao and Hu Shih were most indicative of the generation shift. Liang regarded Lu Hsiao-man's divorce as shamefully immoral and repeatedly chided Hsü for his behavior. On the other hand, Hu was supportive after the romance had become a fact. Under Hu's and Chang P'eng-ch'un's persistent persuasion, Liang presided over the wedding with Hu serving as the official witness. With Hsü's prior knowledge and consent, Liang delivered a scathing lecture at the wedding on the moral inadequacies of his disciple. But Hu Shih never passed judgment on Hsü and rendered every help to his troubled friend. In December, 1926, Hu wrote Hsü's good friend Leonard K. Elmhirst in England, suggesting that Elmhirst help the Hsüs get away from China and spend two or three years in England and continental Europe. Hsü himself acknowledged in his letter to Elmhirst that Hu was one of "one or two friends" sympathetic with him. In March, 1927, Elmhirst, in answer to Hu's suggestion, offered Hsü money to cover travel expenses to Europe.[35] Thus, Hu Shih was opposed to divorce only as a general principle, as he was critical of some of his fellow returned students for too readily abandoning their uneducated wives. He was no longer able to pass a concrete judgment, as Liang Ch'i-ch'ao was able to, on a divorce case in which his friend was involved. Immediately after Hsü Chih-mo died in a plane crash on November 19, 1931, Hu Shih wrote a moving eulogy praising Hsü's pristine pursuit of "love," "freedom," and "beauty."[36]

Of course, Hu Shih, Hsü Chih-mo, and others misled many of us by often talking about their personal affairs in a grandiloquent language. Hsü, certainly one of the most defiant and individualistic May Fourth personalities, even justified his divorce in social and national terms. He wrote his wife Chang Yu-i in March, 1922:

> Both of us have boundless futures. . . . Both of us have minds set on reforming society; both of us have minds set on achieving well-being for mankind. This all hinges on our setting ourselves as examples. With courage and resolution, with respect to our personalities, we must get a free divorce, thereby terminating pain and initiating happiness.[37]

Was Hsü really thinking of the happiness of mankind and national well-being when he pursued different women and fought for his divorce? But how embarrassing and selfish it was for a Chinese to discuss his personal matters as personal matters. Similarly, Hu Shih told us that he strove to be a scientist and left his widowed mother to study in America not for personal fulfillment but for national salvation. Shall we say that one of the most painful and persistent protests in modern China—protest against familial ethics, parental authority, and the arranged marriage—was not so much nationalistically motivated as existentially motivated?

While the May Fourth generation was more existentially oriented, the earlier reform generation was certainly more committed to the collective good. K'ang Yu-wei, Yen Fu, and Liang Ch'i-ch'ao did their best to practice the age-honored tradition of combining scholarship and governmental service. Even in the bleakest moments they did not attempt to sever their ties with politics. Yen Fu suffered a lifelong frustration as a political outsider. To members of the reform generation, intellectual activity and political service were not mutually exclusive but rather reinforced each other, and they often switched back and forth between the two. Liang Ch'i-ch'ao spent long years laying an intellectual foundation for the reform movement of 1898 in which he was an active participant. After it failed, he again devoted himself to practical scholarship in an engaged manner. Then in July, 1907, the *New Citizen* ceased publication, four months after a fire damaged its office. With the demise of this journal, Liang passed the height of his intellectual influence. From then on, he again became involved in politics.

Thus, Liang departed from politics not because he wanted to, but because opportunities were shut off. And for all the setbacks and discouraging development of events, his departure proved to be always temporary. Following the Republican Revolution, he became active in party politics, served in the governments of Yüan Shih-k'ai and Tuan Ch'i-jui, and took part in the military campaign against Yüan.

The May Fourth generation, on the other hand, was characterized by a profound feeling of political alienation. This happened in a relatively short time, although it had been in the working for a longer period. The disappearance of the traditional examination system, while having little psychological impact on the aspiring elite at the time, turned out in the long run to be one of the most pivotal events in modern China. The examination system defined the place of the elite in Chinese society. When the system was abolished in 1905, it signaled the fragmentation of functions of the leadership class. The elite, in other words, was left to redefine itself, and its social functions, intellectual obligations, and political roles were all open to speculation. The demise of the examination system was followed, six years later, by that of the imperial system. The latter can be properly described as an institution of "universal kingship," for "the king, perceived as the link between the cosmos and the people, also exercised a religio-spiritual authority."[38] Its collapse had a devastating effect on the elite class. The Revolution of 1911 did nothing to help the situation. Instead of making China a modern nation-state, the founding of the republic turned out to be the culmination of the process of breakdown of the tradition. Finally, Yüan Shih-k'ai's manipulation and the thrashing about of the warlords without meaningful goals further benumbed the elite class.

Under such circumstances, there was a withdrawal from politics among a sizable number of the newly emerging intelligentsia and an obsession with so-called cultural endeavors. Hu Shih, by rejecting the civil service examination and striving to be a scientist, had made the decision at the very outset not to engage in politics. To be sure, his elitist personality helped explain much about his aloofness, but his perception of reality was a far more important factor in determining his attitude toward politics. He considered the situation so hopeless that he would not even "talk" politics for twenty years. Opportunities presented to him—various university presidencies, ambassadorships, foreign ministership, and the first presidency under the nationalist constitution—which would have generated irrepressible envy of the members of the reform generation were dubiously perceived by Hu to be dilemmas and even deadly traps. When he did become involved in politics, he did so halfheartedly. Of course, many May Fourth figures soon began to take an active part in politics. Yet the very fact that it took a difficult struggle before they decided to partake bespoke a fundamental change of attitude toward politics.

It hardly needs to be emphasized that Hu Shih's withdrawal from politics differed from that of a traditional eremite. The latter withdrew to protest corrupt and authoritarian government, to show his loyalty to the previous dynasty or to the principle of loyalty itself, to fulfill filial obligations, or to protect his purity. The motivating force was mostly Confucian and, to a lesser extent, Taoist and Buddhist.[39] Like an eremite in traditional times, Hu's refusal to serve in the nationalist government was in part to protest its evils, and his overwhelming concern was to retain his independence. But when Hu assessed politics, he was not appreciably under the influence of Confucianism, much less Buddhism or Taoism. He had no intrinsic feeling of loyalty toward any particular government, and devotion to the principle of loyalty had become an idea alien to him.

Hu Shih's focus had shifted from the state to society and his effort was to work for the good of society from the outside, not within it. Having excluded politics, intellectual activity became his only endeavor. And in the area of intellectual opinions, the May Fourth generation contrasted sharply with their immediate predecessors. While the general direction and content of the criticisms of the traditional culture by the two groups were similar, there were nonetheless significant differences. Democracy and science for the first time were consciously advocated in the reform era, but they became apotheosized in the May Fourth period. Moreover, the purpose, intensity, and bitterness of the criticism of Chinese culture that characterized the May Fourth era were by and large absent from the reform generation. Writings of T'an Ssu-t'ung, K'ang Yu-wei, Yen Fu, and Liang Ch'i-ch'ao did much to undermine the validity and respectability of tradition, yet these men also reaffirmed certain elements in the past which, in their view, were eternal. An outstanding example was their conviction that Confucian philosophy and Buddhism had more to offer than Western ideas in areas of private morality and personal cultivation. Therefore, although their criticism of tradition was severe, the attachment to it by the reform generation was at the same time deep and passionate.

Hu Shih, too, tried to find what he regarded as the eternal values in the tradition, but he did so either in a detached, academic manner or when he felt threatened by his Western colleagues. And the values he found in Chinese culture, such as logic, the scientific spirit and method, and the tradition of democracy, were in fact Western values which he hoped the Chinese would adopt. When Hu spoke of the Chinese culture with contemporary China in mind, his dominant mood was one of mordancy and cruelty. Compare on the one hand the most radical writings of the reform generation and on the other Hu's repeated description of Chinese culture as being characterized by foot binding and concubinage, and Lu Hsün's charge against Chinese culture as "cannibalistic," and the difference in the temper of the two generations becomes unequivocal.

Inevitably, an intellectual approach without a meaningful social and political connection only sharpened Hu's feeling of impotence. His pungent assault on Chinese culture, his espousal of Ibsenism, and his emphasis on fiction and the vernacular were meant as much to change the Chinese mentality as to unleash his own disillusionment. Reformers of the 1898 generation wrote to express reform ideas. One of Liang's most important essays on literary reform, "Fiction Seen in Relation to the Guidance of Society," discussed the value of fiction entirely in terms of social well-being and national revival.[40] Moreover, merely unleashing his disillusionment was not enough; Hu often had to block out reality to find respite and temporary peace. Here classical scholarship assumed the role of calming nerves and benumbing senses. The popularity of science reached an unprecedented level not only because it was considered a cure-all for China's cultural diseases and practical problems but also because it offered something unique: it presumably gave the May Fourth elite extraordinary power to transform society while enabling him to transcend the suffocating social and political web.

Walter Kaufmann observes that "alienation is a central feature of human existence."[41] Throughout Chinese history, there were always a small number of literati who protested the ideological rigidity, the unreasonableness of certain demands, and the injustice of society. Wm. Theodore de Bary speaks of

> a recognizable pattern of alienation among members of the educated class of Ming and Ch'ing China, typified by the sensitive, highly intelligent child of a well-to-do family on the decline, who feels a fundamental conflict between his own individuality or intellectual integrity and what he must do in order to succeed in the world and discharge his family responsibilities.[42]

In the eighteenth century, as Paul Ropp has described, Wu Ching-tzu and a few of his contemporaries satirized superstition, criticized the examination system and the elite class, and advocated equality and individualism. "Wu Ching-tzu rejected government service as his goal" and was "too pessimistic to suggest reforms" for the examination system.[43] Ideas of the members of the reform generation deviated even more from the Confucian culture.

But compared with the May Fourth cultural radicals, those individuals mentioned above were less estranged. "If Wu Ching-tzu sensed the decadence of Chinese civilization in his time, he saw this phenomenon chiefly as the malfunction of an irreplaceable ideal of a ritualized world."[44] Though both Wu and Ts'ao Hsüeh-ch'in

> find intellectually that the inevitable erosion of time and skepticism regarding reality badly shake the total vision of life, they are still willing to adhere to this shattered vision of life in a more limited version, which still comforts them with lyric reveries in time of crisis. When they give us their fragmentary visions or illusions, they also truthfully confide to us their broken hopes.[45]

Indeed, Wu and Ts'ao criticized their society chiefly because they encountered obstacles in their personal lives: repeated setbacks in examination attempts and irreversible decline of family fortunes. They had no radically different alternative value for comparison or choice. While members of the reform generation opened up a new avenue by exposing themselves to Western ideas, their acceptance of the West was selective, and their personal lives were too comfortably embedded in tradition to break with it abruptly.

It was in the May Fourth era that alienation became more profound and a truly common experience shared by a growing number of intellectuals. Hu Shih tried to disassociate himself from the values of the past even though he had had one of the most illustrious careers of his generation. Instead of feeling comfortable in Chinese society, he felt debilitated, so much so that this feeling generated a sense of incomprehensibility, in the mental rather than intellectual meaning of the word, of external events. He was so disillusioned that, in his mind, no alternative would really make things better. For the first time, the feeling of estrangement had deeply permeated both the personal life and intellectual outlook of the May Fourth generation. Inevitably, an existential individualism emerged. All of Hu's reform ideas were simultaneously designs to gratify his innermost cravings. The May Fourth elite expressed their personal feelings and fought for their concerns with greater passion than any of their predecessors.

Abbreviations

CSM	*Chinese Students' Monthly.*
HCN	*Hsin ch'ing-nien* 新青年.
HSWT	Hu Shih. *Hu Shih wen-ts'un* 胡適文存 (Collected writings of Hu Shih). 4 vols. Taipei, 1971.
HSWT, erh-chi	Hu Shih. *Hu Shih wen-ts'un, erh-chi* 胡適文存, 二集 (Collected writings of Hu Shih, second collection). 4 chüan. Shanghai, 1924.
HY	*Hsin-yüeh yüeh-k'an* 新月月刊.
NLCP	*Nu-li chou-pao* 努力週報.
TLPL	*Tu-li p'ing-lun* 獨立評論.

Notes

Preface

1. Jerome B. Grieder, *Hu Shih and the Chinese Renaissance: Liberalism in the Chinese Revolution, 1917–1937* (Cambridge, Mass.: Harvard University Press, 1970). The reader will quickly note my heavy indebtedness to Professor Grieder's book for insight and source material.
2. There are exceptions, of course. Wong Young-tsu has argued that cosmopolitan thinking was one of the important strains of thought in the late Ch'ing. See Wong Young-tsu, "The Ideal of Universality in Late Ch'ing Reformism," in *Reform in Nineteenth-Century China*, ed. Paul A. Cohen and John E. Schrecker (Cambridge, Mass.: Harvard University Press, 1976), pp. 150–59; Wong Young-tsu (Wang Yung-tsu), "Wan-Ch'ing pien-fa ssu-hsiang hsi-lun" (An analysis of the reformist thought in the late Ch'ing), in *Chin-tai Chung-kuo ssu-hsiang jen-wu lun: wan-Ch'ing ssu-hsiang* (On the thought and personalities of modern China: thought in the late Ch'ing) (Taipei, 1980), pp. 85–132.

Chapter 1

1. My narrative of Hu Shih's family background is brief to avoid repetition. For an intimate and detailed account, see Grieder, *Hu Shih*. Hu Shih himself produced three autobiographical items: Hu Shih, *Ssu-shih tzu-shu* (Autobiography at forty) (Shanghai, 1933; Taipei reprint, 1974); Hu Shih, "My Credo and Its Evolution," in *Living Philosophies: A Series of Intimate Credos* (New York: Simon and Schuster, 1931), pp. 235–64; Hu Shih, *The Personal Reminiscences of Dr. Hu Shih (1891–1962)*, interviewed, compiled, and edited by Te-Kong Tong [T'ang Te-kang], with Dr. Hu's corrections in his own handwriting, 1959. Typescript in the archive of the Chinese Oral History Project, East Asian Institute, Columbia University; microform by the Microfilming Corporation of America, New Jersey (hereafter this item will be referred to as *Oral History*). The

last item is translated as Hu Shih, *Hu Shih k'ou-shu tzu-chuan* (The oral autobiography of Hu Shih), trans. with notes by T'ang Te-kang (Taipei, 1981).
2. Hu Shih, "My Credo and Its Evolution," p. 239.
3. Hu Shih, *Ssu-shih tzu-shu*, pp. 19–26.
4. Ibid., pp. 26–30.
5. Hu Shih, "My Credo and Its Evolution," p. 243.
6. Hu Shih, *Ssu-shih tzu-shu*, p. 41; Hu Shih, "My Credo and Its Evolution," p. 243.
7. Hu Shih, "My Credo and Its Evolution," pp. 243–44. See also Hu Shih, *Ssu-shih tzu-shu*, pp. 42–44.
8. Hu Shih, *Ssu-shih tzu-shu*, pp. 27, 28, 33, 42, 44–47; Hu Shih, "My Credo and Its Evolution," pp. 245–46.
9. Hu Shih, "My Credo and Its Evolution," p. 246; Hu Shih, *Ssu-shih tzu-shu*, p. 49.
10. Hu Shih, "My Credo and Its Evolution," p. 246; Hu Shih, *Ssu-shih tzu-shu*, p. 49.
11. Hu Shih, *Ssu-shih tzu-shu*, p. 63.
12. Ibid., pp. 49–92.
13. Ibid., pp. 51, 55, 62, 65, 86–88.
14. Ibid., p. 55.
15. Ibid.
16. Ibid.
17. Benjamin I. Schwartz, *In Search of Wealth and Power: Yen Fu and the West* (Cambridge, Mass.: Harvard University Press, 1964); D. W. Y. Kwok, *Scientism in Chinese Thought, 1900–1950* (New Haven: Yale University Press, 1965).
18. Science was loosely defined by the Chinese. Almost any discipline not belonging to the humanities, the social sciences, or law was "science." I will use the term in this sense throughout the book.
    When Chiang Meng-lin came to the United States in 1908, he majored in agriculture at the University of California, Berkeley, before transferring to education. Chiang Monlin (Chiang Meng-lin), *Tides from the West: A Chinese Autobiography* (New Haven: Yale University Press, 1947). In Japan, Kuo Mo-jo concentrated on medicine while spending most of his time writing poetry and translating Western literary works. He refused to transfer to literature despite extreme hardship caused by daily contact with medical science. He received his medical degree without ever practicing it, and he is known because of his works in history, literature, and archaeology. Ch'eng Fang-wu, a close friend of Kuo's, specialized in and was much troubled by ordnance making while indulging himself in Tolstoi. For both men's experiences, see Kuo Mo-jo, *T'ung-nien shih-tai* (The years of my boyhood) (Shanghai, 1940); Kuo Mo-jo, *Ke-ming ch'un-ch'iu* (The revolutionary years) (Shanghai, 1957); Kuo Mo-jo, *Ch'uang-tsao shih-nien* (Ten years of creation) (Shanghai, 1932). Like Kuo, Lu Hsün majored in medicine in Japan. He changed

to literature after a traumatic experience as a medical student. See Leo Ou-fan Lee, "Genesis of a Writer: Notes on Lu Xun's Educational Experience, 1881–1909," in *Modern Chinese Literature in the May Fourth Era,* ed. Merle Goldman (Cambridge, Mass.: Harvard University Press, 1977), pp. 161–88. Wang Kuo-wei, who was to become one of the most gifted scholars in twentieth-century China, departed for Japan in 1901 and enrolled in a physics school to concentrate on science. See Wang Te-i, *Wang Kuo-wei nien-p'u* (A chronological biography of Wang Kuo-wei) (Taipei, 1967); Tu Ching-i, "Conservatism in a Constructive Form: The Case of Wang Kuo-wei (1877–1927)," *Monumenta Serica* 28 (1969): 188–214.

19. Charlotte Furth, "May Fourth in History," in *Reflections on the May Fourth Movement: A Symposium,* ed. Benjamin I. Schwartz (Cambridge, Mass.: Harvard University Press, 1972), p. 62.
20. Hu Shih, "My Credo and Its Evolution," p. 247; Hu Shih, "Ch'ung-pai ying-hsiung" (Hero worship), *Ching-yeh hsün-pao* 25 (1906–8): 47–48.
21. Hu Shih, *Ssu-shih tzu-shu,* pp. 56, 57; Hu Shih, "Hun-yin p'ien" (On marriage), *Ching-yeh hsün-pao* 25 (1906–8): 1–5.
22. Hu Shih, *Ssu-shih tzu-shu,* p. 56; Hu Shih, "My Credo and Its Evolution," pp. 247–48.
23. Hu Shih, *Ssu-shih tzu-shu,* pp. 56–57; Hu Shih, "My Credo and Its Evolution," p. 248.
24. On Social Darwinism in China in the late nineteenth and early twentieth centuries, see Benjamin I. Schwartz, *In Search of Wealth and Power;* and Lin Yü-sheng, *The Crisis of Chinese Consciousness: Radical Antitraditionalism in the May Fourth Era* (Madison: University of Wisconsin Press, 1979).
25. On Social Darwinism in America from 1860 to 1915, see Richard Hofstadter, *Social Darwinism in American Thought* (Boston: Beacon Press, 1955).

    That the same philosophy created such opposite views is not surprising at all. Hofstadter reminds us:
    There was nothing in Darwinism that inevitably made it an apology for competition or force. Kropotkin's interpretation of Darwinism was as logical as Sumner's. . . . Darwinism had from the first this dual potentiality; intrinsically it was a neutral instrument, capable of supporting opposite ideologies. (p. 201)
26. Hu Shih, *Ssu-shih tzu-shu,* pp. 52, 53, 57–60; Hu Shih, "My Credo and Its Evolution," p. 246.
27. Liang Ch'i-ch'ao, "Hsin-min i" (On new citizen), in Liang Ch'i-ch'ao, *Yin-ping-shih wen-chi* (Collected essays of Liang Ch'i-ch'ao) (Taipei reprint, 1960, 16 vols in 8), *ts'e* 7, pp. 104–7. The passage is quoted in Hu Shih, *Ssu-shih tzu-shu,* p. 58.
28. Hu Shih, *Ssu-shih tzu-shu,* p. 59.
29. Liang Ch'i-ch'ao, "Lun Chung-kuo hsüeh-shu ssu-hsiang pien-ch'ien chih ta-shih" (General trends of the development of Chinese scholarship), in

Liang Ch'i-ch'ao, *Yin-ping-shih wen-chi*, *ts'e* 7, pp. 1–104. Hu Shih discussed it in *Ssu-shih tzu-shu*, pp. 59–61.
30. The Kuomintang party archive in Taiwan has five issues of *Ching-yeh hsün-pao* in which I found thirteen essays by Hu Shih.
31. The literary revolution will be discussed in greater detail in a later chapter.
32. Hu Shih, *Ssu-shih tzu-shu*, p. 75.
33. Lin Shu, "Lun ku-wen pai-hua chih hsiang hsiao-chang" (On the rise and fall of the classical language and the vernacular), in *Wen-hsüeh lun-cheng chi* (A collection of essays on the literary debate), ed. Cheng Chen-to, pp. 96–99. This is vol. 2 of Chao Chia-pi, ed., *Chung-kuo hsin wen-hsüeh ta-hsi* (A comprehensive compendium of modern Chinese literature), 10 vols. (Shanghai, 1935).
34. Hu Shih, *Ssu-shih tzu-shu*, pp. 73–74.
35. Hu Shih (signed Tieh-erh), "Lun hui-ch'u shen-fo" (On destroying god and Buddha), *Ching-yeh hsün-pao* 28 (1906–8): 1–5; Hu Shih (signed Shih-chih), "Wu-kuei ts'ung-hua" (On the nonexistence of the spirit), *Ching-yeh hsün-pao* 25 (1906–8): 27–28, and 28 (1906–8): 37–38; Hu Shih, *Ssu-shih tzu-shu*, pp. 69–74. The quote is from the first item listed above, p. 4. Emphasis in original.
36. Hu Shih, "My Credo and Its Evolution," p. 249.
37. Hu Shih, *Ssu-shih tzu-shu*, pp. 61–62.
38. Hu Shih, "Hun-yin p'ien," pp. 1–5.
39. Hu Shih, *Ssu-shih tzu-shu*, pp. 74–75.
40. Liang Ch'i-ch'ao, "Yü chih ssu-sheng kuan" (My view of life and death), in Liang Ch'i-ch'ao, *Yin-ping-shih wen-chi*, *ts'e* 17, pp. 1–12.
41. Hu Shih, *Ssu-shih tzu-shu*, p. 65; Hu Shih, *Chung-kuo kung-hsüeh hsiao-shih* (A history of the China National Institute), n.p., 1929.
42. Hu Shih, *Ssu-shih tzu-shu*, pp. 53–54.
43. Ibid., pp. 65, 83–92; Hu Shih, *Chung-kuo kung-hsüeh hsiao-shih*, p. 6.
44. Hu Shih, *Ssu-shih tzu-shu*, p. 30.
45. Ibid., p. 65.
46. Li Ao, *Hu Shih p'ing-chuan* (A critical biography of Hu Shih) (Taipei, 1964), p. 230.

Chapter 2

1. Hu Shih, "My Credo and Its Evolution," pp. 249–50.
2. A more detailed but substantively similar account is given in Hu Shih, *Ssu-shih tzu-shu*, pp. 83–99.
3. Benjamin I. Schwartz, "Introduction," in *Reflections on the May Fourth Movement: A Symposium*, ed. Benjamin I. Schwartz (Cambridge, Mass.: Harvard University Press, 1972), pp. 2–3. Also see Benjamin I. Schwartz, "The Limits of 'Tradition versus Modernity' as Categories of

Explanation: The Case of the Chinese Intellectuals," *Daedalus* 101.2 (Spring, 1972): 71–88.
4. Benjamin I. Schwartz, *In Search of Wealth and Power*, pp. 73, 127, and passim.
5. Liang Ch'i-ch'ao, "P'ien-fa t'ung-i" (A general treatise on reform), in Liang Ch'i-ch'ao, *Yin-ping-shih wen-chi*, ts'e 1, pp. 1–92.
6. Chang Hao, *Liang Ch'i-ch'ao and Intellectual Transition in China, 1890–1907* (Cambridge, Mass.: Harvard University Press, 1971), p. 160.
7. Quoted in ibid. Hu Shih cited part of this passage in his *Ssu-shih tzu-shu*, p. 59.

Liang, of course, always had some misgivings about the American type of democracy, and they were intensified by his firsthand observations in 1903 when he toured the United States. He perceptively noted some of the fundamental shortcomings of democracy and was far from sanguine about the possibility of its implementation in China. He was alarmed by the "monstrous" growth of the trust, its frightening impact on international economy and politics, the United States naval expansion, and Theodore Roosevelt's imperialistic attitude. However, Liang was able to reconcile political opposition to America with cultural admiration. His refusal to endorse democracy in China was contingent rather than intrinsic. America's democratic tradition went back to the colonial days, he said, and the Anglo-Saxon race had always possessed the self-governing ability, whereas China had no such tradition or quality. He declared,

Ah! republicanism, republicanism, I love you so much! but not so much as I love my fatherland. . . . Republicanism, republicanism, I cannot bear to defile your noble name again. [If I were to advocate your cause for my country,] future generations of political commentators would have one more reason to curse you.

Liang was also awed by America's potential and its economic achievements: the United States possessed "vast territory" and "unlimited natural resources," it had already surpassed Great Britain in national wealth, and the American people had the greatest consuming power. See Liang Ch'i-ch'ao, "Cheng-chih-hsüeh ta-chia Po-lun-chih-li chih hsüeh-shuo" (The theory of the great political scientist Bluntchli), in Liang Ch'i-ch'ao, *Yin-ping-shih wen-chi*, ts'e 13, pp. 67–89; Liang Ch'i-ch'ao, "Erh-shih shih-chi chih chü-ling—t'o-la-ssu" (The monster of the twentieth century—the trust), in Liang Ch'i-ch'ao, *Yin-ping-shih wen-chi*, ts'e 14, pp. 33–61.

8. See Charlotte Furth, *Ting Wen-chiang: Science and China's New Culture* (Cambridge, Mass.: Harvard University Press, 1970). A short biography of Ting can also be found in Howard L. Boorman, ed., *Biographical Dictionary of Republican China*, 4 vols. (New York: Columbia University Press, 1967–71).
9. Chang Hao, *Liang Ch'i-ch'ao*, p. 148. Philip C. Huang discusses in great detail Japan's influence on Liang without, however, distinguishing influ-

ence in practical matters from influence in values. See Philip C. Huang, *Liang Ch'i-ch'ao and Modern Chinese Liberalism* (Seattle: University of Washington Press, 1972).
10. Chiang Monlin, *Tides from the West*, p. 59, and passim.
11. Wang Te-i, *Wang Kuo-wei nien-p'u*, pp. 11–18; Tu Ching-i, "Conservatism in a Constructive Form."
12. See Ch'en Tu-hsiu's biography in Howard L. Boorman, *Biographical Dictionary*.
13. Shih Chao-chi (Alfred Sao-ke Sze), *Shih Chao-chi tsao-nien hui-i lu* (Memoir of Shih Chao-chi: the early years) (Taipei, 1967), p. 38.

Shih himself took his B.A. and M.A. from Cornell University in 1901 and 1902, respectively. Among his important posts were: minister to the United States, 1921–29, 1933–35; first ambassador to the United States, 1935–37; minister to Great Britain, 1914–21.

For Tuan-fang's background, see Arthur W. Hummel, ed., *Eminent Chinese of the Ch'ing Period* (1644–1912), 2 vols. (Washington, D. C.: Government Printing Office, 1943; Taipei reprint 1970, 2 vols. in 1).
14. Chiang Monlin, *Tides from the West*, pp. 60, 67.
15. Y. C. Wang, *Chinese Intellectuals and the West, 1872–1949* (Chapel Hill: University of North Carolina Press, 1966), pp. 72–73, 510.
16. Kuo Mo-jo, *T'ung-nien shih-tai*, p. 142.
17. Yen Fu, "Chiu-wang chüeh-lun" (On our salvation), in Yen Fu, *Yen Chi-tao shih-wen-ch'ao* (A collection of Yen Fu's prose and poetry) (Shanghai, 1922; Taipei reprint, n.d.), pp. 104-29.
18. Liang Ch'i-ch'ao, "P'ien-fa t'ung-i."
19. Ernest P. Young, "Nationalism, Reform, and Republican Revolution: China in the Early Twentieth Century," in *Modern East Asia: Essays in Interpretation*, ed. James B. Crowley (New York: Harcourt, Brace and World, 1970), p. 151.
20. Hu Shih (signed Tieh-erh), "Ai kuo" (Patriotism), *Ching-yeh hsün-pao* 34 (1906-8): 4–5.
21. Hu Shih (signed Shih-an), "Chung-kuo te cheng-fu" (The Chinese government), *Ching-yeh hsün-pao* 28 (1906-8): 33.
22. Erik H. Erikson, *Gandhi's Truth: On the Origins of Militant Nonviolence* (New York: W. W. Norton and Co. 1969), p. 135.
23. Hu Shih, *Ssu-shih tzu-shu*, pp. 92–93.
24. Ibid., p. 95.
25. Ibid., pp. 98–99; Ts-zun Z. Zee and Lui-ngau Chang, "The Boxer Indemnity Students of 1910," *CSM*, 6.1 (November 10, 1910): 16.
26. Hu Shih, *Ts'ang-hui-shih cha-chi*, 4 vols. (Shanghai, 1939). Reissued as *Hu Shih liu-hsüeh jih-chi* (Hu Shih's diary while studying abroad), 4 vols. (Taipei, 1973), 1:231. (Hereafter this item will be cited as *Diary*).
27. Ts-zun Z. Zee and Lui-ngau Chang, "Boxer Indemnity Students," pp. 16–17.
28. For background of the remission of the Boxer indemnity, see Michael H.

Hunt, "The American Remission of the Boxer Indemnity: A Reappraisal," *Journal of Asian Studies* 31.3 (May, 1972): 539–59.
29. Hu Shih, *Ssu-shih tzu-shu*, pp. 98, 99.
30. Hu Shih, "Hsien-mu hsing-shu" (Reflections on my late mother's life), *HSWT* 1 (dated December, 1918): 789.

Chapter 3

1. *Diary*, p. 1145.
2. *Diary*, p. 1145. Translation is from Grieder, *Hu Shih*, pp. 41–42.
3. Quoted in Leo Ou-fan Lee, "Genesis of a Writer," pp. 177–78.
4. Chiang Monlin, *Tides from the West*, pp. 72–73.
5. Kuo Mo-jo, *Ch'uang-tsao shih-nien;* Kuo Mo-jo, *T'ung-nien shih-tai;* Kuo Mo-jo, *Ke-ming ch'un-ch'iu*.
6. Hu Shih, "My Credo and Its Evolution," p. 252.
7. *Diary*, p. 226.
8. Hu Shih, "My Credo and Its Evolution," p. 252; *Oral History*, p. 50.
9. *Oral History*, pp. 45–46, 48–49.
10. Hu Shih, "My Credo and Its Evolution," p. 252.
11. *Oral History*, pp. 45–46; *Diary*, p. 38.
12. *Diary*, pp. 96–98.
13. Kuo Mo-jo, *Ch'uang-tsao shih-nien;* Kuo Mo-jo, *T'ung-nien shih-tai;* Kuo Mo-jo, *Ke-ming ch'un-ch'iu*.
14. See Chao's biography in Boorman, *Biographical Dictionary*. Hu Shih discussed Chao's earlier background and activities in *Diary*, pp. 230–31, 834–35.
15. *Diary*, passim.
16. Ibid., pp. 230–31.
17. Grieder bases his observation of Hu's academic performance on Hu's Cornell transcripts in his possession. Grieder, *Hu Shih*, p. 41.
18. *Diary*, pp. 229–30.
19. Ibid.; *Oral History*, p. 52. Both report the event of winning the prize. Hu's original essay is, Hu Shih (using the pseudonym Bernard W. Savage), "A Defense of Browning's Optimism," the Corson Browning Prize Essay, 1914. Department of Manuscripts and University Archives, Cornell University Libraries, Cornell University.
20. The event of winning the prize is reported in *Diary*, pp. 951–53. The original essay is Hu Shih (Suh Hu), "Is There a Substitute for Force in International Relations?" in *Hu Shih Items*, microfilm from the Patterson Scrapbook; and the Hu Shih misc., E. E. Barker, Collector. Collection of Regional History and University Archives, Cornell University.

    The essay was published as a special issue, International Conciliation. Special Bulletin, New York: American Association for International Conciliation, Prize Essay, International Polity Club Competition,

Awarded June, 1916. A translation of this essay appears as Hu Shih (Suh Hu), *Ha algum substituto efficaz que se imponha á forca nas relacoes internacionaes?* American Association for International Conciliation, Pan-American Division, bulletin no. 13 (New York, 1917).
21. J. L. Harbour, "High Achievements of Mr. Suh Hu," in *Hu Shih Items.* This is a newspaper item written on October 10, 1914.
22. *Diary,* pp. 165–66.
23. Ibid., p. 376.
24. Quoted in Elmer Eugene Barker, "Hu Shih, Incurable Optimist: Personal Recollections of a Great Humanist's Intellectual Development," in *Hu Shih Items,* p. 2.

Chapter 4

1. *Diary,* pp. 4, 12.
2. Ibid., pp. 42–50.
3. Ibid., p. 44.
4. Ibid., pp. 48–49.
5. *Oral History,* pp. 27–29.
6. *Diary,* p. 45.
7. F. Oliver Brachfeld, *Inferiority Feelings in the Individual and the Group,* translated from the French by Marjorie Gabain (London: Routledge and Kegan Paul, 1951; reprint ed. Westport, Conn.: Greenwood Press, 1972), p. 255.
8. *Diary,* pp. 43–44.
9. Erik H. Erikson, *Childhood and Society* (New York: W. W. Norton and Co., 1963), p. 254.
10. William W. Comfort received his B.A. (1894) from Haverford College and M.A. (1896) and Ph.D. (1902) from Harvard. He taught French at Cornell University until 1917 when he was appointed president of Haverford where he served until his retirement in 1940. See the *National Cyclopedia of American Biography.* Hu and Comfort developed a lasting friendship. Hu's second son, Hu Ssu-tu, attended Haverford (1941–42) during Hu's ambassadorship to Washington.
11. *Diary,* passim.
12. Ibid., pp. 134–35, 377–79, 420–21.
13. Ibid., p. 102.
14. Ibid., p. 131.
15. Ibid., pp. 134–35.
16. Ibid., pp. 377–79.
17. Ibid., pp. 455–56. English and emphasis are Hu's own.
18. Ibid., p. 486. English and emphasis are Hu's own.
19. Ibid. English and emphasis are Hu's own.
20. Hu Shih, "The Ideal Missionary," an address given at the First Baptist

Church, Ithaca, New York, February 2, 1913, pp. 4–5. Reproduced in *Hu Shih Items*.
21. *Diary*, pp. 598–600. English is Hu's own.
22. Chow Tse-tsung, *The May Fourth Movement: Intellectual Revolution in Modern China* (Cambridge, Mass.: Harvard University Press, 1960), pp. 291–92.
23. This compliment was extended to him by a friend of his. See *Diary*, pp. 376–77.
24. Ibid., pp. 157–60.
25. Ibid., p. 199.
26. Ibid., pp. 468–70.
27. Robert Jay Lifton, "America in Vietnam—The Counterfeit Friend," in Robert Jay Lifton, *History and Human Survival: Essays on the Young and Old, Survivors and the Dead, Peace and War, and on Contemporary Psychohistory* (New York: Vintage Books, 1971), p. 229.
28. *Diary*, pp. 600–601. English is Hu's own.
29. Hu Shih, "The Ideal Missionary," pp. 5–6.
30. *Diary*, p. 601. English is Hu's own.
31. Ibid., pp. 601–2. Emphasis is mine.
32. On the anti-Christian movement, see Chow Tse-tsung, *The May Fourth Movement*, pp. 321–27; Chang Ch'in-shih, ed., *Kuo-nei chin-shih-nien lai chih tsung-chiao ssu-ch'ao* (Religious thought in China over the past ten years) (Peking, 1927); Yamamoto Tatsuro and Yamamoto Sumiko, "The Anti-Christian Movement in China, 1922–1927," *Far Eastern Quarterly* 12.2 (February, 1953):133–48; Jessie Lutz, *China and the Christian Colleges, 1850–1950* (Ithaca, New York: Cornell University Press, 1971); Philip West, *Yenching University and Sino-Western Relations, 1916–1952* (Cambridge, Mass.: Harvard University Press, 1976).
33. Hu Shih, "Chin-jih chiao-hui chiao-yü te nan-kuan" (Present crisis in Christian education), *HSWT* 3 (1926): 728–30.
34. Hu Shih, "*K'o-hsüeh yü jen-sheng-kuan* hsü" (Preface to *Science and the Philosophy of Life*), *K'o-hsüeh yü jen-sheng-kuan* (Science and the Philosophy of Life), 2 vols. (Shanghai, 1923), 1:1–29.
35. Hu Shih, "Chin-jih chiao-hui chiao-yü te nan-kuan" (1926), pp. 730–31.
36. Ibid., pp. 731–33.
37. Hu Shih, *Hu Shih te jih-chi* (Hu Shih's unpublished diaries, 1921–40), deposited at the Library of Congress. Entry for April 7, 1922. English is Hu's own.
38. Hu Shih, "Chin-jih chiao-hui chiao-yü te nan-kuan" (1926), pp. 733–34.
39. Ibid.
40. Ibid., pp. 734-35.
41. Hu Shih, "China and the Missionaries," *Spectator* (London) 5138 (December 18, 1926): 1107; Hu Shih, "China and Christianity," *Forum* 78.1 (July, 1927): 1–2; Hu Shih, "The Task of Modern Religion," *Journal of Religion* 14.1 (January, 1934): 104–8.

42. Hu Shih, "Chu-ho nü ch'ing-nien-hui" (Tendering our congratulations to the YWCA), *HSWT* 3 (1928): 737.
43. Hu Shih, "Tz'u-yu te wen-t'i" (The question of adoring the young), *HSWT* 3 (1929): 739–43.
44. Philip West, *Yenching University,* p. 93.
45. See Hu Shih, "Hsin wen-hua yün-tung yü Kuomintang" (The new culture movement and the Kuomintang), *HY* 2.6–7 (September, 1929): 1–15.
46. Ibid., p. 6.
47. Ibid., p. 4. The scholar Hu alluded to was Ku Chieh-kang.
48. Yeh Ch'u-ts'ang, "Yu tang te li-hsing lai wan-hui feng-ch'i" (Restore public morals by means of the party effort), *Che-chiang min-pao* (Oct. 10, 1929), pasted in Hu Shih, *Hu Shih te jih-chi.*
49. Ch'en Tu-hsiu, "Chi-tu-chiao yü Chung-kuo-jen" (Christianity and the Chinese people), *HCN* 7.3 (February 1, 1920): 15–20.
50. Ch'en Tu-hsiu, "Chi-tu-chiao yü Chi-tu chiao-hui" (Christianity and the Christian church), in Ch'en Tu-hsiu, *Tu-hsiu wen-ts'un* (Collected essays of Ch'en Tu-hsiu), 3 *chüan* (Shanghai, 1922; Hong Kong reprint, 1965), 1:659–62.
51. Anna Freud, *The Ego and the Mechanisms of Defense* (New York: International Universities Press, 1946), p. 113.
52. Ibid., pp. 118–19.
53. Philip West, *Yenching University,* passim; Hu Shih, "Ts'ung ssu-li hsüeh-hsiao t'an tao Yen-ching ta-hsüeh" (Yenching University in the light of private schools), *TLPL* 108 (July 8, 1934): 2–5.

Chapter 5

1. Hu Sung-p'ing, *Hu Shih hsien-sheng nien-p'u chien-pien* (A brief chronological biography of Mr. Hu Shih) (Taipei, 1971), p. 3.
2. *Diary,* pp. 248–49, 853.
3. Elmer Eugene Barker, "Hu Shih, Incurable Optimist," p. 7.
4. Hu took both languages at Cornell and translated some short stories from French in his student days. Originally published in various journals, these translations are gathered in Hu Shih, trans., *Tuan-p'ien hsiao-shuo* (Short stories) (Taipei, 1972).
5. Hu Shih, "Hsien-mu hsing-shu" (1918), p. 790; Hu Sung-p'ing, *Hu Shih,* p. 15.
6. Hu Shih, "Hun-yin p'ien" (1906–8), p. 4. Emphasis in original.
7. Hu Shih, "Hsin-hun tsa-shih" (Poems in various styles on being newly married), *HCN* 4.4 (April 15, 1918): 339–40.
8. Hu Shih, "Hun-yin p'ien" (1906–8), p. 3.
9. Ibid., pp. 1, 3. Emphasis in original.
10. *Diary,* p. 74.
11. Ibid., pp. 103–4.

12. Ibid., p. 154. See also Hu Shih, "Marriage Customs in China," *Cornell Era*, (June, 1914), 610–11; reproduced in *Hu Shih Items*.
13. *Diary*, pp. 168–69; Hu Shih, "Marriage Customs in China."
14. *Diary*, p. 253.
15. Hu Shih, "Marriage Customs in China," p. 610.
16. Robert Jay Lifton, "Youth and History: Individual Change in Postwar Japan," in Robert Jay Lifton, *History and Human Survival*, p. 36.
17. Hu Shih, "Marriage Customs in China," p. 610.
18. Ibid.
19. *Diary*, p. 129, entry for December 3, 1912.
20. Ibid., pp. 395–96.
21. Ibid., pp. 253–54.
22. Chou Ts'e-tsung (Chow Tse-tsung) has also suggested this in his "Hu Shih-chih hsien-sheng te k'ang-i yü jung-jen" (Mr. Hu Shih's protestation and tolerance), *Hai-wai lun-t'an* 3.5 (May 1, 1962): 21–38.
23. *Diary*, pp. 428–29, 958–59, 1137, and passim.
24. Ibid., p. 749. The relationship between Hu and Williams grew so serious that Hu's mother tried to intervene. Chang Yüan-hsi, who knew Hu intimately, had the following interesting recollection:
    One day [when I was a student at Cornell] a friend took me to the L. E. Pattersons for tea. Mr. Patterson showed me his two "adopted sons" in an album. . . . One of the two was Mr. Hu Shih, and the other my eldest brother.
    [In the first album] was a letter in Chinese which Mr. Patterson asked me to read carefully and translate for him. He then requested that I compare my translation with the one that Mr. Hu provided years ago. After all these, Patterson said: "I have had this in mind for twenty years, but now I am convinced that Hu Shih did not lie to me." That letter in Chinese was from Mr. Hu's mother in Anhwei. I still remember that it began with "there is a certain Miss Williams. . . ." And it continued that "according to Chinese custom, once a betrothal is formalized, it cannot be nullified."
    See Chang Yüan-hsi, "Wo so chi-te te Hu Shih-chih hsien-sheng chi-chien shih" (The things I remember about Mr. Hu Shih), *Chuan-chi wen-hsüeh* 32.6 (June, 1978): 48–49.
25. *Diary*, p. 524.
26. Ibid., pp. 250–52. Part of the translation is adopted, with revision, from Grieder, *Hu Shih*, p. 102.
27. *Diary*, pp. 390–92.
28. Ibid., pp. 707–9.
29. Ibid., pp. 806–7.
30. Ibid., pp. 390–92.
31. Ibid., pp. 392–93.
32. Ibid., pp. 647–48.
33. Ibid., p. 392. The original is in Francis Bacon, *The Works of Francis*

Bacon, Lord Chancellor of England, with a Life of the Author, by Basil Montagu, Esquire, 3 vols. (Philadelphia: M. Murray, 1876), 1:16.
34. *Diary,* p. 411. Part of the translation is adopted, with revision, from Grieder, *Hu Shih,* p. 103.
35. *Diary,* pp. 441–42.
36. Ibid., pp. 756–58.
37. For the psychological quest for immortality, see Robert Jay Lifton, "On Death and Death Symbolism," in Robert Jay Lifton, *History and Human Survival,* pp. 156–86.
38. Hu Shih, *Ssu-shih tzu-shu,* pp. 32–33.
39. *Diary,* p. 102.
40. Ibid., pp. 68, 225.
41. Ibid., p. 225.
42. Ibid., pp. 225–26.
43. Ibid., p. 226.
44. Elmer Eugene Barker, "Hu Shih, Incurable Optimist," p. 7. This remark was apparently made in 1911. Hu was born in December, 1891 and Chiang Tung-hsiu was a few months older then he.
45. *Diary,* pp. 35, 248–49. Hu did not quote the poem in its entirety. My translation here has been aided by Kenneth P. H. Ho, trans., *The Nineteen Ancient Poems* (Hong Kong: Kelly and Walsh, 1977), p. 67.
46. *Diary,* pp. 620–21, 853.
47. Ibid., p. 853.
48. Ibid., pp. 442–43.
49. Ibid.
50. Ibid., p. 443. Translation is that of Grieder, *Hu Shih,* p. 12.
51. *Diary,* pp. 448–49. John Viscount Morley, *On Compromise* (London: MacMillan and Co., 1923), pp. 137, 138. The book was first published in 1874.
52. *Diary,* pp. 536–37.
53. Ibid., pp. 471–72.
54. Ibid., pp. 290, 620–21.
55. Ibid., pp. 647–48. Translations are adopted, with revision, from Grieder, *Hu Shih,* pp. 352–53.
56. *Diary,* p. 648.
57. Ibid., pp. 702–3.
58. Ibid., pp. 705–7. English is Hu's own. Hu gave a copy of this poem to Elmer Eugene Barker and expressly told him that it was written for Chiang Tung-hsiu. Both the poem and Barker's recollection in this regard can be found in Elmer Eugene Barker, "Hu Shih, Incurable Optimist," pp. 7–8.
59. Hu Shih, "Ping-chung te Tung-hsiu shu" (Receiving a letter from Tung-hsiu while I am ill), in Hu Shih, *Ch'ang-shih chi* (A collection of experiments) (Shanghai, 1920; Taipei, 1971), pp. 111–12. Part of the translation is from Grieder, *Hu Shih,* p. 353.

Notes to Pages 74–77   235

60. Erik H. Erikson, *Gandhi's Truth*, p. 153. Emphasis in original.
61. It should be noted, though only tangentially, that Edith Clifford Williams and Chiang Tung-hsiu were not the only women in Hu's life. He became a good friend of Nellie B. Sergent during the summer school in 1914 at Cornell. In that year, he wrote almost as many letters to her as he did to Williams. *Diary*, p. 764, entry for August 27, 1915. Then there was the talented Ch'en Heng-che (Sophia H. Chen Zen), a student at Vassar College in 1915–16 who married Hu's Cornell schoolmate Jen Hung-chün (H. C. Zen) in 1920 and in the same year became the first woman appointed to the faculty of Peking National University. Elmer Eugene Barker mentioned Hu's interest in Ch'en. Both C. T. Hsia and T'ang Te-kang have some interesting speculations about the romance between Hu and Ch'en. See Hsia Chih-ch'ing, "*Hu Shih tsa-i* hsü" (Foreword to *Miscellaneous reminiscences of Hu Shih*), in T'ang Te-kang, *Hu Shih tsa-i* (Miscellaneous reminiscences of Hu Shih) (Taipei, 1979), and T'ang Te-kang, *Hu Shih tsa-i*. Hu Shih himself provided the best clue to his feeling toward Ch'en Heng-che. His unpublished diary has the following entry (July 31, 1921):

> Received a letter from Tung-hsiu, learning that Shu-yung [Jen Hung-chün] and So-fei [Ch'en Heng-che] just had a girl. I named our daughter [who died in infancy] Su-fei [Sophia] after So-fei [Sophia].

62. Hu Shih, "Chen-ts'ao wen-t'i" (The question of chastity), *HCN* 5.1 (July 15, 1918): 9–18.
63. Ibid.
64. Hu Shih, "Mei-kuo te fu-jen" (American women), *HCN* 5.3 (September 15, 1918): 231–42.
65. Ibid.
66. Ibid.
67. Hu Shih, "The Greatest Event in Life," in A. E. Zucker, *The Chinese Theater* (Boston: Little, Brown, and Co., 1925), pp. 119–28. This is a farce in one act written in early 1919. The Chinese version is Hu Shih, "Chung-shen ta-shih" (The greatest event in life), *HCN* 6.3 (March 15, 1919): 343–51.
68. Hu Shih, "Li Ch'ao chuan" (A biography of Li Ch'ao), *Hsin-ch'ao* 2.2 (December, 1919): 266–75.
69. Hu Shih, "I-ko wen-t'i" (One big question), *HSWT* 1 (1919): 805–12.
70. Hu Shih, "Hsien-mu hsing-shu" (1918); Hu Shih, "Shih-erh-yüeh i-jih tao-chia" (Arriving home on December first), *Hsin-ch'ao* 1.2 (February, 1919): 281.
71. Hu Shih, "Wo tui sang-li te i-tien i-chien" (Some of my ideas on funeral rites), *HCN* 6.6 (November 1, 1919): 641–50.
72. Grieder, *Hu Shih*, p. 354.
73. Hu Shih, "Wo-te erh-tzu" (My son), in Hu Shih, *Ch'ang-shih chi* (1919), pp. 177–79.

74. Hu Shih, "Wo-te erh-tzu" (My son), *HSWT* 1:687–92.
75. Hu Shih, "Mei-kuo te fu-jen" (1918), p. 238. Translations are those of Grieder, *Hu Shih,* p. 354.
76. Hu Shih, "Chen-ts'ao wen-t'i" (1918); Hu Shih, "Lun chen-ts'ao wen-t'i" (On the question of chastity), *HSWT* 1 (1919): 676–84.
77. Hu Shih, "Lun nü-tzu wei ch'iang-pao so-wu" (On women assaulted by violence), *HSWT* 1 (1919): 685–86.
78. Hu Shih, "Mei-kuo te fu-jen" (1918).
79. Hu Shih, "Pu-hsiu—wo-te tsung-chiao" (Immortality—my religion), *HCN* 6.2 (February 15, 1919): 96–105.
80. Grieder, *Hu Shih,* p. 352.
81. Lewis S. Gannett, "Hu Shih: Young Prophet of Young China," *New York Times Magazine,* March 27, 1927, p. 10.
82. Chang Yüan-hsi hinted that Hu had girl friends when he was touring the United States in the late 1930s. See Chang Yüan-hsi, "Wo so chi-te te Hu Shih-chih hsien-sheng chi-chien shih." And Hu visited brothels, at least briefly. He wrote the following as part of his reflections on the year 1924:
    My health has not been recovered. Earlier this year, the doctor said that I had symptoms of tuberculosis . . . [Dr.] Esser, noticing the tubercle on my neck, suspected that I had venereal disease. Six blood tests yielded no conclusion.
    See Hu Shih, "I-chiu erh-ssu nien te nien-p'u" (A chronological biography of the year 1924), in his *Hu Shih te jih-chi.*
    And the August 23, 1926 entry in his *Hu Shih te jih-chi* has this to say: Wrote a long letter to Lewis Gannett last night. We were together in Shanghai in February. To let him know conditions in China, one night I took him to the home of two prostitutes, Yang Lan-ch'un and Kuei Heng. Gannett, a friend of long standing, wrote from Peking on March 5 and exhorted me not to waste energy on meaningless plays.
    While some people may wish to pass judgment on Hu's behavior, no judgment will gainsay his painful personal struggle and deep concern about the issues of marriage, family, and women's status.

Chapter 6

1. Hu Shih, "Ai kuo" (1906–8), p. 3. Emphasis in original.
2. Ibid., pp. 4–6. Hu Shih (signed Shih-chih), "Chung-kuo ti-i wei-jen Yang Ssu-sheng chuan" (A biography of Yang Ssu-sheng), *Ching-yeh hsün-pao* 25 (1906–8): 9–12.
3. On the cosmopolitan movement, see Hu Shih (Suh Hu), "The International Student Movement," *CSM* 9.1 (November 10, 1913): 37–39; Louis P. Lochner, *The Cosmopolitan Club Movement* (New York: American Association for International Conciliation, 1912); Louis P. Lochner, *In-*

ternationalism Among Universities, Vol. 3, no. 7, pt. 2 (Boston: World Peace Foundation, 1913); Efisio Giglio-Tos, *Appel pour le Désarmement et pour la Paix: Les Pionniers de la Société Des Nations et de la Fraternité Internationale; d'après les arcives de la "Corda Fratres," Fédération Internationale des Etudiants, 1898-1931* (Torino: Tipografia A. Kluc, 1931).
4. Giglio-Tos, *Appel pour le Désarmement*, p. 59.
5. Ibid., p. 84.
6. Ibid. p. 187. Originally in English.
7. *Diary*, p. 10.
8. Ibid., pp. 71, 418.
9. Ibid., pp. 136-38.
10. Giglio-Tos, *Appel pour le Désarmement*, pp. 190, 192.
11. Ibid., pp. 174, 177, 178. Hu's picture can be found in the group at the White House and with the Secretary of State. Hu also related the event in *Oral History*.
12. Giglio-Tos, *Appel pour le Désarmement*, p. 194; *Diary*, pp. 235-36.
13. *Diary*, pp. 504-11.
14. The event and the summary of the essay are recorded in *Diary*, pp. 951-53.
15. Nasmyth obtained his B.A. (1906), M.A. (1908), and Ph.D. (1909) from Cornell. He was twice president of the Association of Cosmopolitan Clubs and served as director of the World Peace Foundation of Boston. See the *National Cyclopedia of American Biography*.
16. *Diary*, p. 439.
17. Ibid., pp. 495-502. The original poem is in *Hu Shih Items*.
18. *Diary*, pp. 232-35. The *Ithaca Journal* containing Hu's letter is reproduced in *Hu Shih Items*.
19. *Diary*, pp. 314-15, entry for July 26, 1914; p. 509, entry for January 4, 1915. On the latter date, Dr. Washington Gladden condemned, at the eighth convention of the Association of Cosmopolitan Clubs held in Columbus, Ohio, the "double standard" of political morality in international conduct. Hu responded, in private, that "men of wisdom tend to agree."
20. Ibid., pp. 425-26. Schurman (1854-1942), trained at the University of London (B.A., 1877 and M.A., 1878) and the University of Edinburgh (Sc.D., 1878), was appointed Sage Professor of Philosophy and head of the department in 1886. He became dean of the Sage School of Philosophy in 1890. In 1892, he became the third president of Cornell, resigning in 1920. A year later, he became minister to China. Between 1925 and 1930, he was ambassador to Germany. *National Cyclopedia of American Biography*.
21. *Diary*, p. 1054; *Oral History*, pp. 36, 37.
22. *Diary*, pp. 111-15.
23. Ibid., pp. 395-96, 1054.
24. Ibid., p. 71.

25. Ibid., p. 113.
26. Ibid., pp. 481–84, 301, Hu quoted Wilson's speeches at length.
27. Ibid., pp. 636–45.
28. Ibid., p. 645.
29. Ibid., pp. 1080–82, 1083–85.
30. Erik H. Erikson, *Gandhi's Truth*, p. 433.
31. *Diary*, p. 110.
32. Ibid., pp. 139–40.
33. Ibid., p. 332.
34. Ibid., p. 433.
35. Hu Shih, "The International Student Movement" (1913), pp. 38, 39. Emphasis in original.
36. *Diary*, p. 533.
37. Ibid., pp. 431–35.
38. Ibid., pp. 551–52.
39. Ibid., pp. 436, 465.
40. Ibid., p. 331.
41. Ibid., 465–66.
42. Hu Shih (Suh Hu), "A Plea for Patriotic Sanity: An Open Letter to All Chinese Students," *CSM* 10.7 (April, 1915): 425–26. Emphasis in original.
43. *Diary*, p. 491.
44. See the note in H. K. Kwong, "What is Patriotic Sanity? A Reply to Suh Hu," *CSM* 10.7 (April, 1915): 427–30. Kwong, who was an editor of the publication and had read Hu's original article before the deletion, rebutted Hu sharply.

    If you will study Japan's history of expansion of the last thirty years and her imperialistic policy, you will think your doctrine of non-resistance is after all rested on the wings [of] philosophers' fancy and scholars' dreams. . . . We are prepared to suffer "devastation, and devastation, and devastation," but we are not prepared to be chained and bound as slaves. . . . Fortunately, we are made of different materials from Suh Hu—not of wood and stone but of blood and flesh. We have senses and feelings. We do not pretend to be deaf and dumb, when the situation requires us to express what is in us.
45. "Tsingtau and After," signed "A Friend of China," *New Republic* 2.14 (February 6, 1915): 20–21.
46. Hu Shih (Suh Hu), "Letter to the *New Republic*," *New Republic* 2.17 (February 27, 1915): 103. The same letter also appears in *CSM* 10.6 (March, 1915): 389–90.
47. *Diary*, pp. 431–33, 676. Ralph Norman Angell (1872?–1967), journalist, author, and leader of peace movements, was born in England and emigrated to America at seventeen. He was knighted in 1931 and awarded the Nobel Prize for Peace two years later. *Contemporary Authors—Permanent Series*.

48. This is taken from Norman Angell, *The Great Illusion: A Study of the Relation of Military Power to National Advantage* (New York: G. P. Putnam's Sons, 1913 [1910]); see also *Diary*, pp. 676–78.
49. John Dewey, "Force, Violence, and Law," *New Republic* 5 (January 22, 1916): 295–97; John Dewey, "Force and Coercion," *International Journal of Ethics* 26.3 (April, 1916): 359–67.

    Hu cited "Force and Coercion" in his "Is There a Substitute for Force in International Relations?" and referred to the influence of both essays on him in later writings. See Hu Shih, "Instrumentalism as a Political Concept," in *Studies in Political Science and Sociology* (Philadelphia: University of Pennsylvania Press, 1941), p. 4, and *Oral History*, p. 72.
50. Hu Shih (Suh Hu), "A Chinese Philosopher on War: A Popular Presentation of the Ethical and Religious Views of Mo-Ti," *CSM* 2.6 (April, 1916): 408–12.
51. Hu Shih, "Is There a Substitute for Force in International Relations?" (1916). Emphasis in original.
52. Ibid.
53. *Diary*, p. 1138.
54. Hu Shih, "Is There a Substitute for Force in International Relations?" (1916). Emphasis in original.
55. Hu Shih, "Wu-li chieh-chüeh yü chieh-chüeh wu-li" (Resolving problems by force, and resolving the problem of force), *HCN* 5.6 (December 15, 1918): 605–8.
56. Hu Shih, "My Credo and Its Evolution," p. 251.
57. Hu told Elmer Eugene Barker that he was "an incurable optimist." The phrase subsequently became the subtitle of Barker's essay in memory of Hu. Jerome B. Grieder insists that "optimism" was one of Hu's persistent characteristics.
58. *Diary*, p. 26.
59. T. Iyenaga, "Japan's Position in the World War," *New York Times*, March 24, 1915; *Diary*, pp. 525–27.
60. *Diary*, p. 525.
61. *New York Evening Post*, Nov. 15, 1915; *Diary*, pp. 812–15.
62. *New York Evening Post*, Nov. 23, 1915; *Diary*, p. 815.
63. *Diary*, p. 815.
64. Ibid., pp. 584–85.
65. Ibid., pp. 587–89.
66. Ibid., pp. 625–26.
67. Erik H. Erikson, *Gandhi's Truth*, p. 205.
68. Robert Jay Lifton, *Death in Life: Survivors of Hiroshima* (New York: Vintage Books, 1969), p. 369.
69. *Diary*, pp. 683–84.
70. Ibid., pp. 148–49.
71. Ibid., p. 315.
72. Ibid., pp. 1102–5.

73. Hu Shih, "Ni mo wang-chi" (You should not forget), *HCN* 5.3 (September 15, 1918): 244–45.
74. Rupert Emerson, *From Empire to Nation: The Rise to Self-Assertion of Asian and African Peoples* (Boston: Beacon Press, 1960), p. 96.
75. Ibid., p. 95.
76. *Diary,* p. 1025.
77. Ibid.
78. Hu Shih, trans., "Erh yü-fu" (Deux Amis), *HCN* 3.1 (March 1, 1917): 23–29.
79. *Diary, tzu-hsü,* p. 6.
80. Hu Shih, "Wu-li chieh-chüeh yü chieh-chüeh wu-li" (1918).
81. Hu Shih, "Kuo-chi te Chung-kuo" (China among the nations), *NLCP* 22 (October 1, 1922): 1–2. Hu quoted this same passage and repeated the same argument eleven years later. See his "Pa Chiang T'ing-fu hsien-sheng te lun-wen" (An epilogue to Mr. Chiang T'ing-fu's essay), *TLPL* 45 (April 9, 1933): 6–8.
82. Hu Shih, *Hu Shih te jih-chi,* entry for August 1, 1930.
83. Hu Shih, "Lun tui-Jih wai-chiao fang-chen" (On China's Japan policy), *TLPL* 5 (June 19, 1932): 2–5.
84. Hu Shih, "Nei-t'ien tui shih-chieh te t'iao-chan" (Uchida's challenge to the world), *TLPL* 16 (September 4, 1932): 2–3.
85. Hu Shih, "Chiu-ching na i-ko t'iao-yüeh shih fei-chih?" (Which treaty is after all a scrap of waste paper?), *TLPL* 19 (September 25, 1932): 2–7.
86. Hu Shih, "I-ko tai-piao shih-chieh kung-lun te pao-kao" (A report that represents world public opinion), *TLPL* 21 (October 9, 1932): 2–6.
87. Hu Shih, "Wo-men k'o-i teng-hou wu-shih nien" (We can wait fifty years!), *TLPL* 44 (April 2, 1933): 2–5.
88. Ibid.
89. Hu Shih, "Shih-chieh hsin hsing-shih li te Chung-kuo wai-chiao fang-chen" (China's foreign policy in the new international situation), *TLPL* 78 (November 26, 1933): 2–5.
90. Hu Shih, "Wo-te i-chien yeh pu-kuo ju-tz'u" (My opinions are simply these), *TLPL* 46 (April 16, 1933): 2–5.
91. Hu Shih, "Lun tui-Jih wai-chiao fang-chen" (1932).
92. Hu Shih, "I-ko tai-piao shih-chieh kung-lun te pao-kao" (1932).
93. Hu Shih, "Ch'üan-kuo chen-ching i-hou" (Following the shock of the entire nation), *TLPL* 41 (March 21, 1933): 2–8. The figures here are all Hu's own. Whether they were correct or not is beside the point that I want to make.
94. Ibid.
95. Grieder, *Hu Shih,* p. 250.
96. Hu Shih, *Hu Shih te jih-chi,* entry for September 19, 1931.
97. Hu Shih, "Ts'an-t'ung te hui-i yü fan-hsing" (Grievous recollections and reflections), *TLPL* 18 (September 18, 1932): 8–13.
98. Hu Shih, *Hu Shih te jih-chi,* entry for March 2, 1933.

99. Hu Shih, "Ching-kao Jih-pen kuo-min" (An appeal to the Japanese people), *TLPL* 178 (November 24, 1935): 10–14. The article was finished in early October for the Japanese press which expurgated three paragraphs. The Chinese version is therefore slightly different.
100. Hu Shih, "Hua-pei wen-t'i" (The question of North China), *TLPL* 179 (December 1, 1935): 2–3.
101. Hu Shih, "Ta Shih-fu Kao-hsin hsien-sheng" (A reply to Mr. Murobushi Koshin), *TLPL* 180 (December 8, 1935): 5–8.
102. *Foreign Relations of the United States, Diplomatic Papers, 1935*, Vol. 3: *The Far East* (Washington, D. C.: Government Printing Office, 1953), pp. 400–401.
103. Peter Gay, *The Enlightenment: An Interpretation. The Rise of Modern Paganism* (New York: Alfred A. Knopf, 1966), p. 13.
104. Quoted in Gay, *The Enlightenment*.
105. Robert Jay Lifton, *Death in Life*, p. 391.

Chapter 7

1. *Diary*, pp. 1053–54.
2. Ibid., pp. 100, 105–6, 196–98, 268–70.
3. *Oral History*, pp. 36, 37.
4. *Diary*, pp. 121, 124, 130.
5. Ibid., pp. 807–8.
6. Ibid., pp. 808–9.
7. Ibid., p. 809. Translations are those of Grieder, *Hu Shih*, p. 54.
8. *Diary*, pp. 809–10.
9. Ibid., p. 1054.
10. Bernard R. Crick, *In Defense of Politics* (Baltimore: Penguin Books, 1964), pp. 123–24.
11. Grieder, *Hu Shih*, p. 127.
12. *Diary*, pp. 1056–57.
13. Ibid., pp. 1158–64.
14. Ibid., p. 1054.
15. Ibid., p. 82.
16. Hu Shih (Suh Hu), "A Republic for China," in *Hu Shih Items*. Originally published in the *Cornell Era*, (January, 1912), pp. 240–42.
17. Hu Shih (Suh Hu), "China and Democracy," *Outlook* 3 (September 1, 1915): 27–28. Emphasis in original. See also *Diary*, pp. 741–48.
18. Hu Shih (Suh Hu), "Manufacturing the Will of the People: A Documentary History of the Recent Monarchical Movement in China," *Journal of Race Development* 7.3 (January, 1917): 319–28. See also Hu Shih (Suh Hu), "Analysis of the Monarchical Restoration in China," in *Hu Shih Items*. Originally published in the *Columbia Spectator*, (January 14, 1916).

19. Hu Shih (Suh Hu), "A Philosopher of Chinese Reactionism," *CSM* 2.1 (November, 1915): 16–19.
20. Hu Shih, "China and Democracy" (1915), p. 28. Emphasis in original.
21. Ibid.
22. *Diary*, pp. 493–94.
23. Ibid., p. 833.
24. Liang Ch'i-ch'ao, "Cheng-chih chih chi-ch'u yü yen-lun-chia chih chih-chen" (The foundation of politics and the guide for a political commentator), in Liang Ch'i-ch'ao, *Yin-ping-shih wen-chi, ts'e* 33:31–40. Hu quoted Liang in *Diary*, pp. 650–53.
25. *Diary*, pp. 842–43, entry for January 31, 1916. A similar letter was written to Edith Clifford Williams on January 11. See *Diary*, pp. 821–22.
26. Ibid., pp. 453–54.
27. Ibid., pp. 926–27.
28. Ibid., p. 1147.
29. See Hu Shih, "Wo-te ch'i-lu" (My predicament), *NLCP* 7 (June 18, 1922): 3–4, and Hu Shih, *Ting Wen-chiang te chuan-chi* (A biography of Ting Wen-chiang) (Taipei, 1973), pp. 35–36.
30. Hu Shih, "Wo-te ch'i-lu" (1922).
31. Lin Yü-sheng, *The Crisis of Chinese Consciousness,* p. 41.
32. Ibid., p. 27.
33. Ibid., p. 41.
34. *Diary*, pp. 653–54.
35. Hu Shih, "Wo-te ch'i-lu" (1922).
36. Ibid.
37. Hu Shih, "To yen-chiu hsieh wen-t'i, shao t'an hsieh chu-i" (Study more problems, talk less of isms), *Mei-chou p'ing-lun* 31 (July 20, 1919); *T'ai-p'ing yang* 2.1 (May 5, 1920): 1–10. Hu Shih, "San lun wen-t'i yü chu-i" (A third discussion of problems and isms), *Mei-chou p'ing-lun* 36 (August 24, 1919); *T'ai-p'ing yang* 2.1 (May 5, 1920): 15–21. Hu Shih, "Ssu lun wen-t'i yü chu-i: lun shu-ju hsüeh-li te fang-fa" (A fourth discussion of problems and isms: on the methods of importing theories), *Mei-chou p'ing-lun* 37 (August 31, 1919); *T'ai-p'ing yang* 2.1 (May 5, 1920): 21–25. Li Ta-chao, "Tsai lun wen-t'i yü chu-i" (Another discussion of problems and isms), *Mei-chou p'ing-lun* 35 (August 17, 1919); *T'ai-p'ing yang* 2.1 (May 5, 1920): 10–15.
38. Hu Shih, "To yen-chiu hsieh wen-t'i, shao t'an hsieh chu-i" (1919).
39. Hu Shih, "Wo-te ch'i-lu" (1922).
40. William James, *Pragmatism and Four Essays from The Meaning of Truth* (Cleveland: World Publishing Co., 1955), p. 35.
41. Barry Keenan, *The Dewey Experiment in China: Educational Reform and Political Power in the Early Republic* (Cambridge, Mass.: Harvard University Press, 1977).
42. Hu Shih, "Che i-chou" (This week), *NLCP* 7 (June 18, 1922).
43. Hu Shih et al., "Cheng tzu-yu te hsüan-yen" (A manifesto of struggle for

freedom), *Tung-fang tsa-chih* 17.16 (August 25, 1920): 133–34. The manifesto was cosigned by six others: Chiang Meng-lin, Li Ta-chao, Kao I-han, Wang Cheng, T'ao Lü-kung, and Chang Tsu-hsün.

44. Hu Shih, *Ting Wen-chiang te chuan-chi* (1973), pp. 35–36. Hu was here recalling Ting's conversation by memory. Ting wrote a little later after the conversation with Hu:

> We must realize that politics is our only goal and that to reform politics is our only duty. Don't be deceived that a political reform must start with industry and education. Look at these few years: since there has been no way out for politics, are not industry and education daily facing the possibility of bankruptcy? While we can say that good politics must begin with a good education and industry, we can also say, conversely, that to have a good education and industry, we must first have good politics. By doing this, we are really setting up a circuitous trap in which we turn around all day long and of which we can never get out.

See Ting Wen-chiang, "Shao-shu jen te tse-jen" (The responsibility of the elite minority), *NLCP* 67 (August 26, 1923).

45. Hu Shih, *Hu Shih te jih-chi,* entry for August 5, 1921.
46. Hu Shih, "Hou nu-li ko" (A second song of endeavor), *NLCP* 4 (May 28, 1922).
47. Hu Shih, "Nu-li ko" (A song of endeavor), *NLCP* 1 (May 7, 1922).
48. Ting Wen-chiang, "I-ko wai-kuo p'eng-yu tui-yü i-ko liu-hsüeh-sheng te chung-kao" (Counsels of a foreign friend to a Chinese graduate from abroad), *NLCP* 42 (March 4, 1923).
49. Hu Shih, *Hu Shih te jih-chi,* entry for May 27, 1922.
50. Ibid., entry for August 3, 1926.
51. Ibid., entry for April 28, 1928.
52. Frederic Wakeman, Jr., "The Price of Autonomy: Intellectuals in Ming and Ch'ing Politics," *Daedalus* 101.2 (Spring, 1972): 36.
53. Hu Shih, "Cheng-lun-chia yü cheng-tang" (Political commentators and political parties), *NLCP* 5 (June 4, 1922).
54. Ibid.
55. Hu Shih et al., "Wo-men te cheng-chih chu-chang" (Our political proposals), *NLCP* 2 (May 14, 1922).
56. Ibid.
57. For the chronology of these events, see Hu Shih, "Che i-chou," *NLCP*. Ts'ai Yüan-p'ei's letter of resignation to the president and his public proclamation were quoted in full in Hu Shih, "Che i-chou," *NLCP* 38 (January 21, 1923).
58. Hu Shih, "Che i-chou," *NLCP* 13 (July 30, 1922).
59. Hu Shih, "Che i-chou," *NLCP* 38 (January 21, 1923). Ts'ai's letter of resignation reads, in part:

> Yüan-p'ei, realizing the difficulties of the time, lamenting the hopelessness of attaining political decency, unwilling to eke out a

living by getting into the same stream and tainting myself, unable to withstand the condemnation of the fellow countrymen and my own conscience if I supported such a crumbling educational system under the present educational authority, has decided that the only thing proper is to withdraw myself in order to show my due respect for education and my fellow countrymen.

For more of Hu's thoughts on the subject, see Hu Shih, "Ts'ai Yüan-p'ei yü Pe-ching chiao-yü chieh" (Ts'ai Yüan-p'ei and the educational circle of Peking), *NLCP* 39 (January 28, 1923).

60. Ts'ai Yüan-p'ei, "Ts'ai Yüan-pei te hsüan-yen" (Ts'ai Yüan-p'ei's proclamation), *NLCP* 39 (January 28, 1923).
61. Hu Shih, "Che i-chou," *NLCP* 39 (January 28, 1923).
62. Ibid.
63. In February, 1922, Hu learned that some American diplomats in China favored him to be the president of Tsinghua University. "I will absolutely not accept it," he vowed. See Hu Shih, *Hu Shih te jih-chi*, entry for February 25, 1922. In September of the same year, Hu declined Wang Ch'ung-hui's invitation to be the deputy minister of education. Ibid., entry for September 4, 1922. In May, 1928, Ts'ai Yüan-p'ei had a long talk with Hu, urging him to be the chancellor of Sun Yat-sen University in Canton, which Hu refused. Ibid., entry for May 19, 1928. In July, 1928, "I swear I will not do it. . . . There is absolutely no room for discussion," Hu said when he was asked to head Anhwei University. Ibid., entries for July 3 and 4, 1928.
64. Ibid., entry for April 26, 1928. Hu served on the post for two years until May, 1930.
65. Grieder, *Hu Shih,* p. 304. For the premiership, see the *China Weekly Review* 112.1 (December 4, 1948), and T'ao Hsi-sheng, "Kuan-yü tun-ch'ing Hu hsien-sheng ch'u-jen hsing-cheng-yüan-chang chi ch'i-t'a" (The invitation to Hu Shih to head the Executive Yüan, and other recollections), *Chuan-chi wen-hsüeh* 28.5 (May, 1976): 18–21.
66. Grieder, *Hu Shih,* p. 305.
67. This was Chiang Kai-shek's speech before the Central Executive Committee of the Kuomintang on April 4, 1948. The text is translated in *United States Relations with China, with Special Reference to the Period 1944–1949* (Washington, D. C.: Government Printing Office, 1949), p. 848.
68. Ibid.
69. Ibid., pp. 273, 849.
70. Ibid.
71. Ibid., p. 846. John Leighton Stuart, *Fifty Years in China: The Memoirs of John Leighton Stuart, Missionary and Ambassador* (New York: Random House, 1954), p. 193.

Stuart further noted that Chiang answered "Communist criticism of 'personal rule' by attempting to seek less significant position in [the] new government." *United States Relations with China,* p. 850. Stuart himself

also exerted pressure on Chiang by publicly rebuking the Kuomintang leadership for not making better use of enlightened and liberal intellectuals. Stuart's "personal message to the people of China," issued in February, 1948. *United States Relations with China,* pp. 985–87.
72. *United States Relations with China,* p. 850.
73. Elmer Eugene Barker, "Hu Shih, Incurable Optimist," pp. 13–13a.
74. Ibid., p. 5.
75. *Foreign Relations of the United States, Diplomatic Papers, 1942: China* (Washington, D.C.: Government Printing Office, 1956), pp. 132–34.
76. Hu Shih, "Che i-chou," *NLCP* 7 (June 18, 1922).
77. Hu Shih, "Jen-ch'üan yü yüeh-fa" (Human rights and provisional constitution), *HY* 2.2 (April 10, 1929): 1–8.
78. Hu Shih, "Wo-men shen-mo shih-hou ts'ai k'o yu hsien-fa?" (When can we have a constitution?), *HY* 2.4 (June 10, 1929): 1–8.
79. Hu Shih, "Chih-nan, hsing i pu-i" (Knowledge is difficult, but action is not easy either), *HY* 2.4 (June 10, 1929): 1–15.
80. Hu Shih, "Hsin wen-hua yün-tung yü Kuomintang" (1929).
81. Newspaper clipping with Ch'en's motion is pasted in Hu Shih, *Hu Shih te jih-chi,* entry for March 26, 1929. See also Hu Shih, "Jen-ch'üan yü yüeh-fa" (1929).
82. Duplicate copy of the letter to Wang is pasted in Hu Shih, *Hu Shih te jih-chi,* entry for March 26, 1929. See also Hu Shih, "Jen-ch'üan yü yüeh-fa" (1929).
83. *Kuo-wen chou-pao*'s reply that the censor refused to give permission for the letter to be published is pasted in Hu Shih, *Hu Shih te jih-chi,* entry for March 29, 1929. See also Hu Shih, "Jen-ch'üan yü yüeh-fa" (1929).
84. Ch'en Te-cheng's essay, "Hu shuo" (Nonsense), *Min-kuo jih-pao hsing-ch'i p'ing-lun* 2.46 (April 1, 1929), is pasted in Hu Shih, *Hu Shih te jih-chi,* entry for April 1, 1929.
85. See newspaper clippings pasted in Hu Shih, *Hu Shih te jih-chi,* throughout August and September, 1929, and January, 1930. These included newspaper articles and party resolutions.
86. Newspaper clipping reporting the resolution is pasted in *Hu Shih te jih-chi,* entry for August 29, 1929.
87. Newspaper clipping reporting this is pasted in *Hu Shih te jih-chi,* entry for September 22, 1929.
88. Newspaper clipping reporting this is pasted in *Hu Shih te jih-chi,* entry for September 26, 1929.
89. Original document of the Ministry of Education and Hu's reply to Chiang Meng-lin are pasted in *Hu Shih te jih-chi,* entry for October 4, 1929.
90. Hu Shih, "Wo-men tsou na-t'iao lu?" (Which road shall we follow?), *HY* 2.10 (December 10, 1929): 1–16.
91. Quoted in Liang Ch'i-ch'ao, "K'ai-ming chuan-chih lun" (On enlightened despotism), in Liang Ch'i-ch'ao, *Yin-ping-shih wen-chi, ts'e* 17, p. 13.
92. Ibid.

93. Hu Shih, *Hu Shih te jih-chi,* entry for September 18, 1926. English is Fu's as recorded by Hu.
94. Chiang T'ing-fu, "Chih-shih chieh-chi yü cheng-chih" (The intelligentsia and politics), *TLPL* 51 (May 21, 1933): 15–19.
95. Chiang T'ing fu, "Ke-ming yü chuan-chih" (Revolution and despotism), *TLPL* 80 (December 10, 1933): 2–5.
96. Chiang T'ing-fu, "Lun chuan-chih ping ta Hu Shih-chih hsien-sheng" (On despotism, in reply to Mr. Hu Shih), *TLPL* 83 (December 31, 1933): 2–6.
97. *Diary,* pp. 493–94.
98. Hu Shih, "China and Democracy" (1915). Emphasis in original.
99. Hu Shih, "*Cheng-chih kai-lun* hsü" (Preface to *Introduction to politics* [by Chang Wei-tz'u]), *HSWT, erh-chi, chüan* 3 (1923): 17–24.
100. Hu Shih, "Tsai lun chien-kuo yü chuan-chih" (Another discussion of national reconstruction and despotism), *TLPL* 82 (December 24, 1933): 2–5; Hu Shih, "Chung-kuo wu tu-ts'ai te pi-yao yü k'o-neng" (There is no need or feasibility for China to be autocratic), *TLPL* 130 (December 9, 1934): 2–6; Hu Shih, "Ta Ting Tsai-chün hsien-sheng lun min-chu yü tu-ts'ai" (A rejoinder to Mr. Ting Tsai-chün and a discussion of democracy and autocracy), *TLPL* 133 (December 30, 1934): 7–9.
101. Hu Shih, "Wo-men neng hsing te hsien-cheng yü hsien-fa" (The constitutional government and the constitution that we can implement), *TLPL* 242 (July 11, 1937): 12–13.
102. Ch'ien Tuan-sheng, "Min-chu cheng-chih hu? Chi-ch'üan kuo-chia hu?" (Democracy or a totalitarian state?), *Tung-fang tsa-chih* 31.1 (January 1, 1934): 17–25.
103. Hu Shih, "Cheng-chih t'ung-i te t'u-ching" (The path to political unification), *TLPL* 86 (January 21, 1934): 2–7.
104. Hu Shih, "Chung-kuo wu tu-ts'ai te pi-yao yü k'o-neng" (1934).
105. Hu Shih, "Ta Ting Tsai-chün hsien-sheng lun min-chu yü tu-ts'ai" (1934).
106. See, for example, Ch'ien Tuan-sheng, "Min-chu cheng-chih hu? Chi-ch'üan kuo-chia hu?"; Ch'ien Tuan-sheng, "Tui-yü liu-chung ch'üan-hui te ch'i-wang" (Our hopes for the sixth plenary sessions), *TLPL* 162 (August 4, 1935): 5–9.
107. Hu Shih, "Tsai lun chien-kuo yü chuan-chih" (1933).
108. Hu Shih, "Chung-kuo wu tu-ts'ai te pi-yao yü k'o-neng" (1934); Hu Shih, "Wang-Chiang t'ung-tien li t'i-ch'i te tzu-yu" (On the freedom discussed in the Wang-Chiang telegram), *TLPL* 131 (December 16, 1934): 3–6.
109. Hu Shih, "Tsai lun wu-wei te cheng-chih" (Another discussion of *wu-wei* politics), *TLPL* 89 (February 25, 1934): 2–6.
110. Hu Shih, "Chien-she yü wu-wei" (Construction and *wu-wei*), *TLPL* 94 (April 1, 1934): 2–5.
111. Hu Shih, "Tsai lun wu-wei te cheng-chih" (1934).
112. Hu Shih, "Ts'ung nung-ts'un chiu-chi t'an-tao wu-wei te cheng-chih" (*Wu-wei* politics in light of the rural relief), *TLPL* 49 (May 7, 1933): 2–6.
113. Ibid.

114. Hu Shih, "Wu-li t'ung-i lun" (On unification by force), *TLPL* 85 (January 14, 1934): 2–7.
115. Chiang T'ing-fu, "Lun chuan-chih ping ta Hu Shih-chih hsien-sheng"; Ch'ien Tuan-sheng, "Min-chu cheng-chih hu? Chi-ch'üan kuo-chia hu?"
116. Chiang T'ing-fu, "Chih-shih chieh-chi yü cheng-chih."
117. Chiang T'ing-fu, "Lun chuan-chih ping ta Hu Shih-chih hsien-sheng."
118. Hu Shih, "Cheng-chih kai-ke te ta-lu" (The great road toward the reform of political institutions), *TLPL* 163 (August 11, 1935): 2–9.
119. Hu Shih, "Ts'ung i-tang tao wu-tang te cheng-chih" (Form one-party politics to politics without parties), *TLPL* 171 (October 6, 1935): 10–12. Translations are adopted, with revision, from Grieder, *Hu Shih,* pp. 272–73.
120. Hu Shih, "Ts'ung i-tang tao wu-tang te cheng-chih" (1935).
121. Grieder, *Hu Shih,* pp. 273–74.
122. Ibid., p. 274.
123. Hu Shih, *Hu Shih te jih-chi,* entry for February 13, 1932.
124. Hu Shih, "Cheng-chih kai-ke te ta-lu" (1935).
125. *China Weekly Review* 106.12 (August 23, 1947).
126. Hu Shih, "Kung-tu chu-i shih-hsing te kuan-ch'a" (Observations on the work-study program), *HCN* 7.5 (April 1, 1920): 817–21.
127. Hu Shih, Chiang Meng-lin, "Wo-men tui-yü hsüeh-sheng te hsi-wang" (Our hopes for the students), *Tung-fang tsa-chih* 17.11 (June 10, 1920): 107–12; Hu Shih, "Huang Li-chou lun hsüeh-sheng yün-tung" (Huang Li-chou on student movement), *HSWT, erh-chi, chüan* 3, pp. 11–15; Hu Shih, "Lun hsüeh-ch'ao" (On the student movement), *TLPL* 9 (July 17, 1932): 6–9; Hu Shih, "Wang-Chiang t'ung-tien li t'i-ch'i te tzu-yu"; Hu Shih, "Wei hsüeh-sheng yün-tung chin i-yen" (A word to the student movement), *TLPL* 182 (December 22, 1935): 4–7; Hu Shih, "Tsai lun hsüeh-sheng yün-tung" (Another discussion of the student movement), *TLPL* 183 (December 29, 1935): 2–4.
128. Hu Shih, Chiang Meng-lin, "Wo-men tui-yü hsüeh-sheng te hsi-wang"; Hu Shih, "Wei hsüeh-sheng yün-tung chin i-yen"; Hu Shih, "Tsai lun hsüeh-sheng yün-tung"; Hu Shih, "Ai-kuo yün-tung yü ch'iu-hsüeh" (The patriotic movement and getting an education), *Hsien-tai p'ing-lun* 2.39 (September 5, 1925): 5–9; Hu Shih, "So-wei chiao-yü te fa-hsi-ssu-ti-hua" (The so-called fascistization of education), *TLPL* 8 (July 10, 1932): 14–15.
129. Hu Shih, "Ai-kuo yün-tung yü ch'iu-hsüeh" (1925).
130. Hu Shih, "Tseng-yü chin-nien te ta-hsüeh pi-yeh-sheng" (An offering to this year's university graduates), *TLPL* 7 (July 3, 1932): 2–5.
131. Hu Shih, "Tseng-yü chin-nien te ta-hsüeh pi-yeh-sheng" (An offering to this year's university graduates), in Hu Shih, *Hu Shih wen-ts'un wai-pien* (Collected essays of Hu Shih, a supplement) (Taipei, 1970), pp. 85–89. Dated June 24, 1934.
132. Hu Shih, "Hsieh tsai Hsü Mei nü-shih te wen-chang te hou-mien" (A rejoinder to Madam Hsü Mei's essay), in Hu Shih, *Hu Shih wen-ts'un wai-pien,* pp. 91–93. Dated July 8, 1934.

133. These events are discussed in Grieder, *Hu Shih*, pp. 301–2.
134. Hu Shih, "Min-ch'üan te pao-chang" (The protection of civil rights), *TLPL* 38 (February 19, 1933): 2–5.
135. Ibid.
136. Hu's published writings on the subject need not be mentioned. His private feelings can be found in Hu Shih, *Hu Shih te jih-chi,* entries for August 21, 1926; May 4, 1928; September 4, 1930; May 12, 1935.
137. Hu Shih, "Wang-Chiang t'ung-tien li t'i-ch'i te tzu-yu."
138. *Chinese Press Review* (Chunking) 238 (September 4, 1945): 6.
139. *Chinese Press Review* (Nanking) 457 (July 7, 1947): 5.

Chapter 8

1. The following episode divulged his feeling about his contribution to China's new literature. On the train from Shanghai to Peking on February 26, 1929, he came across the Swedish explorer Sven Hedin, who was a member of the Nobel Prize committee. Hedin intimated that he might nominate Hu for the prize in literature and suggested that Hu translate his works into English. This led Hu to reflect in private:
   I have my own opinions about this matter. If they should nominate me because of my contributions in the literary revolution, I would not decline the prize. But I am not thick-skinned enough to want to translate my works simply because, as they might think, I would be eager to win the prize. I am not qualified to be considered a creative writer. (*Hu Shih te jih-chi,* entry for February 26, 1929)
   No sooner had the significance of the literary revolution become clear than Hu began to write his own version of its history for future historians, often resorting to the third person singular.
2. *Diary,* pp. 1002–3, entry for August 21, 1916; Hu Shih, "T'ung-hsin" (Correspondence), *HCN* 2.2 (October 1, 1916): 181–83. See also Hu Shih, "Wen-hsüeh kai-liang ch'u-i" (A preliminary discussion of literary reform), *HCN* 2.5 (January 1, 1917): 407–17. Except for my deletion of one sentence, translations are those of Achilles Fang, "From Imagism to Whitmanism in Recent Chinese Poetry: A Search for Poetics that Failed," in *Indiana University Conference on Oriental-Western Literary Relations,* ed. Horst Frenz and G. L. Anderson (Chapel Hill: University of North Carolina Press, 1955), pp. 177–89.
3. *Diary,* p. 956.
4. Hu Shih, "The Renaissance in China," *Journal of the Royal Institute of International Affairs* 5.6 (November, 1926): 273. See also Hu Shih, "Tao-yen" (Introduction), in Hu Shih, ed., *Chien-she li-lun chi* (Essays on the theories concerning a constructive literature), vol. 1 of Chao Chia-pi, ed., *Chung-kuo hsin wen-hsüeh ta-hsi* (A comprehensive compendium of modern Chinese literature), 10 vols. (Shanghai, 1935).

5. *Diary*, pp. 1151–55. Hu was to repeat this point many times later.
6. Hu Shih, "The Renaissance in China" (1926), p. 273.
7. *Diary*, p. 956.
8. Ibid., pp. 737–41.
9. Ibid., p. 25.
10. Ibid., pp. 193–95.
11. Ibid., pp. 305–6.
12. Ibid., p. 306.
13. Ibid., pp. 309–10.
14. Ibid., p. 321.
15. Ibid., p. 691.
16. Hu Shih, "My Credo and Its Evolution," p. 254.
17. *Diary*, p. 307.
18. Throughout this chapter, I use *realism* and *naturalism* interchangeably because Hu Shih himself thought that the two were essentially identical. Only once in his writings did he ever make a distinction between realism and naturalism. See Hu Shih, *Hu Shih te jih-chi*, entry for July 22, 1921.

    Hu concurred with Ch'en Tu-hsiu in Hu Shih, "T'ung-hsin" (1916). For Ch'en's realist view of literature, see his "Hsien-tai Ou-chou wen-i shih-t'an" (A discussion of modern European literature), *HCN* 1.3 (November 5, 1915): 225–26; 1.4 (December 15, 1915): 319–20. Ch'en stated simplistically,

    > Due to the rise of science since the end of the nineteenth century, the real nature of the universe and human life has been increasingly uncovered. This is a so-called naked age and an age in which false masks have been stripped. This spirit has noisily spread throughout Europe. All the old moral principles, old thoughts, and old institutions handed down from antiquity are being destroyed. Literature and the arts have also followed the current and passed from romanticism to realism and further to naturalism.

    Ch'en sang generous praise of such writers as Emile Zola, the Goncourts, Flaubert, Daudet, Turgenev, and Maupassant. "All modern Eurpoean writers, whatever school they belong to, have been influenced by naturalism." Ch'en was of the opinion that Tolstoi, Zola, and Ibsen were the three greatest literary men of the world and that Ibsen, Turgenev, Wilde, and Maeterlinck were the four writers most representative of the modern world.

    See also Ch'en Tu-hsiu, "Wen-hsüeh ke-ming lun" (On the literary revolution), *HCN* 2.6 (February 1, 1917): 487–90.
19. René Wellek, "The Concept of Realism in Literary Scholarship," in his *Concepts of Criticism*, ed. Stephen G. Nichols, Jr. (New Haven: Yale University Press, 1963), pp. 222–55.
20. Lilian R. Furst and Peter N. Skrine, *Naturalism* (London: Methuen and Co., 1971).
21. Hu Shih, "Wen-hsüeh kai-liang ch'u-i," pp. 409–10.

22. Hu Shih, "*Shui-hu chuan* k'ao-cheng" (A study of *Water Margin*), *HSWT* 1:500–547.
23. Hu Shih, "*Hung-lou meng* k'ao-cheng" (A study of *Dream of the Red Chamber*), *HSWT* 1:575–620.
24. Hu Shih, "Wen-hsüeh chin-hua kuan-nein yü hsi-chü kai-liang" (The concept of progress in literature and the reform of drama), *HCN* 5.4 (October 15, 1918): 340.
25. Hu Shih, "Wu Ching-tzu chuan" (A biography of Wu Ching-tzu), *HSWT* 1:779–86.
26. Hu Shih, "Wu-shih nien lai Chung-kuo chih wen-hsüeh" (Chinese literature in the past fifty years), in *Tsui-chin chih wu-shih nien: Shen-pao kuan wu-shih chou-nien chi-nien* (The past fifty years: commemorating the fiftieth anniversary of *Shen-pao*) (Shanghai, 1923), p. 17. For a discussion of the T'ung-ch'eng school, see Yeh Lung, *T'ung-ch'eng pai wen-hsüeh shih* (A history of the literature of T'ung-ch'eng school) (Hong Kong, 1975).
27. Hu Shih, "*Hsi-yu chi* k'ao-cheng" (A study of *Journey to the West*), *HSWT* 2:354–90.
28. Hu Shih, "A Chinese Declaration of the Rights of Women," *Chinese Social and Political Science Review* 8.2 (April, 1924): 100–109; Hu Shih, "*Ching-hua yüan* te yin-lun" (A study of *Flowers in the Mirror*), *HSWT* 2:400–433.
29. Hu Shih, "*Kuan-ch'ang hsien-hsing chi* hsü" (A study of *Panorama of Officialdom*), *HSWT* 3:514–28.
30. Hu Shih, "Wu-shih nien lai Chung-kuo chih wen-hsüeh," pp. 1–23.
31. Hu Shih, "*Erh-nü ying-hsiung chuan* hsü" (A study of *Tales of Heroic Young Lovers*), *HSWT* 3:473–513.
32. C. T. Hsia, *A History of Modern Chinese Fiction* (New Haven: Yale University Press, 1971), p. 15.
33. Hu Shih, "I-pu-sheng chu-i" (Ibsenism), *HCN* 4.6 (June 15, 1918): 532.
34. Hu Shih, "*Kuan-ch'ang hsien-hsing chi* hsü."
35. Hu Shih, "Chien-she te wen-hsüeh ke-ming lun" (On a constructive literary revolution), *HCN* 4.4 (April 15, 1918): 329.
36. Hu Shih, "The Social Message in Chinese Poetry," *Chinese Social and Political Science Review* 7.1 (January, 1923): 78.
37. Hu Shih, "The Greatest Event in Life"; Hu Shih, "Chun-shen ta-shih"; Hu Shih, "I-ko wen-t'i."
38. Leo Lee, *The Romantic Generation of Modern Chinese Writers* (Cambridge, Mass.: Harvard University Press, 1973), p. 276.
39. Huang Yüan-yung, "Shih-yen—chih *Chia-yin tsa-chih* chi-che" (A letter to the *Chia-yin* magazine), *Chia-yin tsa-chih* 1.10 (October 10, 1915). Hu quoted this passage in Hu Shih, "The Renaissance in China," p. 270; Hu Shih, "The Chinese Renaissance," *China Year Book*, 1924–1925, pp. 643; Hu Shih, "The Literary Renaissance," in *Symposium on Chinese Culture,* ed. Sophia H. Chen Zen (Shanghai: China Institute of Pacific Relations, 1931), p. 150.

40. Hu Shih, "The Chinese Renaissance," p. 643; Hu Shih, "The Literary Renaissance," pp. 150–51.
41. Hu Shih, "The Chinese Renaissance," p. 641.
42. Hu Shih, "Pi-shang liang-shan: wen-hsüeh ke-ming te k'ai-shih" (Forced into outlawry: the origins of the literary revolution), *Tung-fang tsa-chih* 31.1 (January 1, 1934): 19–20.
43. *Diary*, pp. 908–18, entry for May 18 and May 29, 1916.
44. Hu Shih, "Chien-she te wen-hsüeh ke-ming lun," p. 319. Translated in William Theodore de Bary, ed., *Sources of Chinese Tradition*, 2 vols. (New York: Columbia University Press, 1966), 2:164.
45. Hu Shih, *Pai-hua wen-hsüeh shih* (A history of vernacular literature) (Shanghai, 1928), pp. 3–4, Preface, p. 11.
46. Hu Shih, "Chien-she te wen-hsüeh ke-ming lun," pp. 331–32.
47. Hu Shih, "T'ung-hsin" (Correspondence), *HCN* 3.4 (June 1, 1917): 400–401.
48. Hu Shih, "Wen-hsüeh chin-hua kuan-nien yü hsi-chü kai-liang," pp. 339–40.
49. Hu Shih, *The Chinese Renaissance* (Chicago: University of Chicago Press, 1934), p. 44.
50. Hu Shih, "Wen-hsüeh kai-liang ch'u-i," p. 409; Hu Shih, "Li-shih te wen-hsüeh kuan-nien lun" (On the historico-evolutionary concept of literature), *HCN* 3.3 (May 1, 1917): 233.
51. Hu Shih, "Ta Huang Chüeh-seng chün che-chung te wen-hsüeh ke-hsin lun" (A reply to Mr. Huang Chüeh-seng's eclectic view on literary reform), *HCN* 5.3 (September 15, 1918): 323–24.
52. Hu Shih, "Chung-hsüeh kuo-wen te chiao-shou" (Teaching Chinese at the secondary school level), *HCN* 8.1 (September 1, 1920): 17–28.
53. John Northam, *Ibsen: A Critical Study* (Cambridge, England: Cambridge University Press, 1973), pp. 221–23.
54. Hu Shih, "I-pu-sheng chu-i," p. 536.
55. Ibid., pp. 531–32. The original is in *The Collected Works of Henrik Ibsen* (New York: Charles Scribner's Sons, 1902), 11:415–16.
56. Hu Shih, "I-pu-sheng chu-i," p. 532.
57. Ibid., pp. 544–45. Henrik Ibsen, *Letters of Henrik Ibsen*, trans. J. N. Laurvik and M. Morison (New York: Fox, Duffield and Co., 1905), p. 218.
58. This is the very last sentence that the defiant Dr. Stockmann says in "An Enemy of the People."
59. Leo Lee, *The Romantic Generation of Modern Chinese Writers*, p. 251.
60. Hu Shih, "I-pu-sheng chu-i," p. 545. Translations are adopted, with revision, from Grieder, *Hu Shih*, p. 95.
61. Lilian R. Furst and Peter N. Skrine, *Naturalism*.
62. Wang Ching-hsüan (Ch'ien Hsüan-t'ung), "Wen-hsüeh ke-ming chih fan-hsiang" (A response to the literary revolution), *HCN* 4.3 (March 15, 1918): 289–92. Liu Pan-nung's untitled rejoinder to Wang Ching-hsüan is in *HCN* 4.3 (March 15, 1918): 292–309.

63. Hu Shih, "T'ung-hsin" (Correspondence), *HCN* 3.3 (May 1, 1917): 280. It should be pointed out that Lin Shu at this time was only a mild critic of the literary revolution. Disturbed by the ruse of Ch'ien Hsüan-t'ung and Liu Pan-nung, he began to attack the new literature violently. See his two short stories, "Ching-sheng" (Ching-sheng the giant), in Hu Shih, ed., *Chien-she li-lun chi*, pp. 202–3, and "Yao-meng" (The nightmare), in Cheng Chen-to, pp. 435–37. Under fictitious names, he implicated and attacked Ts'ai Yüan-p'ei, Ch'en Tu-hsiu, Hu Shih, and Ch'ien Hsüan-t'ung. Lin even vaguely appealed to the Anfu Clique for possible intervention in the affairs of Peking University. See also Chow Tse-tsung, *The May Fourth Movement*, pp. 66–68.
64. Hu Shih, "Intellectual China in 1919," *Chinese Social and Political Science Review* 5.4 (December, 1919): 345.
65. Hu Shih, "Wu-shih nien lai Chung-kuo chih wen-hsüeh," p. 23. Translations are those of Chow Tse-tsung, *The May Fourth Movement*, p. 282. Lu Hsün's remark about Mei and the *Hsüeh-heng* group was more pungent: "What I respect in you gentlemen is only that you still have the courage to publish such articles." Cited in Chow Tse-tsung, *The May Fourth Movement*, p. 282.
66. Ibsen, "An Enemy of the People," in *Six Plays of Henrik Ibsen*, trans. Eva Le Gallienne (New York: Modern Library, 1957). Emphasis in original.

Chapter 9

1. Hu Shih, "Chieh-shao wo tzu-chi te ssu-hsiang" (Introducing my own thought), *HY* 3.4 (n.d.): 1–18. Dated November 27, 1930.
2. *Diary, tzu hsü*, pp. 5–6.
3. Hu Shih, "Shih-yen chu-i" (Experimentalism), *HCN* 6.4 (April 15, 1919): 385–401; Hu Shih, "Tu-wei lun ssu-hsiang" (Dewey on thinking), *Hsin Chung-kuo* 1.2 (November 30, 1919): 1–6; Hu Shih, "Tu-wei hsien-sheng yü Chung-kuo" (Mr. Dewey and China), *Tung-fang tsa-chih* 18.13 (July 10, 1921): 121–22; Hu Shih, "The Political Philosophy of Instrumentalism," in *The Philosopher of the Common Man: Essays in Honor of John Dewey to Celebrate His Eightieth Birthday* (New York: G. P. Putnam's Sons, 1940), pp. 205–19; Hu Shih, "Instrumentalism as a Political Concept," in *Studies in Political Science and Sociology* (Philadelphia: University of Pennsylvania Press, 1941), pp. 1–6; Hu Shih, "John Dewey in China," in *Philosophy and Culture—East and West: East-West Philosophy in Practical Perspective*, ed. Charles A. Moore (Honolulu: University of Hawaii Press, 1962), pp. 762–69.
4. For example, Irene Eber ("Hu Shih and Chinese History: The Problem of *Cheng-li kuo-ku*," *Monumenta Serica*, 27 [1968]) discusses Hu's scholarship entirely in light of the Deweyan philosophy. Laurence A. Schneider (*Ku Chieh-kang and China's New History: Nationalism and the Quest for*

Alternative Tradition [Berkeley: University of California Press, 1971]) does so to a lesser extent.
5. Hu Shih, *Ssu-shih tzu-shu*, p. 74.
6. *Oral History*, pp. 110, 124, 125.
7. Grieder, *Hu Shih*, pp. 43–44.
8. Hu Shih, "My Credo and Its Evolution," p. 252.
9. *Diary*, p. 167. Translated in Grieder, *Hu Shih*, pp. 48–49.
10. *Diary*, p. 168.
11. Ibid., pp. 263–65.
12. Since there have been some important studies on the language and literature reform prior to the May Fourth period, I have kept my discussion of the subject to the minimum. Primary sources on the subject are too numerous to cite here. A convenient collection of materials on language reform is *Ch'ing-mo wen-tzu kai-ke wen-chi* (Materials on language reform in the late Ch'ing) (Peking, 1958). Two of the earliest studies of the background of the literary revolution are A Ying (Ch'ien Hsing-ts'un), *Wan-Ch'ing hsiao-shuo shih* (A history of fiction in the late Ch'ing period) (Hong Kong reprint, 1966); and Wu Wen-ch'i, *Chin pai-nien lai te Chung-kuo wen-i ssu-ch'ao* (The literary trend in China during the past hundred years) (n.p., 1940–41). Other useful studies include T'an Pi-an, *Wan-Ch'ing te pai-hua wen yün-tung* (The vernacular movement in the late Ch'ing) (Wuhan, 1956); Milena Dolezelova-Velingerova, "The Origins of Modern Chinese Literature," in *Modern Chinese Literature in the May Fourth Era*, ed. Merle Goldman (Cambridge, Mass.: Harvard University Press, 1977), pp. 17–35; C. T. Hsia, "Yen Fu and Liang Ch'i-ch'ao as Advocates of New Fiction," in *Chinese Approaches to Literature from Confucius to Liang Ch'i-ch'ao*, ed. Adele Austin Rickett (Princeton: Princeton University Press, 1978), pp. 221–57; Mabel Lee, "Liang Ch'i-ch'ao (1873–1929) and the Literary Revolution of Late-Ch'ing," in *Search for Identity: Modern Literature and the Creative Arts in Asia*, ed. A. R. Davis (Sydney, Australia: Angus and Robertson, 1974), pp. 203–24; Masuda Hajime, "Ryo Kei-cho ni tsuite—bungakushi teki ni mite" (On Liang Ch'i-ch'ao—from the standpoint of the history of literature), *Jimbun kenkyu* 6.6 (July, 1955): 49–66.
13. Wu Wen-ch'i, *Chin pai-nien lai te Chung-kuo wen-i ssu-ch'ao*, p. 32.
14. Hu Shih discussed in his diary more than once Ma Chien-chung, *Ma shih wen-t'ung* (Ma's grammar), 10 vols. (Shanghai, 1898).
15. *Diary*, pp. 758–59.
16. Hu Shih (Suh Hu), "The Problem of the Chinese Language: The Teaching of Chinese As It Is," *CSM* 2.8 (June, 1916): 567–72.
17. *Diary*, pp. 981–82.
18. Ibid., pp. 1071–73.

Hu copied in his diary these Imagist credos from a New York newspaper. (Emphasis on the word *exact* is original. All the other emphases are Hu's.)

On the whole, one cannot help admiring the spirit that animates the "new poets" in spite of some of their ludicrous failures to reach a new and higher poetry in their verse. They at least aim for the real, the natural; their work is a protest against the artificial in life as well as poetry. It is curious to note, moreover, that the principles upon which they found their art are simply, as Miss Lowell, quoted by Professor Erskine, tells us, "the essentials of all great poetry, indeed of all great literature." These six principles of imagism are from the preface to "Some Imagist Poets":

1. To *use the language of common speech, but to employ always the exact word, not the nearly exact nor the merely decorative word.*
2. To *create new rhythms—as the expression of new moods—*and not to copy old rhythms, which merely echo old moods. We do not insist upon "free verse" as the only method of writing poetry. *We fight for it as for a principle of liberty.* We believe that the individuality of a poet may often be better expressed in free verse than in conventional forms. In poetry a new cadence means a new idea.
3. To allow *absolute freedom in the choice of the subject.*
4. To *present an image* (hence the name "Imagist"). We are not a school of painters, but we believe that *poetry should render particular exactly and not deal in vague generalities,* however magnificent and sonorous.
5. To produce *poetry that is hard and clear,* never blurred nor indefinite.
6. Finally, most of us believe that *concentration* is of the very essence of poetry.

The six Imagist principles are from Amy Lowell, ed., *Some Imagist Poets: An Anthology,* 3 vols. (Boston: Houghton and Mifflin Co., 1915–17), Preface. For Imagism, see also Ezra Pound, "A Few Don'ts by An Imagiste," *Poetry: A Magazine of Verse* 1 (March 1913): 200–206.

But one can also make too much of the connection between Imagism and Hu's literary revolution. Achilles Fang goes so far as to say that the literary revolution "was inspired by a poetic movement in full swing at the time in England and America—Imagism. . . . Ezra Pound was the godfather, and Amy Lowell the god-mother, of the Chinese literary revolution of 1917" (Fang, "From Imagism to Whitmanism," pp. 179, 181).

My purpose here, of course, is not to settle the issue of the origins of the literary revolution, but to point out the complexity of this movement.

19. In April, 1916, Hu first likened *pai-hua* literature to the vulgate literature in Renaissance Europe. See *Diary,* pp. 862–67. The comparability of the two remained one of his central arguments ever after.
20. *Diary, tzu-hsü,* pp. 5–6.
21. John Dewey, *Logic: The Theory of Inquiry* (New York: Henry Holt and Co., 1938).

22. John Dewey, *Reconstruction in Philosophy* (Boston: Beacon Press, 1948), pp. 94–95. Emphasis in original.
23. Carl L. Becker, *The Heavenly City of the Eighteenth-Century Philosophers* (New Haven: Yale University Press, 1932), pp. 88–89.
24. T'an Ssu-t'ung, "Jen-hsüeh" (A study of benevolence), in T'an Ssu-t'ung, *T'an Ssu-t'ung ch'üan-chi* (Complete works of T'an Ssu-t'ung) (Peking, 1954).
25. Hu Shih, *The Development of the Logical Method in Ancient China* (Shanghai: Oriental Book Co., 1922), pp. 6–7.
26. Ibid., pp. 7–8, and passim.
27. Ibid.
28. Ibid., pp. 56, 69. Hu Shih, "Mo-chia che-hsüeh" (The philosophy of Mohism), *T'ai-p'ing yang* 1.11 (April 15, 1919): 1–24; 1.12 (July 15, 1919): 1–22.
29. Hu Shih, *Chung-kuo che-hsüeh shih ta-kang* (An outline history of Chinese philosophy) (Shanghai: Commercial Press, 1919); reissued with a new preface by Hu under the title *Chung-kuo ku-tai che-hsüeh shih* (A history of ancient Chinese philosophy) (Taipei: Commercial Press, 1958).
30. Hu Shih, "Ch'ing-tai hsüeh-che te chih-hsüeh fang-fa" (The scholarly methodology of Ch'ing-period scholars), *HSWT* 1:383–412. Dated November 3, 1921; Hu Shih, "Tai Tung-yüan te che-hsüeh" (The philosophy of Tai Tung-yüan), *Kuo-hsüeh chi-k'an* 2.1 (December, 1925); reprinted as an independent book by Taipei: Commercial Press, 1967; Hu Shih, *Chung-kuo chung-ku ssu-hsiang hsiao-shih* (A short history of medieval Chinese thought) (Taipei, 1969); Hu Shih, "Fei Ching-yü yü Fei Mi: Ch'ing-hsüeh te liang-ko hsien-ch'ü che" (Fei Ching-yü and Fei Mi: two pioneers of the Ch'ing Learning), *HSWT* 2:48–90. Dated September 17, 1924.
31. Hu Shih, "Shuo ju" (On *ju*), *HSWT* 4:1–103. Dated May 19, 1934.
32. Hu Shih, "Chung-kuo ku-tai cheng-chih ssu-hsiang-shih te i-ko k'an-fa" (An interpretation of the political philosophy of ancient China), *Tzu-yu Chung-kuo* 10.7 (April 1, 1954): 6–10.

The purpose of this chapter is not to summarize Hu's position on every issue pertaining to Chinese culture, but to show how and why his positions changed under different circumstances. Issues which in my opinion are not directly related to this purpose, such as Hu Shih's role in the controversy on "total Westernization" in the mid-1930s, will therefore not be discussed.

33. Hu Shih and Ch'en Tu-hsiu, "T'ung-hsin" (Correspondence), *HCN* 5.4 (October 15, 1918): 433. Translated in Lin Yü-sheng, *The Crisis of Chinese Consciousness*, p. 96.
34. Hu Shih, "*Wu Yü wen-lu hsü*" (Preface to the *Collected essays of Wu Yü*), in Wu Yü, *Wu Yü wen-lu* (Collected essays of Wu Yü) (Shanghai, 1921), pp. 1–7.
35. Hu Shih, "*K'o hsüeh yu jen-sheng-kuan hsü*."
36. Hu Shih, "Wo-men tui-yü Hsi-yang chin-tai wen-ming te t'ai-tu" (Our

attitude toward modern Western civilization), *Hsien-tai p'ing-lun* 4.83 (July 10, 1926): 3–11; Hu Shih, "Kindai Seiyo bummei ni taisuru gojin no taido" (Our attitude toward modern Western civilization), *Kaizo* 8.8 (August, 1926): 4–17; Hu Shih, "The Civilizations of the East and the West," in *Whither Mainkind: Panorama of Modern Civilization,* ed. Charles A. Beard (New York: Longmans, Green and Co., 1928), pp. 25–41.

37. Hu Shih, "Ts'an-t'ung te hui-i yü fan-hsing."
38. Quoted in Hu Shih, "Hsin-hsin yü fan-hsing" (Faith and reflection), *TLPL* 103 (June 3, 1934): 2–6.
39. Ibid.
40. Hu Shih, "Tsai lun hsin-hsin yü fan-hsing (Another discussion of faith and reflection), *TLPL* 105 (June 17, 1934): 2–6.
41. Hu Shih, "San lun hsin-hsin yü fan hsing" (A third discussion of faith and reflection), *TLPL* 107 (July 1, 1934): 2–6.
42. Lin Yü-sheng, *The Crisis of Chinese Consciousness,* p. 98.
43. Hu Shih, "San lun hsin-hsin yü fan-hsing."
44. Hu Shih, "Social Changes and Science," *Free China Review* 7.3 (March, 1962): 39–41.
45. Hu Shih, *The Development of the Logical Method in Ancient China,* p. 9.
46. Lin Yü-sheng, *The Crisis of Chinese Consciousness,* pp. 101, 93–95.
47. Hu Shih (Suh Hu), "A Republic for China," in *Hu Shih Items*. Originally published in the *Cornell Era,* January, 1912, pp. 240–42.
48. Ibid.
49. Hu Shih (Suh Hu), "The Confucianist Movement in China: An Historical Account and Criticism," *CSM* 9.7 (May 12, 1914): 533–36.
50. Ibid. Emphasis in original.
51. Ibid.
52. Hu Shih, *The Chinese Renaissance,* p. 26.
53. See, for example, Hu Shih, "Historical Foundations for a Democratic China," in *Edmund J. James Lectures on Government,* 2d series (Urbana: University of Illinois Press, 1941), pp. 53–64; Hu Shih, "The Struggle for Intellectual Freedom in Historical China," *World Affairs* 105.3 (September, 1942):170–73; Hu Shih, "Women's Place in Chinese History," paper read in December, 1940 at the Cosmopolitan Club in New York City and in 1945 before the American Association of University Women. Printed in 1954 according to the 1945 version.
54. Hu Shih, *The Development of the Logical Method in Ancient China,* p. 9. Emphasis in original.
55. Hu Shih, "The Civilizations of the East and the West," p. 25.
56. The Japanese version is Hu Shih, "Kindai Seiyo bummei ni taisuru gojin no taido." The two Chinese essays are Hu Shih, "Wo-men tui-yü Hsi-yang chin-tai wen-ming te t'ai-tu" and Hu Shih, "Man-yu te kan-hsiang" (Impressions of ramblings), *Hsien-tai p'ing-lun* 6.140 (August 13, 1927): 9–12; 6.141 (August 20, 1927): 11–13; 6.145 (September 17, 1927): 12–15.
57. Hu Shih, "The Civilizations of the East and the West."

58. Hu Shih, "Conflict of Cultures," in *China Christian Year Book* (Shanghai: Christian Literature Society, 1929), pp. 112–21.
59. Hu Shih, "Religion and Philosophy in Chinese History," in *Symposium on Chinese Culture,* ed. Sophia H. Chen Zen, pp. 25–28. See also Hu Shih, "The Indianization of China: A Case Study in Cultural Borrowing," in *Independence, Convergence, and Borrowing in Institutions, Thought, and Art* (Cambridge, Mass.: Harvard University Press, 1937), pp. 219–47.
60. Hu Shih, "Chih-hsüeh te fang-fa yü ts'ai-liao" (The methods and materials of scholarship), *HY* 1.9 (November 10, 1928): 1–14.
61. Hu Shih, "The Scientific Spirit and Method in Chinese Philosophy," in *The Chinese Mind: Essentials of Chinese Philosophy and Culture,* ed. Charles A. Moore (Honolulu: University of Hawaii Press, 1967), pp. 104–31. Emphasis in original.
62. Quoted in *Ibid.*
63. Ibid.
64. Hu Shih, "Confucianism and Modern Scientific Thinking," in *Modern Trends in World-Religions,* ed. Albert Eustace Haydon (Chicago: University of Chicago Press, 1934), pp. 46–51.
65. Ibid.
66. Ibid. For more information on the matter, see also Hu Shih, "The Task of Confucianism," in Albert Eustace Haydon, *Modern Trends,* pp. 245–50; Hu Shih, "Confucianism and Social Economic Problems," in Albert Eustace Haydon, *Modern Trends,* pp. 81–86.
67. Lin Yü-sheng, *The Crisis of Chinese Consciousness,* pp. 93, 94–95.

Chapter 10

1. John K. Fairbank, Edwin O. Reischauer, and Albert M. Craig, *East Asia: Tradition and Transformation* (Boston: Houghton Mifflin Co., 1973), p. 558.
2. Susanne K. Langer, *Philosophy in a New Key: A Study in the Symbolism of Reason, Rite, and Art* (Cambridge, Mass.: Harvard University Press, 1957), p. 287.
3. Robert Jay Lifton, *History and Human Survival,* pp. 153, 163.
4. *Diary,* p. 484.
5. Ibid., p. 570. See also ibid., p. 577 and Hu Shih, "A Plea for Patriotic Sanity."
6. *Diary,* pp. 832–33.
7. Hu Shih, "Ai-kuo yü-tung yü ch'iu-hsüeh."
8. Hu Shih, "Tseng-yü chin-nien te ta-hsüeh pi-yeh-sheng" (An offering to this year's university graduates), *TLPL* 7 (July, 1932): 2–5.
9. Ibid.
10. Hu Shih, *Hu Shih kei Chao Yüan-jen te hsin* (Hu Shih's letters to Chao Yüan-jen), released by Chao Yüan-jen (Taipei, 1972), p. 20.

11. Ibid., p. 30. English in the parenthesis is Hu's own.
12. Ibid., p. 41. These letters also offer glimpses of Hu's difficulties in other areas.
13. Liu K'ai, "Pei-shou Mei-kuo ch'ao-yeh ching-chung te wai-chiao-chia" (The diplomat widely respected in America), *Chuan-chi wen-hsüeh* 28.5 (May, 1976): 15–17.
14. Pai Hsien-yung, "Tung yeh" (Winter nights), in Pai Hsien-yung, *Taipei jen* (Taipei residents) (Taipei, 1971), pp. 197–217. Translation is adopted, with revision, from "Winter nights," in *Chinese Stories from Taiwan, 1960–1970*, ed. Joseph S. M. Lau (New York: Columbia University Press, 1976), pp. 337–54.
15. Hu Shih, "Chih-hsüeh te fang-fa yü ts'ai-liao."
16. Fu Ssu-nien, "Li-shih yü-yen yen-chiu-so kung-tso chih chih-ch'ü" (The main goals of the Institute of History and Philology, Academia Sinica), in Fu Ssu-nien, *Fu Meng-chen hsien-sheng chi* (Collected writings of Fu Ssu-nien), 6 vols. (Taipei, 1952), 4:169–82.
17. Ting Ling, "I-chiu-san-ling nien ch'un Shanghai" (Shanghai, spring 1930), in Ting Ling, *Ting Ling tuan-p'ien hsiao-shuo chi* (A collection of the short stories of Ting Ling) (Peking, 1954), p. 154. Translated in Leo Lee, *The Romantic Generation of Modern Chinese Writers*, pp. 271–72.
18. Hsia Tsi-an, *The Gate of Darkness: Studies on the Leftist Movement in China* (Seattle: University of Washington Press, 1968), p. 187.
19. Hu Shih, "*K'o-hsüeh yü jen-sheng-kuan* hsü," 1:2–3.
20. Hu Shih, "Lun kuo-ku hsüeh—ta Mao Tzu-shui" (On classical scholarship—a rejoinder to Mao Tzu-shui), *HSWT* 1:440–42.
21. Hu Shih, "Yen-chiu kuo-ku te fang-fa" (Methodology for the study of classical scholarship), *Tung-fang tsa-chih* 18.16 (August 25, 1921): 112–14.
22. Hu Shih, "I-ko tsui-ti hsien-tu te kuo-hsüeh shu-mu" (A minimal bibliography of the classical scholarship), *HSWT, erh-chi*, 1:165–236.

Chapter 11

1. Grieder, *Hu Shih*, p. 313.
2. Benjamin I. Schwartz, *Reflections on the May Fourth Movement*, pp. 2–3.
3. Ibid., p. 4.
4. Benjamin I. Schwartz, *In Search of Wealth and Power*, p. 25.
5. By the time Hu Shih was preparing for his son's education, a grasp of the English language and going abroad to study in a Western country had become absolute necessities.

    In September, 1929, Hu took his son, Hu Tsu-wang, ten and a half then, to Professor T. Neil Johnson of Hu-chiang University (University of Shanghai), a missionary college, to have his English tested. Hu Shih and his wife wanted their son to attend Hu-chiang's affiliated middle school where Hu Tsu-wang could live in the dormitory. Johnson, however, suggested that, because of his age, Hu Tsu-wang go to Hu-chiang's affiliated elementary school. But the elementary school had no dormitory, and daily commuting in the big city for a ten-year-old would be too hard. Johnson then mentioned that a Mr. Tu, a physics professor whose wife happened to be an American, probably could accommodate Hu Tsu-wang. Hu Shih asked that Johnson make inquiries for him. It also occurred to Hu Shih that he should consider the Chao Sung-nans of Paris. Because their son died in a car accident, the Chaos vowed to assume the responsibility for the education in France of the child of a Chinese friend. "But no one is willing to send one's young son or daughter to them in Paris," Hu said, apparently speaking of his own feeling. (Hu Shih, *Hu Shih te jih-chi,* entries for September 7 and 8, 1929.)

The arrangement to have his son live with the Tu family, however, did not work out. Hu Shih then took Hu Tsu-wang to take the entrance examination for Hu-chiang's middle school. "The test lasted from nine in the morning till four in the afternoon" (Ibid., entry for September 10, 1929).

Hu Tsu-wang successfully passed the examination, and on September 12,

> we took Tsu-wang to begin his new school. [Chiang] Tung-hsiu and I then returned home for lunch. I opened the Jewish brandy that Mr. Abraham gave us last month, and I poured two glasses. Handing one to Tung-hsiu, I said, "We hope that our son succeed." Instantaneously, her eyes turned red and tears came down. (Ibid., entry for September 12, 1929.)

These four items in Hu Shih's diary capture the essence of the modern Chinese tragedy. Hu was willing to have his son live with a family that he did not even know personally. The Chao Sung-nans' compensation for their son was to have another Chinese youngster educated in France, and Hu Shih at least considered such a possibility for his son. To receive a Western education, a ten-year-old Chinese had to take a test that lasted almost a whole day. Finally, although Chiang Tung-hsiu was perhaps not sophisticated enough to comprehend the meaning of the entire episode, she felt sad enough to shed tears.

6. Quoted in Michael H. Hunt, "The American Remission of the Boxer Indemnity," p. 550.
7. Ibid., pp. 557–58.
8. Letter of Howard Comfort, son of William W. Comfort, to the author, dated April 13, 1979.
9. Chang Yüan-hsi, "Wo so chi-te Hu Shih-chih hsien-sheng chi-chien shih," pp. 48–49.

Hu's feeling toward the Pattersons can be seen from his diary of September 14, 1914, which reads:

> Received a phone call from Mrs. Patterson, inviting me to dinner on Thursday evening. Because of a prior engagement, I had to decline. She then proposed Friday evening. It then occurred to me that Thursday is December 17 which will be my birthday and that

Mrs. Patterson is really preparing a dinner party to celebrate it. Being a traveler abroad, I have long forgotten this kind of thing. But a friend is concerned and loving enough to make efforts to help mitigate my homesickness and console my lonely feeling. How can I forget such thoughtfulness! As I was thinking, I nearly came to tears. The Pattersons treat me like a member of their family, as if I were part of their flesh and blood. I reciprocate them in the same manner.

10. *Diary*, p. 789.
11. See a brief summary in *Diary*, p. 516, entry for January 27, 1915.
12. Ibid., pp. 565–66.
13. Ibid., p. 579.
14. Hu Shih, "Cheng-ch'u hsüeh-shu tu-li te shih-nien chi-hua" (A ten-year plan to acquire the independence of scholarship), in Hu Shih, *Hu Shih te shih-lun i-chi* (Hu Shih's essays on current affairs, first series) (n.p., 1948), pp. 39–44.
15. Quoted in Ernest P. Young, *The Presidency of Yuan Shih-k'ai: Liberalism and Dictatorship in Early Republican China* (Ann Arbor: University of Michigan Press, 1977), p. 11.
16. Leo Lee, *The Romantic Generation of Modern Chinese Writers*, p. 156.
17. The two bibliographies referred to are *Columbia University Masters' Essays and Doctoral Dissertations on Asia, 1875–1956* (New York: Columbia University Libraries, 1957), which is compiled by Howard Linton; and Yüan T'ung-li, comp., *A Guide to Doctoral Dissertations by Chinese Students in America, 1905–1960* (Washington, D. C.: Sino-American Cultural Society, 1961).

Problems surrounding Hu's degree are discussed in T'ang Te-kang (T. K. Tong), *Hu Shih tsa-i*, pp. 38–43; and Hsia Chih-ch'ing (C. T. Hsia), "Hu Shih po-shih hsüeh-wei k'ao-cheng" (An investigation of Hu Shih's Ph.D. degree), *Chuan-chi wen-hsüeh* 33.5 (November, 1978): 28–35. T'ang Te-kang is the first person to have learned of Hu's degree problems in the late 1950s when Yüan T'ung-li asked for his help in locating records on Hu. Although T'ang tells us that Hu did receive a Ph.D. in 1927, T'ang's language is highly ambiguous and would not explain why neither Linton nor Yüan could find any record pertaining to Hu's degree. Linton's bibliography has no entry on Hu, while Yüan's lists both 1917 and 1927 as the years in which Hu received his degree. C. T. Hsia, too, insists that Hu earned a Ph.D. in 1927. Hsia's conclusion is based on known materials, not on official records, and dubious logic. Among Hsia's proofs is a letter of L. Carrington Goodrich written to Hsia testifying that Hu did receive his Ph.D. in 1927.

I did not conduct an investigation of my own because my purpose is no more than to point out one of Hu's burdens as a returned student as reflected in the circumstances surrounding his Ph.D. degree. Whether Hu earned a Ph.D. in 1927 or never had one would not have altered my conclusion.

Notes to Pages 209–15   261

18. Hsiao Kung-chuan, *A Modern China and a New World: K'ang Yu-wei, Reformer and Utopian, 1858–1927* (Seattle: University of Washington Press, 1975), pp. 111–12, 113, 165–68.
19. Paul A. Cohen, *Between Tradition and Modernity: Wang T'ao and Reform in Late Ch'ing China* (Cambridge, Mass: Harvard University Press, 1974), pp. 20–21.
20. Schwartz, *In Search of Wealth and Power*, p. 50.
21. Chang Hao, *Liang Ch'i-ch'ao*, pp. 157, 167.
22. Hsiao Kung-chuan, *A Modern China*, p. 437. K'ang Yu-wei's utopian ideal was spelled out in great detail in his *Ta-t'ung shu* (A treatise on universal peace), ed. Ch'ien An-ting (Shanghai, 1935). The book was completed in 1902. For cosmopolitanism in the late Ch'ing, see Wong Young-tsu, "The Ideal of Universality in Late Ch'ing Reformism" and "Wan-ch'ing pien-fa ssu-hsiang hsi-lun."
23. Hsiao Kung-chuan, *A Modern China*, p. 409.
24. Kao I-han, "Kuo-chia fei jen-sheng chih kuei-su lun" (Nation-state is not the ultimate focus of loyalty in life), *HCN* 1.4 (December 15, 1915): 287–94.
25. Ch'en Tu-hsiu, "Ai-kuo-hsin yü tzu-chüeh-hsin" (Patriotism and self-awareness), *Chia-yin tsa-chih* 1.4 (November 10, 1914): 1–6. See also Ch'en Tu-hsiu, "Wo chih ai-kuo chu-i" (My conception of patriotism), *HCN* 2.2 (October 1, 1916): 107–12; Ch'en Tu-hsiu, "Wo-men chiu-ching ying-tang pu ying-tang ai-kuo?" (Should we or should we not be patriotic?), in Ch'en Tu-hsiu, *Tu-hsiu wen-ts'un*, 1:647–50; Ch'en Tu-hsiu, "Hsüeh-sheng-chieh ying-kai p'ai-ch'ih ti Jih-huo" (The Japanese goods that Chinese student circles should boycott), *HCN* 7.2 (January 1, 1920): 313–14.
26. Schwartz, *In Search of Wealth and Power*, p. 25.
27. Ibid.
28. K'ang Yu-wei, *Ta-t'ung shu*, p. 249.
29. Ibid., pp. 193–253.
30. Ibid., p. 253. Translated in Hsiao Kung-chuan, *A Modern China*, pp. 467–68.
31. For a brief account of K'ang's taking concubines, see Hsiao Kung-chuan, *A Modern China*, p. 10.
32. Liang's letter to Hsü Chih-mo was first disclosed by Hu Shih in December, 1931, in his "Chui-tao Chih-mo" (Mourning for Chih-mo), in Hsü Chih-mo, *Hsü Chih-mo ch'üan-chi* (The complete works of Hsü Chih-mo), ed. Chiang Fu-ts'ung and Liang Shih-ch'iu, 6 vols. (Taipei, 1969), 1:355–67. Part of the translation is Leo Lee's, *The Romantic Generation of Modern Chinese Writers*, p. 136.
33. Chang Chün-ku, *Hsü Chih-mo chuan* (A biography of Hsü Chih-mo) (Taipei, 1970).
34. Leo Lee, *The Romantic Generation of Modern Chinese Writers*, pp. 136–37.
35. Leo Lee gives a delightful account of Hsü Chih-mo's romance with Lu

Hsiao-man. For Liang Ch'i-ch'ao's and Hu Shih's roles in the romance, see Hsü Chih-mo, *Hsü Chih-mo ch'üan-chi*, 1:623; and Ting Wen-chiang, *Liang Jen-kung hsien-sheng nien-p'u ch'ang-pien ch'u-kao* (First draft of a chronological biography of Liang Ch'i-ch'ao), 2 vols. (Taipei, 1959), 1:710. For Hsü Chih-mo's and Hu Shih's correspondence with Elmhirst, see Hsü Chih-mo, *Hsü Chih-mo Ying-wen shu-hsin chi* (A collection of Hsü Chih-mo's letters in English), ed. Liang Hsi-hua (Taipei, 1979).
36. Hu Shih, "Chui-tao Chih-mo."
37. Quoted in Leo Lee, *The Romantic Generation of Modern Chinese Writers*, p. 134.
38. Lin Yü-sheng, *The Crisis of Chinese Consciousness*, pp. 12-13.
39. For discussions of eremitism in traditional China, see Frederick W. Mote, "Confucian Eremitism in the Yüan Period," *The Confucian Persuasion*, ed. Arthur F. Wright (Stanford, California: Stanford University Press, 1960), pp. 202–40; and Li Chi, "The Changing Concept of the Recluse in Chinese Literature," *Harvard Journal of Asiatic Studies* 24 (1962–63): 234–47.
40. Liang Ch'i-ch'ao, "Lun hsiao-shuo yü chün-chih chih kuan-hsi" (Fiction seen in relation to the guidance of society), in Liang Ch'i-ch'ao, *Yin-ping-shih wen-chi*, ts'e 10, pp. 6–10.
41. Walter Kaufmann, "The Inevitability of Alienation" in Richard Schacht, *Alienation* (Garden City, New York: Doubleday and Co., 1970), p. lviii.
42. William Theodore de Bary "Individualism and Humanitarianism in Late Ming Thought," in *Self and Society in Ming Thought*, ed. William Theodore de Bary (New York: Columbia University Press, 1970), p. 189.
43. Paul S. Ropp, *Dissent in Early Modern China: Ju-lin wai-shih and Ch'ing Social Criticism* (Ann Arbor: University of Michigan Press, 1981), pp. 241, 118.
44. Lin Shuen-fu, "Ritual and Narrative Structure in *Ju-lin wai-shih*," in *Chinese Narrative: Critical and Theoretical Essays*, ed. Andrew H. Plaks (Princeton: Princeton University Press, 1977), p. 265.
45. Kao Yu-kung, "Lyric Vision in Chinese Narrative Tradition: A Reading of *Hung-lou meng* and *Ju-lin wai-shih*," in Plaks, *Chinese Narrative*, pp. 242–43.

Glossary

A Hsing 阿馨
ai 愛
Anfu 安福
Ariga Nagao 有賀長雄

bushido 武士道
Butsuri Gakko 物理學校

Chang Chia-ao (Kia-gnau) 張嘉璈
Chang Chün-mai (Carsun Chang)
　張君勱
Chang Hsün 張勳
Chang P'eng-ch'un 張彭春
Chang Ping-lin 章炳麟
Chang Shih-chao 章士釗
Chang Tso-lin 張作霖
Chang Tsu-hsün 張祖訓
Chang Wei-tz'u 張慰慈
Chang Yu-i 張幼儀
Chao Sung-nan 趙頌南
Ch'en Chiung-ming 陳炯明
Ch'en Heng-che (Sophia H. Chen Zen)
　陳衡哲
Chen-ju tao 眞如島
Ch'en-pao 晨報
Ch'en Shao-t'ang 陳紹唐
Ch'en Te-cheng 陳德徵
Ch'en T'ien-hua 陳天華
Ch'eng-Chu 程朱
Ch'eng-chung 澄衷
Ch'eng Fang-wu 成仿吾
Ch'eng I-ch'uan 程伊川

Ch'eng Lo-t'ing 程樂亭
cheng-ming 正名
Chi-ch'i 績溪
Chia Pao-yü 賈寶玉
Chiang Meng-lin 蔣夢麟
Chiang Tung-hsiu 江冬秀
chiao 敎
chih-hsing ho-i 知行合一
chih-kuo p'ing t'ien-hsia 治國平天下
Ch'in 秦
Chin-pu tang 進步黨
Ching-shang 經上
ching-shih hsüeh-p'ai 經世學派
Ch'iu-shih (Academy) 求是
Chou Ping-lin 周炳琳
Chu Hsi 朱熹
Chu-ko Liang 諸葛亮
chün-tzu 君子
Chün-yen 俊彥
Chung 鍾
chung 忠
Chung-kuo hsin kung-hsüeh
　中國新公學
*Chung-kuo min-ch'üan pao-chang
　t'ung-meng* 中國民權保障同盟

*Erh-shih nien mu-tu chih kuai hsien-
　chuang* 二十年目覩之怪現狀

Fan Chen 范縝
fang kao-li chai 放高利債
Fang Pao 方苞

Fu Chün-chien 傅君劍
Fukuoka 福岡

Hai-ning 海寧
Han Wu-ti 漢武帝
Hiroshima 廣島
Hsiang-ch'i-lou chien-ch'i 湘綺樓箋啟
hsiao 孝
Hsiao-ching 孝經
Hsiao-hsüeh chi-chu 小學集註
Hsin-hsüeh wei-ching k'ao 新學僞經考
Hsin-min shuo 新民說
hsiu-ts'ai 秀才
Hsüan-tsung 玄宗
Hsüeh-heng 學衡
Hsün-tzu 荀子
Hu-chiang 滬江
Hu Ch'uan 胡傳
Hu Shih lai-wang shu-hsin hsüan
　胡適來往書信選
hu-shuo po-shih 胡說博士
Hu Ssu-tu 胡思杜
Hu Tsu-wang 胡祖望
Huang Hsing 黃興
Hung-hsing 洪騂
Hung-teng chiao 紅燈教

I-ching 易經

Jehol 熱河
jen 仁
Jen Hung-chün (Shu-yung)
　任鴻雋(叔永)

k'ang-li erh chien shih-yu
　伉儷而兼師友
Kao Sheng 高升
Kao-tzu 告子
Ke-ming chün 革命軍
K'o-hsüeh she 科學社
Ku Chieh-kang 顧頡剛
ku-shih 古詩
Ku Wei-chün 顧維鈞
Kuei Heng 桂姮
K'ung-chiao hui 孔教會
K'ung-tzu kai-chih k'ao 孔子改制考

Kuo-wen chou-pao 國聞週報
Kyushu 九州

Li-chi 禮記
Li Ju-chen 李汝珍
Li Po 李白
Li Po-yüan 李伯元
liang 凉
liang-ch'i hsien-mu 良妻賢母
Liang Ssu-ch'eng 梁思成
Lin Ch'ang-min 林長民
Lin chiang hsien 臨江仙
Lin Hui-yin 林徽音
Lin Tai-yü 林黛玉
Lin Yutang 林語堂
Lo Chen-yü 羅振玉
Lo Wen-kan 羅文幹

Manchukuo 滿洲國
Mao I 毛義
Mei-ch'i 梅溪
Mei-fu kung-ssu 美孚公司
Mei Kuang-ti 梅光廸
Men 穈
Min-kuo jih-pao hsing-ch'i p'ing-lun
　民國日報星期評論

Nan-yang 南陽
niang 娘
Nieh-hai hua 孽海花

Ou-yang Hsiu 歐陽修

Pei-hai 北海
Po Chü-i 白居易

Sakyamuni 釋迦牟尼
san-huang wu-ti 三皇五帝
Shansi 山西
Shih-chi 史記
Shih-ching 詩經
Shih Nai-an 施耐庵
Shih-pao 時報
Shih-shih hsin-pao 時事新報
shih-tao jen-hsin 世道人心

Shih-yün ho-pi 詩韻合璧
Shinto 神道
Shou-chen 守眞
Shou-huan 守煥
Shou-sheng 壽生
Shu-ching 書經
Shui-ching chu 水經注
So-fei 莎菲
Soong Ch'ing-ling 宋慶齡
ssu-erh pu-hsiu 死而不朽
Ssu-ma Kuang 司馬光
Ssu-shu 四書
Su-fei 素菲
Sun Ching-ts'un 孫競存
Sun Fo (Sun K'o) 孫科
Sun Heng 孫恆
Sun Yat-sen 孫逸仙
Sung Yüan hsüeh-an ts'ui-yü 宋元學案粹語

t'ai-chi 太極
Tai Chi-t'ao 戴季陶
T'ai-hsing 泰興
T'ai-tung 泰東
T'ang Erh-ho 湯爾和
T'ang Ts'ai-ch'ang 唐才常
Tangku 塘沽
T'ao Lü-kung (Meng-ho) 陶履恭(孟和)
taotai 道臺
T'ao Yüan-ming 陶淵明
t'ien 天
Tien Ah-may (Tien Ya-mei) 田亞梅
T'ien-pao 天寶
tsa-chü 雜劇
Ts'ao Hsüeh-ch'in 曹雪芹
Ts'ao Ju-lin 曹汝霖
Tseng Kuo-fan 曾國藩
Tso-chuan 左傳
Tsou Jung 鄒容
tsung-li 總理
tu-chün 督軍
T'u-shu chi-ch'eng 圖書集成

Tuan Ch'i-jui 段祺瑞
Tuan-fang 端方
Tu Fu 杜甫
T'ung-meng hui 同盟會
Tung Pi-wu 董必武
Tung-wen hsüeh-she 東文學社
tz'u 詞
Tzu-chih t'ung-chien 資治通鑑

Uchida Yasuya (Kosai) 內田康哉

wai-kuo nu-ts'ai 外國奴才
Wang An-shih 王安石
Wang Cheng 王徵
Wang Chih-ch'un 王之春
Wang Ching-wei 汪精衞
Wang Ch'ung-hui 王寵惠
Wang Jen-ch'iu (K'ai-yün) 王壬秋(闓運)
Wang Keng 王賡
Wang T'ao 王韜
Wang Yang-ming 王陽明
wei-yen ta-i 微言大義
Wen-k'ang 文康
Wen-ming hsiao-shih 文明小史
Wu Chih-hui 吳稚暉
Wu Chu-kuo 吳柱國
wu-hou chu-i 無後主義
Wu Ju-lun 吳汝綸
Wu P'ei-fu 吳佩孚
Wu T'ing-fang 伍廷芳

yamen 衙門
Yang Ch'üan 楊銓
Yang Lan-ch'un 楊蘭春
Yang T'ien-tse 楊天擇
Yao Nai 姚鼐
Yen Hsi-shan 閻錫山
Yin 殷
Yokohama 橫濱
Yü Chin-lei 余嶔磊
yüan-ch'i 元氣
Yüan Shih-k'ai 袁世凱

Bibliography

A Ying 阿英 (Ch'ien Hsing-ts'un) 錢杏村. *Wan-Ch'ing hsiao-shuo shih* 晚淸小說史 (A history of fiction in the late Ch'ing period). Hong Kong reprint, 1966.
Angell, Norman. *The Great Illusion: A Study of the Relation of Military Power to National Advantage*. New York: G. P. Putnam's Sons, 1913.
―――. *After All: The Autobiography of Norman Angell*. New York: Farrar, Straus and Young, n.d. Preface dated 1951.
Bacon, Francis. *The Works of Francis Bacon, Lord Chancellor of England, with a Life of the Author*, by Basil Montagu, Esquire. 3 vols. Philadelphia: M. Murray, 1876.
Barker, Elmer Eugene. "Hu Shih, Incurable Optimist: Personal Recollections of a Great Humanist's Intellectual Development." In *Hu Shih Items*, pp. 1–19.
Becker, Carl L. *The Heavenly City of the Eighteenth-Century Philosophers*. New Haven: Yale University Press, 1932.
Boorman, Howard L., ed. *Biographical Dictionary of Republican China*. 4 vols. New York: Columbia University Press, 1967–71.
Chang Ch'in-shih 張欽士, ed. *Kuo-nei chin-shih-nien lai chih tsung-chiao ssu-ch'ao* 國內近十年來之宗敎思潮 (Religious thought in China over the past ten years). Peking, 1927.
Chang Chün-ku 章君榖. *Hsü Chih-mo chuan* 徐志摩傳 (A biography of Hsü Chih-mo). Taipei, 1970.
Chang Hao, *Liang Ch'i-ch'ao and Intellectual Transition in China, 1890–1907*. Cambridge, Mass.: Harvard University Press, 1971.
Chang Hsi-jo 張熙若. "Min-chu cheng-chih tang-chen shih yu-chih te cheng-chih ma?" 民主政治當眞是幼稚的政治嗎？ (Is democracy really kindergarten politics?). *TLPL* 239 (June 20, 1937): 3–6.
―――. "Wo wei-shen-mo hsiang-hsin min-chih" 我爲什麼相信民治 (Why I believe in democracy). *TLPL* 240 (June 27, 1937): 2–5.
Chang Yüan-hsi 章元義. "Wo so chi-te te Hu Shih-chih hsien-sheng chi-chien shih" 我所記得的胡適之先生幾件事 (The things I remember about Mr. Hu Shih). *Chuan-chi wen-hsüeh* 傳記文學 32.6 (June, 1978): 48–49.
Chao Chia-pi 趙家璧, ed. *Chung-kuo hsin wen-hsüeh ta-hsi* 中國新文學大系 (A comprehensive compendium of modern Chinese literature). 10 vols. Shanghai, 1935–36.

Ch'en Chih-mai 陳之邁. "Min-chu yü tu-ts'ai chih t'ao-lun" 民主與獨裁之討論 (The discussion on democracy and autocracy). *TLPL* 136 (January 20, 1935):4–11.

———. "Cheng-chih kai-ke te pi-yao" 政制改革的必要 (On the need for reform of the political system). *TLPL* 162 (August 4, 1935):2–5.

Ch'en Tu-hsiu 陳獨秀. "Ai-kuo-hsin yü tzu-chüeh-hsin" 愛國心與自覺心 (Patriotism and self-awareness). *Chia-yin tsa-chih* 甲寅雜誌 1.4 (November 10, 1914).

———. "Hsien-tai Ou-chou wen-i shih-t'an" 現代歐洲文藝史譚 (A discussion of modern European literature). *HCN* 1.3 (November 5, 1915):225–26; and 1.4 (December 15, 1915):319–20.

———. "Wo chih ai-kuo chu-i" 我之愛國主義 (My conception of patriotism). *HCN* 2.2 (October 1, 1916):107–12.

———. "Wen-hsüeh ke-ming lun" 文學革命論 (On the literary revolution). *HCN* 2.6 (February 1, 1917):487–90.

———. "Wo-men chiu-ching ying-tang pu ying-tang ai-kuo?" 我們究竟應當不應當愛國？(Should we or should we not be patriotic?). In Ch'en Tu-hsiu, *Tu-hsiu wen-ts'un* 獨秀文存 (Collected essays of Ch'en Tu-hsiu). 3 *chüan*. Shanghai, 1922. Hong Kong reprint, 1965, *chüan* 1, pp. 647–50.

———. "Hsüeh-sheng-chieh ying-kai p'ai-ch'ih ti Jih-huo" 學生界應該排斥底日貨 (The Japanese goods that Chinese student circles should boycott). *HCN* 7.2 (January 1, 1920):313–14.

———. "Chi-tu-chiao yü Chung-kuo-jen" 基督教與中國人 (Christianity and the Chinese people). *HCN* 7.3 (February 1, 1920):15–22.

———. "Chi-tu-chiao yü Chi-tu chiao-hui" 基督教與基督教會 (Christianity and the Christian church). In Ch'en Tu-hsiu, *Tu-hsiu wen-ts'un*, *chüan* 1, pp. 659–62.

Cheng Chen-to 鄭振鐸, ed. *Wen-hsüeh lun-cheng chi* 文學論爭集 (A collection of essays on the literary debate). Shanghai, 1935. Vol. 2 of Chao Chia-pi, ed. *Chung-kuo hsin wen-hsüeh ta-hsi*.

———. "Tao-yen" 導言 (Introduction). In Cheng Chen-to, pp. 1–22.

Chiang Monlin (Chiang Meng-lin). *Tides from the West: A Chinese Autobiography*. New Haven: Yale University Press, 1947.

Chiang T'ing-fu 蔣廷黻. "Chih-shih chieh-chi yü cheng-chih" 知識階級與政治 (The intelligentsia and politics). *TLPL* 51 (May 21, 1933):15–19.

———. "Ke-ming yü chuan-chih" 革命與專制 (Revolution and despotism). *TLPL* 80 (December 10, 1933):2–5.

———. "Lun chuan-chih ping ta Hu Shih-chih hsien-sheng" 論專制並答胡適之先生 (On despotism, in reply to Mr. Hu Shih). *TLPL* 83 (December 31, 1933):2–6.

Ch'ien Hsüan-t'ung 錢玄同. "Chung-kuo chin-hou chih wen-tzu wen-t'i" 中國今後之文字問題 (China's language in the future). *HCN* 4.4 (April 15, 1918):381–87.

Ch'ien Tuan-sheng 錢端升. "Min-chu cheng-chih hu? Chi-ch'üan kuo-chia hu?" 民主政治乎？極權國家乎？(Democracy or a totalitarian state?). *Tung-fang tsa-chih* 東方雜誌 31.1 (January 1, 1934):17–25.

———. "Tui-yü liu-chung ch'üan-hui te ch'i-wang" 對於六中全會的期望 (Our

hopes for the sixth plenary sessions). *TLPL* 162 (August 4, 1935): 5–9.
China Weekly Review. (Formerly *Millard's Review*). Shanghai, 1917–49.
Ch'ing-mo wen-tzu kai-ke wen-chi 清末文字改革文集 (Materials on language reform in the late Ch'ing). Peking, 1958.
Ch'iu T'ing-liang 裘廷梁. "Lun pai-hua wei wei-hsin chih pen" 論白話爲維新之本 (On *pai-hua* as the foundation of modernity). In Chien I-chih 簡夷之 et al., eds. *Chung-kuo chin-tai wen lun hsüan* 中國近代文論選 (A selection of modern Chinese essays). 2 vols. Peking, 1962. 1:176–80.
Chou Min-chih 周明之. "Wu-ssu shih ch'i ssu-hsiang wen-hua te ch'ung-t'u—i Hu Shih te hun-yin wei li" 五四時期思想文化的衝突—以胡適的婚姻爲例 (Cultural and intellectual conflicts in the May Fourth period: the case of Hu Shih's marriage). In *Wu-ssu yen-chiu lun-wen chi* 五四研究論文集 (Essays in commemoration of May Fourth), edited by Wang Yung-tsu (Wong Young-tsu) 汪榮祖. Taipei, 1979. Pp. 177–208.
Chou Tso-jen 周作人. "Jih-pen te hsin-ts'un" 日本的新村 (Japan's new village). *HCN* 6.3 (March 15, 1919): 297–308.
———. "Fang Jih-pen hsin-ts'un chi" 訪日本新村記 (A visit to the new village in Japan). *Hsin-ch'ao* 新潮 2.1 (October, 1919): 69–80.
———. "Hsin-ts'un te ching-shen" 新村的精神 (The spirit of the new village). *HCN* 7.2 (January 1, 1920): 129–34.
Chow Tse-tsung. *The May Fourth Movement: Intellectual Revolution in Modern China*. Cambridge, Mass.: Harvard University Press, 1960.
———. (Chou Ts'e-tung) 周策縱. "Hu Shih-chih hsien-sheng te k'ang-i yü jung-jen" 胡適之先生的抗議與容忍 (Mr. Hu Shih's protestation and tolerance). *Hai-wai lun-t'an* 海外論壇 3.5 (May 1, 1962): 21–38.
Chung-kuo ta-t'ung ssu-hsiang tzu-liao 中國大同思想資料 (Historical materials on utopian thought in China). Shanghai, 1959.
Cohen, Paul A. *Between Tradition and Modernity: Wang T'ao and Reform in Late Ch'ing China*. Cambridge, Mass.: Harvard University Press, 1974.
Columbia University Masters' Essays and Doctoral Dissertations on Asia, 1875–1956. New York: Columbia University East Asiatic Library, 1957.
Crick, Bernard. *In Defense of Politics*. Baltimore: Penguin Books, 1964.
de Bary, William Theodore, ed. *Sources of Chinese Tradition*. 2 vols. New York: Columbia University Press, 1966.
———. "Individualism and Humanitarianism in Late Ming Thought." In *Self and Society in Ming Thought*, edited by William Theodore de Bary. New York: Columbia University Press, 1970. Pp. 145–247.
———. "Neo-Confucian Cultivation and the Seventeenth-Century 'Enlightenment.'" In *The Unfolding of Neo-Confucianism*, edited by William Theodore de Bary. New York: Columbia University Press, 1975. Pp. 141–216.
Dewey, John. *Reconstruction in Philosophy*. Boston: Beacon Press, 1948.
———. "Force, Violence and Law." *New Republic* 5 (January 22, 1916): 295–97.
———. *Essays in Experimental Logic*. Chicago: University of Chicago Press, 1916.
———. "Force and Coercion." *International Journal of Ethics* 26.3 (April, 1916): 359–67.
———. *Logic: The Theory of Inquiry*. New York: Henry Holt and Co., 1938.

Dictionary of American Biography. New York: Charles Scribner's Sons, 1928—.
Dolezelova-Velingerova, Milena. "The Origins of Modern Chinese Literature." In *Modern Chinese Literature in the May Fourth Era*, edited by Merle Goldman. Cambridge, Mass.: Harvard University Press, 1977. Pp. 17–35.
Eber, Irene. "Hu Shih and Chinese History: The Problem of *Cheng-li kuo-ku*." *Monumenta Serica* 27 (1968):169–207.
Emerson, Rupert. *From Empire to Nation: The Rise to Self-Assertion of Asian and African Peoples*. Boston: Beacon Press, 1960.
Erikson, Erik H. *Childhood and Society*. New York: W. W. Norton and Company, 1963.
———. *Gandhi's Truth: On the Origins of Militant Nonviolence*. New York: W. W. Norton and Company, 1969.
Fairbank, John K., Edwin O. Reischauer, and Albert M. Craig. *East Asia: Tradition and Transformation*. Boston: Houghton Mifflin Company, 1973.
Fang, Achilles. "From Imagism to Whitmanism in Recent Chinese Poetry: A Search for Poetics That Failed." In *Indiana University Conference on Oriental-Western Literary Relations*, edited by Horst Frenz and G. L. Anderson. Chapel Hill: University of North Carolina Press, 1955. Pp. 177–89.
Foreign Relations of the United States, Diplomatic Papers, 1935. Vol. 3: *The Far East*. Washington, D.C.: Government Printing Office, 1953.
Foreign Relations of the United States, Diplomatic Papers, 1942: China. Washington, D.C.: Government Printing Office, 1956.
Freud, Anna. *The Ego and the Mechanisms of Defense*. Trans. from the German by Cecil Baines. New York: International Universities Press, 1966.
Fu Ssu-nien 傅斯年. "Li-shih yü-yen yen-chiu-so kung-tso chih chih-ch'ü" 歷史語言研究所工作之旨趣 (The main goals of the Institute of History and Philology, Academia Sinica). In Fu Ssu-nien, *Fu Meng-chen hsien-sheng chi* 傅孟眞先生集 (Collected writings of Fu Ssu-nien). 6 vols. Taipei, 1952. 4:169–82. Dated October, 1928.
Furst, Lilian R., and Peter N. Skrine. *Naturalism*. London: Methuen and Co., 1971.
Furth, Charlotte. *Ting Wen-chiang: Science and China's New Culture*. Cambridge, Mass.: Harvard University Press, 1970.
———. "May Fourth in History." In *Reflections on the May Fourth Movement: A Symposium*, edited by Benjamin I. Schwartz. Cambridge, Mass.: Harvard University Press, 1972. Pp. 59–68.
Gannett, Lewis S. "Hu Shih: Young Prophet of Young China." *New York Times Magazine*, March 27, 1927. Pp. 10, 20.
———. *Young China*. New York: The Nation, Inc., 1927.
Gay, Peter. *The Enlightenment: An Interpretation. The Rise of Modern Paganism*. New York: Alfred A. Knopf, 1966.
Giglio-Tos, Efisio. *Appel pour le Désarmement et pour la Paix: Les Pionniers de la Société Des Nations et de la Fraternité Internationale; d'après les arcives de la "Corda Fratres," Fédération Internationale des Etudiants, 1898–1931*. Torino: Tipografia A. Kluc, 1931.
Grieder, Jerome B. *Hu Shih and the Chinese Renaissance: Liberalism in the Chinese Revolution, 1917–1937*. Cambridge, Mass.: Harvard University Press, 1970.

Harbour, J. L. "High Achievements of Mr. Suh Hu." In *Hu Shih Items*. Dated October 10, 1914.
Ho, Kenneth P. H., trans., *The Nineteen Ancient Poems*. Hong Kong: Kelly and Walsh, 1977.
Hofstadter, Richard. *Social Darwinism in American Thought*. Boston: Beacon Press, 1955.
Hsia, C. T. "Yen Fu and Liang Ch'i-ch'ao as Advocates of New Fiction." In *Chinese Approaches to Literature from Confucius to Liang Ch'i-ch'ao*, edited by Adele Austin Rickett. Princeton: Princeton University Press, 1978. Pp. 221–57.
──────. *A History of Modern Chinese Fiction*. New Haven: Yale University Press, 1971.
Hsia Chih-ch'ing (C. T. Hsia) 夏志清. "Hu Shih po-shih hsüeh-wei k'ao-cheng" 胡適博士學位考證 (An investigation of Hu Shih's Ph.D. degree). *Chuan-chi wen-hsüeh* 33.5 (November 1978): 28–35.
──────. "*Hu Shih tsa-i* hsü" 胡適雜憶序 (Foreword to *Miscellaneous reminiscences of Hu Shih*). In T'ang Te-kang (T. K. Tong) 唐德剛, *Hu Shih Tsa-i* 胡適雜憶 (Miscellaneous reminiscences of Hu Shih). Taipei, 1979.
Hsia Tsi-an. *The Gate of Darkness: Studies on the Leftist Literary Movement in China*. Seattle: University of Washington Press, 1968.
Hsiao Kung-chuan. *A Modern China and a New World: K'ang Yu-wei, Reformer and Utopian, 1858–1927*. Seattle: University of Washington Press, 1975.
Hsü Chih-mo 徐志摩. *Hsü Chih-mo ch'üan-chi* 徐志摩全集 (The complete works of Hsü Chih-mo). Edited by Chiang Fu-ts'ung 蔣復璁 and Liang Shih-ch'iu 梁實秋. 6 vols. Taipei, 1969.
──────. *Hsü Chih-mo Ying-wen shu-hsin chi* 徐志摩英文書信集 (A collection of Hsü Chih-mo's letters in English). Edited by Liang Hsi-hua 梁錫華. Taipei, 1979.
Hu Shih 胡適 (signed Shih-an 適广). "Chung-kuo te cheng-fu" 中國的政府 (The Chinese government). *Ching-yeh hsün-pao* 競業旬報 28 (1906–8): 33–35.
────── (signed Tieh-erh 鐵兒). "Hun-yin p'ien" 婚姻篇 (On marriage). *Ching-yeh hsün-pao* 25 (1906–8): 1–5.
────── (signed Shih-chih 適之). "Chung-kuo ti-i wei-jen Yang Ssu-sheng chuan" 中國第一偉人楊斯盛傳 (A biography of Yang Ssu-sheng). *Ching-yeh hsün-pao* 25 (1906–8): 9–12.
────── (signed Shih-chih). "Ch'ung-pai ying-hsiung" 崇拜英雄 (Hero worship). *Ching-yeh hsün-pao* 25 (1906–8): 47–48.
────── (signed Shih-chih). "Wu-kuei ts'ung-hua" 無鬼叢話 (On the nonexistence of the spirit). *Ching-yeh hsün-pao* 25 (1906–8): 27–28; and 28 (1906–8): 37–39.
────── (signed Tieh-erh). "Lun hui-ch'u shen-fo" 論毀除神佛 (On destroying god and Buddha). *Ching-yeh hsün-pao* 28 (1906–8): 1–5.
────── (signed Tieh-erh). "Ai kuo" 愛國 (Patriotism). *Ching-yeh hsün-pao* 34 (1906–8): 1–6.
────── (signed Hsing 騂). "Tui-yü Chung-kuo kung-hsüeh feng-ch'ao chih kan-yen" 對於中國公學風潮之感言 (Reflections on the student strike at the China National Institute). *Ching-yeh hsün-pao* 34 (1906–8): 21–25.
────── (Suh Hu). "A Republic for China." In *Hu Shih Items*. Originally published in *Cornell Era*, January, 1912, pp. 240–42.

——— (Suh Hu). "The Ideal Missionary," an address given at the First Baptist Church, Ithaca, New York, February 2, 1913. 8pp. In *Hu Shih Items*.
——— (Suh Hu). "The International Student Movement." *CSM* 9.1 (November 10, 1913): 37–39.
——— (Suh Hu). "The Confucianist Movement in China: An Historical Account and Criticism." *CSM* 9.7 (May 12, 1914): 533–36.
——— (using the pseudonym Bernard W. Savage). "A Defense of Browning's Optimism," the Corson Browning Prize Essay, 1914. Department of Manuscripts and University Archives, Cornell University Libraries, Cornell University.
——— (Suh Hu). "Marriage Customs in China." In *Hu Shih Items*. Originally in *Cornell Era*, June, 1914, pp. 610–11.
——— (Suh Hu). "Japan and Kiao-chau." *CSM* 10.1 (October, 1914): 27.
——— (Suh Hu). "History of the German Leased Territory of Kiao-chau." *CSM* 10.2 (November, 1914): 68–69.
——— (Suh Hu). "The Philosophy of Browning and Confucianism." Essay read before the Browning Society of Boston, January 19, 1915. In *Hu Shih Items*.
——— (Suh Hu). "Letter to the *New Republic*." *New Republic* 2.17 (February 27, 1915): 103; *CSM* 10.6 (March, 1915): 389–90.
——— (Suh Hu). "A Plea for Patriotic Sanity: An Open Letter to All Chinese Students." *CSM* 10.7 (April, 1915): 425–26.
——— (Suh Hu). "China and Democracy." *Outlook* 3 (September 1, 1915): 27–28.
——— (Suh Hu). "A Philosopher of Chinese Reactionism." *CSM* 2.1 (November, 1915): 16–19.
———. Letter to the *New York Evening Post*, November 23, 1915.
——— (Suh Hu). "Analysis of the Monarchical Restoration in China." In *Hu Shih Items*. Originally in *Columbia Spectator*, January 14, 1916.
——— (Suh Hu). "A Chinese Philosopher on War: A Popular Presentation of the Ethical and Religious Views of Mo-Ti." *CSM* 11.6 (April, 1916): 408–12.
——— (Suh Hu). "Classical Confucianism." *CSM* 11.7 (May, 1916): 510–13.
——— (Suh Hu). "Is There a Substitute for Force in International Relations?" International Polity Club Competition, Prize Essay. New York: American Association for International Conciliation, 1916. Reproduced in *Hu Shih Items*.
——— (Suh Hu). "The Problem of the Chinese Language: The Teaching of Chinese As It Is." *CSM* 11.8 (June, 1916): 567–72.
———. "T'ung-hsin" 通信 (Correspondence). *HCN* 2.2 (October 1, 1916): 181–83.
——— (Suh Hu). "Manufacturing the Will of the People: A Documentary History of the Recent Monarchical Movement in China." *Journal of Race Development* 7.3 (January, 1917): 319–28.
——— (Suh Hu). "Classical Confucianism." *Monist* 27.1 (January, 1917): 157–60.
———. "Wen-hsüeh kai-liang ch'u-i" 文學改良芻議 (A preliminary discussion of literary reform). *HCN* 2.5 (January 1, 1917): 407–17.
———. "Ping-chung te Tung-hsiu shu" 病中得冬秀書 (Receiving a letter from Tung-hsiu while I am ill). In Hu Shih, *Ch'ang-shih chi* 嘗試集 (A collection of experiments). Shanghai, 1920; Taipei, 1971. Pp. 111–12. Dated January 16, 1917.

———, trans. "Erh yü-fu" 二漁夫 (Deux Amis). *HCN* 3.1 (March 1, 1917): 23–29.
———. "Li-shih te wen-hsüeh kuan-nien lun" 歷史的文學觀念論 (On the historico-evolutionary concept of literature). *HCN* 3.3 (May 1, 1917): 233–35.
———. "T'ung-hsin" 通信 (Correspondence). *HCN* 3.3 (May 1, 1917): 279–82.
———. "T'ung-hsin" 通信 (Correspondence). *HCN* 3.4 (June 1, 1917): 399–401.
——— (Suh Hu). *Ha algum substituto eficaz que se imponha á forca nas relacoes internacionaes?* American Association for International Conciliation, Pan-American Division, bulletin no. 13. New York, 1917.
———. "Kuei-kuo tsa-kan" 歸國雜感 (Random reflections on returning home). *HCN* 4.1 (January 15, 1918): 25–31.
———. "Chien-she te wen-hsüeh ke-ming lun" 建設的文學革命論 (On a constructive literary revolution). *HCN* 4.4 (April 15, 1918): 317–34.
———. "Hsin-hun tsa-shih" 新婚雜詩 (Poems in various styles on being newly married). *HCN* 4.4 (April 15, 1918): 339–40.
———. "Chung-kuo chin-hou chih wen-tzu wen-t'i" 中國今後之文字問題 (China's language in the future). *HCN* 4.4 (April 15, 1918): 387–88.
———. "Lun tuan-p'ien hsiao-shuo" 論短篇小說 (On short story). *HCN* 4.5 (May 15, 1918): 429–41.
———. "I-pu-sheng chu-i" 易卜生主義 (Ibsenism). *HCN* 4.6 (June 15, 1918): 531–49.
———. "Chen-ts'ao wen-t'i" 貞操問題 (The question of chastity). *HCN* 5.1 (July 15, 1918): 9–18.
———. "Hsin wen-hsüeh wen-t'i chih t'ao-lun" 新文學問題之討論 (A discussion of the problems of new literature). *HCN* 5.2 (August 15, 1918): 179–82.
———. "Mei-kuo te fu-jen" 美國的婦人 (American women). *HCN* 5.3 (September 15, 1918): 231–42.
———. "Ni mo wang-chi" 你莫忘記 (You should not forget). *HCN* 5.3 (September 15, 1918): 244–45.
———. "Ta Huang Chüeh-seng chün che-chung te wen-hsüeh ke-hsin lun" 答黃覺僧君折衷的文學革新論 (A reply to Mr. Huang Chüeh-seng's eclectic view on literary reform). *HCN* 5.3 (September 15, 1918): 320–24.
———. "Wen-hsüeh chin-hua kuan-nien yü hsi-chü kai-liang" 文學進化觀念與戲劇改良 (The concept of progress in literature and the reform of drama). *HCN* 5.4 (October 15, 1918): 331–44.
——— and Ch'en Tu-hsiu. "T'ung-hsin" 通信 (Correspondence). *HCN* 5.4 (October 15, 1918): 431–33.
———. "Wu-li chieh-chüeh yü chieh-chüeh wu-li" 武力解決與解決武力 (Resolving problems by force, and resolving the problem of force). *HCN* 5.6 (December 15, 1918): 605–8.
———. "Hsien-mu hsing-shu" 先母行述 (Reflections on my late mother's life). *HSWT* 1: 787–91. Dated December, 1918.
———. "Shih-erh-yüeh i-jih tao-chia" 十二月一日到家 (Arriving home on December first). *Hsin-ch'ao* 1.2 (February, 1919): 281.
———. "Pu-hsiu—wo-te tsung-chiao" 不朽—我的宗教 (Immortality—my religion). *HCN* 6.2 (February 15, 1919): 96–105.
———. "The Greatest Event in Life." In *The Chinese Theater*, edited by A. E. Zucker. Boston: Little, Brown and Co., 1925. Pp. 119–28.

———. "Chung-shen ta-shih" 終身大事 (The greatest event in life). *HCN* 6.3 (March 15, 1919): 343–51.

———. "Lun chen-ts'ao wen-t'i" 論貞操問題 (On the question of chastity). *HSWT* 1:676–84. Dated April, 1919.

———. "Shih-yen chu-i" 實驗主義 (Experimentalism). *HCN* 6.4 (April 15, 1919): 385–401.

———. "Wo-te erh-tzu" 我的兒子 (My son). In Hu Shih, *Ch'ang-shih chi*, pp. 177–79. Dated June, 1919.

———. "To yen-chiu hsieh wen-t'i, shao t'an hsieh chu-i" 多研究些問題，少談些主義 (Study more problems, talk less of isms). *Mei-chou p'ing-lun* 每週評論 31 (July 20, 1919); *T'ai-p'ing yang* 太平洋 2.1 (May 5, 1920): 1–10.

———. "Wo-te erh-tzu" 我的兒子 (My son). *HSWT* 1:687–92. Dated June, 1919.

———. "Hsü I-sun chuan" 許怡蓀傳 (A biography of Hsü I-sun). *Hsin Chung-kuo* 新中國 1.4 (August 15, 1919): 17–26.

———. "Lun kuo-ku hsüeh—ta Mao Tzu-shui" 論國故學，答毛子水 (On classical scholarship: a rejoinder to Mao Tzu-shui). *HSWT* 1:440–42. Dated August 16, 1919.

———. "San lun wen-t'i yü chu-i" 三論問題與主義 (A third discussion of problems and isms). *Mei-chou p'ing-lun* 36 (August 24, 1919); *T'ai-p'ing yang* 2.1 (May 5, 1920): 15–21.

———. "Ssu lun wen-t'i yü chu-i: lun shu-ju hsüeh-li te fang-fa" 四論問題與主義：論輸入學理的方法 (A fourth discussion of problems and isms: on the methods of importing theories). *Mei-chou p'ing-lun* 37 (August 31, 1919); *T'ai-p'ing yang* 2.1 (May 5, 1920): 21–25.

———. "Wo tui sang-li te i-tien i-chien" 我對喪禮的一點意見 (Some of my ideas on funeral rites). *HCN* 6.6 (November 1, 1919): 641–50.

———. "Mo-chia che-hsüeh" 墨家哲學 (The philosophy of Mohism). *T'ai-p'ing yang* 1.11 (April 15, 1919): 1–24; 1.12 (July 15, 1919): 1–22.

———. "Tu-wei lun ssu-hsiang" 杜威論思想 (Dewey on thinking). *Hsin Chung-kuo* 1.2 (November 30, 1919): 1–6.

———. "Hsin ssu-ch'ao te i-i" 新思潮的意義 (The meaning of the new thought). *HCN* 7.1 (December 1, 1919): 9–16.

———. "Li Ch'ao chuan" 李超傳 (A biography of Li Ch'ao). *Hsin-ch'ao* 2.2 (December, 1919): 266–75.

———. "Lun nü-tzu wei ch'iang-pao so-wu" 論女子為強暴所汙 (On women assaulted by violence). *HSWT* 1:685–86. Dated 1919.

———. "I-ko wen-t'i" 一個問題 (One big question). *HSWT* 1:805–12. Dated 1919.

———. (Hu Suh). "Intellectual China in 1919." *Chinese Social and Political Science Review* 5.4 (December, 1919): 345–55.

———. *Chung-kuo che-hsüeh shih ta-kang* 中國哲學史大綱 (An outline history of Chinese philosophy). Shanghai: Commercial Press, 1919; reissued, with a new preface by Hu Shih, under the title *Chung-kuo ku-tai che-hsüeh shih* 中國古代哲學史 (A history of ancient Chinese philosophy). Taipei: Commercial Press, 1958.

———. "Fei ko-jen chu-i te hsin sheng-huo" 非個人主義的新生活 (A new life of nonindividualism). *Hsin-ch'ao* 2.3 (April, 1920):467–77. Dated January 26, 1920.

———. "Kung-tu chu-i shih-hsing te kuan-ch'a" 工讀主義試行的觀察 (Observations on the work-study program). *HCN* 7.5 (April 1, 1920):817–21.

——— and Chiang Meng-lin. "Wo-men tui-yü hsüeh-sheng te hsi-wang" 我們對於學生的希望 (Our hopes for the students). *Tung-fang tsa-chih* 17.11 (June 10, 1920):107–12.

———. "*Shui-hu chuan* k'ao-cheng" 水滸傳考證 (A study of *Water Margin*), *HSWT* 1:500–547. Dated July 27, 1920.

——— et al. "Cheng tzu-yu te hsüan-yen" 爭自由的宣言 (A manifesto of struggle for freedom). *Tung-fang tsa-chih* 17.16 (August 25, 1920):133–34.

———. "Chung-hsüeh kuo-wen te chiao-shou" 中學國文的教授 (Teaching Chinese at the secondary school level). *HCN* 8.1 (September 1, 1920):17–28. Dated March 24, 1920.

———. "Wu Ching-tzu chuan" 吳敬梓傳 (A biography of Wu Ching-tzu). *HSWT* 1:779–86. Dated November, 1920.

———. "Pu-hsiu—wo-te tsung-chiao" 不朽—我的宗教 (Immortality—my religion). *HSWT* 1:693–702. Dated May, 1921.

———. "Huang Li-chou lun hsüeh-sheng yün-tung" 黃梨洲論學生運動 (Huang Li-chou on student movement). *HSWT, erh-chi, chüan* 3, pp. 11–15. Dated May 2, 1921.

———. "*Wu Yü wen-lu* hsü" 吳虞文錄序 (Preface to the *Collected essays of Wu Yü*). In Wu Yü 吳虞. *Wu Yü wen-lu* 吳虞文錄 (Collected essays of Wu Yü). Shanghai, 1921. Pp. 1–7. Dated June 16, 1921.

———. "Kuo-yü wen-fa te yen-chiu fa" 國語文法的研究法 (The method of studying the grammar of the national language). *HCN* 9.3 (July 1, 1921):293–303; 9.4 (August 1, 1921):433–48.

———. "Yen-chiu kuo-ku te fang-fa" 研究國故的方法 (Methodology for the study of classical scholarship). *Tung-fang tsa-chih* 18.16 (August 25, 1921):112–14.

———. "Ch'ing-tai hsüeh-che te chih-hsüeh fang-fa" 清代學者的治學方法 (The scholarly methodology of Ch'ing-period scholars). *HSWT* 1:383–412. Dated November 3, 1921.

———. "*Hung-lou meng* k'ao-cheng" 紅樓夢考證 (A study of *Dream of the Red Chamber*). *HSWT* 1:575–620. Dated November 12, 1921.

———. *Hu Shih te jih-chi* 胡適的日記 (Hu Shih's unpublished diaries, 1921–40), deposited at the Library of Congress.

———. (Hu Suh). "The Literary Revolution in China." *Chinese Social and Political Science Review* 6.2 (1922):91–100. Dated February, 1922.

———. "Tu-wei hsien-sheng yü Chung-kuo" 杜威先生與中國 (Mr. Dewey and China). *Tung-fang tsa-chih* 18.13 (July 10, 1921):121–22.

———."Wu-shih nien lai Chung-kuo chih wen-hsüeh" 五十年來中國之文學 (Chinese literature in the past fifty years), in *Tsui-chin chih wu-shih nien: Shen-pao-kuan wu-shih chou-nien chi-nien* 最近之五十年：申報館五十週年紀念 (The past half century: commemorating the fiftieth anniversary of *Shen-pao*).

Shanghai, 1923. Pp. 1–23. Dated March 3, 1922.

———. "Nu-li ko" 努力歌 (A song of endeavor). *NLCP* 1 (May 7, 1922).

——— et al. "Wo-men te cheng-chih chu-chang" 我們的政治主張 (Our political proposals). *NLCP* 2 (May 14, 1922).

———. "*San-kuo-chih yen-i* hsü" 三國志演義序 (An introduction to *Romance of the Three Kingdoms*). *HSWT* 2:467–75. Dated May 16, 1922.

———. "Hou nu-li ko" 後努力歌 (A second song of endeavor). *NLCP* 4 (May 28, 1922).

———. "Kuan-yü 'Wo-men te cheng-chih chu-chang' te t'ao-lun" 關於"我們的政治主張"的討論 (Discussions of 'Our political proposals'). *NLCP* 4 (May 28, 1922): et seq.

———. "Cheng-lun-chia yü cheng-tang" 政論家與政黨 (Political commentators and political parties). *NLCP* 5 (June 4, 1922).

———. "Cheng-chih yü chi-hua" 政治與計劃 (Politics and planning). *NLCP* 7 (June 18, 1922).

———. "Wo-te ch'i-lu" 我的歧路 (My predicament). *NLCP* 7 (June 18, 1922): 3–4.

———. "Wang Mang: i-ch'ien chiu-pai nien ch'ien te i-ko she-hui-chu-i-che" 王莽：一千九百年前的一個社會主義者 (Wang Mang, the socialist emperor of nineteen centuries ago). *HSWT* 2:20–27. Dated September 3, 1922.

———. "Hu Shih hsien-sheng tao-ti tsen-yang?" 胡適先生到底怎樣？(How *Is* Mr. Hu Shih?). *NLCP* 36 (January 7, 1923).

———. "The Social Message in Chinese Poetry." *Chinese Social and Political Science Review* 7.1 (January 1923):66–79.

———. "Che i-chou" 這一週 (This week). *NLCP* 7 (June 18, 1922) to 48 (April 1, 1923).

———. "Tsai lun chung-hsüeh te kuo-wen chiao-hsüeh" 再論中學的國文教學 (Again on teaching Chinese at the secondary school level). *HSWT* 2:484–94. Dated August 17, 1922.

———. "Wu-shih nien lai chih shih-chieh che-hsüeh" 五十年來之世界哲學 (World philosophy in the past fifty years). In *Tsui-chin chih wu-shih nien: Shen-pao-kuan wu-shih chou-nien chi-nien* 最近之五十年：申報館五十週年紀念 (The past half century: Commemorating the fiftieth anniversary of *Shen-pao*). Shanghai, 1923. Pp. 1–16. Dated September 5, 1922.

———. "Lien-sheng tzu-chih yü chün-fa ko-chü—ta Ch'en Tu-hsiu" 聯省自治與軍閥割據—答陳獨秀 (Federative provincial self-government and warlord separatism—a rejoinder to Ch'en Tu-hsiu). *NLCP* 19 (September 10, 1922).

———. "Kuo-chi te Chung-kuo" 國際的中國 (China among the nations). *NLCP* 22 (October 1, 1922).

———. *The Development of the Logical Method in Ancient China*. Shanghai: Oriental Book Co., 1922.

———. "Ts'ai Yüan-p'ei yü Pe-ching chiao-yü chieh" 蔡元培與北京教育界 (Ts'ai Yüan-p'ei and the educational circle of Peking). *NLCP* 39 (January 28, 1923).

———. "*Kuo-hsüeh chi-k'an* fa-k'an hsüan-yen" 國學季刊發刊宣言 (Manifesto of *Kuo-hsüeh chi-k'an*). *HSWT* 2:1–18. Dated January, 1923.

———. "*Hsi-yu chi* k'ao-cheng" 西遊記考證 (A study of *Journey to the West*).

HSWT 2:354–90. Dated February 4, 1923.

———. "I-ko tsui-ti hsien-tu te kuo-hsüeh shu-mu" 一個最低限度的國學書目 (A minimal bibliography of the classical scholarship). *HSWT erh-chi, chüan* 1, pp. 165–236. Dated February, 1923.

———. "*Ching-hua yüan* te yin-lun" 鏡花緣的引論 (A study of *Flowers in the Mirror*). *HSWT* 2:400–433. Dated March, 1923.

———. "Yü I-han teng ssu-wei te hsin" 與一涵等四位的信 (Letter to [Kao] I-han and others). *HSWT, erh-chi, chüan* 3, pp. 141–44. Dated October 9, 1923.

———. "I-nien-pan te hui-ku" 一年半的回顧 (Reflecting upon the past year and a half). *NLCP* 75 (October 21, 1923).

———. "*K'o-hsüeh yü jen-sheng-kuan* hsü" 科學與人生觀序 (Preface to *Science and the Philosophy of Life*). *K'o-hsüeh yü jen-sheng-kuan* 科學與人生觀 (Science and the philosophy of life). 2 vols. Shanghai, 1923. 1:1–29.

———. "*Cheng-chih kai-lun* hsü" 政治概論序 (Preface to *Introduction to Politics* [by Chang Wei-tz'u]). *HSWT, erh-chi, chüan* 3, pp. 17–24. Dated November 17, 1923.

———. "A Chinese Declaration of the Rights of Women." *Chinese Social and Political Science Review* 8.2 (April, 1924):100–109.

———. "Fei Ching-yü yü Fei Mi: Ch'ing-hsüeh te liang-ko hsien-ch'ü che" 費經虞與費密：清學的兩個先驅者 (Fei Ching-yü and Fei Mi: two pioneers of the Ch'ing Learning). *HSWT* 2:48–90. Dated September 17, 1924.

———. "The Chinese Renaissance." *China Year Book*, 1924–25. Pp. 633–51.

———. "Ai-kuo yün-tung yü ch'iu-hsüeh" 愛國運動與求學 (The patriotic movement and getting an education). *Hsien-tai p'ing-lun* 現代評論 2.39 (September 5, 1925):5–9.

———. "*Lao-ts'an yu-chi* hsü" 老殘遊記序 (A study of *Travels of Lao-ts'an*). *HSWT* 3:529–53. Dated November 7, 1925.

———. "*Erh-nü ying-hsiung chuan* hsü" 兒女英雄傳序 (A study of *Tales of Heroic Young Lovers*). *HSWT* 3:473–513. Dated December, 1925.

———. "Tai Tung-yüan te che-hsüeh" 戴東原的哲學 (The philosophy of Tai Tung-yüan). *Kuo-hsüeh chi-k'an* 國學季刊 2.1 (December, 1925):1–123. Published as an independent book by Taipei: Commercial Press, 1967.

———. *Sinological Research at the Present Time*. Peking: Peking Leader Press, 1925.

———. "Chin-jih chiao-hui chiao-yü te nan-kuan" 今日教會教育的難關 (Present crisis in Christian education). *HSWT* 3:728–36. Dated March 9, 1926.

———. "Wo-men tui-yü Hsi-yang chin-tai wen-ming te t'ai-tu" 我們對於西洋近代文明的態度 (Our attitude toward modern Western civilization). *Hsien-tai p'ing-lun* 4.83 (July 10, 1926):3–11.

———. "Kindai Seiyo bummei ni taisuru gojin no taido" 近代西洋文明に対する吾人の態度 (Our attitude toward modern Western civilization). *Kaizo* 改造 8.8 (August, 1926):4–17.

———. "The Renaissance in China." *Journal of the Royal Institute of International Affairs* 5.6 (November, 1926):265–83.

———. "China and the Missionaries." *Spectator* (London) 5138 (December 18, 1926):1107.

———. "China and Christianity." *Forum* 78.1 (July, 1927): 1–2.
———. "Man-yu te kan-hsiang" 漫遊的感想 (Impressions of ramblings). *Hsien-tai p'ing-lun* 6.140 (August 13, 1927): 9–12; 6.141 (August 20, 1927): 11–13; 6.145 (September 17, 1927): 12–15.
———. "*Kuan-ch'ang hsien-hsing chi* hsü" 官場現形記序 (A study of *Panorama of Officialdom*). *HSWT* 3: 514–28. Dated October 12, 1927.
———. "Chi-ko fan li-hsüeh te ssu-hsiang-chia" 幾個反理學的思想家 (Some anti-*li-hsüeh* thinkers). *HSWT* 3: 53–107. Dated February 7, 1928.
———. "Ch'ing ta-chia lai chao-chao ching-tzu" 請大家來照照鏡子 (Please let us look in the mirror). *HSWT* 3: 16–23. Dated June 24, 1928.
———. "Chu-ho nü ch'ing-nien-hui" 祝賀女青年會 (Tendering our congratulations to the YWCA). *HSWT* 3: 737–38. Dated June 24, 1928.
———. "Ming chiao" 名教 (The worship of written words). *HY* 1.5 (July 10, 1928): 1–13.
———. "Chih-hsüeh te fang-fa yü ts'ai-liao" 治學的方法與材料 (The methods and materials of scholarship). *HY* 1.9 (November 10, 1928): 1–14.
———. *Pai-hua wen-hsüeh shih* 白話文學史 (A history of vernacular literature). Shanghai, 1928.
———. "The Civilizations of the East and the West." In *Whither Mankind: A Panorama of Modern Civilization*, edited by Charles A. Beard. New York: Longmans, Green and Co., 1928. Pp. 25–41.
———. "Jen-ch'üan yü yüeh-fa" 人權與約法 (Human rights and provisional constitution). *HY* 2.2 (April 10, 1929): 1–8.
———. "Wo-men shen-mo shih-hou ts'ai k'o yu hsien-fa?" 我們什麼時候才可有憲法? (When can we have a constitution?). *HY* 2.4 (June 10, 1929): 1–8.
———. "Chih nan, hsing i pu-i" 知難,行亦不易 (Knowledge is difficult, but action is not easy either). *HY* 2.4 (June 10, 1929): 1–15.
———. "'Jen-ch'üan yü yüeh-fa' te t'ao-lun" "人權與約法"的討論 (Discussions of 'Human rights and the provisional constitution'). *HY* 2.4 (June 10, 1929): 1–5.
———. "Hsin wen-hua yün-tung yü Kuomintang" 新文化運動與國民黨 (The new culture movement and the Kuomintang). *HY* 2.6–7 (September, 1929): 1–15.
———. "Tz'u-yu te wen-t'i" 慈幼的問題 (The question of adoring the young). *HSWT* 3: 739–43. Dated October, 1929.
———. "Wo-men tsou na-t'iao lu?" 我們走那條路 (Which road shall we follow?). *HY* 2.10 (December 10, 1929): 1–16.
———. *Chung-kuo kung-hsüeh hsiao-shih* 中國公學校史 (A history of the China National Institute). N.p., 1929.
———. "Conflict of Cultures." *China Christian Year Book*. Shanghai: Christian Literature Society, 1929. Pp. 112–21.
———. "Chieh-shao wo tzu-chi te ssu-hsiang" 介紹我自己的思想 (Introducing my own thought). *HY* 3.4 (n.d.): 1–18. Dated Nov. 27, 1930.
———. *Chung-kuo chung-ku ssu-hsiang-shih ch'ang-pien* 中國中古思想史長編 (A history of medieval Chinese thought). Taipei, 1971. (1930).
———. "*Hsing-shih yin-yüan chuan* k'ao-cheng" 醒世姻緣傳考證 (A study of *A Romance to Awaken the World*). *HSWT* 4: 329–95. Dated December 13, 1931.

———. "Chui-tao Chih-mo" 追悼志摩 (Mourning for Chih-mo). In Hsü Chih-mo 徐志摩, *Hsü Chih-mo ch'üan-chi* 徐志摩全集 (The complete works of Hsü Chih-mo). Edited by Chiang Fu-ts'ung 蔣復璁 and Liang Shih-ch'iu 梁實秋. 6 vols. Taipei, 1969. 1:355–67. Dated December 3, 1931.

———. "Confucianism." *Encyclopedia of the Social Sciences.* New York: MacMillan Co., 1931. 4:198–201.

———. "My Credo and Its Evolution." In *Living Philosophies: A Series of Intimate Credos.* New York: Simon and Schuster, 1931. Pp. 235–64.

———. "Religion and Philosophy in Chinese History." In *Symposium on Chinese Culture*, edited by Sophia H. Chen Zen. Shanghai: China Institute of Pacific Relations, 1931. Pp. 25–58.

———. "The Literary Renaissance." In *Symposium on Chinese Culture*, edited by Sophia H. Chen Zen. Shanghai: China Institute of Pacific Relations, 1931. Pp. 150–64.

———. "Hsien-cheng wen-t'i" 憲政問題 (The question of constitutional government). *TLPL* 1 (May 22, 1932):5–7.

———. "Lun tui-Jih wai-chiao fang-chen" 論對日外交方針 (On China's Japan policy). *TLPL* 5 (June 19, 1932):2–5.

———. "Tseng-yü chin-nien te ta-hsüeh pi-yeh-sheng" 贈與今年的大學畢業生 (An offering to this year's university graduates). *TLPL* 7 (July 3, 1932):2–5.

——— (signed Shih-chih 適之). "So-wei chiao-yü te fa-hsi-ssu-ti-hua" 所謂教育的法西斯蒂化 (The so-called fascistization of education). *TLPL* 8 (July 10, 1932):14–15.

——— (signed Ts'ang-hui 藏暉). "Lun hsüeh-ch'ao" 論學潮 (On the student movement). *TLPL* 9 (July 17, 1932):6–9.

———. "Ling-hsiu jen-ts'ai te lai-yüan" 領袖人才的來源 (The sources of leadership talent). *TLPL* 12 (August 7, 1932):2–5.

———. "Nei-t'ien tui shih-chieh te t'iao-chan" 內田對世界的挑戰 (Uchida's challenge to the world). *TLPL* 16 (September 4, 1932):2–3.

———. "Chung-kuo cheng-chih ch'u-lu te t'ao-lun" 中國政治出路的討論 (A discussion of the way out for Chinese politics). *TLPL* 17 (September 11, 1932): 2–6.

———. "Ts'an-t'ung te hui-i yü fan-hsing" 慘痛的回憶與反省 (Grievous recollections and reflections). *TLPL* 18 (September 18, 1932):8–13.

———. "Chiu-ching na i-ko t'iao-yüeh shih fei-chih?" 究竟那一個條約是廢紙? (Which treaty is after all a scrap of waste paper?). *TLPL* 19 (September 25, 1932): 2–7.

———. "I-ko tai-piao shih-chieh kung-lun te pao-kao" 一個代表世界公論的報告 (A report that represents world public opinion). *TLPL* 21 (October 9, 1932):2–6.

———. "T'ung-i te lu" 統一的路 (The road to unification). *TLPL* 28 (November 27, 1932):2–6.

———. *Chung-kuo chung-ku ssu-hsiang hsiao shih* 中國中古思想小史 (A short history of medieval Chinese thought). Taipei, 1969. Dated 1932.

———. "Conflict of Cultures." In *Problems of the Pacific, 1931, Proceedings of the Fourth Conference of the Institute of Pacific Relations, Hangchow and Shanghai, China, October 21 to November 2*, edited by Bruno Lasker. Chicago: University of Chicago Press, 1932. Pp. 471–77.

———. "Kuo-min ts'an-cheng-hui ying-kai ju-ho tsu-chih" 國民參政會應該如何組織 (How the National People's Assembly should be organized). *TLPL* 34 (January 8, 1933):2–5.

———. "Kuo-lien t'iao-chieh te ch'ien-tu" 國聯調解的前途 (The prospect of the mediation by the League of Nations). *TLPL* 36 (January 22, 1933):2–5.

———. "Min-ch'üan te pao-chang" 民權的保障 (The protection of civil rights). *TLPL* 38 (February 19, 1933):2–5.

———. "Kuo-lien pao-kao-shu yü chien-i-an te shu-p'ing" 國聯報告書與建議案的述評 (A discussion and criticism of the report and proposals of the League of Nations). *TLPL* 39 (February 26, 1933):2–7.

———. "Ch'üan-kuo chen-ching i-hou" 全國震驚以後 (Following the shock of the entire nation). *TLPL* 41 (March 12, 1933):2–8.

———. "Jih-pen-jen ying-kai hsing-hsing le!" 日本人應該醒醒了 (The Japanese must wake up!). *TLPL* 42 (March 19, 1933):2–4.

———. "Wo-men k'o-i teng-hou wu-shih nien" 我們可以等候五十年 (We can wait fifty years!). *TLPL* 44 (April 2, 1933):2–5.

———. "Pa Chiang T'ing-fu hsien-sheng te lun-wen" 跋蔣廷黻先生的論文 (An epilogue to Mr. Chiang T'ing-fu's essay). *TLPL* 45 (April 9, 1933):6–8.

———. "Wo-te i-chien yeh pu-kuo ju-tz'u" 我的意見也不過如此 (My opinions are simply these). *TLPL* 46 (April 16, 1933):2–5.

———. "Ts'ung nung-ts'un chiu-chi t'an-tao wu-wei te cheng-chih" 從農村救濟談到無爲的政治 (*Wu-wei* politics in light of the rural relief). *TLPL* 49 (May 7, 1933):2–6.

———. "Chih-hsien pu-ju shou-fa" 制憲不如守法 (Enacting a constitution is not so good as obeying the law). *TLPL* 51 (May 10, 1933):2–4.

———. "Pao-ch'üan Hua-pei te chung-yao" 保全華北的重要 (The importance of defending North China). *TLPL* 52–53 (June 4, 1933):2–6.

———. "Chien-kuo wen-t'i yin-lun" 建國問題引論 (An introduction to the question of national reconstruction). *TLPL* 77 (November 19, 1933):2–7.

———. "Shih-chieh hsin hsing-shih li te Chung-kuo wai-chiao fang-chen" 世界新形勢裡的中國外交方針 (China's foreign policy in the new international situation). *TLPL* 78 (November 26, 1933):2–5.

———. "Fu-chien te ta pien-chü" 福建的大變局 (The great revolt in Fukien). *TLPL* 79 (December 3, 1933):2–4.

———. "Chien-kuo yü chuan-chih" 建國與專制 (National reconstruction and despotism). *TLPL* 81 (December 17, 1933):2–5.

———. "Tsai lun chien-kuo yü chuan-chih" 再論建國與專制 (Another discussion of national reconstruction and despotism). *TLPL* 82 (December 24, 1933):2–5.

———, trans. *Tuan-p'ien hsiao-shuo* 短篇小說 (Short stories). Taipei, 1972. Originally published as *Tuan-p'ien hsiao-shuo ti-i chi* 短篇小說第一集 (Short stories, first collection). Shanghai, 1919. And *Tuan-p'ien hsiao-shou ti-erh chi* 短篇小說第二集 (Short stories, second collection). Shanghai, 1933.

———. *Ssu-shih tzu-shu* 四十自述 (Autobiography at forty). Shanghai, 1933; Taipei reprint, 1974.

———. "Pi-shang liang-shan:wen-hsüeh ke-ming te k'ai-shih" 逼上梁山:

文學革命的開始 (Forced into outlawry: the origins of the literary revolution). *Tung-fang tsa-chih* 31.1 (January 1, 1934):15–31.

———. "Wu-li t'ung-i lun" 武力統一論 (On unification by force). *TLPL* 85 (January 14, 1934):2–7.

———. "Cheng-chih t'ung-i te t'u-ching" 政治統一的途徑 (The path to political unification). *TLPL* 86 (January 21, 1934):2–7.

———. "The Task of Modern Religion." *Journal of Religion* 14.1 (January, 1934):104–8.

———. "Tsai lun wu-wei te cheng-chih" 再論無爲的政治 (Another discussion of *wu-wei* politics). *TLPL* 89 (February 25, 1934):2–6.

———. "Kuo-chi liu-yen chung te i-ko meng-hsiang" 國際流言中的一個夢想 (A wishful thinking amidst the international rumor). *TLPL* 90 (March 4, 1934): 2–5.

———. "Chien-she yü wu-wei" 建設與無爲 (Construction and *wu-wei*). *TLPL* 94 (April 1, 1934):2–5.

———. "Wei Hsin sheng-huo yün-tung chin i-chieh" 爲新生活運動進一解 (A word on the New Life Movement). *TLPL* 95 (April 8, 1934):17–20.

———. "Lun hsien-fa ch'u-kao" 論憲法初稿 (On the draft constitution). *TLPL* 96 (April 15, 1934):2–6.

———. "Hsieh-ho wai-chiao yüan-lai hai-shih chiao-t'u wai-chiao" 「協和外交」原來還是「焦土外交」(The conciliatory diplomacy is after all a scorched earth diplomacy). *TLPL* 98 (April 29, 1934):2–6.

———. "Chin-jih chih wei-chi" 今日之危機 (The present-day crisis). *TLPL* 99 (May 5, 1934):2–4.

———. "Shuo ju" 說儒 (On *ju*). *HSWT* 4:1–103. Dated May 19, 1934.

———. "Chieh-chüeh Chung-Jih te jen-ho hsüan-an" 解決中日的「任何懸案」(Solve the pending questions between China and Japan). *TLPL* 102 (May 27, 1934):2–3.

———. "Hsin-hsin yü fan-hsing" 信心與反省 (Faith and reflection). *TLPL* 103 (June 3, 1934):2–6.

———. "K'an le ts'ai-chün hui-i te cheng-lun i-hou" 看了裁軍會議的爭論以後 (Reflections on the disputes at the disarmament conference). *TLPL* 104 (June 10, 1934):2–3.

———. "Tsai lun hsin-hsin yü fan-hsing" 再論信心與反省 (Another discussion of faith and reflection). *TLPL* 105 (June 17, 1934):2–6.

———. "Tseng-yü chin-nien te ta-hsüeh pi-yeh-sheng" 贈與今年的大學畢業生 (An offering to this year's university graduates). In Hu Shih, *Hu Shih wen-ts'un wai-pien* 胡適文存外編 (Collected essays of Hu Shih, a supplement). Taipei, 1970. Pp. 85–89. Dated June 24, 1934.

———. "San lun hsin-hsin yü fan-hsing" 三論信心與反省 (A third discussion of faith and reflection). *TLPL* 107 (July 1, 1934):2–6.

———. "Ts'ung ssu-li hsüeh-hsiao t'an tao Yen-ching ta-hsüeh" 從私立學校談到燕京大學 (Yenching University in the light of private schools). *TLPL* 108 (July 8, 1934):2–5.

———. "Hsieh tsai Hsü Mei nü-shih te wen-chang te hou-mien" 寫在徐梅女士的文章的後面 (A rejoinder to Madam Hsü Mei's essay). In Hu Shih, *Hu Shih wen-ts'un wai-pien.* Pp. 91–93. Dated July 8, 1934.

———. "Cheng-cheng san-nien le!" 整整三年了 (Fully three years!). *TLPL* 119 (September 23, 1934):2–4.

———. "Lun Kuo-lien ta-hui te liang-chien-shih" 論國聯大會的兩件事 (On the two events that took place at the League of Nations' Assembly meeting). *TLPL* 120 (September 30, 1934):2–3.

———. "Cheng-chih t'ung-i te i-i" 政治統一的意義 (The meaning of political unification). *TLPL* 123 (October 21, 1934):2–4.

———. "Pei-kuan sheng-lang-li te lo-kuan" 悲觀聲浪裡的樂觀 (Optimism in the midst of a wave of pessimism). *TLPL* 123 (October 21, 1934):15–18.

———. "Shei chiao ch'ing-nien hsüeh-sheng tsao chia wen-p'ing te?" 誰教青年學生造假文憑的 (Who is forcing the students to manufacture false diplomas?). In Hu Shih, *Hu Shih wen-ts'un wai-pien*, pp. 101–5. Dated December 2, 1934.

———. "Chung-kuo wu tu-ts'ai te pi-yao yü k'o-neng" 中國無獨裁的必要與可能 (There is no need or feasibility for China to be autocratic). *TLPL* 130 (December 9, 1934):2–6.

———. "Wang-Chiang t'ung-tien li t'i-ch'i te tzu-yu" 汪蔣通電裡提起的自由 (On the freedom discussed in the Wang-Chiang telegram). *TLPL* 131 (December 16, 1934):3–6.

———. "Kuo-chi wei-chi te pi-chin" 國際危機的逼近 (The approaching international crisis). *TLPL* 132 (December 23, 1934):2–4.

———. "Ta Ting Tsai-chün hsien-sheng lun min-chu yü tu-ts'ai" 答丁在君先生論民主與獨裁 (A rejoinder to Mr. Ting Tsai-chün and a discussion of democracy and autocracy). *TLPL* 133 (December 30, 1934):7–9.

———. "Confucianism and Modern Scientific Thinking." In *Modern Trends in World-Religions*, edited by Albert Eustace Haydon. Chicago: University of Chicago Press, 1934. Pp. 46–51.

———. "Confucianism and Social Economic Problems." In *Modern Trends in World-Religions*, edited by Albert Eustace Haydon. Chicago: University of Chicago Press, 1934. Pp. 81–86.

———. "The Task of Confucianism." In *Modern Trends in World-Religions*, edited by Albert Eustace Haydon. Chicago: University of Chicago Press, 1934. Pp. 245–50.

———. *The Chinese Renaissance.* Chicago: University of Chicago Press, 1934.

———. "I-nien lai kuan-yü min-chih yü tu-ts'ai te t'ao-lun" 一年來關於民治與獨裁的討論 (Discussions in the past year concerning democracy and autocracy). *Tung-fang tsa-chih* 32.1 (January 1, 1935):15–23.

———. "An Optimist Looks at China." *Asia* 35.3 (March, 1935):139–42.

———. "Ts'ung min-chu yü tu-ts'ai chih t'ao-lun li ch'iu-te i-ko kung-t'ung cheng-chih hsin-yang" 從民主與獨裁之討論裡求得一個共同政治信仰 (A common political belief derived from the debate concerning democracy and autocracy). *TLPL* 141 (March 10, 1935):16–18.

———. "Pien-chi hou-chi" 編輯後記 (Editor's notes). *TLPL* 142 (March 17, 1935):24.

———. "Chung-Jih t'i-hsi: ta k'o-wen" 中日提攜：答客問 (Sino-Japanese mutual assistance: an interview). *TLPL* 143 (March 25, 1935):2–3.

———. "Shih-p'ing so-wei 'Chung-kuo pen-wei chih wen-hua chien-she'" 試評所謂"中國本位之文化建設" (A critique of so-called cultural reconstruction on a Chinese base). *TLPL* 145 (April 7, 1935):4–7.

———. "Pien-chi hou-chi" 編輯後記 (Editor's notes). *TLPL* 146 (April 14, 1935): 20–21.

———. "Chi-nien 'Wu-ssu'" 紀念五四 (Commemorating May Fourth). *TLPL* 149 (May 5, 1935):2–8.

———. "Ko-jen tzu-yu yü she-hui chin-pu: tsai t'an Wu-ssu yün-tung" 個人自由與社會進步：再談五四運動 (Individual freedom and social progress: more on the May Fourth movement). *TLPL* 150 (May 12, 1935):2–5.

———. "Chin-jih ssu-hsiang-chieh te i-ko ta pi-ping" 今日思想界的一個大弊病 (A great malady among intellectuals today). *TLPL* 153 (June 2, 1935):2–5.

———. "Ch'en-mo te jen-shou" 沉默的忍受 (Silent endurance). *TLPL* 155 (June 16, 1935):2–3.

———. "Ch'ung-fen shih-chieh-hua yü ch'üan-p'an hsi-hua" 充分世界化與全盤西化 (Sufficient modernization and total Westernization). *HSWT* 4:541–44. Dated June 22, 1935.

———. "Ta Ch'en Hsü-ching hsien-sheng" 答陳序經先生 (A reply to Mr. Ch'en Hsü-ching). *TLPL* 160 (July 21, 1935):15–16.

———. "Cheng-chih kai-ke te ta-lu" 政制改革的大路 (The great road toward the reform of political institutions). *TLPL* 163 (August 11, 1935):2–9.

———. "Su-o ke-ming wai-chiao-shih te yu i-yeh chi ch'i chiao-hsün" 蘇俄革命外交史的又一頁及其教訓 (Another page from the history of Soviet Russian revolutionary diplomacy, and what it teaches us). *TLPL* 163 (August 11, 1935):15–18.

———. "Kuo-lien te t'ai-t'ou" 國聯的抬頭 (The League of Nations rises). *TLPL* 170 (September 29, 1935):2–7.

———. "Ts'ung i-tang tao wu-tang te cheng-chih" 從一黨到無黨的政治 (From one-party politics to politics without parties). *TLPL* 171 (October 6, 1935): 10–12.

———. "Tsai chi Kuo-lien te t'ai-t'ou" 再記國聯的抬頭 (Again on the rise of the League of Nations). *TLPL* 172 (October 13, 1935):2–6.

———. "Ching-kao Jih-pen kuo-min" 敬告日本國民 (An appeal to the Japanese people). *TLPL* 178 (November 24, 1935):10–14.

———. "Hua-pei wen-t'i" 華北問題 (The question of North China). *TLPL* 179 (December 1, 1935):2–3.

———. "Ta Shih-fu Kao-hsin hsien-sheng" 答室伏高信先生 (A reply to Mr. Murobushi Koshin). *TLPL* 180 (December 8, 1935):5–8.

———. "Wei hsüeh-sheng yün-tung chin i-yen" 爲學生運動進一言 (A word to the student movement). *TLPL* 182 (December 22, 1935):4–7.

———. "Tsai lun hsüeh-sheng yün-tung" 再論學生運動 (Another discussion of the student movement). *TLPL* 183 (December 29, 1935):2–4.

———. "Ting Tsai-chün che-ko jen" 丁在君這個人 (This man Ting Tsai-chün). *TLPL* 188 (February 16, 1936):9–15.

———, ed. *Chien-she li-lun chi* 建設理論集 (Essays on the theories concerning a constructive literature). Shanghai, 1935. Vol. 1 of Chao Chia-pi.

———. "Tso-yen" 導言 (Introduction). In Hu Shih, ed., *Chien-she li-lun-chi*, pp. 1–32.

———. "Tung-ching te ping-pien" 東京的兵變 (The military coup in Tokyo). *TLPL* 191 (March 8, 1936):2–5.

———. "T'iao-cheng Chung-Jih kuan-hsi te hsien-chüeh t'iao-chien" 調整中日關係的先決條件 (Preconditions for improving Sino-Japanese relations). *TLPL* 197 (April 19, 1936):3–5.

———. "Kuan-yü 't'iao-cheng Chung-Jih kuan-hsi te hsien-chüeh t'iao-chien'" 關於「調整中日關係的先決條件」(An elaboration of "Preconditions for improving Sino-Japanese relations). *TLPL* 200 (May 10, 1936):2–5.

———. "Kuo-lien hai k'o-i t'ai-t'ou" 國聯還可以抬頭 (The League of Nations can still hold on its own). *TLPL* 202 (May 24, 1936):2–5.

———. "Ching-kao Sung Che-yüan hsien-sheng" 敬告宋哲元先生 (An appeal to Mr. Sung Che-yüan). *TLPL* 204 (June 7, 1936):2–3.

———. "Kuo-yü yü han-tzu" 國語與漢字 (The national language and the Chinese character). *TLPL* 207 (June 28, 1936):4–6.

———. "Jih-pen pa-ch'üan te shuai-lo yü T'ai-p'ing-yang te kuo-chi hsin hsing-shih" 日本霸權的衰落與太平洋的國際新形勢 (The decline of Japanese hegemony and the new international situation in the Pacific). *TLPL* 230 (April 18, 1937):2–8.

———. "Chung-Jih wen-t'i te hsien chieh-tuan" 中日問題的現階段 (The current status of the Sino-Japanese issue). *TLPL* 231 (April 25, 1937):2–3.

———. "Lun-tun te Ying-Jih t'an-p'an" 倫敦的英日談判 (The British-Japanese negotiation in London). *TLPL* 235 (May 23, 1937):2–3.

———. "Tsai t'an-t'an hsien-cheng" 再談談憲政 (Talking again about constitutional government). *TLPL* 236 (May 30, 1937):5–7.

———. "Wo-men neng hsing te hsien-cheng yü hsien-fa" 我們能行的憲政與憲法 (The constitutional government and the constitution that we can implement). *TLPL* 242 (July 11, 1937):12–13.

———. "The Indianization of China: A Case Study in Cultural Borrowing." In *Independence, Convergence, and Borrowing in Institutions, Thought, and Art*. Cambridge, Mass.: Harvard University Press, 1937. Pp. 219–47.

———. "Ts'ung Niu-yüeh sheng-hui Albany hui Niu-yüeh shih" 從紐約省會 Albany 回紐約市 (Returning to New York City from Albany). In Hu Shih, *Ch'ang-shih hou chi* 嘗試後集 (A collection of experiments, second series). Taipei, 1971. P. 59. Dated April 19, 1938.

———. "The Westernization of China and Japan." *Amerasia*, July, 1938, pp. 243–47.

———. *Ts'ang-hui-shih cha-chi* 藏暉室劄記. 4 vols. Shanghai, 1939. Reissued as *Hu Shih liu-hsüeh jih-chi* 胡適留學日記 (Hu Shih's diary while studying abroad). 4 vols. Taipei, 1973.

———. "The Political Philosophy of Instrumentalism." In *The Philosopher of the Common Man: Essays in Honor of John Dewey to Celebrate His Eightieth Birthday*. New York: G. P. Putnam's Sons, 1940. Pp. 205–19.

———. "Instrumentalism as a Political Concept." In *Studies in Political Science and Sociology*. Philadelphia: University of Pennsylvania Press, 1941. Pp. 1–6.

———. "Historical Foundations for a Democratic China." In *Edmund J. James Lectures on Government*. 2d series. Urbana: University of Illinois Press, 1941. Pp. 53–64.

———. "China, Too, Is Fighting to Defend a Way of Life." San Francisco: Grabhorn Press, 1942. An address by His Excellency, Dr. Hu Shih, Ambassador of the Republic of China to the United States of America, delivered at Washington, D. C., March 23, 1942.

———. "The Struggle for Intellectual Freedom in Historical China." *World Affairs* 105.3 (September, 1942): 170–73.

———. "Women's Place in Chinese History." Paper read in December, 1940, at the Cosmopolitan Club in New York City and in 1945 before the American Association of University Women. Printed in 1954 according to the 1945 version.

———. "The Concept of Immortality in Chinese Thought." *Harvard Divinity School Bulletin*, 1945–46, pp. 23–42.

———. "Ch'ing-nien-jen te k'u-men" 青年人的苦悶 (The depression of the youth), in Hu Shih, *Hu Shih te shih-lun i-chi* 胡適的時論一集 (Hu Shih's essays on current affairs, first series). N.p.: 1948. Pp. 11–16. Dated June, 1947.

———. "Cheng-ch'ü hsüeh-shu tu-li te shih-nien chi-hua" 爭取學術獨立的十年計劃 (A ten-year plan to acquire the independence of scholarship). In Hu Shih, *Hu Shih te shih-lun i-chi*, pp. 39–44. Dated September, 1947.

———. "Chinese Thought." In *China*, edited by Harley Farnsworth McNair. Berkeley: University of California Press, 1951. Pp. 221–30.

———. "The Natural Law in the Chinese Tradition." *Natural Law Institute Proceedings* 5 (1953): 119–53.

———. "An Oriental Looks at the Modern Western Civilization." In *Modern Education and Human Values*, Pitcairn-Crabbe Foundation Lecture Series. Vol. 5. Pittsburgh: University of Pittsburgh Press, 1954. Pp. 47–60.

———. "Authority and Freedom in the Ancient Asian World." In *Man's Right to Knowledge*. 1st series: *Tradition and Change*. New York: Columbia University Press, 1954. Pp. 40–45.

———. "Chung-kuo ku-tai cheng-chih ssu-hsiang-shih te i-ko k'an-fa" 中國古代政治思想史的一個看法 (An interpretation of the political philosophy of ancient China). *Tzu-yu Chung-kuo* 自由中國 10.7 (April 1, 1954): 6–10.

———. "The Right to Doubt in Ancient Chinese Thought." *Philosophy East and West* 12.4 (January 1963): 295–300. Paper read at the Sixth Annual Meeting of the Far Eastern Association in 1954.

———. "The Scientific Spirit and Method in Chinese Philosophy." In *The Chinese Mind: Essentials of Chinese Philosophy and Culture*, edited by Charles A. Moore. Honolulu: University of Hawaii Press, 1967. Pp. 104–31. Paper delivered at the East-West Philosophy Conference, 1959.

———. "John Dewey in China." In *Philosophy and Culture—East and West: East-West Philosophy in Practical Perspective*, edited by Charles A. Moore. Honolulu: University of Hawaii Press, 1962. Pp. 762–69. Public lecture delivered during the Third East-West Philosophers' Conference at the University of Hawaii in 1959.

———. *The Personal Reminiscences of Dr. Hu Shih (1891–1962)*. Interviewed, compiled, and edited by Te-kong Tong (T'ang Te-kang) with Dr. Hu's corrections in his own handwriting. New York: Chinese Oral History Project, East Asian Institute of Columbia University, 1959. Microform produced by Microfilming Corporation of America, New Jersey.

———. "The Chinese Tradition and the Future." *Report and Proceedings, Sino-American Conference on Intellectual Cooperation*, held at the University of Washington, July 10–15, 1960. Seattle, Washington: Department of Publication and Printing, University of Washington, 1962. Pp. 13–22.

———. "Social Changes and Science." *Free China Review* 7.3 (March, 1962):39–41.

———. *Hu Shih kei Chao Yüan-jen te hsin* 胡適給趙元任的信 (Hu Shih's letters to Chao Yüan-jen). Released by Chao Yüan-jen. Taipei, 1972.

———. *Ting Wen-chiang te chuan-chi* 丁文江的傳記 (A biography of Ting Wen-chiang). Taipei, 1973.

———. *Hu Shih k'ou-shu tzu-chuan* 胡適口述自傳 (The oral autobiography of Hu Shih). Translated with notes by T'ang Te-kang 唐德剛. Taipei, 1981.

Hu Shih Items, microfilm from the Patterson Scrapbook; and the Hu Shih misc., E. E. Barker, Collector. Collection of Regional History and University Archives, Cornell University.

Hu Sung-p'ing 胡頌平. *Hu Shih hsien-sheng nien-p'u chien-pien* 胡適先生年譜簡編 (A brief chronological biography of Mr. Hu Shih). Taipei, 1971.

Huang Yüan-yung 黃遠庸. "Shih-yen—chih *Chia-yin tsa-chih* chi-che" 釋言—致甲寅雜誌記者 (A letter to the *Chia-yin* magazine). *Chia-yin tsa-chih* 1.10 (October 10, 1915).

Huang, Philip C. *Liang Ch'i-ch'ao and Modern Chinese Liberalism*. Seattle: University of Washington Press, 1972.

Hummel, Arthur W., ed. *Eminent Chinese of the Ch'ing Period (1644–1912)*. 2 vols. Washington, D.C.: Government Printing Office, 1943; Taipei reprint, 1970, 2 vols. in 1.

Hunt, Michael H. "The American Remission of the Boxer Indemnity: A Reappraisal." *Journal of Asian Studies* 31.3 (May, 1972):539–59.

Ibsen, Henrik. *The Collected Works of Henrik Ibsen*. New York: Charles Scribner's Sons, 1907. Vol. 11.

———. *Letters of Henrik Ibsen*. Translated by J. N. Laurvik and M. Morison. New York: Fox, Duffield and Co., 1905.

———. *Six Plays of Henrik Ibsen*. Translated by Eva Le Gallienne. New York: Modern Library, 1957.

Iyenaga, T. "Japan's Position in the World War." *New York Times*, March 24, 1915.

James, William. *Pragmatism and Four Essays from The Meaning of Truth*. Cleveland: World Publishing Co., 1955.

K'ang Yu-wei 康有爲. *Ta-t'ung shu* 大同書 (A treatise on universal peace). Edited by Ch'ien An-ting 錢安定. Shanghai, 1935.

Kao I-han 高一涵. "Kuo-chia fei jen-sheng chih kuei-su lun" 國家非人生之歸宿論 (Nation-state is not the ultimate focus of loyalty in life). *HCN* 1.4 (December 15, 1915):287–94.

Kao Yu-kung. "Lyric Vision in Chinese Narrative Tradition: A Reading of *Hung-lou Meng* and *Ju-lin wai-shih*." In *Chinese Narrative: Critical and Theoretical Essays*, edited by Andrew H. Plaks. Princeton: Princeton University Press, 1977. Pp. 227–43.

Kaufmann, Walter. "The Inevitability of Alienation." In Richard Schacht, *Alienation*. Garden City, New York: Doubleday and Company, 1970. Pp. xv–lviii.

Keenan, Barry. *The Dewey Experiment in China: Educational Reform and Political Power in the Early Republic*. Cambridge, Mass.: Harvard University Press, 1977.

Keniston, Kenneth. *The Uncommitted: Alienated Youth in American Society*. New York: Harcourt, Brace and World, 1965.

Kuo Mo-jo 郭沫若. *Ch'uang-tsao shih-nien* 創造十年 (Ten years of creation). Shanghai, 1932.

———. *T'ung-nien shih-tai* 童年時代 (The years of my boyhood). Shanghai, 1940.

———. *Ke-ming ch'un-ch'iu* 革命春秋 (The revolutionary years). Shanghai, 1957.

Kuo Shao-yü 郭紹虞. "Hsin-ts'un yen-chiu" 新村研究 (A study of the new village). *Hsin-ch'ao* 2.1 (October, 1919): 59–67.

Kwok, D. W. Y. *Scientism in Chinese Thought, 1900–1950*. New Haven: Yale University Press, 1965.

Kwong, H. K. "What is Patriotic Sanity? A Reply to Suh Hu." *CSM* 10.7 (April, 1915): 427–30.

Langer, Susanne K. *Philosophy in a New Key: A Study in the Symbolism of Reason, Rite, and Art*. Cambridge, Mass.: Harvard University Press, 1957.

Lee, Leo Ou-fan. *The Romantic Generation of Modern Chinese Writers*. Cambridge, Mass.: Harvard University Press, 1973.

———. "Genesis of a Writer: Notes on Lu Xun's Educational Experience, 1881–1909." In *Modern Chinese Literature in the May Fourth Era*, edited by Merle Goldman. Cambridge, Mass.: Harvard University Press, 1977. Pp. 161–88.

Lee, Mabel. "Liang Ch'i-ch'ao (1873–1929) and the Literary Revolution of Late-Ch'ing." In *Search for Identity: Modern Literature and the Creative Arts in Asia*, edited by A. R. Davis. Sydney, Australia: Angus and Robertson, 1974. Pp. 203–24.

Levenson, Joseph R. *Confucian China and Its Modern Fate: A Trilogy*. Berkeley: University of California Press, 1958–65.

———. *Liang Ch'i-ch'ao and the Mind of Modern China*. Berkeley: University of California Press, 1967.

Li Ao 李敖. *Hu Shih p'ing-chuan* 胡適評傳 (A critical biography of Hu Shih). Taipei, 1964.

Li Chi. "The Changing Concept of the Recluse in Chinese Literature." *Harvard Journal of Asiatic Studies* 24 (1962–63): 234–47.

Li Ta-chao 李大釗. "Tsai lun wen-t'i yü chu-i" 再論問題與主義 (Another discussion of problems and isms). *Mei-chou p'ing-lun* 35 (August 17, 1919); *T'ai-p'ing yang* 2.1 (May 5, 1920): 10–15.

Liang Ch'i-ch'ao 梁啓超. "Lun hsiao-shuo yü chün-chih chih kuan-hsi" 論小說與羣治之關係 (Fiction seen in relation to the guidance of society). In Liang Ch'i-ch'ao, *Yin-ping-shih wen-chi* 飲冰室文集 (Collected essays of Liang Ch'i-ch'ao).

Taipei reprint, 1960, 16 vols. in 8. *Ts'e* 10, pp. 6–10. Dated 1902.

———. "K'ai-ming chuan-chih lun" 開明專制論 (On enlightened despotism). In Liang Ch'i-ch'ao, *Yin-ping-shih wen-chi. Ts'e* 17, pp. 13–83. Dated 1905.

———. "Erh-shih shih-chi chih chü-ling—t'o-la-ssu" 二十世紀之巨靈—托辣斯 (The monster of the twentieth century—the trust). In Liang Ch'i-ch'ao, *Yin-ping-shih wen-chi. Ts'e* 14, pp. 33–61. Dated 1903.

———. "Cheng-chih-hsüeh ta-chia Po-lun-chih-li chih hsüeh-shuo" 政治學大家伯倫知理之學說 (The theory of the great political scientist Bluntchli). In Liang Ch'i-ch'ao, *Yin-ping-shih wen-chi. Ts'e* 13, pp. 67–89. Dated 1903.

———. "Yü chih ssu-sheng kuan" 余之死生觀 (My view of life and death). In Liang Ch'i-ch'ao, *Yin-ping-shih wen-chi. Ts'e* 17, pp. 1–12. Dated 1904.

———. "P'ien-fa t'ung-i" 變法通議 (A general treatise on reform). In Liang Ch'i-ch'ao, *Yin-ping-shih wen-chi. Ts'e* 1, pp. 1–92. Dated 1896.

———. "Cheng-chih chih chi-ch'u yü yen-lun-chia chih chih-chen" 政治之基礎與言論家之指針 (The foundation of politics and the guide for a political commentator). In Liang Ch'i-ch'ao, *Yin-ping-shih wen-chi. Ts'e* 33, pp. 31–40. Dated 1915.

———. "Hsin-min i" 新民議 (On new citizen). In Liang Ch'i-ch'ao, *Yin-ping-shih wen-chi. Ts'e* 7, pp. 104–7. Dated 1902.

———. "Lun Chung-kuo hsüeh-shu ssu-hsiang pien-ch'ien chih ta-shih" 論中國學術思想變遷之大勢 (General trends of the development of Chinese scholarship). In Liang Ch'i-ch'ao, *Yin-ping-shih wen-chi. Ts'e* 7, pp. 1–104. Dated 1902.

Lifton, Robert Jay. *Death in Life: Survivors of Hiroshima.* New York: Vintage Books, 1969.

———. *History and Human Survival: Essays on the Young and Old, Survivors and the Dead, Peace and War, and on Contemporary Psychohistory.* New York: Vintage Books, 1971.

Lin Shu 林紓. "Ching-sheng" 荊生 (Ching-sheng the giant). In *Chien-she li-lun chi*, edited by Hu Shih. Pp. 202–3.

———. "Yao-meng" 妖夢 (The nightmare). In *Wen-hsüeh lun-cheng chi*, edited by Cheng Chen-to. Pp. 435–37.

———. "Lun ku-wen pai-hua chih hsiang hsiao-chang" 論古文白話之相消長 (On the rise and fall of the classical language and the vernacular). In *Wen-hsüeh lun-cheng chi*, edited by Cheng Chen-to. Pp. 96–99.

Lin Shuen-fu. "Ritual and Narrative Structure in *Ju-lin wai-shih*." In *Chinese Narrative: Critical and Theoretical Essays*, edited by Andrew H. Plaks. Pp. 244–65.

Lin Yü-sheng. *The Crisis of Chinese Consciousness: Radical Antitraditionalism in the May Fourth Era.* Madison: University of Wisconsin Press, 1979.

Liu Hsin-huang 劉心皇. *Hsü Chih-mo yü Lu Hsiao-man* 徐志摩與陸小曼 (Hsü Chih-mo and Lu Hsiao-man). Taipei, 1965.

Liu K'ai 劉鍇. "Pei-shou Mei-kuo ch'ao-yeh ching-chung te wai-chiao-chia" 備受美國朝野敬重的外交家 (The diplomat widely respected in America). *Chuan-chi wen-hsüeh* 28.5 (May, 1976): 15–17.

Liu Pan-nung 劉半農. Liu's untitled rejoinder to Wang Ching-hsüan 王敬軒. *HCN* 4.3 (March 15, 1918): 292–309.

Lochner, Louis P. *The Cosmopolitan Club Movement.* New York: American Association for International Conciliation, 1912.
———. *Internationalism Among Universities.* Vol. 3, no. 7, pt. 2. Boston: World Peace Foundation, 1913.
Lowell, Amy, ed. *Some Imagist Poets: An Anthology.* 3 vols. Boston: Houghton and Mifflin Co., 1915–17.
Lu Hsün 魯迅, trans. "I-ko ch'ing-nien te meng" 一個青年的夢 (A youth's dream). *HCN* 7.2 (January 1, 1920):223–61; 7.3 (February 1, 1920):417–48; 7.4 (March 1, 1920):641–64; 7.5 (April 1, 1920):765–809.
Lutz, Jessie. *China and the Christian Colleges, 1850–1950.* Ithaca, New York: Cornell University Press, 1971.
Ma Chien-chung 馬建忠. *Ma shih wen-t'ung* 馬氏文通 (Ma's grammar). 10 vols. Shanghai, 1898.
Masuda Hajime 增田涉. "Ryo Kei-cho ni tsuite—bungakushi teki ni mite" 梁啓超について—文学史的にみて (On Liang Ch'i-ch'ao—from the standpoint of the history of literature). *Jimbun Kenkyu* 人文研究 6.6 (July, 1955):49–66.
Morley, John Viscount. *On Compromise.* London: MacMillan and Co., 1923.
Mote, Frederick W. "Confucian Eremitism in the Yüan Period." In *The Confucian Persuasion*, edited by Arthur F. Wright. Stanford, Calif.: Stanford University Press, 1960. Pp. 202–40.
Murobushi Koshin 室伏高信. "Ta Hu Shih-chih shu" 答胡適之書 (A reply to Hu Shih-chih). *TLPL* 180 (December 8, 1935):8–12.
———. "Tsai ta Hu Shih-chih shu" 再答胡適之書 (Another reply to Hu Shih-chih). *TLPL* 192 (March 15, 1936):15–19.
Mushakoji Saneatsu 武者小路實篤. "Yü Chih-na wei-chih te yu-jen" 與支那未知的友人 (A letter to Chinese friends unknown to me). *HCN* 7.3 (February 1, 1920):411–16. Includes comments by Chou Tso-jen, Ts'ai Yüan-p'ei, and Ch'en Tu-hsiu.
National Cyclopedia of American Biography. New York: J. T. White and Co. 1893–
Nivison, David S. "The Problem of 'Knowledge' and 'Action' in Chinese Thought Since Wang Yang-ming." In *Studies in Chinese Thought*, edited by Arthur F. Wright. Chicago: University of Chicago Press, 1953. Pp. 112–45.
Northam, John. *Ibsen: A Critical Study.* Cambridge, England: Cambridge University Press, 1973.
Oliver Brachfeld, F. *Inferiority Feelings in the Individual and the Group.* Translated from the French by Marjorie Gabain. London: Routledge and Kegan Paul, 1951; reissued by Westport, Conn.: Greenwood Press, 1972.
Pai Hsien-yung 白先勇. "Tung yeh" 冬夜 (Winter nights). In *Pai Hsien-yung, Taipei jen* 台北人 (Taipei residents). Taipei, 1971. Pp. 197–217. Translated as "Winter Nights." In *Chinese Stories from Taiwan, 1960–1970*, edited by Joseph S. M. Lau. New York: Columbia University Press, 1976. Pp. 337–54.
Pound, Ezra. "A Few Don'ts by An Imagiste." *Poetry: A Magazine of Verse* 1 (March, 1913):200–206.
Rawlinson, John L. "Reflections on Biography and Autobiography: The Case of Hu Shih." *Asian Profile* 4.2 (April, 1976):96–113.
Ropp, Paul S. *Dissent in Early Modern China: Ju-lin wai-shih and Ch'ing Social*

Criticism. Ann Arbor: University of Michigan Press, 1981.

Schacht, Richard. *Alienation*. Garden City, N. Y.: Doubleday and Co. 1970.

Schneider, Laurence A. *Ku Chieh-kang and China's New History: Nationalism and the Quest for Alternative Tradition*. Berkeley, Calif.: University of California Press, 1971.

Schwartz, Benjamin I. "Some Polarities in Confucian Thought." In *Confucianism in Action*, edited by David S. Nivison and Arthur F. Wright. Stanford, Calif.: Stanford University Press, 1959. Pp. 50–62.

———. *In Search of Wealth and Power: Yen Fu and the West*. Cambridge, Mass.: Harvard University Press, 1964.

———. "Introduction." In *Reflections on the May Fourth Movement: A Symposium*, edited by Benjamin I. Schwartz. Cambridge, Mass.: Harvard University Press, 1972. Pp. 1–13.

———. "The Limits of 'Tradition versus Modernity' as Categories of Explanation: The Case of the Chinese Intellectuals," *Daedalus* 101.2 (Spring, 1972): 71–88.

———. "Notes on Conservatism in General and in China in Particular." In *The Limits of Change: Essays on Conservative Alternatives in Republican China*, edited by Charlotte Furth. Cambridge, Mass.: Harvard University Press, 1976. Pp. 3–21.

———. "History and Culture in the Thought of Joseph Levenson." In *The Mozartian Historian: Essays on the Works of Joseph R. Levenson*, edited by Maurice Meisner and Rhoads Murphey. Berkeley, Calif.: University of California Press, 1976. Pp. 100–112.

Shih, Vincent Y. C. "A Talk with Hu Shih." *China Quarterly* 10 (April–June, 1962): 149–65.

Shih Chao-chi (Alfred Sao-ke Sze) 施肇基. *Shih Chao-chi tsao-nien hui-i lu* 施肇基早年回憶錄 (Memoir of Shih Chao-chi: the early years). Taipei, 1967.

Sichel, Edith. *The Renaissance*. London: Oxford University Press, 1914.

Stuart, John Leighton. *Fifty Years in China: The Memoirs of John Leighton Stuart, Missionary and Ambassador*. New York: Random House, 1954.

T'an Pi-an 譚彼岸. *Wan-Ch'ing te pai-hua wen yün-tung* 晚清的白話文運動 (The vernacular movement in the late Ch'ing). Wuhan, 1956.

T'an Ssu-t'ung 譚嗣同. "Jen-hsüeh" 仁學 (A study of benevolence). In T'an Ssu-t'ung, *T'an Ssu-t'ung ch'üan-chi* 譚嗣同全集 (Complete works of T'an Ssu-t'ung). Peking, 1954. Pp. 3–90.

T'ang Te-kang (T. K. Tong) 唐德剛. *Hu Shih tsa-i* 胡適雜憶 (Miscellaneous reminiscences of Hu Shih). Taipei, 1979.

T'ao Hsi-sheng 陶希聖. "Kuan-yü tun-ch'ing Hu hsien-sheng ch'u-jen hsing-cheng-yüan-chang chi ch'i-t'a" 關於敦請胡先生出任行政院長及其他 (The invitation to Hu Shih to head the Executive Yüan, and other recollections). *Chuan-chi wen-hsüeh* 28.5 (May, 1976): 18–21.

Ting Ling 丁玲. "I-chiu-san-ling nien ch'un Shanghai" 一九三〇年春上海 (Shanghai, spring 1930). In Ting Ling, *Ting Ling tuan-p'ien hsiao-shuo chi* 丁玲短篇小說集 (A collection of the short stories of Ting Ling). Peking, 1954. Pp. 150–231.

Ting Wen-chiang 丁文江. "I-ko wai-kuo p'eng-yu tui-yü i-ko liu-hsüeh-sheng te

chung-kao" 一個外國朋友對於一個留學生的忠告 (Counsels of a foreign friend to a Chinese graduate from abroad). *NLCP* 42 (March 4, 1923).
———. "Shao-shu jen te tse-jen" 少數人的責任 (The responsibility of the elite minority). *NLCP* 67 (August 26, 1923).
———. "Chung-kuo cheng-chih te ch'u-lu" 中國政治的出路 (The way out for Chinese politics). *TLPL* 11 (July 31, 1932):2–6.
———. "Min-chu cheng-chih yü tu-ts'ai cheng-chih" 民主政治與獨裁政治 (Democracy and autocracy). *TLPL* 133 (December 30, 1934):4–7.
———. "Tsai lun min-chu yü tu-ts'ai" 再論民主與獨裁 (Another discussion of democracy and autocracy). *TLPL* 137 (January 27, 1935):19–22.
———. *Liang Jen-kung hsien-sheng nien-p'u ch'ang-pien ch'u-kao* 梁任公先生年譜長編初稿 (First draft of a chronological biography of Liang Ch'i-ch'ao). 2 vols. Taipei, 1959.
Ts'ai Yüan-p'ei 蔡元培. "Ts'ai Yüan-p'ei te hsüan-yen" 蔡元培的宣言 (Ts'ai Yüan-p'ei's proclamation). *NLCP* 39 (January 28, 1923).
"Tsingtau and after." Signed "A Friend of China." *New Republic* 2.14 (February 6, 1915):20–21.
Tu Ching-i. "Conservatism in a Constructive Form: The Case of Wang Kuo-wei (1877–1927)." *Monumenta Serica* 28 (1969):188–214.
United States Relations with China, with Special Reference to the Period 1944–1949. Washington, D.C.: Government Printing Office, 1949.
Wakeman, Frederic, Jr. "The Price of Autonomy: Intellectuals in Ming and Ch'ing Politics." *Daedalus* 101.2 (Spring, 1972):35–70.
Wang Ching-hsüan 王敬軒 (Ch'ien Hsüan-t'ung 錢玄同). "Wen-hsüeh ke-ming chih fan-hsiang" 文學革命之反響 (A response to the literary revolution). *HCN* 4.3 (March 15, 1918):289–92.
Wang Te-i 王德毅. *Wang Kuo-wei nien-p'u* 王國維年譜 (A chronological biography of Wang Kuo-wei). Taipei, 1967.
Wang, Y. C. *Chinese Intellectuals and the West, 1872–1949.* Chapel Hill: University of North Carolina Press, 1966.
Wellek, René. "The Concept of Realism in Literary Scholarship." In his *Concepts of Criticism*, edited by Stephen G. Nichols, Jr. New Haven: Yale University Press, 1963. Pp. 222–55.
West, Philip. *Yenching University and Sino-Western Relations, 1916–1952.* Cambridge, Mass.: Harvard University Press, 1976.
Wong Young-tsu. "The Ideal of Universality in Late Ch'ing Reformism." In *Reform in Nineteenth-Century China*, edited by Paul A. Cohen and John E. Schrecker. Cambridge, Mass.: Harvard University Press, 1976. Pp. 150–59.
———. (Wang Yung-tsu) 汪榮祖. "Wan-Ch'ing pien-fa ssu-hsiang hsi-lun" 晚清變法思想析論 (An analysis of the reformist thought in the late Ch'ing). In *Chin-tai Chung-kuo ssu-hsiang jen-wu lun: wan-Ch'ing ssu-hsiang* 近代中國思想人物論：晚清思想 (On the thought and personalities of modern China: thought in the late Ch'ing). Taipei, 1980. Pp. 85–132.
Wu Ching-ch'ao 吳景超. "Ke-ming yü chien-kuo" 革命與建國 (Revolution and national construction). *TLPL* 84 (January 7, 1934):2–5.
Wu Wen-ch'i 吳文祺. *Chin pai-nien lai te Chung-kuo wen-i ssu-ch'ao*

近百年來的中國文藝思潮 (The literary trend in China during the past hundred years). N.p., 1940–41.
Yamamoto Tatsuro and Yamamoto Sumiko. "The Anti-Christian Movement in China, 1922–27." *Far Eastern Quarterly* 12.2 (February, 1953): 133–48.
Yeh Ch'u-ts'ang 葉楚傖. "Yu tang te li-hsing lai wan-hui feng-ch'i" 由黨的力行來挽回風氣 (Restore public morals by means of the party effort). *Che-chiang min-pao* 浙江民報, October 10, 1929. Pasted in Hu Shih, *Hu Shih te jih-chi*.
Yeh Lung 葉龍. *T'ung-ch'eng p'ai wen-hsüeh shih* 桐城派文學史 (A history of the literature of T'ung-ch'eng school). Hong Kong, 1975.
Yen Fu 嚴復. "Chiu-wang chüeh-lun" 救亡決論 (On our salvation). In Yen Fu, *Yen Chi-tao shih-wen ch'ao* 嚴幾道詩文鈔 (A collection of Yen Fu's prose and poetry). Shanghai, 1922; Taipei reprint, n.d. Pp. 104–29. Dated 1895.
Young, Ernest P. "Nationalism, Reform, and Republican Revolution: China in the Early Twentieth Century." In *Modern East Asia: Essays in Interpretation*, edited by James B. Crowley. New York: Harcourt, Brace and World, 1970. Pp. 151–79.
———. *The Presidency of Yuan Shih-k'ai: Liberalism and Dictatorship in Early Republican China*. Ann Arbor: University of Michigan Press, 1977.
Yüan T'ung-li, comp. *A Guide to Doctoral Dissertations by Chinese Students in America, 1905–1960*. Washington, D.C.: Sino-American Cultural Society, 1961.
Zee, Ts-zun Z., and Lui-ngau Chang. "The Boxer Indemnity Students of 1910." *CSM* 6.1 (November 10, 1910): 16–19.

Index

Academia Sinica, 143, 197, 203
Adams, John Quincy, Jr., 206
Alsace, 141
American Association for International Conciliation, 35, 85
American Civil Liberties Union, 143
Anarchism, 110, 118
Anfu Clique, 117, 252
Angell, Ralph Norman, 92, 238
Anglo-French invasions, 97
Anhwei, 3, 6, 14, 17, 154, 206
Anhwei University, 244
Anna Karenina, 151
Anti-Christian movement, 49, 52, 53, 55, 57
Antisuffragettes, 108, 109
Ariga Nagao (1860–1921), 111
Arranged marriage, 60, 61, 62, 63, 71, 75, 76, 213, 215
Association of Cosmopolitan Clubs, 83, 84, 85, 237

Bacon, Francis, 35, 66, 95
Barker, Elmer Eugene, 69, 126, 183, 205, 234, 235, 239
Becker, Carl, 171
Before Dawn, 151
Begbie, H., 43
Belgium, 90, 91, 95, 102
Bentham, Jeremy, 10
Bosanquet, Bernard, 168

Boxer indemnity scholarship, 10, 20, 21, 25, 27, 28, 29, 34, 41, 204, 205, 228
Boxer movement, 50, 51, 97
Bradley, Francis, 168
Brandes, Georg, 162
Brief History of Enlightenment, 159
Brieux, Eugene, 151, 152
British-American Tobacco Company, 51
British Labor party, 144
Browning, Robert, 35
Bryan, William Jennings, 84
Buddha, 5, 12, 13, 26, 50, 64
Buddhism, 4, 5, 11–13, 15, 19, 41, 42, 44, 47, 50, 56, 87, 171, 172, 174, 178, 186, 187, 198, 209, 217, 218
Bull Moose button, 86
Bunyan, John, 43
Byron, George Gordon, 67, 194, 196, 200, 207

Cambridge University, 206, 213
Capitalism, 101
Carlyle, Thomas, 89
Carnegie Endowment for International Peace, 92
Cartwright, Edmund, 184
Cavour, Camillo de, 67
Chang, Carsun. *See* Chang Chün-mai
Chang Chia-ao, 213

293

294   Index

Chang Chün-mai (1886–1969), 180, 213
Chang Hao, 22
Chang Hsün (1854–1923), 115
Chang Kia-gnau. *See* Chang Chia-ao
Chang Loy, 36, 105
Chang P'eng-ch'un, 214
Chang Ping-lin, 21, 203
Chang Shih-chao (1881–), 157, 158
Chang Tso-lin (1873–1928), 52
Chang Tsu-hsün, 243
Chang Wei-tz'u, 117, 132
Chang Yu-i, 213, 215
Chang Yüan-hsi, 233, 236
Chao Sung-nan, 259
Chao Yüan-jen (Chao Yuen-ren, Y. R. Chao, 1892–1982), 34, 35, 168, 192
Ch'en Chiung-ming, 10
Ch'en Heng-che (1890–), 235
Ch'en Jung-kun, 11
Ch'en-pao. See *Peking Morning Post*
Ch'en Shao-t'ang, 39, 41, 42
Ch'en Te-cheng, 128, 129
Ch'en T'ien-hua, 130
Ch'en Tu-hsiu (1879–1942), 23, 55, 56, 116, 117, 152, 164, 169, 175, 211, 249, 252
Ch'eng-Chu Neo-Confucianism, 12, 40, 42
Ch'eng-chung school, 6, 7
Ch'eng Fang-wu (1894–), 9, 34, 224
Ch'eng I-ch'uan (Ch'eng I, 1033–1107), 12
Ch'eng Lo-t'ing, 41
Chi-ch'i (Anhwei province), 3, 13
Chia Pao-yü, 153
Chiang Kai-shek (1887–1975), 124, 125, 126, 131, 134, 142, 143, 145, 244–45
Chiang Meng-lin (Chiang Monlin, 1886–1964), 9, 22, 23, 31, 119, 129, 224, 243, 245
Chiang T'ing fu (1895–1965), 131, 132, 136

Chiang Tung-hsiu, 58, 59, 66, 68, 69, 70, 72, 74, 76, 78, 80, 235, 259
Ch'ien Hsüan-t'ung (1887–1939), 164, 169, 252
Ch'ien Tuan-sheng, 132, 133, 136
Chin-pu tang. See Progressive party
China National Institute, 7, 9, 16, 17, 20, 39, 124, 129
Chinese Christian Students' Association, 39
Chinese Communists, 101, 115, 128, 130, 135, 139, 142, 144, 145, 146, 244. *See also* Chinese Marxists
Chinese League for the Protection of Civil Rights, 142–43
Chinese Marxists, 118, 119. *See also* Chinese Communists
Chinese Students' Alliance, 84
Chinese Students' Association, 169
Chinese Students' Monthly, 34, 91
Ching-hua yüan. See *Flowers in the Mirror*
Ching-yeh hsün-pao. See *Struggle, The*
Ch'iu-shih Academy, 23
Ch'iu T'ing-liang, 11
Chou Ping-lin, 138
Chou Shu-jen. *See* Lu Hsün
Christianity, 15, 87, 171, 181, 208, 209
Chu Hsi (1130–1200), 4, 12, 43
Chu-ko Liang (181–234), 190, 191
Ch'uang-tsao chi-k'an. See *Creation Quarterly*
Ch'uang-tsao chou-k'an. See *Creation Weekly*
Ch'uang-tsao jih-pao. See *Creation Daily*
Chuang-tzu (369–286 B.C.), 172
Chung-kuo hsin kung-hsüeh. See New China National Institute
Chung-kuo kung-hsüeh. See China National Institute
Chung-kuo min-ch'üan pao-chang

t'ung-meng. *See* Chinese League for the Protection of Civil Rights
Civil Service Examination, 5, 6, 16, 17, 23, 24, 25, 26, 28, 32, 155, 157, 185, 204, 216, 217, 219
Classic of Changes, 3
Classic of Documents, 3
Classic of Filial Piety, 3
Classic of Songs, 3, 161
Classical literature, 154, 159, 160, 164
Collected Essays of Wu Yü, 175
Columbia University, 30, 63, 69, 87, 107, 108, 129, 131, 205, 206, 208
Comfort, Howard, 259
Comfort, William Wistar, 43, 205, 230
Commentary on the Book of Waterways, 192, 193
Commercial Press, 6, 54
Comprehensive Mirror for Aid in Government, The, 4, 161
Concubinage, 177, 212, 218
Condorcet, Marquis de, 71
Confucian Society, 47
Confucianism, 9, 12, 15, 18, 19, 42, 43, 47, 48, 56, 67, 116, 122, 171, 172, 173, 174, 181, 182, 187, 188, 194, 209, 217, 218, 219
Confucius (551–479 B.C.), 12, 47, 67, 96, 97, 116, 150, 171, 172, 173, 174, 175, 183, 209
Confucius as Reformer, 171
Conservatism, 179, 180. *See also* Cultural conservatism; Kuomintang conservatism
Cornell Cosmopolitan Club, 46, 83, 84, 85, 86, 87
Cornell Daily Sun, 65, 86, 87, 96
Cornell Era, 111
Cornell University, 27, 33, 34, 35, 36, 39, 40, 46, 52, 59, 63, 69, 73, 86, 92, 107, 111, 166, 168, 205, 206, 208; College of Arts and Sciences, 33, 35; Russell Sage School of Philosophy, 35, 168, 237; New York State College of Agriculture, 30, 32–33
Corson, Hiram, 35
Cosmopolitan Student, 85
Cosmopolitanism, 36, 64, 211, 233
Crandall, C. L., 73, 74
Creation Daily, 34
Creation Quarterly, 34
Creation Society, 34
Creation Weekly, 34
Creighton, James E., 33, 168
Crescent, 115, 129
Crick, Bernard, 109
Crisis of Chinese Consciousness, The, 115
Cultural conservatism, 53, 54. *See also* Conservatism; Kuomintang conservatism

Damaged Goods, 151
Darwin, Charles, 10, 35
Daudet, Alphonse, 249
de Bary, William Theodore, 219
De l'esprit des lois, 9, 14, 58
Decatur, Stephen, 86
Decline and Fall of the Roman Empire, The, 89
Democracy, 111, 112, 124, 130, 132, 133, 136, 176, 180, 183, 184, 185, 194, 207, 217, 218
Democracy and despotism, debate on, 130–38
Descartes, René, 10, 67
Despotism, 130, 131, 153
Development of the Logical Method in Ancient China, The, 167
Dewey, John, 92, 108, 109, 118, 119, 167, 168, 169, 170, 171, 207
Dickens, Charles, 9, 35
Dictatorship, 112, 130, 131–32, 133, 134, 136, 138
Diderot, Denis, 106
Doll's House, A, 151
Dream of the Red Chamber, 4, 151, 153, 156, 157, 159

Dumas, Alexandre (fils), 9
Dumas, Alexandre (père), 9

Edwards, Dwight, 51
Eight-legged essay, 24, 154, 157, 176, 177
Elitism, 18, 19, 103, 109, 134, 136, 142
Elmhirst, Leonard K., 214, 215
Endeavor, 115, 120, 122
"Enemy of the People, An," 151, 164
English, popularity of, in China, 22–23, 25, 26, 258
Erh-nü ying-hsiung chuan. See *Tales of Heroic Young Lovers*
Erh-shih nien mu-tu chih kuai-hsien-chuang. See *Eyewitnessed Strange Phenomena of the Past Twenty Years*
Erikson, Erik H., 74, 88, 96
Esperanto, 84
Euclid, 177
Evolution and Ethics, 9
Examination Yüan, 137
Executive Yüan, 125, 137
Experimentalism, 118, 167
Eyewitnessed Strange Phenomena of the Past Twenty Years, 159

Fairbank, John K., 189
Fan Chen (fl. 483–505), 5, 11, 168
Fang Pao (1668–1749), 154
Faust, 34
Fédération Internationale des Étudiants, 83, 84, 89
Feudalism, 178
First Higher School of Tokyo, 32
Fitschen, Mrs. Frederick, 67
Five Classics, 11
Five Power Constitution, 137
Flaubert, Gustave, 249
Flowers in the Mirror, 154, 157
Flowers in the Sea of Sin, 159
Foot binding, 176, 177, 178, 184, 185, 212, 218

Ford, Henry, 184
Fosdick, Harry Emerson, 43
Four Books, 3, 11, 12
Franco-Prussian War, 103, 141
Franklin, Benjamin, 181
Freud, Anna, 56, 57
Fu, Chün-chien, 7, 8
Fu Ssu-nien (1896–1950), 131, 144, 197, 198, 199, 200
Fulton, Robert, 184

Gandhi, Mahatma, 74, 88, 96, 124
Gannett, Lewis Stiles, 80, 236
Gay, Peter, 106
George, Henry, 35
Ghosts, 151
Gibbon, Edward, 67, 89
Giglio-Tos, Efisio, 83
Gilman, Daniel Coit, 206–7
Gladden, Washington, 237
Goethe, Johann Wolfgang von, 34, 35, 190, 191
Gogol, Nikolai, 150
Goncourt, Edmond de, 249
Goncourt, Jules de, 249
Goodnow, Frank Johnson, 111
Goodrich, L. Carrington, 260
Gradualism, 119
Great Britain, 133, 145, 150, 204, 206, 208, 211, 214, 215, 227, 228
Great Illusion, The, 92
Grieder, Jerome B., 77, 80, 104, 109, 137, 138, 167, 223
Grote, George, 89
Guide to Doctoral Dissertations by Chinese Students in America, 1905–1960, A, 208
Gulliver's Travels, 155

Han-fei-tzu (d. 233 B.C.), 172
Han Learning, 174, 186, 187
Han Wu-ti (141–87 B.C.), 159
Hargreaves, James, 184
Harvard University, 34, 36, 62, 194, 206

Hauptmann, Gerhart, 151, 152
Hawthorne, Nathaniel, 151
Hedin, Sven, 248
Hiram Corson Browning Prize, 35
Historical Records, 153
History of [Ancient] *Chinese Philosophy, A,* 167
History of Greece, A, 89
Hobbes, Thomas, 10, 67
House of Seven Gables, The, 151
Hsi-yu chi. See *Journey to the West*
Hsia, C. T., 235, 260
Hsiao-ching. See *Classic of Filial Piety*
Hsiao-hsüeh chi-chu, 4, 12
Hsiao Kung-chuan, 209, 210, 212
Hsin-ch'ao, 76
Hsin ch'ing-nien, 149, 161, 175
Hsin-hsüeh wei-ching k'ao. See *Study of the Forged Classics of the Hsin Period*
Hsin-min shuo. See *New Citizen*
Hsin-yüeh yüeh-k'an. See *Crescent*
Hsü Chih-mo (1896–1931), 208, 213, 214, 215
Hsü I-sun, 39, 41, 47, 112, 190, 191
Hsü Mei, 141
Hsüeh-heng, 164
Hsün-tzu (ca. 300 to ca. 230B.C.), 13, 116, 172, 173
Hu-chiang University, 258–59
Hu Ch'uan, 3
Hu Shih (1891–1962): family background, 3: early schooling, 3–4, 5–11; interest in English, 7, 25; interest in mathematics and science, 7–9; on human nature, 13–14 (*see also* pessimism); at Cornell, 30–36; perception of Western culture, 42, 175–76; and cosmopolitanism, 46, 210–11; ability of French, 58; ability of German, 58; reserved personality, 61; pacifism, 90, 100, 103, 105; and Japan, 90–91, 95–96, 100–106; pessimism, 94, 97, 103–4, 125, 141–42, 143, 164; defended foreign interests in China, 101; elitist tendency, 108–9, 139, 142; emphasis on intellectual reform, 112–17, 119–20, 157–58, 163, 191–92; aversion to modern Chinese history, 189–91; and independence of China's higher education, 206–7; problems concerning his Ph.D. degree, 208, 260; visited brothels, 236
—and Buddhism, 4–5, 11–13, 168, 186; reassessment of Confucianism, 40, 172–73, 181–82; attitude toward Confucianism as a state religion, 46–47; criticism of Chinese culture, 52–53, 54–55, 56–57, 175–80; defended Chinese culture, 180–88
—relationship with his mother, 3–4, 5, 20, 68–73, 77; on marriage, 14, 60–63, 75, 213–15; conception of children, 14, 66–68, 77–78; and "social immortality," 14–15, 65–66, 67–68, 79–80; conception of family, 64–65; and freedom of women, 65–66, 75, 79; contemplated bachelorhood, 66–68
—influence of Lin Shu on, 9; influence of Yen Fu on, 9–10, 14; influence of Liang Ch'i-ch'ao on, 10–11, 14–15, 16; influence of John Dewey on, 167–70; attacked by Lin Shu, 252
—perception of the United States, 25–28, 40–41, 46, 86–88; admired Theodore Roosevelt, 86–87; admired Woodrow Wilson, 86–88; interest in American politics, 107–8; and suffragette movement in America, 107–8; impact of long stay in America on, 204–6
—conversion to Christianity, 39–40; decline of religious fervor, 43; criticism of Christianity, 43–49,

49–57, 181; defended missionary, 48–49, 52–53, 56–57
—cultural inferiority complex, 42–43, 56–57; defensive psychology, 60–61; mentality as a returned student, 207–8 (*see also* perception of Western culture)
—and vernacular fiction, 4; early writings in the vernacular, 11–15; and realism and naturalism, 150–52, 162; and Ming-Ch'ing fiction, 152–56; criticism of Chinese literary heritage, 158–61; and opponents of literary revolution, 164; and origins of literary revolution, 169–70; and Nobel Prize for literature, 248
—early attitude toward politics, 16–18; perception of Yüan Shih-k'ai, 46–47, 111, 113–14; and the Kuomintang, 53–55, 134–38 (*see also* Kuomintang); ambivalence toward China, 97–100, 209–10; perception of the 1911 revolution, 111, 114; and the debate on "problems and isms," 118; and the Chinese presidency, 124–26; reluctance to be identified with Chinese government, 126; ambassadorship to Washington, 126, 183; relation with authority in power, 127–38; in the debate on democracy versus dictatorship, 130–38; and student activism, 138–42; and KMT-CCP conflict, 144–45; political opportunities, 124–26, 244
Hu Tsu-wang, 77, 258–59
Huang Hsing (1874–1916), 111, 181
Huang Tsun-hsien (1848–1905), 11
Huang Yüan-yung, 157, 158
Hugo, Victor, 9
Hume, David, 106
Hung-lou meng. See *Dream of the Red Chamber*

Hung-teng chiao. See Red Lanterns
Huxley, Thomas Henry, 9, 141, 167

I-ching. See *Classic of Changes*
Ibsen, Henrik, 150, 151, 152, 161, 162, 163, 164, 249
Ibsenism, 161, 162, 218
Imagism, 170, 253–54
Impeachment Yüan, 137
Imperialism, 101, 140, 203, 210
Independent Critic Association, 138
Individualism, 10, 62, 64, 79, 174, 175, 197, 219, 220
Inspector General, The, 150
Institute of Eastern Language, 23
Intellectual Trends in the Sung and Yüan Dynasties, 175
International Club, 83, 85
Introduction to Politics, 132
Ithaca, 30, 33, 43, 45, 60, 63, 69, 84, 86, 89, 107, 110, 205, 206
Ithaca Journal, 86
Iyenaga, T., 95

Jackson, Henry E., 44, 45
James, Edmund J., 204
James, William, 118
Japan, 22, 23, 24, 32, 90, 91, 92, 94, 95, 96, 100, 101, 102, 103, 104, 105, 106, 177, 182, 189, 192, 194, 211
Japan Critic, 104
Jefferson, Thomas, 144, 145
Jen, 173, 174, 177
Jen Hung-chün (1886–1961), 168, 235
Jesus, 44, 45, 55, 67, 90, 96
Johns Hopkins University, 206
Johnson, Nelson T., 105
Johnson, T. Neil, 258
Journey to the West, 154, 159
Ju, 174
Ju-lin wai-shih. See *Scholars, The*
Judaism, 105
Judicial Yüan, 128, 137

K'ang Yu-wei (1858–1927), 5, 21, 154, 171, 181, 203, 204, 209, 210, 211, 212, 215, 218
Kant, Immanuel, 10, 67, 85, 95
Kao I-han (1885–), 117, 210, 243
Kao-tzu, 13
Kaufmann, Walter, 219
Ke-ming chün. See *Revolutionary Army, The*
Kiao-chau, 95
"Kindergarten politics," 132, 133, 134, 135
KMT-CCP conflict, 142, 144, 145
K'o-hsüeh. See *Science*
K'o-hsüeh she. See *Science Society*
Koo, Wellington. *See* Ku Wei-chün
Kropotkin, Peter, 225
Ku Chieh-kang (1895–), 232
Ku-shih, 8
Ku Wei-chün (1887–), 23
Kuan-ch'ang hsien-hsing chi. See *Panorama of Officialdom*
Kuei Heng, 236
K'ung-chiao hui. See *Confucian Society*
K'ung-tzu kai-chih k'ao. See *Confucius as Reformer*
Kuo Mo-jo (1892–), 9, 24, 32, 33, 34, 224
Kuo-wen chou-pao, 128
Kuomintang, 49, 53, 54, 115, 125, 127, 128, 129, 130, 134, 135, 136, 137, 138, 142, 143, 144, 145, 176, 226, 245
Kuomintang conservatism, 54. *See also* Cultural conservatism
Kwok, D. W. Y., 8
Kyushu Imperial University, 33

Lan Chih-hsien, 118
Langer, Susanne, 190
Lao-ts'an yu-chi. See *Travels of Lao-ts'an*
Lao-tzu (604?–531?B.C.), 67, 90, 96, 174

League of Nations, 93, 101, 102
League to Enforce Peace, 88
Lee, Leo Ou-fan, 157
Legislative Yüan, 125, 137
Levenson, Joseph R., 196
Li Ch'ao, 76
Li-chi. See *Record of Rituals*
Li Ju-chen (ca. 1763 to ca. 1830), 154, 157
Li Po (701–62), 67, 150
Li Po-yüan (Pao-chia, 1867–1906), 151
Li Ta-chao (1889–1927), 117, 118, 243
Liang Ch'i-ch'ao (1873–1929), 5, 9, 10, 11, 14, 15, 16, 21, 22, 24, 66, 112, 130, 154, 156, 168, 180, 203, 204, 210, 213, 214, 215, 216, 218, 227
Liang Shu-ming (1893–), 180
Liang Ssu-ch'eng, 213, 214
Liberal party, 122
Liberalism, 15, 174, 203
Lifton, Robert Jay, 48, 61, 96, 190
Lin Ch'ang-min (1876–1925), 213
Lin Hui-yin, 213, 214
Lin Shu (1852–1924), 9, 11, 154, 164, 252
Lin Tai-yü, 153
Lin Yü-sheng, 115, 116, 117, 178, 180
Lin Yutang (1895–), 105
Link, The, 151
Linton, Howard P., 208
Literary revolution, 4, 119, 169, 252
Liu Pan-nung (1891–1934), 164, 252
Lo Chen-yü (1866–1940), 23
Lo Wen-kan (1888–1941), 123
Lochner, Louis Paul, 36, 85
Locke, John, 67
Lorraine, 141
Lowell, Amy, 254
Lu Hsiao-man, 214
Lu Hsün (1881–1936), 9, 31, 116, 218, 224

Lusitania, 88
Luxemburg, 90

Ma Chien-chung (1844–1900), 169
Maeterlinck, Maurice, 150, 249
Manchukuo, 102
Manchuria, 102, 103
Manchurian Incident, 102, 104, 176
Mao I, 70
Mao Tse-tung (1893–1976), 144, 153
Mao Tzu-shui, 198
Marshall mission, 142
Marxism, 49, 56, 118
Maupassant, Guy de, 100, 249
May Fourth generation, 9, 21, 207, 213, 215, 216, 217, 220
May Fourth movement, 9, 11, 21, 33, 50, 54, 139, 157, 161, 163, 164, 169, 172, 175, 179, 194, 195, 196, 210, 211, 212, 215, 217, 218, 219, 220
May 30th Incident, 140
Mei-ch'i school, 6
Mei-chou p'ing-lun. See *Weekly Critic*
Mei-fu kung-ssu. See Standard Oil Company
Mei Kuang-ti (1890–1945), 164, 170, 180
Mencius, 13, 111, 116, 150, 163, 173, 180, 183
Mexico, 101
Mill, John Stuart, 9
Ming-Ch'ing fiction, 152, 155, 156, 157, 161, 163
Mr. Ace, 39
Mr. Mercer, 39, 40, 41
Mo-tzu, 93, 161, 172, 174, 175, 177
Modernization of China, 52, 56, 166, 180, 182, 183, 185, 189
Mohism, 172, 173
Monarchical movement, 110, 111, 112, 113, 114, 158, 191
Montesquieu, C. L., 9, 14, 58, 180

More, Thomas, 95
Morley, John Viscount, 71
Morrison, George Ernest, 207
Mott, John R., 40
Mukden incident, 105
Murobushi Koshin, 104, 105
"My country, right or wrong," 86, 87, 93, 97

Nanking, 126, 129
Napoleon Bonaparte, 96
Nasmyth, George William, 85, 90, 92, 237
National Assembly, 115, 125, 126, 138
Nationalism, 49, 50, 84, 89, 90, 94, 98, 100, 168, 176, 189, 203, 210
Nationalist government of China, 126, 130, 217
Naturalism, 150, 151, 152, 153, 155, 164, 249
Neo-Confucianism, 50, 53, 154, 173, 176. See also Ch'eng-Chu Neo-Confucianism
Neo-Mohism, 172
New China National Institute, 7, 17, 26
New Citizen, 10, 21, 216
New Culture movement, 9, 21, 54, 58, 164
New Republic, 91
New York Evening Journal, 107
New York Evening Post, 95
New York Times, 95, 107
New York Tribune, 107
Newton, Sir Isaac, 67, 74
Nieh-hai hua. See *Flowers in the Sea of Sin*
Nietzsche, Friedrich, 34
Nineteen Ancient Poems, 70
Nonresistance, 90, 91, 92, 93, 96, 100, 124
Northam, John, 161
Northrop, Filmer S. C., 187
Nu-li chou-pao. See *Endeavor*

Oliver Brachfeld, F., 42
On Liberty, 9
Opium War, 97
Orth, Samuel P., 107
Ottomeir, 26
Ou-yang Hsiu (1007–72), 116
"Our Attitude toward Modern Western Civilization," 176
"Our Political Proposals," 122, 123
Outlook, 111
Oxford University, 206, 208

Pai Hsien-yung, 193, 195
Pai-hua, 11, 73, 150, 163, 168, 169, 170. See also Vernacular literature
Panorama of Officialdom, 151, 155, 157, 159
Pascal, Blaise, 67
Pasteur, Louis, 141
Patriotism, 83, 89, 106, 210, 211
Patterson, Mr. and Mrs. L. E., 205, 233, 259–60
Peita. See Peking National University
Peking, 6, 10, 20, 27, 29, 41, 51, 129, 139, 143, 193, 214, 236, 248
Peking Morning Post, 123
Peking National University, 58, 123, 129, 142, 192, 193, 198, 235, 252
Phi Beta Kappa, 28, 35, 58
Philippines, The, 87, 94
Pilgrim's Progress, 43
Pitt, William, 67
Plato, 35, 44, 95, 173
Po Chü-i (772–846), 150
Pound, Ezra, 254
Pragmatism, 167, 168, 170, 172, 174
Princeton University, 193, 214
Princeton-Yenching Foundation, 51
Progressive party, 47
Proudhon, Pierre Joseph, 110

Rationalism, 50, 51, 172, 176
Realism, 151, 152, 155, 157, 162, 249
Record of Rituals, 3

Red Lanterns, 51
Reform generation of 1898: compared with May Fourth generation, 203–20; nationalism of, 209–10; attitude toward marriage, 211–15; attitude toward political involvement, 215–16, 216–18, 220; mentioned, 21
Reform movement of 1898, 23, 169, 203, 209, 216, 218
Reid, Gilbert, 43
Renaissance, 157, 170, 194
Republican China, 111, 121, 136, 193, 195
Republican revolution. See Revolution of 1911
Revolution of 1911, 50, 110, 111, 114, 121, 158, 180, 207, 216
Revolutionary Army, The, 16, 17
Robinson, Fred, 33, 69, 205
Robinson, James R., 67
Rockefeller Foundation, 206
Romance of the Three Kingdoms, 4
Romanticism, 157
Roosevelt, Theodore, 40, 86, 87, 107, 227
Ropp, Paul, 219
Rousseau, Jean-Jacques, 10
Rubaiyat of Omar Khayyam, 34
Russell, Bertrand, 34, 35, 90, 207
Russo-Japanese War, 16, 104

St. Augustine, 95
Sakyamuni, 67, 90–91
Sampson, Martin, 36
San-huang wu-ti, 54
San-kuo yen-i. See *Romance of the Three Kingdoms*
Scholars, The, 4, 150, 153, 154, 155, 157, 159
Schumm, George, 110
Schumm, Paul B., 110
Schurman, Jacob Gould, 86, 237
Schwartz, Benjamin, 8, 21, 203, 204, 209

Science: popularity of, 7–9, 13, 30–32, 33, 34, 197, 198, 199–200; defined, 224
Science, 169
Science Education Conference, 178
Science Readers, The, 13
Science Society, 168, 169
Scott, Sir Walter, 9
Second Mile, The, 43
Sergent, Nellie B., 235
Shakespeare, William, 35
Shanghai, 11, 13, 16, 19, 20, 23, 25, 27, 28, 47, 58, 62, 65, 68, 69, 79, 83, 115, 117, 124, 128, 129, 139, 166, 167, 168, 248
Shaw, George Bernard, 150, 152
Sheldon, Wilmon Henry, 186, 187
Shen-pao, 6
Shih Chao-chi (1877–1958), 23, 228
Shih-chi. See *Historical Records*
Shih-ching. See *Classic of Songs*
Shih Nai-an, 153
Shih-pao, 6
Shih-shih hsin-pao, 6, 34
Shih-yün ho-pi, 8
Shinto, 182
Shu-ching. See *Classic of Documents*
Shui-ching chu. See *Commentary on the Book of Waterways*
Shui-hu chuan. See *Water Margin*
Sigma Xi honor society, 28, 35
Sino-Japanese War (of 1895), 104
Sixth Higher School of Tokyo, 33
Smith, Adam, 67, 74
Smith, Goldwin, 89
Social Darwinism, 10, 203, 225
Socialism, 110, 184
Socrates, 44, 45, 173
Soong Ch'ing-ling (1892–1981), 143
Sorrows of Young Werther, The, 34
Soviet Union, 110, 131, 133, 151
Spencer, Herbert, 67, 110, 135
Spinoza, Benedict, 67
Ssu-ma Kuang (1018–86), 11, 168
Ssu-shu. See *Four Books*

Standard Oil Company, 51
Stephenson, George, 184
Stimson, Henry Lewis, 102
Stockmann, Tomas, 164, 165
Strindberg, August, 151
Struggle, The, 7, 8, 11
Stuart, John Leighton, 57, 125, 244–45
Student movement, 139–42
Study of the Forged Classics of the Hsin Period, 171
Suffragette movement, 108, 109
Sulzer, William, 97
Sumner, William Graham, 225
Sun Ching-ts'un, 10
Sun Fo, 125
Sun Heng, 62
Sun Yat-sen (1866–1925), 5, 13, 54, 111, 114, 127, 131, 137, 143, 181
Sun Yat-sen University, 244
Sung Yüan hsüeh-an ts'ui-yü. See *Intellectual Trends in the Sung and Yüan Dynasties*
Swift, Jonathan, 155
Synthesis of Books and Illustrations of Ancient and Modern Times, 69
Sze, Alfred Sao-ke. See Shih Chao-chi

Ta-t'ung shu, 212
Taft, William Howard, 107
Tai Chi-t'ao (1891–1949), 54
T'ai-tung Publishing Company, 34
Taiwan, 126, 193, 194, 203
Taiwan National University, 193, 198
Tales of Heroic Young Lovers, 155
T'an Ssu-t'ung (1865–1898), 21, 154, 171, 203, 218
T'ang Erh-ho (1877–1943), 123
T'ang Te-kang, 208, 235, 260
T'ang Ts'ai-ch'ang, 26
Tangku Truce, 105
T'ao Lü-kung (Meng-ho, 1887–1960), 243
T'ao Yüan-ming (365–427), 8

Taoism, 44, 47, 50, 56, 87, 217
Tennyson, Alfred, 67, 89, 95
"Three Immortalities," 80
Three Peoples' Principles, 128
Thus Spake Zarathustra, 34
Tien Ah-may, 76
Ting Ling (1907–), 197, 198, 199, 200
Ting Wen-chiang (1887–1936), 22, 103, 119, 120, 132, 207, 243
Tokyo, 23, 31, 32, 33
Tolstoi, Leo, 9, 90, 151, 249
"Total Westernization," 255
Tradition of Tso, 67, 80, 153, 161
Travels of Lao-ts'an, 159
Ts'ai Yüan-p'ei (1876–1940), 114, 123, 124, 143, 243–44, 252
Ts'ao Hsüeh-ch'in, 153, 219
Ts'ao Ju-lin (1876–1966), 194
Tseng Kuo-fan (1811–72), 116, 154
Tsiang, T. F. See Chiang T'ing-fu
Tsinghua University, 34, 131, 199, 208, 244
Tso-chuan. See *Tradition of Tso*
Tsou Jung (1885–1905), 16, 17
Tu Fu (712–70), 67, 150
Tu–li p'ing-lun, 115
T'u-shu chi-ch'eng. See *Synthesis of Books and Illustrations of Ancient and Modern Times*
Tuan Ch'i-jui (1865–1936), 117, 213, 216
Tuan-fang (1861–1911), 23, 228
T'ung-ch'eng school, 154
T'ung-meng hui, 17, 18
Tung Pi-wu, 144
Tung-wen hsüeh-she. See Institute of Eastern Language
Turgenev, Ivan, 249
Twenty-Four Dynastic Histories, 160–61
Twenty-one Demands, 90, 91, 95, 96, 191
Twice-born Men, 43
Tzu-chih t'ung-chien. See *Compre-
hensive Mirror for Aid in Government, The*

Uchida Yasuya (Kosai, 1865–1936), 102
United Nations, 115, 131
United States, 20, 21, 22, 23, 24, 25, 26, 27, 28, 29, 30, 31, 35, 36, 40, 42, 46, 50, 58, 61, 62, 63, 65, 69, 70, 75, 83, 86, 88, 91, 93, 94, 98, 101, 107, 110, 111, 115, 117, 124, 126, 131, 132, 133, 144, 145, 150, 151, 167, 169, 172, 180, 181, 186, 192–93, 203, 204, 205, 215, 227, 236
University of California, Berkeley, 31, 32, 192, 193, 195, 196, 200
University of Chicago, 206
University of Illinois, 204
University of Shanghai. See Hu-chiang University
University of Wisconsin, 83, 85
Utilitarianism, 156, 161, 172
Utopianism, 210, 211

Vassar College, 235
Vernacular literature, 149, 153, 159, 160, 161, 163, 168, 169, 218. See also *Pai-hua*
Voltaire, 52, 67, 171

Wang An-shih (1021–86), 116
Wang Cheng, 243
Wang Chih-ch'un, 16
Wang Ching-hsüan, 164
Wang Ching-wei (1883–1944), 114, 134
Wang Ch'ung-hui (1882–1956), 123, 128, 244
Wang Jen-ch'iu (K'ai-yün, 1833–1916), 97, 98
Wang Keng, 214
Wang Kuo-wei (1877–1927), 9, 11, 21, 23, 156, 169, 203, 225
Wang T'ao (1829–97), 209

Wang Yang-ming (1472–1529), 13, 116
Warlordism, 110, 115, 127
Washington, George, 67, 181
Water Margin, 4, 150, 153, 157, 159
Watt, James, 184
Weaver, The, 151
Weekly Critic, 117, 118
Wellek, René, 152
Wen-k'ang (fl. 1842–51), 155
Wen-ming hsiao-shih. See *Brief History of Enlightenment*
Wilde, Oscar, 249
Williams, Edith Clifford, 63, 64, 65, 66, 68, 69, 70, 71, 72, 75, 76, 87, 113, 191, 205, 235, 242
Williams, H. S., 63
Williams, Mrs. George R., 67
Wilson, Woodrow, 84, 86, 87, 88, 97, 98, 107, 108
Women's movement, 107, 110
Wordsworth, William, 35, 207
World Peace Foundation, 92
World War I, 50, 88, 101, 102–3, 175
Wu Chih-hui (1865–1953), 22
Wu Ching-ch'ao, 132
Wu Ching-tzu (1701–54), 219
Wu Chu-kuo, 193, 194, 195, 196
Wu Ju-lun (1840–1903), 7, 154

Wu P'ei-fu (1872–1939), 52
Wu T'ing-fang (1842–1922), 181
Wu-wei politics, 132, 134, 135, 174
Wu Wen-ch'i, 169
Wu Yü (1871–1949), 175
Wu Yü wen-lu. See *Collected Essays of Wu Yü*

Yang Ch'üan (1893–1933), 143, 168
Yang Lan-ch'un, 236
Yang T'ien-tse, 10
Yao Nai (1732–1815), 154
Yeh Ch'u-ts'ang, 53, 55
Yen Fu (1853–1921), 5, 9, 14, 15, 16, 21, 24, 47, 58, 65, 66, 154, 156, 168, 181, 203, 204, 209, 211, 215, 216, 218
Yen Hsi-shan (1883–1960), 127
Yenching University, 57
Yü Chin-lei, 193, 194, 195, 196, 200
Yüan Shih-k'ai (1859–1916), 46, 47, 90, 96, 97, 99, 101, 110, 111, 113, 114, 131, 158, 181, 191, 207, 216
Yüan T'ung-li, 208, 260

Zen, H. C. *See* Jen Hung-chün
Zen, Sophia H. Chen. *See* Ch'en Heng-che
Zola, Emile, 249

www.ingramcontent.com/pod-product-compliance
Lightning Source LLC
Chambersburg PA
CBHW021136230426
43667CB00005B/136